What a
Time
It
Was!

JEFFREY LYONS

Foreword by Rex Reed

*Leonard Lyons and
the Golden Age
of New York Nightlife*

Leonard Lyons

*now writes
for...*

Abbeville Press Publishers
New York   London

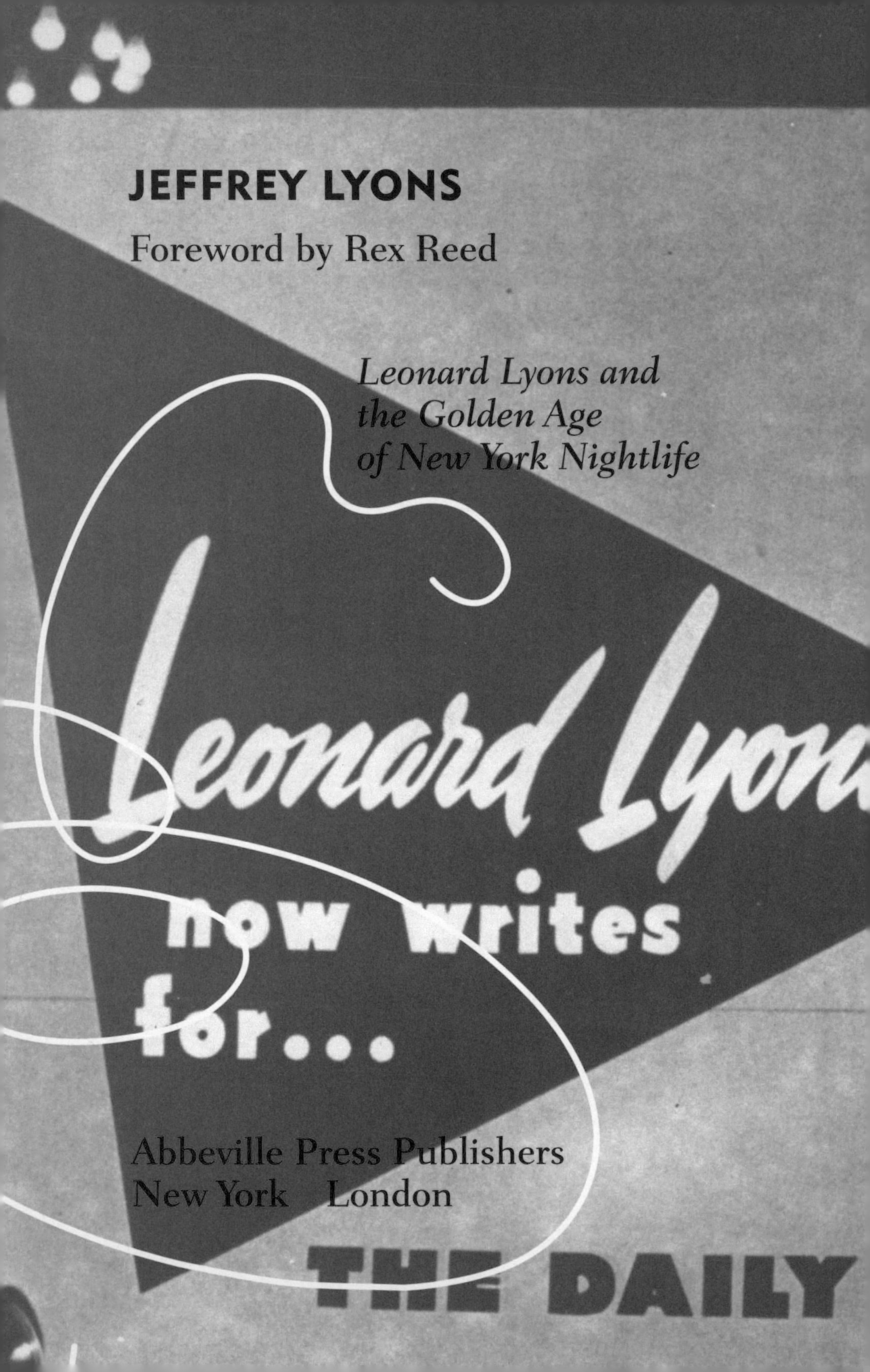

THE DAILY

What a Time It Was!

Inquirer

FRONT COVER: Ecita and her orchestra performing at the Stork Club. Photograph by Alfred Eisenstaedt.
BACK COVER: My father on his terrace, c. 1966.
PAGE 14: Brendan Behan and Bette Davis at Sardi's, New York City, 1960. Photograph by Sam Shaw.
PAGE 50: Joan Crawford and my father on the Warner Bros. studio lot.
PAGE 220: John Huston, *Casino Royale*, London, 1967. Photograph by Sam Shaw.
PAGE 258: Arthur Miller and Marilyn Monroe, New York City, 1957. Photograph by Sam Shaw.
PAGE 302: Eleanor Roosevelt (center) with my mother (second from right) at a United Jewish Appeal event.
PAGE 388: My father (left) and Charles "Lucky" Luciano, captured on a surveillance camera, in Naples, 1953.
PAGE 398: Woody Allen and Paula Prentiss, *What's New Pussycat?*, Paris, 1964. Photograph by Sam Shaw.
PAGE 416: Muhammed Ali, Madison Square Garden, New York City, 1967. Photograph by Sam Shaw.
PAGE 430: Left to right: Lou Gehrig, Joe Cronin, Bill Dickey, Joe DiMaggio, Charlie Gehringer, Jimmie Foxx, and Hank Greenberg at the All-Star Game, July 7, 1937.
PAGE 442: Louis Armstrong and his band, Paris Blues, directed by Martin Ritt and produced by Sam Shaw, Paris, 1960. Photograph by Sam Shaw.

EDITOR: Shannon Connors
TEXT EDITOR: Greg Villepique
DESIGNER: Misha Beletsky
PRODUCTION MANAGER: Louise Kurtz

First published in 2015 by Abbeville Press, 116 West 23rd Street, New York, NY 10011.

For bulk and premium sales and for text adoption procedures, write to Customer Service Manager, Abbeville Press, 116 West 23rd Street, New York, NY 10011, or call 1-800-ARTBOOK.

Visit Abbeville Press online at www.abbeville.com.

First edition
10 9 8 7 6 5 4 3 2 1

ISBN 978-0-7892-1235-1

Library of Congress Cataloging-in-Publication Data

Lyons, Jeffrey.
  What a time it was! : Leonard Lyons and the golden age of New York nightlife / Jeffrey Lyons.
    pages cm
  Includes index.
  ISBN 978-0-7892-1235-1 (hardback)
  1. New York (N.Y.)—Social life and customs—20th century—Anecdotes. 2. Nightlife—New York (State)—New York—History—20th century—Anecdotes. 3. Celebrities—New York (State)—New York—Biography—Anecdotes. 4. New York (N.Y.)—Biography—Anecdotes. 5. Lyons, Leonard, 1906-1976—Anecdotes. 6. Celebrities—Homes and haunts—New York (State)—New York—History—20th century—Anecdotes. 7. Nightclubs—New York (State)—New York—History—20th century—Anecdotes. 8. Restaurants—New York (State)—New York—History—20th century—Anecdotes. I. Lyons, Leonard, 1906-1976. II. Lyons, Jeffrey. Stories my father told me. III. Title.
  F128.5.L966 2015
  974.7″043—dc23
                    2015017462

CONTENTS

Contents

PART III

They Made the Movies

PART IV

Their Pens Were Mightier

PART V

Larger Than Life

Contents

DEDICATION

This is a tribute to my father's life and career, as was the book which preceded it. In his eulogy in October, 1976, New York Mayor John V. Lindsay said: "In a business filled with sharks, he was a prince." My father was and is my role model, and the crowd of 1,000 people who were there that day was a tribute to how he lived his life and did his work. He and my mother Sylvia fulfilled their dream of raising four productive citizens.

I also dedicate this book to my wife Judy and our children, Ben and Hannah. They are the purpose of my life.

My family in the pool at Grossinger's.

FOREWORD

*I*f you came to New York from horizons far away, as I did, the first thing you learned about the city was that if you missed Leonard Lyons, you did so at your own peril. Everything you wanted to know about the Apple in the good old days, when it was still just an apple seed, you learned about first in The Lyons Den.

Now, in this second collection of the juiciest items and anecdotes from the world's most reliable columnist, his son Jeffrey has compiled enough stories to make you wonder where we all went wrong. Instead of bogus phonies, you get the real deal—priceless vignettes about presidents, movie stars, gangsters, five-star generals, and every denizen of Manhattan's after-midnight social scene from Tallulah Bankhead to Mayor Fiorello La Guardia. You visit the Barrymores, chew pearls of wisdom from literary lights like Gertrude Stein and Gore Vidal, and eavesdrop on Greta Garbo.

Make nightly rounds with Leonard Lyons and you'll attend opening nights on Broadway; find yourself a guest of Sherman Billingsley in the sacred sanctions of the Stork Club; go behind the scenes of the feud between Olivia de Havilland and Joan Fontaine; share a joke with Groucho; talk-talk-talk to Zsa Zsa; travel up the river behind bars with Al Capone; play ball with Babe Ruth; enter the ring with Muhammed Ali; and sing along with Toscanini, Gershwin, and Nat King Cole. And that's just for starters.

This book gives the lie to the old saw "Less is more." I couldn't put it down and I still want more!

—Rex Reed

INTRODUCTION

On Tuesday, December 2, 2014, I'd lived as many days as my father. Ironically, the same day I heard a report from London saying that people who work night shifts live shorter lives; the reversal of the normal sleep cycle damages a part of the brain.

My father, Leonard Lyons, worked "the night shift" for forty years writing his column, The Lyons Den, for the *New York Post*. Most of his 12,480 columns, from May 20, 1934, to May 20, 1974, were the result of table-hopping in nightclubs, elegant restaurants, supper clubs, and at Broadway and movie premieres. He found stories on lunchtime rounds too, submitting the rough draft of the column by 6 p.m. six days a week.

A short nap or a half an hour pitching fastballs to his sons across the street in Central Park, and he'd go out again, covering a dozen more places at night. He'd arrive home around 2 a.m., then painstakingly dictate newer stories to the men on the lobster shift—the overnight copy editors on the city desk—so they'd be inserted in the hours before 11 a.m., when the paper hit the street.

If only he'd had a smartphone, a fax, e-mail, even a word processor, he'd have lived a normal lifespan, not a mere seventy years. If only.

But what a life it was! And what a time it was!

While practicing law in the early 1930s, he began dreaming of writing a daily column. He'd never worked on a newspaper or interviewed anyone. He relied on his legal training to search for the truth. Soon he began submitting poems, news items, and anecdotes to the columnists of the day; my mother kept a scrapbook of the ones that were printed. Mark Hellinger in particular used lots of his submissions. Then he wrote a weekly column called East of Broadway for the English page of the *Jewish Daily Forward*.

In 1934, the *New York Post* came under new ownership, and they searched for a competitor to Walter Winchell in the *Daily Mirror*. My father arrived carrying that scrapbook and beat out five hundred other aspirants for a sixty-day tryout. The first person he interviewed was Milton Berle—a great way to begin. He won the job on a Friday afternoon when editor J. David Stern said, "Leonard Sucher, Monday morning, you'll be 'Leonard Lyons.' These things are fated."

As with 2011's *Stories My Father Told Me*, this is about his era as a renowned columnist who knew *everyone*. It was decades before social media. Print ruled the roost. In New York, the stars were out every night. He traveled the world frequently, but the Broadway theater district and the elegant East Side restaurants and nightclubs were his main beat.

While flying to distant movie locations or on inaugural flights, he'd use evergreen columns or guest columnists. They included some of the giants of the day: Ben Hecht, arguably Hollywood's greatest screenwriter; Sinclair Lewis; Margaret Bourke-White; Helen Hayes; James A. Michener; even Salvador Dalí!

He'd find travelers returning to New York and use them as 'pigeons,' giving them manuscript columns for delivery to the *Post*. On Sunday nights, a Western Union messenger would come to our home to pick up the column. For a year or so it was a teenager named Edward Albee, which is why, in his masterpiece, *Who's Afraid of Virginia Woolf?*, the quarreling couple learn of the death of their imaginary son from a Western Union messenger.

Unlike some competitors, my father did not fill his column with vitriol or gossip. "Newsworthy" was his watchword. He never started feuds, but if attacked in print he'd hit back. His main rival was Walter Winchell, who created the gossip column genre and, ironically, won a contest to name my father's column. Winchell was a strange, lonely man, hated by as many as liked. When he attacked FDR, for example, my father revealed that Winchell had never voted in his life.

Winchell attacked Truman's outrage at a scathing review *Washington Post* music critic Paul Hume had given Truman's daughter Margaret's singing recital. Winchell said Truman's angry letter to that paper was "stew stuff," implying the president was tipsy.

My father took Winchell to task in print, and when Winchell phoned asking why he'd dared to interfere, my father replied that the image of a drunken president commanding troops in Korea was *Winchell* interfering, damaging their morale.

The great writer William Saroyan called The Lyons Den "one of the few columns of our time which has both form and style." An English professor at New York University recommended it to his advanced writing class. It wasn't a gossip column, but an invaluable chronicle of the times.

The morning after Pearl Harbor, my father sprang into action calling his sources in the White House and other places in government. The next day's column had *seven* stories about the aftermath of the attack: the work not of a gossip columnist, but of a journalist.

We'd always keep our eyes open for a portable typewriter two ounces lighter than the clumsy ones he used on trips. Pop could type anywhere—on a plane, a ship, or a train, even with his typewriter propped up on a suitcase.

New York was his town. And he made it others' town, too. In October 1957, for example, he walked up Fifth Avenue to a party with Bostonian Maxwell Rabb, secretary to Eisenhower's cabinet. "I love this town," said Rabb. "You can see anything. Today I saw a woman with a small kangaroo on a leash!"

They arrived at the party and there she was, the woman with her kangaroo!

The column was his key to everything. Hemingway taking him around the Paris of his youth and hosting our family at his *finca* near Havana; taking Vivien Leigh to the Stork Club; tea with the Windsors; a tour by Truman of the renovations of the White House; tea with Churchill at 10 Downing Street: all in a day's work.

In Rome one day, he had breakfast with actress Dawn Addams, cocktails with Sophia Loren (even though he was a teetotaler), and dinner with Gina Lollobrigida. Not a bad day, and not an atypical one.

He took Brendan Behan, the Irish poet-playwright, on a one-hour tour of Broadway musicals. Entering, say, *Fiddler on the Roof*, he'd look at his watch, then tell Behan what had happened in the show up to then. They'd see one number from the back, then move on to *The Most Happy Fella* next door, and so on. Six or seven shows in one hour.

A local TV crew filming his evening rounds couldn't keep up, as he table-hopped in one nightspot after another gathering his stories.

As an example of how well liked he was around town, a 1945 *New Yorker* profile told of two men engaged in a fight outside a nightclub just as my father pulled up in a cab. The victor, breathing heavily, paused and said, "Oh, hello, Leonard." The vanquished foe on the ground stirred, turned around, and said, "Oh, hi, Leonard," as my father went inside.

On April 9, 1948, a full-page ad in the *New York Post* blared: "NO

Introduction

KEYHOLE-PEEPER THIS MAN LYONS—HARDEST WORKING COL-
UMNIST IN NEW YORK!" Carl Sandburg termed him "the only living anecdotist of our time."

He described the scope of the column as "covering every field of
human interest."

In October 1963 Albert Finney, still new in town, came to Sardi's,
the theatrical restaurant, where he spotted my father table-hopping, chatting with diners, jotting notes in a small pad, then moving on to the next table.

"What's he doing?" asked Finney, used to the British style of
sensational journalism where sources were rarely checked for
verification.

"Oh, that's Leonard Lyons," said his friend. "He's the Broadway
columnist who knows everyone, and he's getting stories for tomorrow's column. No middleman. Everything exclusive. And no gossip.
All newsworthy stuff. Nothing hurtful."

Finney and my father soon became friends.

In March 1957, he was on a TWA flight headed toward what was
then Ceylon to visit the jungle set of *The Bridge on the River Kwai*.
The long flight gave him time to reflect.

"Give me lights and sound and people, and music into the night,"
he wrote for his "in transit" column. "Late into the night. Peace and
quiet are for death and poets. I prefer crowds, and 'Satchmo' trum-
peting at the moon, streets lit brilliantly, and crowded sidewalks and
laughter coming out of joints in a row."

His favorite song was from *Guys and Dolls*, a show written by his
good friends Frank Loesser and Abe Burrows. "My Time of Day" described his life in New York and his late hours.

What follows are anecdotes about some of the people whose ex-
ploits he chronicled. As they say on *Law and Order*:

"These are their stories."

PART
I

"Of All the

EL MOROCCO

(1931–1981)

Famed for its zebra-striped booths, it was the capital of café society.

"I've seen them all at El Morocco," my father wrote in June 1965, when the ownership changed hands. "The Mountbattens and Vanderbilts, LBJ and the Whitneys, senators, movie stars, industrialists, and always—the beauties."

One New Year's Eve at midnight, an elegant couple in formal attire posed for photographs wearing paper crowns adorned with tinsel. Owner John Perona never released the pictures, however. The couple was the Duke and Duchess of Windsor, beneath the only crowns they'd ever wear.

In November 1956, Judy Garland was there with Anita Ekberg and Ekberg's new husband, Anthony Steel. The voluptuous Swedish actress began to apply more lipstick in an intricate way. "Do you like putting on so much lipstick?" Garland asked.

"Not really," replied Ekberg, "but I sure like the way he takes it off!"

Later that evening, Jerry Lewis was asked if his eyesight had been affected by so many television appearances in front of hot lights. "My eyesight is perfect," he said, then headed to the table where Garland and Ekberg were seated and planted a kiss on the person sitting in between them: my father!

An extremely wealthy woman was told she couldn't get a table at El Morocco. She didn't complain, didn't ask if they knew who she was, but instead simply left, saying, "I just hope the next time I come unannounced, the doorman will spot my license plate."

Her plate read "NY 1." She was Mrs. Averell Harriman, wife of the governor of New York.

On the dance floor one night, Arde Bulova, of the watch company, told a young man: "What's the future President doing dancing here?"

"When I'm President, I won't be coming here," replied John F. Kennedy.

My father and Carroll Baker at El Morocco.

On another night, a rich drunk scattered ten-dollar bills across the dance floor and patronizingly invited the waiters to pick them up. Not one stooped to claim the money.

In 1960, Ireland's ambassador to the UN, Frederick Boland, then serving as president of the General Assembly, was at El Morocco discussing Khrushchev's infamous speech wherein he banged his shoe on the table, while Boland broke his gavel calling for order. Afterward, Boland received thirty-eight gavels from jurists around the world—all unbreakable.

Darryl F. Zanuck was there reminiscing about the vagaries of the film business. In 1931, the Fox production chief had seen a young actor in a West Coast stage production of *The Last Mile* and gave him a film role in *Night Nurse*. Zanuck thought the young actor did fine in his debut.

One of his bosses said, "That guy's ridiculous, with those big ears." Irving Thalberg at MGM disagreed so strongly, he hired the young actor for some movie musicals. That was how, Zanuck recalled, Fox lost Clark Gable to a rival studio.

Late one night, an Italian industrialist suddenly did a somersault, then explained, "When I've had a few, I always do this as a warning that it's time to go home. Before I do something *really* foolish."

Olivia de Havilland recalled one night that when her husband Pierre Galante began wooing her, he sent a limousine to pick her up at the airport, telling her the chauffeur, dressed in a fancy uniform, was part of an honor guard from the French embassy. Later she learned he was really a moonlighting doorman from El Morocco.

In December 1960, a patron was admitted without a jacket and tie: Tenzing Norgay, the Sherpa who guided Sir Edmund Hillary on the first successful ascent of Mount Everest seven years before. Norgay wore traditional Sherpa garb.

For many years, Karl Inwald sang and played the piano in the club's Champagne Room. One night, German count Felix von Luckner suddenly burst into song, accompanying Inwald, who was singing an obscure number by nineteenth-century French composer Charles Gounod.

"I knew that sound," said the count, who'd been a German naval hero in World War I, "because I once sank a ship named the *Charles Gounod* and became interested in the man and his music."

While Toots Shor's was their usual hangout, many heavyweight champions also loved El Morocco, such as Jack Dempsey, Gene Tunney, Rocky Marciano, and Max Baer. Ingemar Johansson loved it there so much that only strenuous objections from his handlers dissuaded him from dancing away the night before his second fight with Floyd Patterson. He lost anyway.

Although thousands of pregnant women danced there, no births were recorded. But there was one suicide attempt and two deaths of customers. One happened when my father was seated with producer Billy Rose and his date, Marlene Dietrich. The man, whose doctors had warned him to take it easy, ignored them and was dancing furiously, then collapsed with a thud. Rose went over to help, but it was too late.

The second death on the dance floor happened near where George Jessel, who'd given hundreds of eulogies, was seated. "Too bad I didn't know the guy," he sighed. "I'd have given his eulogy, and since he died at El Morocco, I'd have begun: 'It is the will of Allah.'"

In November 1962, producer Joe Levine was there and told my father—in strict confidence—that he was planning a musical version of *La Dolce Vita*. "If one of my sources tells me that, Joe," said my father, "I'll print it, but until then, you're story's safe with me."

At the next table sat Richard and Sybil Burton. Sybil said to my father, "Lenny, Joe Levine. He's doing a musical of *La Dolce Vita*."

One night in 1964, Salvador Dalí was at El Morocco and said a group of students from Hunter College had greeted him earlier that day by singing a puzzling song: "Hello, Dolly!" He hadn't heard of the musical.

In October 1964, Jack Lemmon dropped by and recalled he was very familiar with the East Fifty-Fourth Street location. It had once been the Ol' Knick Music Hall, where he'd played the piano for ten dollars a night. Joshua Logan, who cowrote *Mister Roberts*, recalled the night he'd seen Lemmon's performance in the movie version of the play, which won the young actor a Best Supporting Actor Oscar.

"Where, oh where were you when I wrote the Broadway play?" he wondered. (David Wayne played Lemmon's part, Ensign Pulver, on Broadway.)

"I'll tell you where I was," replied Lemmon. "I was right outside the Alvin Theater, trying desperately to get in to see you for an audition for a bit part!"

Orson Welles exchanged cursory nods with an attractive lady at ringside one night. Then he suddenly recalled where he'd last seen her. It was at the Hôtel du Cap in Antibes, on the French Riviera. He'd heard some noise near the balcony outside his window and saw this woman about to leap to her death. Welles climbed out, struggled with her, and finally brought her back into her room. Then he spent an hour dissuading her from suicide. The next day, the hotel manager sent a warning to Welles about his "nocturnal escapades."

One night, the Hope Diamond, arguably the most famous (or infamous) gem in history, made an appearance at El Morocco around the neck of its last private owner, newspaper and mining heiress Evalyn Walsh McLean. She arrived with her daughter and bodyguard, whom my father asked, "If a gunman came in and pointed his pistol at you, who or what would you protect first, Mrs. McLean's daughter or the diamond?"

Without hesitation, the bodyguard replied, "The diamond, of course!"

Mrs. McLean, incidentally, would suffer from the supposed curse of the diamond: her husband ran off with another woman and died in a sanatorium; her son was killed in a car accident; her daughter died of an overdose; and years later, her grandson was killed in Vietnam.

19

She tended to be careless with the gem. She once sent a radio to a friend in the hospital. The patient twisted the dials, but the radio didn't work. Finally, in exasperation, she picked up the radio, shook it, and out plopped the Hope Diamond.

When the son of John Perona sold El Morocco to John Mills (not the actor), the first change was to dim the lights. Some aging ladies had told him the bright lights were unflattering.

But Perona had originally turned up the lights after someone said that Clark Gable might be there. "People come here to see and be seen," he said, "especially if it's someone like Clark Gable."

My father took Vivien Leigh to El Morocco one night in May 1960. As they were leaving, a table of young socialites nearby sent her roses with a note, "To the Most Beautiful Woman in the World."

In September 1963, Rocky Marciano was there, annoyed by the huge purses made by inferior boxers due to closed-circuit TV. "Cassius Clay," he said, "is talking of a four-million-dollar gate when he fights Liston. Had I known that such big money would be around, I'd have stayed around and in shape—just a little bit in shape would've been enough."

In 1968, Maurice Uchitel, the new owner, banned men in light jackets and turtlenecks. One night in May of that year, Rod Steiger arrived in a tan suit, and his wife, actress Claire Bloom, wore a black short-pants suit. The owner made an exception in their cases, saying, "A beautiful woman and a man who's just won an Oscar (for *In the Heat of the Night*) must be deemed well dressed, no matter what they wear."

Shelley Winters arrived in February 1968, talking about her new movie *The Scalp Hunters*. "I've played madams and drug addicts," she said, "but in this role, all I have to do is smoke one cigar after another. At least my bad habits are improving."

When El Morocco closed for the summer in 1969, the veteran maître d', known to all the regulars as Angelo, made a radical change in his attire. He exchanged his white tie and tails, which he wore every night, for shorts, sandals, and a sports shirt; he'd landed a job at Xanadu, a resort hotel in the Bahamas.

LINDY'S

(1921–1969)

Oddly, it was Eugene O'Neill's *Strange Interlude* that helped make Lindy's a New York institution. The play, at the nearby John Golden Theater, ran five and a half hours. Patrons rushed over to Lindy's to eat during the long intermissions, thus creating extra business that other restaurants farther from the theater didn't enjoy.

Leo Lindy was that rare restaurateur who refused to raise prices on New Year's Eve. "I won't make suckers out of my regular customers, nor customers out of suckers," he explained.

One evening, a customer asked for chicken chow mein. "I'll sell that dish when a Chinese restaurant sells blintzes," he proclaimed.

There was a British vaudeville performer named Chaz Chase (no relation to Chevy) who ate flowers, coins, newspapers, even lit cigarettes in his bizarre act. In New York, he rushed into Lindy's. "Give me American food!" he demanded. Then he ate the menu.

Groucho Marx dined nearby at Dinty Moore's one night and, during his meal, more space was needed for late diners. "Do you mind if we move your table a bit, Mr. Marx?" the head waiter asked. "Not at all," replied Groucho. "In fact, I wish you'd move it over to Lindy's."

Lindy never owned a TV. "I don't need one," he said. "Milton Berle—'Mr. Television'—is in here every night."

The wife of insult comic Jack E. Leonard asked a Lindy's waiter to wrap her leftover steak. "It's for our dog," she said. "Does he want a pickle with that?" asked the waiter.

The widow of another Lindy's waiter went to a séance and was promised that her recently departed husband would speak to her from the beyond. She placed her hands on the table and called for him three times. No response. Finally someone in the room said, "He can't come, Edith. It's not his table."

In October 1959, Lindy's signed a contract to cater Northeast Airlines' New York–Miami flights. The dishes, taken from the famed menu, included cheese blintzes. But the first test flight had to turn back at Baltimore, as the story goes; they'd forgotten the sour cream.

When Frank Capra began shooting *Pocketful of Miracles*, with Glenn Ford, Hope Lange, and Bette Davis, the cast and director were greeted by a sixty-pound cheese cake flown to Los Angeles from Lindy's, near where the Damon Runyon story took place.

George Jessel came in one night in April 1965 and mentioned his next tour entertaining troops in Greece, Turkey, and Vietnam. "It's a classified tour," he said, "in which I talk to small groups telling them how lucky they are to be in those dismal places. Then, before they can discover that I'm lying, I move on."

One night, Jimmy Foxx, the Hall of Fame slugger, spoke of his old owner-manager Connie Mack. After Foxx had won two MVP awards and hit fifty-eight home runs in 1932, Mack paid him a paltry eighteen thousand dollars.

"Mr. Mack wasn't tight with a dollar," said Foxx. "But if you wanted *two* dollars, you were in trouble."

When radio DJs began broadcasting from remote locations, one approached Lindy, saying, "If you let me do my show from here, it'll surely boost your business."

"Maybe so," replied Lindy, "but I can't spare a table for you; we're sold out every night."

Someone told my mother she'd seen my father in Lindy's at 3 a.m. the night before with Marlene Dietrich. "Oh, of course," said my mother. "How appropriate to be in the place best known for its cheesecake!"

Lindy sued a Chicago hotel offering "Lindy's Chopped Liver." He'd sampled it, grimaced, then sent them his recipe, stating, "I hope this will improve the quality of your chopped liver and protect my reputation until the outcome of my lawsuit against you."

Lindy's was so successful that Leo retired two cash registers after both had recorded $20 million. The restaurant, now a McDonald's, was in the same building as the Mark Hellinger Theater. Lindy once told a producer of a show there, "If your play flops, you can't blame it on bad location."

The walls had paintings Lindy bought from Vanderbilt and Whitney collections, and Damon Runyon immortalized it in his writings as "Mindy's."

Leo Lindy was dismayed when a magazine showed photos of his blintzes and cream, referring to it as "whipped cream." "*Sour* cream!" he wailed. "Whipped cream with blintzes is like having a Republican president and a Democratic vice president."

In September 1967, some jazz musicians stopped in for a late-night snack, but were told they were out of bagels. "*Lindy's* out of *bagels*?" said one. "That's like Fort Knox running out of gold."

The columnist Heywood Broun was handed a menu at Lindy's, perused it, and finally said to the waiter, "I see nothing to object to."

A lunch patron told of an elderly man greeted by a genie who offered one wish. The man wished for a trio of beautiful women. The genie left for a moment, then returned saying none were available. "No women?" asked the man. "Then get me a Lindy's prune Danish."

Lindy's closed in September 1969.

SARDI'S

(1927–)

Sardi's, on West Forty-Fourth Street, in the middle of the Broadway theater district, is still the Mecca for pre- and post-theater meals. For decades, it's been tradition that following the opening of a new show, the stars enter Sardi's to applause, then nervously wait for the newspapers' reviews. When television critics like me came along (I began in 1970), small TV sets were placed strategically around the restaurant. Sardi's remains a symbol of New York.

Unless he was traveling, my father was there at lunch and every weeknight at eleven thirty for forty years, constantly table-hopping, gathering many of the stories you're reading here. Two photos of him are in a place of honor near the bar, though he was a teetotaler.

Movie mogul Sam Goldwyn lunched there and recalled his film *The Bishop's Wife*. On the first day of shooting, in 1947, Cary Grant, who hadn't yet signed his contract, told Goldwyn he wanted more time to study the role.

Goldwyn showed him a piece of paper.

"What's this?" asked Grant.

"It's David Niven's phone number," said Goldwyn. "I'll give his supporting role to someone else and hand Niven the lead if you don't sign now." Grant quickly signed.

Such was the paranoia during the McCarthy era that in June 1951, actors dining at Sardi's were putting miniature Statues of Liberty on their tables to proclaim their loyalty. Unlike the movie and television industries, however, Broadway producers ignored the blacklist.

In November 1960, the bar at Sardi's received an unusual donation: a dictionary, to settle potential arguments about the derivation or meaning of words. It came from Sardi's next-door neighbor, *The New York Times*.

A veteran customer stopped going there when the men's room was moved upstairs. "I refuse to climb for *that*!" he explained.

In August 1968, my father was sitting between Jane Russell and Jackie Gleason at Sardi's when "The Great One" reached over my father to kiss Russell. The next day, Gleason's conclusion made my father's column: "Russell was sweeter."

One afternoon in June 1962, Irwin Shaw, who wrote *The Young Lions* and *Rich Man, Poor Man*, lunched at Sardi's with his mother. He told her about his new book, new play, and new movie, but she was only concerned with his health, since he'd recently had some ulcers.

"Oh, if only you'd have been a plumber instead of a writer," she sighed. "Plumbers don't get ulcers."

"Mother," he replied, "if I'd been a plumber instead of a successful writer, I wouldn't be invited to the White House next week."

"If you, Irwin, had been a plumber," she replied, "you'd be so good at it the White House would've had you in to fix the pipes."

In October of that year, Greer Garson said she'd just taped a TV drama. "It was great to get back to acting," she said. "In fact, I chewed up the scenery. That's my favorite dish—chewed scenery."

Justice William O. Douglas lunched at Sardi's with Isaac Stern. The jurist recalled that on his recent trip to India, he'd seen experiments on the effect of music on growing plants. Stern, who lived in our building, told my father, "Tell Sylvia to plant her geraniums early this year. I'll play loudly for them."

Henny Youngman lunched there and mentioned a gangster so unimportant in the underworld hierarchy, "he didn't even rate a contract put out on him. Just a memo."

Max Gordon produced Broadway hits like *The Solid Gold Cadillac*, *The Women*, *My Sister Eileen*, and *Born Yesterday*. At lunch at Sardi's he said he'd found amongst his files a 1917 report from an Ohio vaudeville house praising his presentation of a one-act play. "The writer will go far," it read. The writer was Eugene O'Neill. But that same report said another act "needs new material." The act was the Marx Brothers.

In September 1964, Frederick Loewe, who wrote the music for *Brigadoon*, *My Fair Lady*, *Gigi*, and *Camelot*, dined there with friends and announced he would no longer compose anything. "But Fritz, it's a sin to waste a god-given talent," said someone at the table.

"The same god who gave me the talents," Loewe replied, "also gave me the wisdom to quit and enjoy it."

Loewe "enjoyed it" for thirty-four years, reaping millions from subsequent revivals of his musicals, then wrote the songs for *Fosse*, which opened in 1999 and ran 1,093 performances.

In August 1965, Vice President Humphrey and his wife Muriel had a late dinner at Sardi's, preceded and followed by Secret Service men. As they got out of a limousine, Mrs. Humphrey said, "It's not like the old days when we'd go chasing for a cab here in New York in the rain because Hubert wouldn't go with me by bus."

Just then a college student came up and requested an autograph from the vice president, who said, "Those Secret Service guys are glaring at you because whenever anyone gets this close to me, they have to take a cut in salary."

Hal Linden, who starred in *The Rothchilds*, *I'm Not Rappaport*, and *Illya Darling*, came in, saw Sardi's was packed with diners, and began to leave. Then the maître d' called, "Mr. Linden, your table is ready."

"That's when I knew I'd made it on Broadway," he said.

In February 1966, Mrs. Vincent Sardi Jr. was the standby for Margaret Leighton in the Broadway play *Slapstick Tragedy*. Leighton said she'd avoid eating at Sardi's. She did, then became ill, allowing Mrs. Sardi to go on in her stead.

Sheldon Harnick and Joe Stein, the lyricist and book writer for *Fiddler on the Roof*, were in Sardi's going over their schedule of international openings of the show in several Scandinavian countries. "Sheldon," asked Stein, "why do we open our show in all those cold countries in the dead of winter?"

"Because," replied Harnick, "we get a cut of the coat check concession."

Later, they discussed the show's eligibility for the Pulitzer Prize. Before *Fiddler*, it was customary to give the award to shows that dealt with American stories. So they speculated that before each performance, Zero Mostel should tell the audience, "I'm Tevye the milkman. *Now* we're living in Chicago. But *this* is what happened *before* we came to America."

In February 1970, a fire gutted the Sardi's kitchen. When the lunch crowd arrived, Sardi served them sandwiches from Nathan's Famous, the hot dog maker, for free.

One night at Sardi's, playwright Charles MacArthur, the husband of Helen Hayes, met an Englishman who insisted they'd met before in London.

"Oh, it's *you*," replied a smiling MacArthur. "I think it was either at Noël Coward's or at 10 Downing Street, right?"

Later, after the man had left, MacArthur said, "I always say that to people who insist we've met, when I know we haven't. It flatters them."

Elliott Gould lunched there in May 1970 and commented on his producer-star status in *Little Murders*: "I'm more secure as an actor now. As a producer, I know I'd hire me. I'm just not sure I'd ever want to work for me."

In January 1972, Giorgio Tozzi of the Metropolitan Opera was chosen over Vincent Sardi for a TV commercial. "There goes my good table," he said.

THE COPACABANA

(1940–1973)

his was the place where performers played to glittering audiences in the heyday of New York nightclubs. Comedian Joe E. Lewis, multitalented Sammy Davis Jr., and Harry Belafonte were top-liners there in the days when Jules Podell ran the place.

After the war, British producer J. Arthur Rank came to New York, took one look at the Copacabana chorus girls, and said, "*Now* I see what's been missing in British musicals."

Joe E. Lewis was the most frequent performer at the Copa. During one monologue, he was constantly interrupted by a woman heckler who'd obviously had a few. Before he left the stage, he pointed to her. "Oh, yes, lady, I remember you. I haven't seen you in ten years. I didn't remember your face, but I remember that dress."

Another night he spotted the oft-married Zsa Zsa Gabor. "There she is, ladies and gentlemen," Lewis said. "Zsa Zsa. Dedicated to the proposition."

Then he defined outer space as "anything more than thirty feet away from the Copa's bar."

Lewis said of singer Eddie Fisher, "His marriage to Debbie Reynolds ended in failure. His marriage to Elizabeth Taylor—also a failure. He's had more fun failing than I've had winning."

Carl Sandburg told Lewis, "You took ten years off my life tonight. But then I'll go out, read the front pages, see the terrible things in the world that happened while I was inside, and those ten years will come right back."

May 19, 1957, was the most important date in the Copa's history. A group of Yankees were there to see Sammy Davis Jr. perform. In their party was Elston Howard, the team's first African American player. When a drunken heckler began spewing racist cracks at Howard and Davis, a fight broke out. In the middle were the drunk man and Yankee Hank Bauer, the grizzled former marine.

As my father arrived on his rounds, the racist was being carried out on a stretcher. Yogi Berra spotted my father and, hoping to avoid publicity, tried to block his view.

"Hi, Lenny," he said. "What's new?" Well, that fight was new. My father offered to lead the Yankees out of the Copa via a secret passageway he knew from its time as a speakeasy if Yogi provided him exclusive details of what happened.

Beating the horde of reporters who by this time had gathered outside, my father broke the story, saying, "There are now *three* famous battlefields in American history: Gettysburg, Iwo Jima, and the Copacabana."

When Frank Sinatra returned a few years after he'd starred at the Copacabana, a long piece of paper reading "Welcome back!" arrived at his table, signed by every employee.

Brook Benton, who had a string of hits, including "The Boll Weevil Song," was offered a chance to sing there—the Copa was one of the first New York nightclubs to hire African American headliners. "You'll have to pay me a lot more than I got when I sang here the last time," he told Podell. "All those clattering dishes! I was washing dishes in the kitchen."

Sophie Tucker, aka "The Last of the Red-Hot Mamas," entertained there with Helen Keller in the audience. Later the two met and Miss Polly, Keller's companion, told Tucker she'd translated the words Tucker sang in some suggestive songs. Tucker's pianist had noticed this and slowed down his tempo whenever he thought Miss Polly was falling behind.

Later, Keller met Tucker, who asked, "Did you think my songs were too racy?"

"No," replied Keller, "because they seemed to bring joy to everyone."

In February 1961, Podell, planning his daughter's party, offered to hire any entertainer she wanted. She chose a performer unknown to her father: the South Carolina–born, Philadelphia-raised singer Ernest Evans. Soon he was the only performer with five top-selling albums on the charts, using his new name, Chubby Checker.

During a Copa performance by Sammy Davis Jr., he spotted a beautiful blonde. He sighed and told his audience, "She's probably married with a kid." She was May Britt, Davis's actress wife.

In February 1967, Wilt Chamberlain was approached by singer Frankie Laine, who tried to convince "The Stilt" to join in a comedy act at the Copa.

"No, thanks," said Chamberlain. "Who wants to be known as the tallest comedian to bomb at the Copa?"

Phil Silvers played the Copa, and one evening, Charlie Chaplin was in the audience. Afterward, he told Silvers, "Your antics are funny because they speak for the stifled voices of the masses, eloquently expressing the true spirit of the common man."

"Nah," replied the Brooklyn-born Silvers. "All I want is to get a few yuks."

Nat King Cole often followed his engagements there by performing at the Apollo Theater in Harlem, "to give the babysitters a chance to see me," he said.

A party was held there after a school prom. A young patron, presented with the large bill, offered his father's credit card, telling the waiter, "My father allows me to forge his name."

The waiter replied, "Well *my* father doesn't allow me to accept forgeries."

In 1968, London Lee, who came from a rich family, was a rising young comic. He signed for an engagement at the Copa and said, "If I'm a hit, I'll have it made. And if I bomb, I'll buy the place."

Jules Podell spent fifty years in the nightclub business, and compared that to "250 years in any other business."

THE OAK ROOM
AT THE PLAZA HOTEL

(1907–)

lthough nowadays the Plaza's ownership has changed, with some suites converted to condominiums, it remains a throwback to the Gilded Age.

One morning in January 1961, Joseph Pasternak, who produced nearly one hundred movies, was awakened by workmen on a scaffold outside his windows, busy cleaning the Plaza's facade. As he was about to complain, Pasternak heard a worker's radio playing the theme of his new movie *Where the Boys Are*. Opening his window, he invited them to the premiere.

In April 1963, frequent guest Baron Edmond de Rothschild, who lived in a hundred-room chateau near Paris, found himself alone in New York for the weekend. The Plaza was filled, but the management came up with an unusual solution: they booked him at Grossinger's, the lavish upstate New York resort, for a weekend. (Whether he participated in the hotel's signature Simon Says games or took cha-cha lessons next to the outdoor pool isn't known.)

My father was in the Plaza's Oak Room with some friends one night. As they got up to leave, one man and his wife lingered a few moments.

Outside, a prostitute approached my father and said, "What are you doing, honey?" "Waiting for some friends," replied my father. "Oh yeah?" she asked, looking up as the friends approached. She left in a hurry, as soon as she recognized New York City mayor Robert Wagner and his wife, Susan.

On April 24, 1964, Barbra Streisand was at the Oak Room and said, "I'm old! I feel *really* old. No, I'm not twenty-one anymore. I'm twenty-two."

Mario, the longtime maître d' at the Oak Room, overheard two diners mention that they went to psychiatrists because of their inability to sleep. "A waste of money," Mario said. "Just let them work for me for a week as busboys and they'll have no problem sleeping."

W. Somerset Maugham stayed at the Plaza on his trips to New York and once met the owner, Conrad Hilton, there. Hilton asked if there was anything he could to do make Maugham's stay more comfortable.

"As a matter of fact, there is," replied Maugham. "Faster room service for ice water."

"From then on," Maugham recalled, "whenever I even moved my arm toward the phone in my room, ice water came—whether I'd ordered it or not."

One night, a man walked into the Edwardian Room of the Plaza dressed in a casual California style. The maître d' stopped him and quickly handed him a tie. Jack Benny donned it, then walked out.

Mario, the Oak Room maître d', greeted an austere-looking English diner and said, "This way, sir."

"I'm used to being addressed as 'my lord,'" the man said with more than a hint of condescension.

"Sir," replied Mario, "I only have one Lord and I don't expect him tonight here at the Oak Room of the Plaza."

THE STORK CLUB

(1929–1965)

Walk east on Fifty-Third Street between Fifth and Madison Avenues in New York, and you'll see a charming little urban oasis called Paley Park, with a cooling twenty-foot waterfall cascading eighteen hundred gallons per minute, drowning out the street noise. It's named for the founder of CBS, William S. Paley, whose foundation funded its construction in 1967. I wonder if any of the people lunching there on any given day know the history of that site, for it's where the Stork Club once stood.

It was the most elegant of New York's nightspots. By the time I took a date there in 1964, it had begun to lose its luster, but for nearly four decades it was *the* place to see and be seen.

I found a photo of the Stork Club online, captioned, "The Stork Club's Cub Room," taken in November 1944. Orson Welles, sporting a huge cigar, is at the lower left. At the center table, seated on the left, is my father, hard at work on his nightly rounds. He's seen talking to asbestos tycoon Tommy Manville, briefly in between one of his *thirteen* marriages.

I trust that photo wasn't taken on November 5, 1944, for my father's place that night was at Polyclinic Hospital (long gone now) where my mother was giving birth—to me!

Owner Sherman Billingsley was famous for his hand signals, determining where patrons should be seated. If he didn't recognize them he'd send them to a table alongside the kitchen, a location dubbed "Siberia."

No nightclub owner watched his competitors more closely. Billingsley subscribed to clipping services collecting information about other places, even checking their nightly business and clientele. He'd obsessively doodle their floor plans. When El Morocco moved to a new location, Billingsley sketched on a tablecloth its architectural dimensions and kept tabs on the progress of the construction.

During the war, the owner of a competing nightspot was barred from the Stork Club because Billingsley didn't want any of his ideas copied. But the competitor got around that by being named air raid warden for that block. Billingsley then gave him a helmet, complete with a bull's-eye on top.

Ernest Hemingway asked Billingsley to cash a one-hundred-thousand-dollar check he'd just received for the movie rights to a story. "It's early," replied Billingsley. "Wait until closing time at four a.m."

On one of her visits, Helen Keller was introduced to critic George Jean Nathan. "Oh, I remember you," she said. "You once panned a show saying, 'The costumes looked like they'd been designed by Helen Keller.'"

In May 1942, two young British naval officers noticed the doorman writing names on a list: Tallulah Bankhead, circus owner John Ringling North, Brooklyn Dodgers manager Leo Durocher, etc. "All celebrities," said one seaman. "Yes, that's who comes here," replied the doorman.

"Well, my companion here is a celebrity, too, so we want to go inside. You see, he's the officer who loaded the torpedo that sank the German battleship *Bismarck*." The doorman admitted them.

When Hemingway returned to New York after covering the D-Day landings, he ordered vodka. Told they were out of vodka due to wartime restrictions, he said, "Okay, just bring me a potato, a bucket, a knife, and a candle."

In April 1945, former postmaster general James A. Farley was at the Stork Club and was asked whether he was planning on running for mayor. "My wife says no," he replied. "Gracie Mansion [the mayor's residence] is too far from the Stork Club."

During the war, Billingsley received a letter from Lord Beaverbrook, the British publishing tycoon: "I'm in a village here named 'Billingsley.' Its population is 522—about half as many people as visit your club in one night."

Billingsley, who was raised near an American Indian village in Oklahoma, was once asked if the Stork Club ever served Indians. "The last one was the Maharaja of Kapurthala," he said.

Billingsley hated unions, convinced they were run by mobsters. He carried photos of employees with their names, believing that if he called new hires by their first names, they'd be flattered and wouldn't join a union.

The 1945 movie *The Stork Club* starred Betty Hutton and Barry Fitzgerald. Billingsley had the right of approval for the actor who would portray him. William Goodwin, a character actor, was cast, and dutifully went to the club. One look at the actor's abundant hair got him Billingsley's approval.

Billingsley thought the entire world revolved around his club. When the first atomic bomb was dropped on Hiroshima, for example, he began calculating the damage to the Stork Club if a bomb were ever dropped over New York, even calculating likely damage to East Fifty-Third Street.

One night at the Stork Club my father was introduced to one of the few stars he didn't yet know. When he shook hands with Mickey Rooney, he said, "Hi, I'm Leonard Lyons. Nice to meet you, Mickey." Rooney, eighteen years younger than my father, said, "Likewise. But I'm 'Mr. Rooney.'" When I interviewed Rooney years later, he remembered that and laughed.

Oscar Levant, the actor-pianist, got a sixteen-dollar bill and wondered whether to tip three or four dollars. "If I tip three dollars," he said, "the waiter will sneer at me. But if I leave four dollars, I can sneer at the waiter. That's all tipping really means."

Another night, a tall man caught Billingsley's eye. He summoned his head waiter and asked, "Why did you let him in? There's something sinister about him—something I don't like. Show him out!" Then, when playwright Sidney Kingsley entered and spoke to the man, Billingsley quickly countermanded the order. The man was actor Harry Worth, who played a sinister doctor in Kingsley's play *Detective Story*, which Billingsley had seen the night before.

A customer lost an address book there one evening. The waiter brought it to Billingsley, who leafed through it, trying to find the owner. Finally he said, "He can't be important—my name isn't in it."

The next night, Billingsley met a well-known judge and said, "Your Honor, you look so distinguished."

"I hope not," replied the jurist. "That means I'm not enjoying myself tonight."

In February 1950, Billingsley dined at El Patio in Palm Beach, where he found that the head waiter and captains were former Stork Club employees. "It's like being in my place," Billingsley beamed. He noticed that the orchestra had played in the Stork Club and many of the customers were familiar faces. Then Dorothy Lamour walked in. She had started her career as a singer at the Stork. Then her escort entered: John Perona, of the rival El Morocco. *That's* when Billingsley knew he wasn't home.

One night Ben Hecht, who won the first Oscar for Best Screenplay, made his first visit to the Stork Club. As usual, it was jammed. "It's as if the rich were envious of the subways," he observed, "so they created their own version."

Ernest Hemingway came another night and sat next to my father, who was on Hemingway's left. On his right sat a drunken lawyer. The drunk, making some point, touched Hemingway's face. Hemingway warned him to keep his distance, but the lawyer did it again. Then Hemingway turned, delivered a half slap, and told him to stop. The lawyer was so intoxicated, he fell off his chair.

The next day a newspaper—not my father's—reported the story, saying that "a stranger in the Stork Club stepped up to Hemingway and said, 'So you're the tough Hemingway? Let's see how tough you are.' He swung and missed and was flattened by the author." Hemingway called my father, saying he preferred that version.

Emerging from the club one night, my father noticed another drunk rolling in the gutter. Pop went over to help him, only to realize it was Westbrook Pegler, the bombastic columnist who was hated and feared by millions and who, once he was fired by the Hearst newspapers, wound up writing for the far-right-wing John Birch Society. Pegler recognized my father and spewed an anti-Semitic slur. Instead of retaliating in a more conventional way, my father returned inside and brought out as many patrons as possible to see and shame Pegler.

Early in 1950, Joe DiMaggio dined there with Ethel Barrymore. The next night, he and Brooklyn Dodger announcer Red Barber returned and were seated at a table with another actress. Barrymore, seated nearby, sent a note to DiMaggio: "Fickle man."

Bing Crosby was given a party at the Stork Club for two hundred of his closest friends—black tie, of course. One guest had attended an earlier party and had to rush home to put on formal attire. He took a cab, asked the driver to wait, rushed upstairs, changed, and came down. "Hanging out with the upper crust, I see," said the driver to his fare. "I suppose so," replied Winthrop Rockefeller.

During the infamous Red Scare era, Billingsley considered demanding loyalty oaths from his patrons before allowing them in. He barred writers, artists, and anyone else he suspected.

When William Boyd—one of TV's first superstars, as Hopalong Cassidy—was at the Stork Club, he signed autographs for parents of his devoted young fans. Metropolitan Opera star Robert Merrill was among those requesting an autograph. Merrill's date reminded him that he wasn't married nor did he have any children.

"True," he replied, "but someday I *will* be married and have kids, and I want to be ready."

Starting in June 1950, Billingsley cohosted a live CBS-TV series from the club. He was, to put it mildly, new to the young medium, so when the floor director offered to tap him on the shoulder as a cue for him to start talking over the opening credits, Billingsley said, "No, don't just tap me. *Shove* me!" Five years later, he said on the air that he wished he had as much money as Toots Shor, his competitor, owed. At the time, Shor happened to be debt free. Shor sued and won a settlement, and the TV show soon ended.

The Stork Club's phone number in 1950 was PI3-1940. Many of the reservation calls went instead to PI3-1040, which happened to be the number of Mr. Fred, a prominent couturier. Since a number of his customers frequented the Club, he'd dutifully take their reservations and pass them on.

The Windsors arrived in February 1951 and noticed some young partygoers nearby. "Much as I hate youth," the duchess sighed, "I admire it."

Then the duke said he admired witty TV commentators who spoke so easily on their feet. My father reminded the duke of his famous abdication speech on the radio in 1937.

"Yes," replied the duke, "but I was seated for that one."

Then the duke began speaking Spanish to a former ambassador at the table, and my father joined in. The duke asked how my father happened to speak such good Spanish. He explained that he'd practiced law before becoming a columnist and that his firm had been planning to open a new office in San Juan, Puerto Rico. He'd learned Spanish in school and was thus in line for a two-year transfer.

By then, however, he'd met my mother, and a two-year separation was out of the question. So he decided to turn to journalism, rather than leave the girl he would marry.

"So you had a career planned for you, then you met a woman and all your plans changed?" asked the duke. "Fascinating. Do tell!"

The duchess danced with her husband; then Yul Brynner, at the time electrifying Broadway in *The King and I*, cut in.

"She danced tonight with two kings," said a friend, "but only one of them is currently working at it."

Patrons dancing to the music of Ecita and her orchestra
at the Stork Club. Photograph by Alfred Eisenstaedt.

In the summer of 1957, Frank Shields, the tennis star (and grand-father of Brooke Shields), mistook my father for another columnist who'd written a scurrilous story about him. Shields, a notorious drinker, took a swing at my father. A horde of waiters and bouncers tackled Shields, my father wrote, but "only two skinny waiters were needed to hold me back. I kept hollering: 'Just *two*? Bring more waiters! This is embarrassing.'" Shields was then barred from the Stork Club for five years.

A few weeks later, Pop was the catcher on Toots Shor's Crumbums team in a celebrity baseball game against "The Gentlemen of the '21' Club" at Yankee Stadium. It was one of several in which he'd play, staged before the midsummer Yankee-Giant exhibitions billed as "The Mayor's Trophy Game."

Up stepped Shields, playing for "21," unaware that my father, behind Yogi Berra's mask, was catching. Shields hit a screaming line drive up the power alley in left center field and sped around the bases.

Finally, center fielder Joe DiMaggio got to the ball and threw a one-hop laser to my father. My father tossed away his mask, caught the ball, and blocked home, just as Shields was rounding third. Realizing my father was catching and holding the ball, Shields retreated to third.

Toots Shor's Crumbums won, 1–0.

Years after the two Dempsey-Tunney heavyweight championship fights, they were at the Stork Club when an argument broke out and they squared off. Friends interceded, preventing a third fight, which would've had worldwide coverage.

One night in late August 1961, Joe DiMaggio dined there. Billingsley asked Joe, "What's doing with M.M.?" Fully aware of who he meant, DiMaggio nevertheless replied, "Oh, Mantle and Maris? They're doing fine."

When my father brought in the poet and historian Carl Sandburg, Billingsley, not noted for being a voracious reader, asked, "What does he do?" "He writes books," my father replied. "Mostly about Lincoln."

"Tell him to stick in 'Stork Club' once in a while," said Billingsley.

Champagne always went to the tables of VIPs. Billingsley explained by asking, "How much does a movie star make per hour for a personal appearance? For the price of a bottle, I get a star to stay longer. People will pay more just to look at each other than for food or drink."

Louis Marx, the toymaker tycoon, brought in Prince Bernhardt of the Netherlands. My father sat nearby and heard the prince say, "I've read about all the important people who come. Who's here tonight?"

Marx glanced around, at the Samuel Goldwyns, John Steinbecks, Gene Tunneys, and Irving Berlins. Also judges, industrialists, and movie stars. He then called my father over and introduced him. The prince looked puzzled. "*This* is the most important person?" he said.

Marx explained, "Your Highness, you have three daughters. Mr. Lyons has four sons." The prince then arose and bowed to my father.

Every New Year's Eve, table 50 was occupied first by the mayor, then a member of the White House family, and finally the Windsors.

Another night, a stream of big-name patrons came in, and each greeted my father. Billingsley, who didn't recognize any of the writers, artists, musicians, and judges—people of culture—said, "Lenny, you'd make a great doorman."

The era of the Stork Club ended with the rise of TV, the decline of café society, and the arrival of fads like the Twist, danced in discotheques, later called "discos." Television catered to the vast audience Billingsley had barred from entry. Eventually the famous and powerful patrons stopped coming, and he finally closed his beloved club in October 1965. He died a year later, by then a fish out of water.

THE WALDORF ASTORIA

(1893–)

O n one of his visits to the Waldorf Astoria, New York's most famous hotel, Bob Hope looked around the opulent lobby and said, "General MacArthur lives *here*? Ain't the GI Bill wonderful?"

During a performance at the hotel's nightclub, Maurice Chevalier suddenly paused and shook the hand of a man in the audience, saying, "Thank you, merci, thank you!" It was Jesse Lasky, one of Hollywood's pioneers, instrumental in bringing the young Chevalier to America.

The owner of a nearby hotel was asked if he was jealous that President Eisenhower and Queen Elizabeth II stayed at the Waldorf on successive weekends.

"Sure," he joked. "If you really care about such publicity."

The Duke and Duchess of Windsor lent their large Waldorf apartment to a friend while they were abroad. There the woman found the closet surprisingly small. "How do two of the best-dressed people in the world do it out of such a small closet?" she asked. The maid then opened the door to the huge dining room, cleared of everything except rack after rack of clothes.

In August 1960, Senator John F. Kennedy was campaigning hard for the presidency. He gave a speech at a Brandeis University dinner at the Waldorf and was introduced by Harold L. Renfield, who'd bought the liquor companies formerly owned by Joseph P. Kennedy.

Thanking him, Senator Kennedy said, "I never thought I'd get such a nice introduction from someone who's done business with my father and who's doing a better job at it, too."

When Soviet premier Khrushchev came to New York, the police commissioner assigned every Russian-speaking cop to protect him. They all jammed into an elevator at the Waldorf, but the elevator wouldn't work because of the overcrowding. A policeman heard Khrushchev say, "No wonder America can't get a missile off the ground. They can't even get a hotel *elevator* to go up!"

In May 1961, singer Tony Martin was feted at the Waldorf and sat with Roy Hamey, then the general manager of the Yankees. Martin said he was a frustrated ballplayer who once had a tryout with the San Francisco Seals of the Pacific Coast League. The scout's report read: "Third baseman. Switch-hitter. Strikes out both ways. But will sing a helluva song on those bus rides up to Portland."

Richard Burton gave a Hawaiian-themed party at the nearby Hotel Lexington and a drunken guest from the Waldorf staggered in. Women placed leis around him and gave him drinks. Looking bleary eyed at numerous Broadway stars, he tried to hold on to Laurence Olivier for balance, but fell into the indoor pool. Soaking wet, before returning to the Waldorf, he met Burton and said, *"You're* the host? How will I ever explain this to my wife?"

TOOTS SHOR'S

(1940–1971)

ernard "Toots" Shor (1903–1977) presided over an unending stream of sports stars and entertainers for three decades. He often urged my father to let me skip college and law school to work for him. "He'll learn all he has to know workin' for me," he'd say. How can a boy not like someone like that, especially someone who only knew about sports! He was one of the most colorful New Yorkers. His joint was a daily stop on my father's rounds, at lunchtime and in the evenings. There has never been another place like it.

In May 1940, Shor opened his restaurant on West Fifty-First Street. He'd put so much of his money into it, he couldn't afford carfare from his home to the restaurant's opening. His phone had been shut off as well, until the receipts from the first week assured its return.

Bert Lahr, the Cowardly Lion in *The Wizard of Oz*, dined at Shor's in 1940 and scanned the menu, looking for a sandwich. He found one named after him, but complained that it was too expensive.

Several weeks after the Japanese surrender in August 1945, Shor received a letter from General Emmett "Rosie" O'Donnell, who led B-29 bombers over Tokyo: "Dear Toots, In case your friends have kept the news from you . . . the war is over."

Shor accepted an invitation from Mike Todd to attend a performance of *Hamlet* with Maurice Evans. He complained that his seats were too far back. "If this were Madison Square Garden," said Shor, a season ticket holder at every New York sports venue, "I'd be right up front." At intermission, he said, "I'm the only guy in this joint who doesn't know how the play turns out."

Told by his doctor that drinking was harmful, the gruff tavern keeper huffed, "Listen, Doc. I don't knock *your* racket. Don't knock *mine*."

Rogers Hornsby was the National League's answer to Ty Cobb, hitting .424 in one season and .358 for his career—second only to Cobb's record. Lunching at Shor's, he said he never went to the movies during the first part of his career, fearing that the jumpy silent films would hurt his vision.

"And I don't play golf, either," he added. "When I hit a ball, I want to see guys chasin' it." Asked how he spent his off-seasons, he replied, "I'd sit by the window all winter and wait for spring."

In March 1946, Billy Conn, the light heavyweight champion, dined at Shor's, three months before he fought Joe Louis, the heavyweight champ. Somehow, in the dead of a New York winter, the fighter left his coat at his hotel, and Shor lent him his. "Not because I like you," said Shor. "Because I'm betting on you." Conn lost by a knockout.

Joe DiMaggio lunched there frequently and spoke of the magazine article he'd been signed to write called "Lucky to Be a Yankee."

"People think I'm a great writer," said DiMaggio, "as long as I keep hitting."

Early in 1948, Shor ignored advice to put away money for his retirement. "Not me," he said. "I want to live rich and die poor."

A few weeks later, Shor received two invitations from the White House. The first, to an informal reception, was addressed: "Mr. and Mrs. Toots Shor." The second, to a formal dinner, was addressed: "Mr. and Mrs. Bernard Shor." One guest at the formal dinner perused the invitees' list and asked if "Bernard" Shor was Toots. "Someone named Toots at the White House?" the aide huffed. "Certainly *not!*"

In March 1947, on a rare trip to Los Angeles to see actor Pat O'Brien and producer Mark Hellinger, Toots, who called friends and strangers alike "ya creep," spotted a sign that read, "The Original Toots Shor's Restaurant." Naturally he entered, and a tall, beefy Shor look-alike greeted him with "How are ya, ya creep?" It was all a gag by Shor's studio friends.

Shor and DiMaggio were extras in the movie *The Naked City*. All they were asked to do was emerge from the restaurant and walk. They needed five takes.

Yankee Hall of Fame catcher Bill Dickey, who played himself in *Pride of the Yankees*, was no stranger to Shor's. He told Shor he was playing himself again in *The Stratton Story*, about the former White Sox pitcher who lost a leg in a hunting accident, but made it back to the minors despite having a wooden leg. Jimmy Stewart played Stratton. Dickey was told to take a pitch down the middle for a called third strike.

"But I'd never do that," he said. Nonetheless, he followed the director's orders in take after take. "I've struck out more in this movie than in my career," he said.

Muddy Ruel, who caught for six teams between 1915 and 1934, stopped by Shor's and said Hollywood gossip columnist Elsa Maxwell had invited him to lunch to explain baseball to her lady friends.

"When I leave the dugout . . ." he began.

"What's a dugout?" asked one of the women. Ruel then went for his hat and coat, telling Maxwell, "Sorry, ma'am, but there just isn't enough time."

"Whiskey, not a dog, is man's best friend," Shor believed. When a customer ordered a Coke, Shor roared, "A *Coke*? That's a soft drink only for afternoons between three and three oh five."

Veteran umpire Bill Summers told Shor he appeared in *The Kid from Cleveland*. Before his scene, the director told Summers to call the first pitch to Indians star Lou Boudreau a strike, then a ball. This would be followed by Boudreau hitting a home run.

Summers called a strike on the first pitch. But then he called, "Strike two!" "Cut!" called the director. "Bill, stick to the script," he said to the umpire. "That pitch was right over the plate," replied Summers. "Tell your *pitcher* to stick to the script!"

Another umpire, "Beans" Reardon, told Shor he'd just met Chief Justice Fred Vinson. "I told him we have a lot in common," said Reardon. "We both make decisions dressed in black, then face people who squawk at them. But both our decisions are final." He then told Shor that Justice Vinson's wife launched a ship with a champagne bottle swung so skillfully that Yankee co-owner Dan Topping, who was there, invited her to spring training.

Dizzy Dean, the colorful St. Louis Cardinal, told Shor that while broadcasting during the Korean War, to protect national security he was prohibited from describing the weather conditions. So he said, "This game's delayed. I can't tell you why, fans, but look out the window."

A mysterious inscription was carved at the far end of the bar at Shor's: "Over here it's quieter—without the proprietor."

Dr. Ralph Bunche, the UN undersecretary general and winner of the Nobel Peace Prize, lunched there the same day as Moe Berg, the former catcher and World War II spy, a Princeton graduate who was fluent in seven languages, including Sanskrit.

Shor said nothing as he sat between them. "What's wrong, Toots?"

asked Dr. Bunche. "Nothing," he replied. "I'm just wonderin' which of you is smarter."

In February 1949, Shor used a tablecloth to write his suggested Yankee lineup for manager Casey Stengel's upcoming season. Stengel paid his bill and left. Then he hurriedly returned and pulled off the tablecloth, saying, "Sorry, I forgot my pennant."

Billy Martin, the fiery Yankee infielder and future manager, was in Shor's when announcer Mel Allen told him that Earl Warren was confirmed as the new chief justice. "He's now the second most powerful man in the country," said Allen, a lawyer by training.

"Behind Casey Stengel?" asked Martin.

Shor was asked to be a guest on a TV show sponsored by the Police Athletic League. "I'm flattered but troubled," he said, "since this means our youth must be in a bad fix, if a saloonkeeper is considered an inspiration."

When Shor entered a mambo contest at El Morocco, he playfully threatened the judge, "If I don't win, I'll punch you in the nose!" The judge—Aristotle Onassis, never a Shor's customer—didn't realize he was kidding and awarded him first prize.

During the height of the Cold War in 1956, Shor expressed a desire to visit Russia. "All their leaders are photographed holding a drink," he explained. "I like guys who like booze."

Shor didn't object to the city's midnight curfew for nightclubs and bars, in force in 1958. "Any crum who can't get drunk by that hour ain't tryin'," he said.

In August 1958, Shor showed Mickey Mantle how to improve his left-handed swing. President Eisenhower's press secretary, James Haggerty, also at the table, couldn't believe what he was seeing. "Are you actually telling Mickey Mantle how to swing?"

"Sure," replied Shor. "He ain't hittin' my weight even."

Mantle grinned and said to the nearly three-hundred-pound Shor, "Toots, I'll settle for your weight as a lifetime batting average." Mantle hit .304 that year, but settled for a .298 career average. Ignoring Shor's suggestions, he would hit 372 of his 536 home runs left-handed.

Joe Louis sat in Shor's with two men he'd knocked out: "Two-Ton" Tony Galento and Billy Conn. Galento said, "I woulda been champ if the ref hadn't hit me. It musta been the ref, 'cause I never saw the punch from you, Joe." Louis then recalled meeting Jackie Conn, Billy's brother, and telling him, "I hear brother Billy's struck it rich with an oil well. You must be in good shape now, right?"

"Billy sharing his money with me? Joe, you hit him hard, but not *that* hard!"

Visiting Galento's home in Newark, Shor saw a huge photo showing Galento standing over Louis after he'd knocked the champion down in their 1939 bout.

"That doesn't tell the whole story, Tony," said Shor. "You lost on a TKO in the fourth round. Where's the photo of Louis beating *you*?" "Probably at Joe's house," replied Galento.

A drinking companion boasted he'd read all the works of Gene Fowler, William Faulkner, and Ernest Hemingway. To match the boast, Shor phoned Fowler, then Faulkner, and had his friend speak to them. But Mary Hemingway said her husband was out of town. "Two out of three," Shor beamed. "Not bad for a mug like me."

After Jackie Gleason hired a Dixieland band to play there, he realized he'd forgotten to ask Shor. Gleason rushed to the restaurant and found the band playing "When the Saints Go Marching In." Shor roared only one word: "Louder!"

When Shor announced a move to a new location, he was asked about keeping the atmosphere of the old place. "*I'm* the atmosphere," Shor replied.

Edward Bennett Williams was one of the most powerful Washington trial lawyers, who had only two nonpaying clients: a convicted murderer whose appeal would be heard by the Supreme Court and Toots Shor. "Only one client gives me constant aggravation," said Williams. "Toots Shor."

When Shor received a large sum from an investor, he was asked what he'd do with his windfall. "Save it for a sunny day," he said.

One day at lunch, four translators worked in vain to establish communications between two people seated at adjacent tables: Casey Stengel and Gina Lollobrigida.

Shor gave a party for Marilyn Monroe and Joe DiMaggio. "It was easy to tell who'd invited which guests," Shor recalled. "Her pals were the intellectuals who crowded around the buffet. Joe's buddies stayed at the bar."

Yogi Berra and Whitey Ford signed their 1962 contracts at Shor's. Then Ford called Roger Maris, who'd hit a record sixty-one home runs the previous year and won the Most Valuable Player award, saying, "Sorry, Rog, there's no more money for you left in the Yankees' till."

Frank Sinatra gave Shor a private screening of *Come Blow Your Horn*. "You lost me in the first few minutes," said Shor. "Your character kicked two beautiful girls out of your apartment. The Sinatra *I* know would've locked the doors and pulled down the shades."

Shor was honored at a banquet with a parade of tributes. Finally Bob Hope said, "Lucky he's the guest of honor. Otherwise he'd never have been let in." Hope recalled Shor's days as a bouncer: "He hasn't changed. Nowadays, he just throws out a better class of people."

Norman Mailer took a date to Shor's when the air-conditioning was stuck on high. Mailer gallantly draped his jacket around her bare shoulders, but Shor said, "Sorry, but you have to wear a jacket in my joint."

"But haven't you ever heard of Sir Walter Raleigh?" the woman asked.

"Sure," replied Shor, "but if Whitey Ford has to wear a jacket, so does this Walter Raleigh."

When Shor opened his new restaurant in 1964, he received congratulatory messages from President Johnson, J. Edgar Hoover, and Jimmy Hoffa.

In October 1964, Chief Justice Earl Warren told Shor he'd had to miss the World Series opener because the court had reconvened. Shor was astonished that anyone with great seats to the World Series would choose to miss a game, no matter what the reason. "What if your Washington Senators were in the World Series?" he asked the justice.

"The Court would never have to decide whether to hold a session that day because it couldn't happen in my lifetime," Warren replied.

In March 1965, author Quentin Reynolds, whose books included *The Battle of Britain* and *The FBI*, was in Shor's editing a manuscript. He read one of the lines to Shor: "Like seafood and alcohol, they don't mix." Shor promptly ordered oysters and brandy, then dipped each oyster into the drink before eating it. Then he ordered lobster and brandy, and did the same. Finally Reynolds changed the line: "Like oil and water, they don't mix."

Willie Mays was there, willingly signing autographs. "Easy for him. Just four letters in his last name. Not so easy for me," said the Red Sox' Carl Yastrzemski.

Shor was hospitalized for nearly eight weeks with a broken leg. Returning in a wheelchair, he announced he'd been dry for sixty-nine days. "I'll drink again only when I'm able to stand up at my bar. *Then* I'll show these amateurs how to drink," he said. In the 152nd day of his abstinence, Shor was invited to a chamber music concert. "I'm not *that* sober," he replied.

Finally back off the wagon, he explained why: "Through booze I met two chief justices, fifty world champs, six presidents, Joe DiMaggio, and Babe Ruth."

Muhammad Ali hosted a party at Shor's and was introduced to Joe Frazier's manager shortly before their fight. The manager, Yancey Durham, said Frazier would "take you in six rounds."

Ali laughed and said, "Don't even let your fighter *dream* about that."

PART
II

"They Had

"Faces Then"

CARROLL BAKER

(1931–)

In September 1956, *Baby Doll* was the most controversial movie in the world. New York's Cardinal Spellman condemned it as obscene—without bothering to see it. In the film, adapted from a Tennessee Williams play called *27 Wagons Full of Cotton*, Baker played a virgin bride in a story charged with sexual themes. A huge billboard on Broadway showed her reclining in a slip. If displayed vertically, it would've been fifteen stories high.

When Baker's daughter was born, a studio press agent asked if he could announce that baby Blanche was named for Blanche DuBois in Tennessee Williams's *A Streetcar Named Desire*.

"No!" she replied. "Blanche was named for my husband Jack Garfein's mother, who died in Auschwitz."

Pregnant again while filming *But Not for Me*, she found that the baby started kicking every time she did love scenes with Clark Gable, and only stopped with the cameras. After one such scene, her agent kidded: "Wait till your husband Jack hears about *this*!"

"Oh, he won't mind," said Baker. "Fact is, I knew Clark long before I met Jack.

She bought a recording of "Old McDonald Had a Farm" and played it for her young son. When Jack arrived home he was shocked at what he heard. That melody had haunted him since his childhood in a concentration camp. The diplomats imprisoned there had been mocked by being called out periodically and made to repeat the animal sounds in the song.

Baker once visited London with her family. Their children wanted to see the queen. Jack said it was highly unlikely, because she was "busy running the Empire." On their first day, the children and their governess returned from a walk in the park and reported they had indeed seen the queen. Elizabeth had been riding on the bridle path in the park and the children waved. She waved back, and Prince Philip dismounted and shook their hands.

Baker appeared in a workshop production of *A Hatful of Rain* at the Actors Studio, but Shelley Winters played the lead on Broadway

My father and Carroll Baker at El Morocco.

and Eva Marie Saint got the part in the movie. When she saw the film, Baker noticed a huge billboard in the background proclaiming, "Carroll Baker Becomes a Star Overnight."

In December 1958, Baker received a letter from a former boyfriend of her mother's, asking for help setting up a business. "I deserve it," he wrote. "After all, if I'd married your mother, I might've been your father and you'd never have gotten where you are today."

ETHEL BARRYMORE

(1879–1959)

Part of America's most famous acting dynasty, Barrymore first appeared on Broadway in September 1895 as the lead in *The Impudent Young Couple*. She was the first actor with a telephone in her dressing room, when she appeared in 1914's *Tante*.

Things didn't go well on opening night of W. Somerset Maugham's *The Constant Wife*, her thirty-ninth play, in 1926. She knew the author was in the audience, and she kept blowing her lines. Afterward, she threw her arms around Maugham and said, "I've ruined your play, but it'll make millions." She was right. It ran nine months and has been revived four times.

In Hollywood, Barrymore and my father drove past the MGM studios. The gateman, who'd been there for years, had barred many famous stars whose names weren't on his list. "I love him," said Barrymore. "He considers me almost an equal."

Her nephew John Barrymore Jr. was starting out as an actor in summer stock and missed a performance, citing illness. "It's not just 'the show must go on,'" she told him. "People from miles around have paid to see you. It's a matter of the integrity of a given word. A healthy fighter would get no sympathy if just before the opening bell, he announced he just didn't feel like fighting that night."

It was she, not Alice Roosevelt Longworth, who first described Governor Thomas E. Dewey, the two-time Republican presidential candidate, as "looking like the bridegroom on the wedding cake."

Her laugh was so distinctive that Tallulah Bankhead once told her, "You haven't seen my show yet. I'd have heard you."

The Salvation Army once asked Barrymore to do a radio benefit. She recalled that when she was fourteen, performing in a touring company of *The Rivals*, a local Salvation Army band played loudly outside, ruining a performance. "But all is forgiven," she told them.

By May 1948, she'd been retired from Broadway for three years and was offered a return. "You owe it to the theater to come back," the producer begged.

"Young man," she replied, "for fifty years I've worked for applause and cut flowers in my dressing room. I've earned the right to sit in my garden and watch them grow."

A huge baseball fan, Barrymore probably knew more sportswriters than critics. Whenever she'd play Pittsburgh, she made it a point to visit Pirate legend Honus Wagner, "The Flying Dutchman," baseball's greatest shortstop.

My parents gave *two* parties for her at our home. She told my father she enjoyed the food and the atmosphere at the first one, so in 1954, she came again. Danny Kaye was one of the guests, as was British diplomat Sir Gladwyn Jebb. Barrymore and Kaye, a future co-owner of the Seattle Mariners, spent much of the evening explaining baseball's intricacies to the Brit, along with some of its most famous names. One of them was there that night: Joe DiMaggio.

Barrymore returned to Broadway in James Barry's *The Twelve-Pound Look*. It had been nearly thirty years since she'd toured in this play, which at one point required her to carry a portable typewriter onstage. Now in her seventies, she found the typewriter extremely heavy to hold as she stood in the wings awaiting her cue.

Then she stepped onstage to thunderous applause. Suddenly, she said, that typewriter started feeling lighter and lighter. By the time she reached center stage, it almost felt weightless.

Judy Holliday confessed to Tallulah Bankhead that she was always nervous before a curtain. "Nonsense. Sheer nonsense," said Bankhead. "I'm never nervous. Why?" When Holliday relayed this to Barrymore, she responded, "I'll tell you what 'nonsense' is. You go back and tell Tallulah that even I, after seventy-one years on the stage, am nervous."

Once a salesgirl was showing her some dresses, but Barrymore said she preferred the simple dress the salesgirl was wearing. "I got it from a friend at a wholesale house," she said. "I'll phone and see if they have one in your size." After the call, she reported, "They told me they never do it, but since it's for you, Miss Barrymore, they'd make one up."

"Tell them not to," replied Barrymore. "I don't like snobs."

At Sardi's, my father sat with her and she overheard someone at the next table saying, "I've just seen a great play at the Barrymore Theater."

"Excuse me, Leonard," she said, then leaned over and exclaimed in a loud voice, "I heard that! It's the *Ethel* Barrymore Theater!"

JOHN BARRYMORE

(1882–1942)

He was known as "The Great Profile," the quintessential stage actor who, with his brother Lionel and sister Ethel, was part of the second of four generations of American acting royalty. Barrymore made his Broadway debut on December 28, 1903, in something called *Glad of It*, which ran a scant thirty-two performances. His Broadway career included *Richard III* and two productions of *Hamlet*. His greatest movie roles were in *Dinner at Eight* and *Twentieth Century*.

In 1936, Barrymore got married for the fourth time, to actress Elaine Barry. Ben Hecht and Gene Fowler, two of Hollywood's top screenwriters, tried to dissuade him, but he cut them off: "Gentlemen, you're looking at a man about to go over Niagara Falls in a barrel." The marriage lasted only four years.

When Barrymore and Barry became estranged, he poured out his heart to screenwriter Charles MacArthur, who used some of Barrymore's melancholy words in his screenplay for *Wuthering Heights*.

Barrymore worked in movies before teleprompters. He occasionally used a chalkboard held off-camera, explaining, "I have memorized, in my lifetime, the glorious works of Shakespeare, Barrie, and Ibsen. Why should I clutter my mind with the worthless drivel written by high-salaried peasants?"

During a break in filming *The Great Man Votes*, he napped on a cot alongside the set. When he awoke, he bumped his head on a klieg light. "Are you okay?" asked a stagehand.

"A bump? It's nothing," Barrymore assured him. "Remember, I've been married four times."

In the same film, he had a scene in which his only line was "Yes." Director Garson Kanin wondered why he needed that famous off-camera blackboard for just one word.

"Because," replied Barrymore, "there is the chance I might otherwise say 'No'!"

In November 1938, as the film neared completion, promotional appearances were being planned. It was then that the studio learned that he'd never voted.

Early in 1940, Barrymore was starring in *My Dear Children* in Chicago. One night, character actor Victor Francen was in the audience. Barrymore, as usual, had downed a few before the curtain and was slurring his lines. After Act I, Francen went to the box office and said, "Mr. Barrymore is obviously under the weather." He got a refund.

Francen's date that night left her phone number at the box office, asking to be notified on an evening when Barrymore looked sober. It came two weeks later.

Random House published *My Dear Children* with an introduction by Barrymore. The book contained all the ad libs that Barrymore had inserted during the run, recorded at every performance by the stage manager.

During one performance, on March 29, 1940, Barrymore ad-libbed to the audience, "You want a paycheck? He just got knocked out by Joe Louis in the second round," a reference to Johnny Paychek, just decked by the Brown Bomber at nearby Madison Square Garden.

Barrymore invited Eddie Cantor to join him and W. C. Fields for a drink. "No thanks," replied Cantor, well aware that both were as renowned for imbibing as for their acting. "I have to be back at the studio next month."

Mary Pickford, one of Hollywood's first superstars, read about Barrymore's decline in 1940. "When I was fourteen," she recalled, "he was my dream man. Now it saddens me."

"You mean how far he's fallen?" she was asked.

"Yes, and also that I'm no longer fourteen!"

Barrymore once checked into a hospital where the doctor turned to the nurse and requested, "Alcohol sponge."

"That's the best way I've ever been described," said Barrymore.

One night on Broadway, he staggered onto the stage, mumbled a few words, then collapsed, but before the audience could gasp, he arose, winked, and said, "If someone could provide me with a wheelchair, I'll do my imitation of brother Lionel."

Brother Lionel wasn't surprised at John's frequent marriages. "He was that way when he was little, too. He'd break a toy and yell, 'I'm done with this. Take it away and bring me another!'"

Barrymore had a favorite after-hours place in New York where a violinist often played. One night, the musician played a series of songs Barrymore requested, and the star said, "This is a wonderful evening."

Then he spilled his drink and said, "This has become a terrible evening."

A friend asked Barrymore, "Don't you think your drinking's harming your health?"

"There are more old drunks around than old doctors," he replied.

As he approached his one hundredth performance of *Hamlet*, he was reminded that Edwin Booth, regarded as one of the greatest Hamlets, had played it only a hundred times. A friend suggested he end the run at ninety-nine, in tribute to Booth. Barrymore agreed, but then, after his 101st performance, he asked, "Remind me, what was it I agreed to?"

A man said: "Mr. Barrymore, I always wanted to meet you face-to-face." "The Great Profile" cocked his head, turned to the right to show his left side and said: "How's this?"

Barrymore met Albert Einstein in Princeton. The two posed for photographs, and Barrymore spoke in his famous stentorian tone, arching one eyebrow and using flowery language. Einstein, renowned for his complex theories, finally said, "Pardon me, but I don't understand a thing you're saying."

Soon after World War II began, Barrymore and W. C. Fields showed up at an army recruiting station. "Don't tell me," said the sergeant behind the desk. "Did the Japanese send you?"

One of his great regrets was never having played *Macbeth* in the Hollywood Bowl. "How would you use your blackboard there?" he was asked. "I'd hire a plane and use skywriting," he explained.

Jed Harris, the Broadway producer-director, approached Barrymore with a unique offer to do *King Lear* for one night. "That's because I know you," Harris explained, "and I know you would lose interest after opening night. So we'd charge a huge amount for tickets, hire second-rate actors and pay them scale, and we'd make a large profit." The project fell through because by then, Barrymore had lost the ability to memorize dialogue.

An actor from Barrymore's 1923 stage production of *Hamlet*, Frederick Lewis, was asked years later what it was like working with him.

"I'll say this," the actor replied. "Barrymore gave a great performance—of something!"

Frank Morgan, who played the title role in *The Wizard of Oz*, did a radio drama and ran into Barrymore, whose dressing room was across the hall. "This is my first experience on radio," he told Barrymore. "How do you like it?"

"It's like kissing a woman," Barrymore replied. "The first time you like it. Then you go MAD for it."

During a hospital stay, a producer kept trying to visit him but was refused entry for three days. Finally he was admitted. "Why did it take so many tries to visit you?" he asked.

"For three reasons," replied Barrymore. "One: you're a producer—a non-creative peasant. Two: I couldn't get any pleasure out of embracing you. And three: you weren't delivering liquor."

He died three months later.

RED BUTTONS

(1919–2006)

When Aaron Chwatt was a teenage bellhop, a bandleader noticed his red hair and shiny buttons. He gave him the nickname that led to a career in vaudeville, burlesque, Borscht Belt hotels, Broadway, and movies, culminating in an Academy Award for Best Supporting Actor for *Sayonara*. He was also memorable in *Hatari!*, *The Longest Day*, and *Harlow*.

In 1941, he was about to make his Broadway debut, earning $50 a week in *The Admiral Had a Wife*, a farce set at Pearl Harbor, scheduled to open Monday, December 8. That Sunday afternoon, the director assembled the cast and said, "I have bad news: the Japanese have just bombed Pearl Harbor."

"Oh, is *that* all?" said Buttons. "I thought you were going to tell me my laugh lines had been cut."

The show was canceled.

Buttons's trademark gesture was cupping his right ear as he sang, aping a cantor in the synagogue.

One night in 1950, George Burns and Chico Marx were honored at the Friars Club and Buttons was called onstage. He shook Marx's hand and said, "Nice to meet you, Mr. Burns," then shook Burns's hand, saying, "You too, Mr. Marx." Later, told of his gaffe, he joked, "Sorry, I don't own a TV set yet."

During the run of his TV series in 1952, he asked Phil Silvers if he'd seen the episode aired the night before. "Nah," replied his old friend, "I watched the fights. Besides, what would I have seen?" Then he repeated every joke in the show.

When Judy Garland performed at the Palace Theater in September 1956, Buttons and his wife had better seats than the Duke and Duchess of Windsor. "He may outrank me at Buckingham," said Buttons, "but at *this* palace, they treat *me* like a king!"

When he won the Oscar for *Sayonara*, he was about to rise and walk to the stage when Sessue Hayakawa, nominated for playing the brutal commander of a prisoner of war camp in *Bridge on the River Kwai*, and seated right behind Buttons, whispered into Buttons's ear, "Tonight you die, Yankee dog!"

JAMES CAGNEY

(1899–1986)

No other actor had such range as the tough-guy product of Manhattan's Hell's Kitchen, who for decades was one of the most respected stars in Hollywood. In 1921 he made his debut in the ensemble of a Broadway show called *Pitter Patter*, and he appeared onstage throughout the decade before entering the movies. He left an enduring legacy, thanks to his sixty-four films: gangsters, cowboys, fighters, an admiral, and America's song-and-dance man; he could handle them all.

In the first few weeks of The Lyons Den in August 1934, a rival columnist announced that Cagney had given up smoking. My father reported that not only was that story untrue, but in fact Cagney would appear in a series of ads touting Old Gold.

In 1945, Cagney spotted Gertrude Stein's photo on the cover of her new book. He called the person in Hollywood he thought looked exactly like Stein and said, "How'd you like to make a movie about her?"

"What role would I play?" came the reply.

"Why, the starring one, of course," said Cagney. "You look exactly like her."

"No, thanks," laughed Spencer Tracy.

In August 1948, Cagney toured the Motion Picture Actors' Home in Hollywood, and came away depressed. Spencer Tracy said he needn't worry; Cagney had money and could easily afford to move there someday, if necessary.

"But what if I'm not wanted there?" asked Cagney.

"I have a solution," said Tracy. "Buy the place now."

In September 1954, Cagney was preparing for *Run for Cover*. Harold J. Kennedy had a small role, which included a scene with Cagney. In their scene, Cagney's line was "Why did you do it?" He read the line listlessly in rehearsal, and Kennedy wondered how he was such an enormous star. Then director Nicholas Ray called "Action!" and Cagney approached Kennedy as in the run-through. Only this time he grabbed Kennedy's lapels, shook him violently, then hurled him across the room, roaring, "WHY DID YOU DO IT?!"

For years, Mae Clarke was questioned about the famous scene in *The Public Enemy* in which Cagney shoved half a grapefruit into her face. "If he'd splashed me with a glass of orange juice," she'd reply, "we wouldn't be having this conversation."

In early October 1968, Cagney visited the Players Club in New York. "Mr. Cagney, why didn't you come last week?" he was asked. "We showed *Yankee Doodle Dandy*."

"I hate Cagney movies," he replied.

LOUIS CALHERN

(1895–1956)

ouis Calhern was one of Hollywood's most distinguished character actors. Born in Brooklyn, his real name was Carl Henry Vogt. His family moved to St. Louis, where, playing in a high school football game in 1912, he was spotted by a stage manager for a touring company. He had starring roles in *Duck Soup* (with the Marx Brothers), *The Asphalt Jungle*, *Juarez*, *Annie Get Your Gun* (as Buffalo Bill), and *Julius Caesar*, in which he played the title part—seventy-two films in all.

An actress once approached producer Lawrence Langner saying, "I need a Louis Calhern type for the stage adaptation of my book." He looked at her oddly, since she was Ilka Chase, who'd been briefly married to Calhern years before. Her book was called *In Bed We Cry*.

Asked his worst moment in the theater, Calhern said, "I overheard a producer talking with an agent about casting a new show. The agent asked the producer what sort of actor he was looking for, and the producer said, 'A young j155 type.'"

Calhern met his fourth wife, Marianne Stewart, when they were in the play *Jacobowsky and the Colonel*. But their ten-year marriage ended in 1955 when she flew to Mexico to file for a divorce. As soon as her plane arrived in El Paso en route home, she wired her husband: "Paperwork completed. Love."

Asked how he handled frequent flops on Broadway, he said, "Whenever that happened, I'd always be seen wearing a bright, checked suit. An unemployed actor should dress in the winter as if he's on his way to Palm Beach."

In June 1944, Calhern tried an experiment at the Lambs Club, the popular actors' gathering place. He greeted every actor then starring on Broadway and pretended he'd just seen their performance. "What happened during your performance tonight?" Every actor said either "My throat went dry," "My leading lady missed her cue," or "I *told* the director we should've tried a different approach to that scene." Not one would proclaim he'd been flawless, and each one had an excuse.

In May 1948, Calhern arrived early at a Yankee game where his friend William Bendix was filming some scenes for *The Babe Ruth Story*. Later, Bendix, who looked nothing like Ruth and had a clumsy left-handed swing, said, "I felt awful, in front of all those Yankee fans, pretending to be Ruth. They were yelling: 'Phony!'"

"I know what you mean," replied Calhern. "I remember portraying Justice Oliver Wendell Holmes in Washington, D.C., in front of an audience which included the justices of the Supreme Court."

Calhern's first success on Broadway came in *Cobra* in 1924. The morning after it opened, he was awakened by a phone call from a powerful Broadway producer. "Come see me before you talk to anybody else," the producer said. Calhern rushed to the producer's office. "Lou, success is harder to take than failure," he said. "That's all I want you to remember. Now get out of here. I'm busy."

When I was six, in 1950, he let me stand backstage watching his *King Lear*. When he told an actor friend in Hollywood he was about to take on one of the theater's most demanding roles, the actor said, "I've been studying *Lear* for two months and I think I can handle it perfectly."

"My good man," Calhern replied, "I've been studying the role for forty-two *years* and I *still* have much concern."

As rehearsals began, he told the cast he didn't know why they wanted to do the play. "When Sir Henry Irving did it in London in 1892," he explained, "the critics panned him. And over here, critics panned the great Edwin Booth, too. I have no worry, because if it should flop, I still have my fat M G M contract. But the rest of you—I admire your bravery."

At one performance, Calhern had to add an extra line of dialogue. The head usher had forgotten to turn off the electric fans after intermission. It was impossible for the actors to be heard over the din. Not wanting to step out of character, he began, "By the sacred radiance of the sun," then pointed to the troublesome fans and ad-libbed, "... and the roar in the sky." The usher got the message and quickly turned off the fans.

"Actors dramatize and exaggerate," he said. "Discount half the knocks and double the praise." He once heard an actor called a liar for boasting his salary was five thousand a week when in fact it was half that. "To double your own salary isn't lying," Calhern said. "Lying is only when you *triple* it."

"When I was broke, I always felt healthy," he recalled. "But when

I became rich, my new friends insisted on sending me to doctors." He was operated on several times due to injuries suffered in his boxing days. His battered nose threatened his career in films, and when Fox production chief Darryl Zanuck suggested he have surgery to straighten and shorten it, Calhern said, "Sorry. Gutzon Borglum is busy sculpting Mount Rushmore and won't be free for years."

On a return to New York in early November 1952, he got into a limousine and the chauffeur said he, too, was an actor, and had played against Calhern in the Broadway Show Softball League. "I was on the *Carmen Jones* team," he said. "I remember that team— good ballplayers," replied Calhern. "Yes, we *were* a good team," said the driver. "If baseball was our living and acting the sideline, you'd be the chauffeur now and I the passenger."

In 1956, he began filming his role in *High Society*, the musical version of *The Philadelphia Story*. On his first day on the set, he looked around at his costars and sighed, "This is typical of MGM, hiring me to bolster up this weak cast." The movie starred Frank Sinatra, Celeste Holm, Grace Kelly, Bing Crosby, and Louis Armstrong.

CAROL CHANNING

(1921–)

Unlike most Broadway musical stars, she had two signature songs: "Diamonds Are a Girl's Best Friend" and "Hello, Dolly!" She came to New York from Seattle at nineteen after graduating from Bennington College in Vermont. Her big break came when author Anita Loos cast her as Lorelei Lee in the 1949 musical adaptation of her book *Gentlemen Prefer Blondes*.

But a much bigger hit was coming. On January 16, 1964, she opened as Dolly Levi in *Hello, Dolly!*, the musical based on Thornton Wilder's 1955 play *The Matchmaker*, itself a revision of Wilder's *The Merchant of Yonkers* (1938). The show ran an astonishing 2,844 performances. By the time the original production closed on December 27, 1970, the role had been taken over by a slew of stars. Ethel Merman, for whom the part was written, had turned it down, as did Mary Martin, but it became such a smash hit that after Channing left, both would play Dolly. So would Ginger Rogers, Martha Raye, Pearl Bailey, and countless others in national and regional productions.

Channing began her career as a model, seeing it as a way to get acting jobs. "I wanted to assume the character of the clothes I was wearing," she recalled. "When I put on lounging pajamas, I was an Indian princess. For a bridal gown, I pretended I had the sweetness of June Allyson. For a dark business suit, I pretended I was English. Then after that fashion show I got fired."

She modeled for a Mill Valley, California, art group, whose members contributed twenty-five cents apiece to pay for her fee. On the second day, Channing glanced at all the canvases and felt she could do better. So she chipped in her own quarter to pay for another model and began painting.

She sang a pop song in a talent show; though she lost, she received an offer from a Toronto nightclub. She then bought a one-thousand-dollar gown. "The critics didn't think much of my act," she said, "but I got raves in *Women's Wear Daily*."

In her one-woman act called *Show Girl*, in 1961, she spoofed big stars who did one-woman shows at the Palace Theater. Judy Garland, who played the Palace, came backstage and told her, "Your Betty Hutton number was great." Betty Hutton, who also played the Palace, then visited Channing, saying, "Your Judy Garland spoof was a hoot!"

In September 1964, her paintings were exhibited in Chicago. Her style was primitive: "It's Junior Varsity Grandma Moses," she said.

In December 1965, Channing performed *Hello, Dolly!* in St. Louis, sharing the venue with other events. The Kiel Auditorium marquee read: "CAROL CHANNING WRESTLING FRIDAY."

She didn't *really* believe diamonds are a girl's best friend. "A girl's best friend is the man who supplies her with the diamonds."

When she performed that song, she would toss imitation diamonds to the audience. In Chicago, Mrs. Joseph P. Kennedy, the president's mother, caught one, put it on her wrist, and kept it.

Soon after she opened on Broadway in *Hello, Dolly!*, she received a gift from producer David Merrick: an engraved cigarette box from Tiffany's. She didn't smoke, so she used the box as a receptacle for her false eyelashes.

After Elizabeth Taylor saw her in *Hello, Dolly!* in August 1964, she sent Channing a bouquet of white orchids. Later, Channing met Richard Burton and told him, "Your wife is charming and thoughtful."

"Of course," Burton replied. "That's how she got *me!*"

September 10, 1964, was a memorable day for Channing. She and her young son were given a tour of the United Nations, lunched with Undersecretary General Ralph Bunche, and met Secretary General U Thant. Also at lunch was Marc Chagall, who communicated with Channing via her son, who'd summered at camps in France. Then Lady Bird Johnson, the First Lady, called to thank her for singing "Hello, Lyndon!" at the recent Democratic National Convention.

In January 1965, she was visited backstage by a Soviet delegation and told them, "Last week, I had the honor of performing with one of your countrymen: Rudolf Nureyev, at LBJ's inaugural gala." She quickly realized she'd erred in mentioning the ballet star, since Nureyev had defected.

To try to make amends for this diplomatic faux pas, she phoned her friend Dr. Bunche at the UN, who was on his other line with U.S. ambassador Adlai Stevenson. After Dr. Bunche told her not to worry, he resumed his talk with Stevenson, who said, "Why didn't you tell me you had Carol Channing on the other line? I'd much rather talk to *her*!"

Channing somehow made Nixon's infamous "Enemies List." Soon after the existence of the list was made public, she toured in *Lorelei* (a revision of *Gentlemen Prefer Blondes*) and was in Cincinnati when a bouquet of flowers arrived. It was from the White House, with the note, "We may hate you, but the audience loves you."

When she was made an honorary princess of the Cherokee tribe in Oklahoma City, her husband Charles Lowe asked, "Does that mean I'm now 'Prince Charles'?"

In October 1973, Channing injured her arm while performing in *Lorelei* in Chicago. "I've heard of an actress being added to a cast, but never the other way around," she said.

A few weeks later, she met a man who looked familiar. "Didn't we meet at a party in late July 1969?" she asked. "I doubt it," replied Buzz Aldrin, the second man to walk on the moon that week. "I was out of town then."

On New Year's Eve, 1973, Mae West came backstage to pay respects to Channing after a performance of *Lorelei* and said, "I just thought I'd come up and see *you* sometime."

She once gave a command performance and later was asked if she thought the queen was tired of having to shake hands day after day, year after year. "She probably likes that more than having to pose for stamps," Channing replied.

JOAN CRAWFORD

(1904–1977)

Born Lucille Fay LeSueur, in her time she was rivaled only by Bette Davis as Hollywood's biggest star. She made 103 movies and TV shows, winning an Oscar for *Mildred Pierce* in 1945. Despite her sordid seduction of the teenage Jackie Cooper and the now-infamous way she treated her four adopted children, her legacy as a star is untarnished. She was the quintessential mid-century movie star in the way she lived, loved, and worked.

On their last night as husband and wife in April 1939, she dined with Franchot Tone. Onlookers seemed surprised at how happy they appeared, probably because they'd consumed nine Scotches.

After that divorce she began removing the initials "J.C.T." from her towels. Then she stopped her maids from that task after becoming engaged to Phillip Terry.

In January 1940, Crawford was at the Rainbow Room in New York and posed for a photo with Will Hays, head of Hollywood's censorship board. "If one of my pictures ever gets in trouble with your office," she told him afterward, "I'll hold this photo against you."

While married to Tone, Crawford was aware of how attractive he was to women. For instance, a party was thrown for her at El Morocco and Tone had to leave early. He called back to her, "Well, good-bye, darling." Three young women within Crawford's earshot turned and replied, "Good-bye, Franchot."

My father appeared in her 1947 movie *Daisy Kenyon*, playing himself at the Stork Club.

In May of that year, Crawford wore heavy makeup accompanying her husband to a nightclub. Her newly adopted daughter Christina had bitten her on the nose.

In January 1948, she was at a Hollywood party where a young actress stopped her and whispered, "Miss Crawford, there's a smudge under your eye."

"Thanks," replied Crawford. Then she asked, "New in town, aren't you?"

"Yes," replied the starlet. "How'd you know?"

Joan Crawford and my father on the Warner Bros. studio lot.

"Because any girl who's been here longer than a week would let a star walk around with dirt on her face."

A few weeks later she attended a party at the home of Fox studio boss Joseph Schenck, but she felt moody and decided to leave early. She asked the butler to express her regrets. Schenck later called her and she said, "I just wanted to take a drive alone in the rain."

"But you've already done that in *Humoresque* and *Daisy Kenyon*," he replied. "So why do it again?"

Offered a starring role on Broadway, she said, "When I go to the theater I visit friends backstage, then walk out on the empty stage feeling I can do it. It's really simple. Friends in the audience. Read the lines. Curtain. Simple.

"But then, when I'm given a script and start imagining myself on-stage in front of people—I shudder."

In 1959, she attended a Christmas party wearing a huge diamond ring, a large bracelet, and an enormous diamond necklace. She noticed guests staring at the gems and said, "I just enjoy things big!"

Her daughter Christina once told her mother she'd like to try to become a movie star, too, and wondered if she'd ever achieve success and wear the fabulous gowns and jewels her mother did.

"Sure," replied the star, "but you have to work hard at it."

"You mean getting up at five a.m. and working until seven p.m.?" asked the girl. When her mother nodded, Christina said, "Never mind. I'll just borrow yours."

In December 1961, Crawford went to the Peppermint Lounge, the hot place known for the Twist. "But you might be recognized," said a friend. "People will surround you and it'll become a mob."

"I hope so," she replied.

Her first husband was Douglas Fairbanks Jr. Years later, she helped director George Cukor screen-test Lady Sylvia Ashley, who'd been married years before to Douglas Fairbanks Sr. and would later marry Clark Gable. The cameras rolled and Crawford, pursuant to the script, slapped Lady Ashley in the face. "Cut!" said Cukor. "Now let's try that again." After the second slap, Lady Ashley announced, "Thank you. I no longer want to be an actress."

In August 1949, she was at her hairdresser's, Westmore's, in Hollywood. When a phone near her rang, she reached for it playfully and said, "Westmore's of Hollywood. May I help you?"

"This is Greta Garbo," said the voice on the phone. "I want to make an appointment."

"Right, and I'm Joan Crawford," replied Crawford before both hung up. A week or so later, they met at a party and exchanged the story, realizing both had told the truth.

Crawford asked a novelist friend to send her three copies of his book, all inscribed to her, explaining she wanted one for the living room, the second for her kitchen, and the third for her bedroom.

In February 1970, Sir Noël Coward sent her a note that she treasured for the rest of her life. It read, "It suddenly occurred to me that I've loved you for thirty years."

When Christopher Plummer opened on Broadway in a musical version of *Cyrano*, Crawford sent him the following wire: "SEE CELIA'S SPEECH, SHAKESPEARE'S 'AS YOU LIKE IT,' ACT III, SCENE 2, LINE 194."

Shakespeare's text reads: "O wonderful, wonderful, and most wonderful wonderful! and yet again wonderful . . ."

Seven years after his death, a TV tribute to Clark Gable was planned. Crawford, who appeared in eight movies with Gable—more than any other actress—had to decline participation. The show was sponsored by Coca-Cola. Crawford was on the board of directors of its rival, Pepsi-Cola. When she returned to Hollywood in 1962, she explained her absence: "I've been away putting the hard sell on a soft drink."

HUME CRONYN

(1911–2003)

This versatile Canadian-born character actor had a career on stage and screen that lasted almost seventy years. Though his first Broadway role was in 1934, *The Fourposter* (1951), costarring his wife, Jessica Tandy, was his first stage hit. Others included *Hamlet*, as Polonius, opposite Richard Burton, in 1964, and *The Gin Game*, another two-hander with his wife, in 1977.

His films include *The Postman Always Rings Twice*, *Sunrise at Campobello*, *Conrack*, and *Cocoon*. He also costarred in two Hitchcock classics, *Lifeboat* and *Shadow of a Doubt*.

Cronyn was in a play called *Retreat to Pleasure* in 1940. George Matthews played a prizefighter, and one night he forgot his entrance cue. Cronyn quickly realized what had happened and ad-libbed, "You probably want to know what's new. I'll tell you. I met a prizefighter *who should've been here by now!*" Matthews hurried out and the play went on, with the audience none the wiser.

In October 1961, Cronyn arrived in Rome for his role in *Cleopatra*. Asked to describe how he'd endure the long separation from his wife in New York, Cronyn said, "Absence makes the bank account grow fatter."

Eight months later, director Joseph Mankiewicz called, "Cut! Hume, you're done!" Cronyn ripped off his false beard, dove into the Bay of Naples, came up to the surface, and yelled, "I'm flying home *tonight!*"

One of Cronyn's prized possessions was a letter from Sean O'Casey that read, in part, "The theater is no place for a man who bleeds easily."

During Richard Burton's Broadway engagement as Hamlet, the star was suffering from an ailment that he alleviated with several glasses of brandy.

In the scene in which Cronyn, as Polonius, is stabbed to death then dragged across the stage, Cronyn did one of the longest death scenes in Shakespearean history. He staggered slowly, in fits, toward the wings, so that the inebriated Burton only had to drag him two or three feet offstage.

In 1966, the Cronyns were starring in *A Delicate Balance,* by Edward Albee. They lectured at the Yale School of Drama, where Cronyn advised students never to go to opening nights. "See a play four months later," he advised. "It'll be a much smoother, better performance."

"But only if it's still playing," his wife added.

In December of that year, Cronyn and Tandy attended a performance of *I Do! I Do!,* the musical version of *The Fourposter,* in which they'd starred on Broadway. Afterward, Cronyn said to his wife, "I *told* you we should've taken singing lessons!"

BING CROSBY

(1903–1977)

Near the end of every college basketball season, Gonzaga University gets national attention. That's because the school, a private Roman Catholic institution in Spokane, Washington, is often in the postseason NCAA tournament. Other than that, it's obscure except for its alumni: former NFL star Tony Canadeo, former speaker of the House Tom Foley, the popular sixties folk group the Chad Mitchell Trio, and by far its most famous alumnus, Harry Lillis "Bing" Crosby.

Crosby became a singing star on the radio in the thirties, then turned to acting. A 1930 movie called *King of Jazz* starred bandleader Paul Whiteman. Listed thirtieth in the cast, part of "The Rhythm Boys" group, was Crosby, whose number was almost cut.

Three years later, the movie was rereleased under the title *Bing Crosby in 'King of Jazz' with Paul Whiteman.* The poster featured a huge close-up of Crosby with a tiny shot of Whiteman and his band far below. It was the second of an astonishing 232 movies and TV shows for Crosby. He eventually won the Best Actor Oscar for 1944's *Going My Way*.

Several women were selling war bonds outside the El Morocco club in September 1942. "How's business?" Crosby asked.

"Only so-so," they replied. .

"Don't go away," replied Crosby. He went into the nightclub, soon raising $80,000 in donations after singing just a few songs.

In March 1943, there was a fire at Crosby's home and all his records were destroyed. Then a fan contacted him: "Mr. Crosby, I've got a complete collection of your recordings. But I've placed a two-dollar bet on every one of the horses you've raced, and lost every time. If you reimburse me, I'll give you my collection."

Crosby paid up: eighty-four dollars for the forty-two races in which his horses finished out of the money.

Dore Schary, the movie executive and writer, lived down the street, and watched the fire raging as Crosby stood helplessly nearby. Trying to lighten the mood, he said, "Hi, Bing. What's new?"

A few weeks later, Schary was hit by a car. Crosby called his hospital room and said, "Hi, Dore. What's new with *you?*"

That fall, Crosby visited the Treasury Department in Washington, where an official said, "You've got what the public wants." "So do you," replied Crosby.

James Roosevelt, the president's son, served in the South Pacific during World War II, and on one mission he landed on a remote island that was home to a fierce tribe whose sympathies were unknown. He and his men were quickly taken to the chief.

Roosevelt extended his hand and said, "I'm Colonel Roosevelt, U.S.A. America."

"Oh, you must know Bing Crosby," the chief replied.

In October 1944, Crosby returned from entertaining troops in France and a Republican urged him to support New York governor Thomas E. Dewey in the fall elections. "Remember," said the politician, "while you were away, FDR had Sinatra to the White House."

In 1946, Crosby met with Jack Kapp, the head of Decca Records, which Crosby had helped make one of the top labels in the music industry. His contract still had two and a half years to go.

"Bing, you're forty-three, which is getting old for a singer," said Kapp. "And there are younger singers coming up." Crosby nodded apprehensively, especially when Kapp pulled out the contract and said, "I'd like to tear this up.'

Without waiting for Crosby to reply, he tore it up, then quickly pulled out another contract. "Sign this instead. You'll be fifty-three when this one expires and still be the best singer of them all."

Two of Crosby's sons were introduced to Frank Sinatra. One said, "We'd love to see your icebox. Dad says you took the bread and butter from us." The other added, "And it doesn't look like you've been eating any of it yourself."

Early in 1946, director Billy Wilder called Crosby and asked if he'd like Joan Fontaine as his next leading lady. "It doesn't matter," replied the easygoing Crosby. "Just tell me when and where to show up and if you want me fat or skinny." *The Emperor Waltz* costarred Fontaine.

Golfer Byron Nelson was invited to play a round with Crosby and Bob Hope. He declined, saying, "They play golf more frequently than pros and all they want to talk about is golf."

Crosby owned part of the Pittsburgh Pirates. In June 1947, he recorded "The Whiffenpoof Song," which took an hour. That's when

Crosby began looking at his watch, worried he'd miss the Pirates' game against the Brooklyn Dodgers. He recorded the flip side of the record, "Kentucky Babe," in eight minutes, plenty of time to make it to Ebbets Field for the first pitch.

By 1948, Crosby had become the top box office star, despite being middle-aged. For his role in *Anything Goes*, in 1956, the studio decided to pin his ears back with tape and make him wear a toupee and a restraining belt around his waist. But before his first scene he ripped off everything, declaring, "They'll see me as I am."

In October 1952, Crosby was in Paris shooting *Little Boy Lost*. In one scene, he was singing in the street, with no cameras or lights visible. Passersby listened and, not recognizing him, tossed him a few coins.

Crosby and his son Gary met Gene Autry in Paris. "Are you enjoying Paris?" Autry asked.

"Yes," said Crosby, "but since I'm with Gary, we have to see only museums and stuff."

Then Autry asked his son the same question, perhaps with the beautiful young Parisian women in mind.

"I am," sighed Gary, "but since I'm with Dad, all we get to see are museums and stuff."

When Bing and Gary recorded a duet, Bing said: "Take this record home to your mother, just to show her you're not spending all your time shooting pool."

Crosby and Hope often played practical jokes on one another. When Hope visited Moscow in 1958, Crosby sent him a cablegram: "Messages received and are being decoded. Thanks for the information."

At the Paramount commissary he overheard a man at the next table saying, "Everyone is born with the same potential for talent."

"Really?" Crosby leaned over and asked. "Let's hear you croon a tune."

Irving Berlin gave Crosby a painting he'd done and under his signature added four notes of "White Christmas." Crosby recalled his note to Berlin the first time he saw the sheet music for that song: "This one you won't have to worry about."

In July 1967, Crosby's daughter Mary Frances announced she'd appear on a TV show in a sinking boat.

"I remember when she was two and fell into the pool and splashed her way to safety," he said. "She'll make it to shore all right."

Billy Wilder said, "I could walk into a bank with a paper bag containing nothing but an okay from Bing Crosby and I'd say I wanted five million dollars. Any banker would say: 'Crosby? You have an okay from Crosby to star in your movie? Sure. Here's your five million. Now go make your picture!'"

TONY CURTIS

(1925–2010)

The son of Hungarian immigrants, Bronx-born Bernard Schwartz became one of Hollywood's leading men of the 1950s and '60s. In 1935, his poverty-stricken parents briefly put him and his older brother into an orphanage, part of what he later described as his "school of hard knocks" education.

When his brother was killed by a truck in 1938, he became an avid moviegoer to escape his grief. After seeing Tyrone Power in *Crash Dive* in 1943, Schwartz enlisted in the navy and served on a submarine. Then he paid his dues onstage in small productions, catching the eye of agent Joyce Selznick, niece of movie mogul David O. Selznick. He changed his name when he signed a seven-year contract with her uncle at Universal, making his screen debut, in 1949's *City Across the River*, as "Anthony Curtis." He wound up making 122 movies, including *Houdini*, *The Great Impostor*, *The Vikings*, *Spartacus*, *The Defiant Ones* (for which he was Oscar nominated), *The Sweet Smell of Success*, and *Some Like It Hot*.

His Bronx accent was often the butt of jokes. In the 1952 film *Son of Ali Baba*, he famously said, "This is my fathah's palace, and yondah lies the Valley of the Sun."

A young woman arrived at a radio station in St. Louis where Curtis was being interviewed, saying she had come twelve miles just to meet him and ask him a question. The producer took pity on her, and she asked Curtis, "Do you know Tab Hunter?"

In November 1958, Curtis bought a lavish estate and, to show how blessed this son of the Bronx felt, he named it "Gezundt Heights."

In 1966, Curtis said, "I merely learn my lines at night, then come into the studio in the morning. When the director says for me to speak my lines, I speak 'em—and try to give them meaning. Those people who make a *megillah* out of acting! Just learn the lines. The rest is up to the director."

At the time, Curtis was filming *Arrivederci, Baby!*, which costarred English character actor Lionel Jeffries. Jeffries was born in 1926, the year after Curtis, but didn't have leading man looks.

Tony Curtis (bottom) and Burt Lancaster (top), *Trapeze*, Paris, 1955.
Photograph by Sam Shaw.

"You're lucky you lost your hair at nineteen," said Curtis. "That forced you to learn how to act. You can get character roles forever. But me? I'm liable to be selling apples again back in the Bronx when my looks fade."

He never forgot his roots. His father, Emanuel Schwartz, hired a three-piece band to play at his son's confirmation party in 1939 and contracted them until midnight. By nine thirty, all the guests had left and his mother pleaded that they should go home, too.

"No!" said his father. "I paid for music until midnight, and not until then will they leave."

Curtis said the best place to learn acting wasn't in classes, but in local TV or neighborhood theater groups. He learned at the YMHA and at a settlement house. "There," he explained, "they point a finger at you and say, 'You're the good guy today.' Then the next day they point at you and say, 'Today, you're the bad guy.' *That's* good training."

While filming *The Great Race* in 1964, Curtis batted cleanup and played center field on a softball team in London's Hyde Park on Sunday mornings. In one game, he hit a double and, when the next batter singled, rounded third, ignoring the third base coach's signal to stop. He scored easily, then explained, "Their first baseman is [producer] Jerry Bresler. I made two movies for him. I know he weighs everything carefully and never makes quick decisions. That's how I knew he'd hesitate before throwing home."

Curtis and Yul Brynner were in Argentina in 1962 filming *Taras Bulba*, and Curtis used his high school Spanish to invite the president, Arturo Frondizi, to watch them filming. When Frondizi visited the set, Curtis was amazed. "It's not so amazing he's here," said Brynner. "What *is* amazing is that he was able to understand your lousy Spanish."

Curtis made a deal with an auto company that insisted on giving him a bonus: the use of five cars. He already owned two Rolls-Royces and a Bentley, so the new deal gave him a different car for each day of the week, plus one for national holidays and birthdays.

BETTE DAVIS

(1908–1989)

During her heyday as the queen of Warner Bros., when she starred in a series of popular melodramas known as "Warner Bros. Weepers," actor Donald Meek said, "Bette Davis is a magician. At every performance, she makes dozens of handkerchiefs appear out of thin air."

In November 1943, a visiting executive from another studio watched her shoot a scene, then told the assistant director, "I don't think Bette is acting right today. She can do better than that."

"If I tell her that," replied the AD, "she might hit me over the head"—with either of her two Oscars for Best Actress.

During her run on Broadway in Tennessee Williams's *The Night of the Iguana*, in 1962, Davis took ill. Her understudy, Madeline Sherwood, a Canadian actress with a long résumé of her own, explained that she was intimidated by having to go on in Davis's place. But she found a way to overcome her uneasiness. Before the curtain rose, Sherwood stood onstage and shouted to herself, "Damn it all, tonight this is *my* role! *Mine*, not Bette Davis's. All *mine*!"

Margaret Leighton was asked about working with Davis. "We have one thing in common," the elegant English actress said. "She hates women and so do I."

Her Broadway career, though limited, influenced other actresses. One was Margaret Hart, who appeared in *Wine, Women, and Song*. The producers were concerned at the wide variations in her performances. "One day I pretend I'm Bette Davis, and I play it dramatically," she explained. "Another day I pretend I'm Katherine Cornell and play it happy. And when I feel lousy, I play it as myself."

Davis refused to attend a Hal Wallis film festival at New York's Museum of Modern Art that included *Now, Voyager*, Davis's most stylish Warner Bros. Weeper.

"I never like looking at myself," she explained. "I never did."

SAMMY DAVIS JR.

(1925–1990)

f Al Jolson was the most versatile entertainer of the first half of the twentieth century, then Sammy Davis Jr. held that title for the second half. His boundless energy dazzled audiences the world over in movies, onstage, on TV, and on records.

Born in Harlem, the son of vaudeville performers, Davis debuted in 1933 in a short called *Rufus Jones for President*. He starred on Broadway in the appropriately titled *Mr. Wonderful* and a musical version of *Golden Boy*. He could sing, dance, act, tell stories, twirl a baton, and do remarkable impressions.

Davis was a prominent participant in the civil rights movement after facing prejudice in Las Vegas and elsewhere. His films of note include *Robin and the Seven Hoods* and *Ocean's 11*, with his Rat Pack pals, as well as *Anna Lucasta* and *Porgy and Bess*.

Sammy Davis Jr., New York City, 1951. Photograph by Sam Shaw.

83

When Davis was completing an album at Decca Records he asked Frank Sinatra to write the liner notes. Sinatra obliged, writing, "Great! Now come on over to us at Capitol Records."

To demonstrate just how quickly he could draw a pistol, an all-star team of opponents was assembled to challenge him to a draw, including *Gunsmoke*'s James Arness and *Maverick*'s James Garner. Davis outdrew them all.

Davis did a command performance before the king of Sweden. "I'm not nervous," he said beforehand. "I'll just make believe I'm performing with Sinatra."

Early in 1965, Davis was performing eight times a week in *Golden Boy*. The title role, a violinist turned boxer, was grueling even without the fifteen songs he had to perform. Davis would play the role 568 times, an incredible run.

"People tell me at this pace, I could kill myself," he said. "But what a wonderful way to die!"

When another famous singer demanded a full orchestra for a lucrative hotel engagement, the head of the hotel chain refused. "Sammy Davis Jr. substituted here three times last year, using only a pianist—and was never better," he explained.

In May 1968, Davis announced what he wanted on his tombstone: "Yes. He. Did."

OLIVIA DE HAVILLAND

(1916–)

The older sister of Joan Fontaine and the longest-surviving cast member of *Gone with the Wind*, she had a fifty-three-year career and is one of the last links to Hollywood's Golden Age.

During World War II, a tall, slim navy lieutenant asked her at a party to dine with him, but De Havilland declined. He soon left, accidentally opening a closet instead of the exit, sending down a cascade of tennis rackets. Somehow, the young officer, Lieutenant John F. Kennedy, managed to keep his cool.

As a young contract player, De Havilland recalled, "You can't easily absorb the shocks of truth about the adult world. You discover adults do everything your parents told you *not* to do. To find this out at twenty-two is better than finding it out at eighteen."

In July 1957, De Havilland was unable to attend a Paris concert by violinist Yehudi Menuhin. The next day, Menuhin called her and played her a Bach piece over the phone.

When she met the British Queen Mother in 1964, De Havilland did a grand, old-fashioned curtsey, explaining, "I learned that playing the lady-in-waiting to Bette Davis's Elizabeth in *The Private Lives of Elizabeth and Essex*."

When a TV interviewer said something De Havilland interpreted as rude while she was promoting *Lady in a Cage*, she stormed off the set. Over lunch she told her press agents, "Listen, without interruption, to my forty-five minutes of indignation. Then I'll be all right."

With their spouses away, Groucho Marx escorted her to a party. At midnight, she asked him to take her home. "Oh, no," said Groucho. "You're the type of dignified lady it's okay to arrive with—but not the type to leave with."

MARLENE DIETRICH

(1901–1992)

he *Blue Angel* made her a star in 1930, and who could ever forget her throaty voice in *Destry Rides Again*, *Blonde Venus*, *Morocco*, *Witness for the Prosecution*, or *Judgment at Nuremberg*? During World War II, Dietrich was the only German-born star beloved in America. After becoming an American citizen in 1939, she spent the war entertaining American troops.

When Dietrich arrived for her American debut in 1930's *Morocco*, she shot her first scene several times. Director Josef von Sternberg instructed, "Walk through the door, count to three to yourself, then turn around." The camera was focused on her eyes. "Try it again," he said, "but this time count up to *four* before turning." Then it was count up to six, seven, and eight. Finally he asked her to count up to twenty. This was the big scene of the movie, and the critics later observed that in Dietrich's eyes viewers could see years of tragedy.

"At the time," recalled Dietrich, "I thought that if this is how they make movies here, I'm taking the first boat back to Germany."

In 1943, Dietrich was asked to audition for the starring role in *One Touch of Venus* on Broadway. The producers wanted to see if her voice carried through the theater. So late one night, with Kurt Weill accompanying her on the piano, she began. As radiators began to hiss and bang, she sang on. "Can't hear you!" came the cry from the middle of the theater. She sang louder. Then from the balcony came the same cry. Finally, after completing the song at the top of her lungs, she said, "Let's try this tomorrow. I can't stand hissing in a theater, even if it's only coming from a radiator."

Mary Martin eventually got the part and became a star.

In November of that year, Dietrich was filming *Kismet*; after she saw the raw footage, she complained about how she looked. The cameraman had also filmed her in *The Garden of Allah*, one of her favorites. She asked to have the earlier film screened for him to remind him how good she'd looked. Afterward, he diplomatically said, "You see, Miss D., I'm eight years older now."

Marlene Dietrich (center), with my father (left) and
UN Undersecretary General Ralph Bunche (right).

Costar Ronald Colman said, "Every actor has a better side, but
Dietrich, she tries to face the camera head-on."

One afternoon in March 1956, Dietrich made German pastries in
Broadway star Katherine Cornell's kitchen. Then Dietrich discovered her emerald ring was missing. Cornell found it in a delicious
strudel Dietrich had made.

Jean Cocteau, the poet, playwright, director, and artist, put it
best about Dietrich's charisma: "Her name begins like a caress—
and ends like a riding whip."

When asked to compare herself to Zsa Zsa Gabor, she said, "*I'm*
often imitated."

After years of refusing, she finally gave in and signed to appear
in Las Vegas, saying, "I decided it'd be criminal to turn down so
much money."

Ernest Hemingway noticed a road sign near his home in Ketchum, Idaho, that read, "Dietrich, Idaho." He took it down and mailed it to her in New York, addressed to "Dietrich, New York." It arrived a few days later.

When Dietrich signed a contract to appear in a Berlin nightclub, the owner was naturally delighted, saying, "When Berliners learn she's coming home, they'll know the war is finally over."

A few months later, she performed in Israel and was asked her formula for staying young. "I'm not so old that I need a formula," she proclaimed.

When a woman in a hospital told her that her husband left her because she didn't have shapely legs, Dietrich, whose legs were among the most famous in the world, told her, "Men sometimes walk out on women who have the most *beautiful* legs in the world."

When she opened at the Golders Green Hippodrome in London in April 1965, the crush at the stage door after the show was so heavy that Scotland Yard agents were called to help get Dietrich out of the theater. "I'm so thrilled," she told them. "I'd heard the Yard is called in only in cases of big crimes."

Actress Joan Littlewood met her a few weeks later and said, "You must've spent the whole day at the beauty parlor to look so perfect."

"Not at all," replied Dietrich. "I spent the day baking bread. The best way to get a man is: learn to cook."

When a photographer took photos of her with her then-fifteen-year-old daughter, Maria Riva, Dietrich made him promise not to release them, since she was still able to play younger roles. Soon afterward, she spotted one of the photos in a magazine, called the photographer, and told him, "We are no longer friends."

"Since we're no longer friends," he replied, "I can now sell all of them."

"We are friends again," she replied. He didn't sell them.

When Dietrich posed for a photo with Jerusalem mayor Teddy Kollek, he was seated on the floor, in front of her famous legs. Some in Israel objected to this "frivolous" pose. Kollek responded, "If you look, I'm not staring at her legs. I'm looking off in the distance. I assure you I was thinking of the city's new budget."

In the late 1960s, at a party in New York, a woman looked at Dietrich's slim figure with envy. She watched Dietrich take a generous portion of food, then whispered to a friend, "I hope it all goes to her legs."

A few days later, Dietrich saw *Rosencrantz and Guildenstern Are Dead* and visited with the actors backstage. John Wood, who played Guildenstern, had to leave because his fourteen-month-old daughter was ill. The next day, two visitors arrived at the Wood apartment: Dietrich's maid, to relieve the parents of housework, and the pediatrician who cared for Dietrich's grandchildren.

In the movie *The Damned*, Helmut Berger did an impression of Dietrich. The two met in March 1970, just after she'd seen the movie. She told him he was brilliant. "For years, I've been imitated only by women—how boring."

In April 1969, New York's Museum of Modern Art held a Marlene Dietrich film festival. After the credits of the final film, she strode out onto the stage to a thunderous ovation and said, "I don't know if your applause was for the legend, the performer, or me. Frankly, I'm rather fond of the legend."

JIMMY DURANTE

(1893–1980)

The New York State Lottery still uses Durante's unmistakable voice singing "Make Someone Happy" in its TV ads, thirty-five years after his death. His catchphrase was, "Stop da music! *Every*body's tryin' ta get inta de act." His signature song was "Inka Dinka Doo," and there was his mysterious sign-off from his TV show in the 1950s, where, standing in a spotlight wearing a trench coat and fedora, he'd say, "Good night, Mrs. Calabash, wher*ever* you are!"

Durante's memorable films include *The Man Who Came to Dinner*, in which he performed "Did You Ever Have the Feeling That You Wanted to Go?"; *Billy Rose's Jumbo*; and *It's A Mad, Mad, Mad, Mad World*.

He got his start playing piano in a restaurant on Brooklyn's Coney Island, where one of the singing waiters was another future star, Eddie Cantor. Durante and Cantor would ask for requests. One night a patron asked them to play "Hills of Kentucky." Durante began playing a generic tune while Cantor kept singing that title over and over. "That's not the right song," said the patron. "What?" said Durante in mock surprise. "There's *another* 'Hills of Kentucky'?"

Once Durante was at a party attended by Albert Einstein, who surprised everyone by playing a violin to Durante's accompaniment on the piano. It was the oddest of duets: the most brilliant mind of the twentieth century teamed with an eighth-grade dropout. One of them, however, was off beat. Finally Durante said, "Perfessuh, at this racket, you ain't no Einstein."

By 1937, Durante was a star, but his father Bartolomeo, an immigrant barber, still didn't believe his son's career would last, so he refused to retire and always kept the tools of his trade with him.

In Hollywood, Durante introduced his father to Johnny Weissmuller, the movies' most popular Tarzan. Jimmy called Weissmuller "my good friend," so his father replied, "Sit down, Johnny. Any friend of Jimmy is a pal of mine." Then he proceeded to trim Weissmuller's hair.

Jimmy Durante (left), with my parents, c. 1945.

In June 1943, Durante was rummaging through scrapbooks and found something that made him wonder if he might've prevented World War II with a well-placed bomb. It was a newspaper article about a gala in Venice where he'd performed, long before the war. Unknown to Durante, the attendees included Hermann Göring, Rudolf Hess, and Joseph Goebbels.

In a Lyons Den guest column in September 1943, Durante wrote, "My early ambition was to become a professional fighter. My record stands: one fight, two knockouts. One in the ring, and one when I got home."

The first time he played the Palace Theater in New York, Durante waited outside until sunset, just to see his name in lights.

A Hollywood plastic surgeon offered to shorten Durante's trademark nose. "No way," he said. "I'd have to go back to truck drivin'."

Durante dined at Lindy's with his manager Lou Clayton and wondered how he'd face his maker. "Just walk into His office and pretend He's Louis B. Mayer," Clayton advised.

DOUGLAS FAIRBANKS JR.

(1909–2000)

The handsome son of the silent movies' greatest swashbuckler forged his own starring career in a hundred films and TV shows, including *Little Caesar*, *The Prisoner of Zenda*, and *The Corsican Brothers*.

Fairbanks, born Douglas Elton Ullman, lived an incredible life that was rewarded with three stars on the Hollywood Walk of Fame, an honorary British knighthood—rarely given to an American—and the French Legion of Honor.

Fairbanks was a presidential envoy to South America in 1940, a participant in the Allied landings on Sicily and Elba in 1943, as well as a holder of the Croix de Guerre and the rank of captain in the U.S. Navy.

Gunga Din was one of Fairbanks's most famous movies. Costar Cary Grant's contract allowed him approval of all publicity photos. Fifty pictures were taken during the filming, mostly with Fairbanks standing to Grant's right. Protecting his status as a star, Grant ordered them reshot with Fairbanks on his left, thus assuring Grant would be mentioned first in the photo captions.

In late October 1941, Fairbanks reported for duty in Boston as a navy lieutenant. He was greeted by Ensign Franklin D. Roosevelt Jr., who saluted Fairbanks, his superior officer, then sighed: "Here I am, the son of the commander in chief, a guy who's supposed to have some influence, and I've just saluted a movie star."

In November 1942, Fairbanks was stationed in London. Back home in California, government officials kept turning up at his house. They'd been tipped off by British censors who'd spotted a cable he sent to his wife reading, "How are your arms?" It turned out to refer not to munitions, but to a recent series of injections she'd needed.

Fairbanks carried an unusual keepsake: an uncashed check for an amount he'd won in a poker game. It was signed "H.R.H. Edward VIII"—the king who abdicated and became the Duke of Windsor.

In 1951, Fairbanks produced a movie in England called *Another*

Douglas Fairbanks Jr. and Woody Allen on the set of *What's New Pussycat?*, Paris, 1964. Photograph by Sam Shaw.

Man's Poison, with Bette Davis as a mystery writer living in a dark, dank house in the English countryside. It was filmed on a moor near a gloomy village in North Yorkshire, where the lodgings were not yet equipped with central heating. One cold, drizzly, windy morning, Davis and the rest of the cast were shivering, and Fairbanks sent for three large hot water bottles—not for the actors, but for the cameras, explaining, "Cold actors we can work with, but not cold cameras."

Fairbanks attended a formal ball and danced with a friend who seemed awkward and uncomfortable. She explained that she was trying to keep space between them "so everyone can see all your medals."

In the summer of 1967, Fairbanks, a member of the U.S. Navy Reserve, was invited to cruise on a warship in the Mediterranean. A Russian vessel was anchored nearby and Fairbanks, who'd never forgotten his semaphore training, was able to read the message an American flagman was sending to the Russians: "Peek-a-boo!"

Lunching in New York, Fairbanks and an Italian count swapped examples of how long-ago encounters aren't really so distant. Fairbanks said his father recalled meeting Alfred Lord Tennyson's grandson, who reported hearing the poet saying he knew a woman who said, "As my husband said to King Louis XIV . . ."

The count had an even better story: "My nanny's grandmother was lady-in-waiting to Marie Antoinette" (born in 1755).

Fairbanks, by this time letting his gray hair show, got into a cab and the driver, looking in his rearview mirror, said, "I saw your son in a movie the other night on TV. Very promising."

JOSÉ FERRER

(1912–1992)

Born in Santurce, Puerto Rico, in 1912, and educated at Princeton, José Ferrer was not just a great star, but also a producer, director, painter, and winner of an Oscar and three Tony Awards. He set high standards for his actor son Miguel and his nephew by marriage, George Clooney. His classic films include *Moulin Rouge, Cyrano de Bergerac, Lawrence of Arabia,* and *The Caine Mutiny.*

Ferrer won favorable notices for performances on Broadway in *Brother Rat* and *Key Largo.* By the time he got raves for *Charley's Aunt,* his agent thought it was time for Ferrer to get billing above the title. "People now know who he is," explained the agent to the producer. But just as he was pleading his case a package arrived for his client addressed "To: Joe's Furrier."

In May 1944, when fellow actor Kent Smith asked Ferrer to be godfather to Smith's new baby, he beamed. But then he learned he'd have to share the honor with two other stars, Louis Calhern and Myron McCormick. All three demanded top billing.

Two years later, Ferrer was back on Broadway performing as Cyrano de Bergerac, the role that would win him his first Tony and the Oscar for Best Actor. One night, Ferrer came out to the footlights before the start of the play and explained to the audience that he'd lost not one but two of the character's signature oversize noses. He asked their indulgence, got a huge ovation, and then performed the play without the prosthesis.

By December 1948, Ferrer was back on the Broadway boards starring in *The Silver Whistle.* There was a rooster in the play, which crowed at inappropriate moments, even from offstage. A veterinarian solved the problem by injecting it with female hormones. Another tactic used was to turn a flashlight on the bird's cage backstage, tricking it into thinking dawn had arrived. Thus, onstage, the rooster wouldn't interpret the spotlight as a cue to crow.

In Hollywood doing preproduction for the movie version of *Cyrano,* he wanted to prove Angelenos were jaded. So he donned the famous nose and walked down a street. No one paid him any attention.

While he was starring on Broadway in *The Shrike*, a deadly serious play about mental illness, a group of young theatergoers continually laughed at inappropriate moments, threatening to ruin the evening's performance.

Finally Ferrer, noticing the stirring among the adults in the audience, stepped out of character and asked the youngsters to stop, adding, "I remind you that this isn't a movie, or television, where the cast is unaware of audience mood. We can't give our best performance unless you cooperate." Then he stepped back into character. There were no further interruptions.

Ferrer told one of my older brothers, who'd become a theatrical producer, "You dream of playing all the great parts. You've got to get the job. But even that isn't enough. For once the curtain rises, and there are a lot of empty seats in the house, you're just a bum soon to be out of work. You've got to keep your feet in the mud in this business and grow up tall enough to have your head in the clouds."

W. C. FIELDS

(1880–1946)

William Claude Dukenfield was the son of a Civil War veteran of English ancestry. He was one of the comedy stalwarts of Hollywood's Golden Age, as well known for bending his elbow as for his incredible talents as a comedian and juggler.

"On the whole, I'd rather be in Philadelphia" is the epitaph this native of the Philadelphia suburb of Darby proposed for himself in a *Vanity Fair* interview in 1925, but his tombstone actually has only his stage name and birth and death years.

"Never give a sucker an even break" is another of his quotable quips, along with "Never work with children or animals."

One afternoon when he was a vaudeville star, he drank too much, and his colleagues tried to freshen him up for the evening's performance. He refused their help and kept calling for one more drink. Finally they summoned a burly actor who'd been a prizefighter, and he told Fields, "If you don't go to sleep so you can make tonight's show, I'll put you to sleep myself with a poke in the nose." Fields dutifully crawled into bed and closed his eyes.

He made no secret of his drinking habits. Screenwriter Nunnally Johnson, who would write and produce *The Man in the Gray Flannel Suit* and *The Three Faces of Eve*, once dined with Fields. "Aren't you afraid of the DTs?" he asked.

"I don't know," replied Fields. "Out here in Hollywood, it's hard to tell where Hollywood ends and the DTs begin."

Eddie Cantor once asked Fields if it was true that he didn't imbibe anymore. "Any *more*?" replied Fields. "Yes, it's true—I don't drink any 'more.' I just keep drinking the same amount."

Warned that drinking would ruin his constitution, he replied, "Constitution? I'm *waaay* beyond that. I've been living on its bylaws for years."

Fields said he owed his stardom to Cantor. He was onstage in the *Ziegfeld Follies*, doing his juggling act, while backstage, Cantor and Will Rogers cooked up a simple but hilarious practical joke on Fields. They intentionally missed their entrance cue for fifteen minutes, leaving Fields juggling onstage endlessly.

Finally, the juggling exhausted Fields, so he began making the caustic comments—the first time he'd spoken onstage—that would soon make him famous.

While they were filming *My Little Chickadee* in 1940, Fields and his costar, Mae West, didn't get along. In one scene, Fields was supposed to kiss her, but she wouldn't allow it. To show his contempt, he kissed a goat instead. Then, perhaps to honor the goat, she head-butted him.

When *The Bank Dick* was released in November 1940, the screenwriting credit read "Mahatma Kane Jeeves"—a pseudonym for Fields.

Fields had a friend named Hedy Stenuf, an Austrian figure skater who competed in the 1936 Winter Olympics in Germany. In December 1941, when she was skating in a show called *It Happens on Ice*, Fields attended a performance.

"That's the best thing I've seen on ice since my last frozen daiquiri," he told her.

When a young man came to his home claiming to be his son, Fields offered him a drink. "I'll have a Coke," the young man said. "A Coke?" roared Fields. "Get out of my house! Anyone who calls a Coke a drink is no son of mine."

Ed Gardner, star of the popular radio show *Duffy's Tavern*, invited Fields aboard his yacht for a drink. "How far offshore will we be?" asked Fields. "No more than half a mile," replied Gardner.

"Half a mile of water is much too much of a chaser for one drink," said Fields.

When Fields visited the home of his good friend and frequent drinking companion John Barrymore, he suffered a violent attack of hiccups. After home remedies failed, Fields asked Barrymore's brother Lionel for advice. "Only two ways to get rid of the hiccups work," Lionel replied. "Drink a glass of water, or get a good scare."

John Barrymore heard this advice and started toward his kitchen, saying, "I'll get you a glass of water, Bill. That ought to do both. "

Barrymore once explained that his friendship with Fields began when Barrymore spent an evening at the home of his biographer Gene Fowler, who drank him under the table. "What's that got to do with meeting Fields?" he was asked. "Because," replied Barrymore, "under that table, I met W. C. Fields!"

W. C. Fields

In the last year of his life, Fields was stricken with a heavy cold. His physician ordered him to remain in bed and not to drink a drop of liquor. After two weeks of drying out, a friend saw Fields and said, "Bill, you look wonderful. What happened?"

"Oh, I've been sick the past two weeks," replied Fields.

Fields's public persona was that of someone who abhorred Christmas and children. Ironically, he died on Christmas Day, 1946, and left most of his eight-hundred-thousand-dollar estate to a college for orphans.

ALBERT FINNEY

(1936–)

Born in Salford, England, Finney was nineteen when he debuted on the stage of the Birmingham Repertory Theater, in April 1956, as Decius Brutus in *Julius Caesar*. He first acted in London in an Old Vic production of *Caesar and Cleopatra*.

In 1963, he was a sensation on Broadway in *Luther*, playing Martin Luther. Finney had become a baseball fan while in New York, and that fall the New York Yankees were in the World Series. At one point during the run of *Luther*, he held up from his pulpit a document from the pope that excommunicated his character. On the paper, so only he could see it, was written, "The Yankees are ahead."

He returned to Broadway in February 1968 to star in *A Day in the Death of Joe Egg*. Finney requested Sunday performances so he could perform in front of his favorite audience: actors from other Broadway shows.

After a supporting role in *The Entertainer*, Finney's breakthrough in the movies came in 1960 with *Saturday Night and Sunday Morning*. That was followed by an even bigger success: *Tom Jones*, the film version of the ribald classic by Henry Fielding.

First to be shot was a racy bedroom scene with Joan Greenwood. The two actors had never met during table reads before filming.

"How do you do, Miss Greenwood?" said Finney just before the cameras rolled. "I hope you don't think I'm forward, but. . . ." After that, they filmed the famous erotic eating scene.

When Tom Courtenay starred in the film *The Day the Fish Came Out*, he said, "I'm often mentioned as the same type of actor as Albert Finney. The only difference is he gets the girl."

In April 1968, Finney completed his run in *A Day in the Death of Joe Egg* and planned to return to London to direct a film. He decided he'd have to leave his pet hamster in his dressing room to avoid England's strict quarantine laws. To ensure that his successor would continue to care for the hamster, Finney named it Donal Donnelly, a name shared by the incoming star.

ERROL FLYNN

(1909–1959)

Born in Tasmania, Flynn starred in films that defined the swashbuckler genre, such as *Robin Hood, Captain Blood, The Sea Hawk*, and *They Died with Their Boots On*. His torrid private life finally caught up with him, but he was a Hollywood legend.

In late November 1941, Flynn was scheduled to make a personal appearance at the Strand Theater in New York, which was showing *They Died with Their Boots On*, depicting Custer's Last Stand. Flynn was shooting dice that day in a fancy Park Avenue apartment. Ironically, like Custer, he spent five hours shooting, then managed to reach the theater just in time.

The next day, Flynn was given a pair of moccasins and made a blood brother of the Sioux Nation in New York's Central Park. But Chief Rising Sun said that the title of Flynn's movie was a misnomer. "None of the troopers of the Seventh Cavalry died with their boots on," said the chief. "Sioux braves removed their boots and tickled their feet. If they moved, they were tomahawked."

At the Waldorf Astoria, a soldier saw a beautiful woman and, trying an unusual pickup line, said, "I know you. You're the one woman in America who hasn't sued Errol Flynn."

"Oh, but I *have*," she replied. "I'm Lili Damita, his ex-wife."

In February 1943, there was a shortage of hot water in Los Angeles one night, due to a malfunction in the city infrastructure. "I know where the city can get hot water," someone at City Hall said. "Over at Errol Flynn's house. He's always up to his neck in hot water."

That same month, Flynn visited St. Louis to act as master of ceremonies at a war bond drive. After the show, Flynn toured the radio studio with the station executives. Two young page girls timidly approached the movie star and asked, "May we touch you?" "Sure," said Flynn, "just don't tell your lawyers."

Flynn appeared onstage with the Ritz Brothers, the slapstick siblings known for wacky stunts. Flynn stood there, with no dialogue.

Later he explained, "I did that to prove I could've been a star in silent pictures, too."

In 1950 Flynn's children were living with another ex-wife, Nora Eddington, who had by then married singer Dick Haymes (a future husband of Rita Hayworth). Haymes's children were living with *his* ex-wife Joanne Dru, who was married to actor John Ireland. Flynn was sending support checks to Mrs. Haymes while Haymes was sending his support checks to Mrs. Ireland. Any delay by one would set off a chain reaction of other delays.

In 1952, Jack Benny led a troupe of entertainers to Korea, including Flynn. He kept getting long-distance phone calls from mothers looking for their daughters. Benny said, "I, too, get such calls, only mine are from daughters looking for their mothers."

When Orson Welles rented Flynn's yacht for his honeymoon with Rita Hayworth, they discovered a monkey on board. Welles fed and tended it and later received, attached to Flynn's bill, an extra seventy-five-dollar charge, describing the monkey as "entertainment."

Production on Flynn's movie *William Tell* was halted when investors pulled out. Desperate to make the film, he went to Italy to find new money, but failed. "No one believed in a movie about William Tell," he said. "They wouldn't even give me money to buy an apple."

HENRY FONDA

(1905–1982)

Along with his contemporary Jimmy Stewart, Henry Fonda
embodied American cinema in the pre- and postwar eras.
The Nebraska-born actor often returned to Broadway,
where he'd started in 1929's *The Game of Love and Death*,
but it was his performances in films like *Jezebel* and *The Grapes
of Wrath*—as Tom Joad, one of the most beloved performances in
movie history—that made him immortal.

In September 1945, Fonda, who'd enlisted in the navy, was in New
York. He asked a friend which subway would take him to Church
Street in the downtown financial district.

"You're kidding me, aren't you?" replied the friend. "You're Henry
Fonda, a big movie star. Don't you take taxis?"

"Right now," the actor replied, "I'm Henry Fonda, an enlisted
man in the U.S. Navy. I have a wife and three children to take care
of and I've got to live within my navy income. Right now, the subway's fine." While in the navy he didn't stay at the Waldorf as usual,
but in a six-dollar-a-week room at the East Forty-Seventh Street
YMCA.

In August 1948, his daughter, Jane, then eleven, suffered a bro-
ken arm in a fight with a boy at school in Greenwich, Connecticut.
It was a rematch after she'd beaten him in an earlier encounter.
Fifty cents was the going price to watch the second fight.

One night, Fonda went with friends to a small nightclub where
patrons could perform. After several other patrons took their turns,
Fonda's came. Slowly he ascended the small stage and did the only
impromptu thing he could think of: his famous "I'll be there" speech
from *The Grapes of Wrath*.

During his Broadway run in *Mr. Roberts*, Fonda visited a drama
workshop and was so impressed with the teacher, he paid for
a month's tuition for the class. Later, he remembered the young
teacher, Sidney Lumet, and hired him to direct the movie version of
Twelve Angry Men, the only film Fonda ever produced.

In *Stage Struck* (1958), playing a Broadway producer, he had the

My father stopping to speak to Henry Fonda (right) at the 21 Club.

line "Don't be silly, I wouldn't give Garbo ten percent." The studio lawyers asked the film's producer to delete that line, saying Garbo would never consent to the use of her name. Instead, the producer wrote Garbo, asking permission, and was careful to include the fact that it was in a Henry Fonda movie. Several days later, a reply arrived: "Yes!"

In late September 1959, Soviet Premier Khrushchev visited Hollywood and was hosted at a luncheon. Many stars of the day were there, including Kirk Douglas, Nat King Cole, and Fonda. He sat in the back, wearing an earplug. Douglas wondered if Fonda had become hard of hearing. "No," replied Cole. "He's listening to the World Series and sending me signals of how the Dodgers are doing."

In 1960, Fonda was back on Broadway in *Critics' Choice* at the Ethel Barrymore Theater. Fonda's understudy was veteran Jeffrey Lynn, who never got the chance to go on for the star. One night he was called on to display another skill: taping Fonda after he had slipped and cracked two ribs. Fonda went on as scheduled.

By March 1963, Fonda was reassessing his career. "I've reached the age where I'm still the hero, not because I win the lady but because I can still whip the villain."

Fonda met his fifth wife, Shirlee, a flight attendant, at the premiere of *The Longest Day*, in which he played Brigadier General Theodore Roosevelt Jr. She was costar Richard Beymer's date that night. Incredibly, she had never heard of Fonda, and had never seen his movies.

One night in September 1966, Fonda and his wife looked out their window and saw two teenage vandals setting fire to a parked car. The actor rushed down and pursued the hoodlums, who got away. Meanwhile his wife, in nightgown and slippers, put the fire out before it could reach the gas tank. The next day, a city commissioner named Mrs. Fonda the honorary fire commissioner.

On another night in New York, the Fondas were introduced to Thomas Foran and his wife. Mrs. Foran said, "Your son-in-law knows us." Indeed he did. Fonda's son-in-law at the time, Tom Hayden, then married to Jane Fonda, had been prosecuted by the then–U.S. attorney, Tom Foran, in 1969, when Hayden was a member of the so-called Chicago Seven.

During his run on Broadway in *Generation*, in the mid-sixties, a young actor asked Fonda the most important thing a young actor needed to know. "How to become an *old* actor," replied Fonda.

JOAN FONTAINE

(1917–2013)

Born Joan de Beauvoir de Havilland in Tokyo to British parents, she was the younger sister of Olivia de Havilland. Their cousin Geoffrey de Havilland was the aviation pioneer whose company manufactured the De Havilland Mosquito fighter-bombers the RAF flew in World War II. Both sisters would win Oscars five years apart, and they had a lifelong feud. Joan told me in a 1978 interview that she changed her last name so as not to be compared or confused with her sister.

Fontaine's most important films include Hitchcock's classic thrillers *Rebecca* (Hitchcock's American debut) and *Suspicion*. Her role in *Suspicion* won her the Best Actress Oscar in 1942, making her the only actor to win an Oscar in a Hitchcock film.

She once attended a party given for the Shah of Iran and was told to curtsy before him. "Why should I?" she said. "Hell, I don't even curtsy before *Joan Crawford*!"

In March 1965, Fontaine's husband at the time, Al Wright Jr., answered the phone at their home. "Who's calling Mrs. Wright?" he asked. "Mrs. Wrong," came the reply. "Mrs. Wright is in Texas en route to San Francisco," he said. The caller said, "Please tell Mrs. Wright that Mrs. Wrong called." Then she hung up.

The caller was, of course, Fontaine's estranged older sister, Olivia de Havilland. They're the only siblings to win the top acting Oscar, Olivia having won twice, in 1947 for *To Each His Own* and in 1949 for *The Heiress*.

Anthony Perkins explained why he dropped out of Columbia University to take a role on Broadway in *Tea and Sympathy*, in which Fontaine starred. "It would've been impossible to concentrate on trigonometry by day and Joan Fontaine by night."

Fontaine never missed an opportunity to poke fun at her older sister. In February 1962, Fontaine, then forty-five, was offered the role of the mother of a twenty-six-year-old. "I'm not yet ready to play such a role," she said, "but my sister is."

One day Fontaine was playing at a golf course on Long Island

Joan Fontaine and my father, backstage at Broadway's
Tea and Sympathy, c. June 1954.

with a friend. At the eighth hole, a dogleg, he told her: "No woman, not even Babe Didrikson herself, has ever been able to reach this green in two shots."

"I'll bet you a mink coat against a box of expensive cigars that I can make the shot," said Fontaine. She reached the green in two shots and collected that mink coat. She didn't tell her friend that she'd once scored a hole-in-one at the fifteenth at Cypress Point in California, in a foursome with Charles Boyer and her then-husband, actor Brian Aherne.

Twenty-five years after that shot, she returned to Cypress Point. At the fifteenth, her caddy—who hadn't recognized her—said, "That's Joan's hole." She then made a birdie and told the caddy, "Well, only one more than last time."

In October 1968, Fontaine was asked to speculate on Jacqueline Kennedy's choice of Aristotle Onassis for a husband. By this time she'd been married four times and would divorce again the following year. "I can't even explain some of *my* choices," she replied.

CLARK GABLE

(1901–1960)

Born in tiny Cadiz, Ohio, in 1901, the son of an oil driller and a mother who died soon after his birth, his first name was William, but he was called Clark from an early age and became the biggest male star of Hollywood's Golden Age.

Gable and Carole Lombard, his wife, dined at the home of Alfred and Alma Hitchcock. Gable mentioned a trip he'd once made to Quito, Ecuador, where he purchased a shrunken human head. A series of odd mishaps then began to befall him. Suspecting a jinx, he decided to dispose of the souvenir by tossing it into a ravine. But then his conscience troubled him, for this, after all, had been the head of a human being.

"So I retrieved it the very next day," said Gable, "and then Carole and I buried it in the garden of our house." And then Gable gasped, realizing that *this* was the very house, now the home of Hitchcock, master of the macabre.

It was director William Wyler who said, "If you want to sell MGM a story, a screenwriter should know that Gable's at his best, and most popular, in a movie where everything can be solved by his punching someone in the nose."

Soon after Lombard's death in a plane crash, a grieving Gable enlisted in the Army Air Corps. He was held in awe by all, including superiors. An army plane landed in Newfoundland, and out stepped Captain Gable, followed by a colonel—carrying his bags.

Working with Gable and Jane Russell on *The Tall Men*, director Raoul Walsh said, "Of course there'll be love scenes between those two. Good dialogue is a part of the action but no substitute. It's fine for the guy to tell the girl he loves her with a sonnet by Browning, but when you have Gable and Russell, poetry shouldn't overlook the fact that she has a body. And so does he!"

When Gable moved into a new home in Encino, California, he visited everyone in the neighborhood on horseback, introduced himself, and said, "I hope we'll all be happy here and that you'll like us as good neighbors."

Cark Gable (left) and Burt Lancaster (right), *Run Silent, Run Deep*, Los Angeles, 1958. Photograph by Sam Shaw.

One of Gable's neighbors was Buddy Clark, a popular singer who died in a plane crash in October 1949. The next day, Gable rang the doorbell of his home unannounced, walked in, and spent three hours comforting Clark's widow.

"I know how you must feel," he began, for he too had suffered such a loss.

Jack Durant was a popular nightclub comic of that era. He'd been an acrobat and included one stunt in his act: "So I'm not Clark Gable," he'd say to his audience. "But can Gable do this?" And then he'd do a back flip.

One night, Gable was in the audience. When Durant made his joke about Gable and did the flip, Gable walked up to the stage and said, "Yes, I can do that." And he did.

When Gable was an Army Air Corps major, he was in London and paid a visit to Pamela Churchill, the future American ambassador to France, then the daughter-in-law of the prime minister. She apologized for not being able to provide lunch, saying her food supplies were limited due to rationing. "Just a cup of tea will do," said Gable.

The maid, however, wanted to meet Gable and prolong the visit, and promised to find some food. She did: canned ham Pamela Churchill had been saving for VE-Day.

In September 1951, actress Kay Williams announced her separation from her third husband, sugar heir Adolph Spreckels II. He'd complained of her friendship with Gable (whom she later married). A previous husband had divorced her, also citing her friendship with Gable, and asking her, "How could you prefer Gable to me? He has false teeth!"

"So do I," she replied, calmly removing her bridge.

THE GABORS

MAGDA (1915–1997)
ZSA ZSA (1917–)
EVA (1919–1998)

The world viewed the Gabors of Hungary—Zsa Zsa, her look-alike sister Eva, her other sister Magda, and their mother Jolie, a jeweler—as the epitome of glamour. Eva came to America first, in 1939, followed two years later by Zsa Zsa, and finally by Magda in 1946. Their mother Jolie arrived in 1945 from Portugal, where she had fled after the Germans took over Hungary.

Surely a Gabor could never be deemed an *undesirable* alien! The family's ostentatious lifestyle was the fodder for an unending stream of publicity and news items.

Eva a stage, TV, and screen actress, remembered mostly for her TV show *Green Acres*. Her stage debut came in *The Happy Time*, in 1950, which she played for eighteen months. But Linda Christian got the movie role. After watching the film, Eva said, "When I hear another actress's voice answering my cue lines, I die. Even after a love affair ends, I'm not as unhappy as I am leaving a show."

Eva was even a disc jockey on New York's WNEW in 1952. Her show was called *A Little Night Music*. Among her duties was recording an occasional song. On one of her recordings, the station thought there wasn't enough warmth or sex appeal coming through. So she went home and returned wearing a low-cut evening gown. "You just can't *sound* irresistible unless you *feel* irresistible," she explained.

A few weeks later, she was at a party and the host called her "the most glamorous woman in the world." Just then, in walked Marlene Dietrich.

"Repeat what you just said to me!" said Eva.

Married in 1937, at age twenty, to Turkish diplomat Burhan Belge, Zsa Zsa once gave a dinner party at which the two men seated on either side of her began feeling her feet under the table. Or so they thought. Somehow she was able to have them unknowingly playing footsie with each other. You'd have thought George Bernard Shaw and H. G. Wells would've known better.

Zsa Zsa's marriage to George Sanders lasted for six years and four days. Sanders later said they'd been friends before and after their marriage, just not during. Zsa Zsa told him, "The only thing we have in common is your money.

Zsa Zsa made several movies, including *Moulin Rouge* in 1953 and *the* most unintentionally hilarious science fiction movie ever, called *Queen of Outer Space*, in 1958.

Between the sisters, they had nineteen husbands (if you count George Sanders twice, since he married Magda after Zsa Zsa) as well as endless suitors and escorts, and lived in the lavish style of women ten times richer.

In May 1952, a man was described as an "ex-husband of a Gabor." "Which one?" he was asked.

"It doesn't matter," came the reply. "When you marry one Gabor, you've married them all."

On a day off from shooting *Moulin Rouge* in London, Zsa Zsa visited the Shakespeare Memorial Theatre in Stratford-upon-Avon. José Ferrer, who starred as Toulouse-Lautrec in the film, asked if she'd seen Anne Hathaway's cottage.

"No," replied Zsa Zsa. "I didn't have time to go visiting people."

In September 1952, the Hearst newspapers were preparing a series on the Gabors. When she heard about it Eva called her friend, the actress Marion Davies, and said, "I don't care what they write about us, so long as they identify me as an actress."

Late June 1953 found Zsa Zsa staying at the Plaza in New York, then owned by her ex-husband Conrad Hilton. She was billed only five dollars for her suite. She realized what an enviable position she was in. United Artists paid for her hotel, and thus profited through her partial ownership of the Plaza, which was part of her divorce settlement.

In April 1954, Zsa Zsa proclaimed her age as twenty-eight. A suspicious Hungarian publisher did some checking and found a photo of Zsa Zsa as a contestant in 1933's Miss Hungary pageant. "She was the prettiest and ordinarily would've won, but the judges gave the title to another because they felt that her mother tried to influence them." Certainly she didn't win that contest when she was seven. Zsa Zsa was thirty-seven in 1954, not twenty-eight.

In March 1956, Zsa Zsa attended Grace Kelly's wedding shower and gave the soon-to-be-princess some advice: "You have two choices in life—to be chic or sexy. Never both." Then she told the single ladies how to get a man: "Cultivate his mind, but always wear a little perfume."

Zsa Zsa Gabor, New York City, 1959. Photograph by Sam Shaw.

Arriving on the set of a TV film called *Autumn Fever*, costarring her ex-husband George Sanders, Zsa Zsa wore an eyepatch. Sanders suspected she was trying to upstage him.

"So upstage me, George, if you like. Wear *two* patches," she scoffed.

There were Gabor weddings on three consecutive Sundays in the spring of 1956. "It's like a TV series," said one observer. "*The Gabor Weddings!* Every Sunday at three."

In July 1956, Zsa Zsa visited Africa and was asked if she'd been there before. "No, but my diamonds have," she replied.

She inscribed a photo for Jack Brooks, who'd written about her Las Vegas act, but she dated it a decade later. "Why'd you do that?" he asked.

"Because," she explained, "fifteen years from now, you'll find the photo and say, 'My, she looked great just five years ago.'"

Zsa Zsa noticed a sign in a window advertising its Hungarian deer steak as "the tastiest Hungarian dish of them all." "Dahling," she sighed, "that's the billing Hollywood used about *me*!"

When the Hungarian revolution erupted, Milton Berle said, "If you want to see how brave the Hungarians *really* are, go see Zsa Zsa's new act!"

When actress Maria Riva was in her dressing room after a May 1954 performance, she and her mother, Marlene Dietrich, heard a knock at the door.

"It's Gabor," said the voice on the other side.

Riva replied, "If it's Eva, come in. If it's Zsa Zsa, don't bother."

It was Eva.

The following January, Eva arrived early for lunch and hid in the coatroom until her date arrived. "Why didn't you wait here at our table?" he asked. Eva replied, "Because no woman should be seen in public waiting for a man."

Zsa Zsa's singing in *Moulin Rouge* was dubbed by Muriel Smith. Asked at the wrap party to sing, Zsa Zsa refused. "I can't," she explained. "Muriel Smith is in Europe."

She once described herself as "The rich man's Marilyn Monroe."

Jolie observed, "Zsa Zsa was once much heavier. Men loved that. There was more to grab at."

When Magda was about to marry husband number four, she told Jolie she planned to elope. "Who tells their mother they're going to elope?" said Jolie. "You want to elope? So elope."

Magda's courtship took a circuitous route. After a year of dating, she and her beau were engaged. One night, Magda asked him to walk her dog. He did—and disappeared, along with the dog. He had met a lady he knew who lived next door to the Gabors. He married her, soon got divorced, and then married Magda.

Eva was introduced to Mike DiSalle, then running for governor of Ohio. "I'll be appearing in Cincinatti," she told him. "Is that near Ohio?"

"That's *in* Ohio, Miss Gabor," said the future governor.

"Oh? What a coincidence," she replied.

Eva's escort at Sardi's told Magda and her husband that he'd obtained tickets to the World Series between the Yankees and the Milwaukee Braves. "There's only one problem," said Eva. "I can't tell one baseball from another."

Magda urged Eva to go anyway. "They scream 'kickoff' or something and everyone goes mad. It's so American."

Magda said her husband constantly watched baseball on TV. "Sometimes I see a man fall down, poor guy. But my husband calls out: 'Great slide!'"

Then Eva said, "This Joe DiMaggio. In person he's a handsome guy. But can he pitch?"

Magda said, "They have a man who stands behind the catcher wearing a black suit. They call him the judge."

"All in black?" replied Eva. "How drab."

Early in 1958, Eva attended a party in honor of Carol Channing. The theme was "Diamonds Are a Girl's Best Friend." Jeweler Harry Winston supplied each female guest with a box containing an imitation diamond. But one contained a real one-thousand-dollar diamond.

Eva opened hers, took one look, and tossed it away.

"But Eva," her escort said, "that could be the real thing."

"Even if it were," she replied, "I'd never wear a diamond *that* small."

Later that year, Dominican dictator Rafael Trujillo bought Zsa Zsa a convertible. After a test drive with the top down, she told him she was cold, so he bought her a chinchilla coat.

Zsa Zsa had a small role in the Bob Hope–Bing Crosby film *The Road to Hong Kong*, and was told to dress simply for her role as a nurse. She complied, saying the only accessory she wore was a pair of earrings costing a "paltry" twenty-five thousand dollars—costume jewelry for a Gabor. The scene was later cut.

She volunteered as an usher at the gala benefit premiere of *The Miracle Worker*. She explained, "Having men follow me down an aisle is nothing new."

On November 6, 1962, the day after Zsa Zsa married Herbert Hunter, husband number four, Eva sighed, "I'm so tired of all these wedding receptions: hers and mine, hers, then mine again. Every other day."

Cy Howard, who wrote and produced the popular TV series *My Friend Irma*, once dated Zsa Zsa, and said, "When you date a Gabor, you get the feeling your whole formal education has been in vain."

Eva attended the opening of a new play by Noël Coward and said, "If I had his talent, I'd write plays with a great big part for me and very small roles for everyone else."

Eva's fourth husband, Richard Brown, said she had an unusual talent: extrasensory perception. "She could scan a room," he explained, "and find the women I once dated."

Zsa Zsa arrived at a New York nightclub with an escort who'd been feuding with another man, seated nearby. The other man challenged Zsa Zsa's escort to a duel. Zsa Zsa urged him to accept.

"But what if I'm killed?" he asked.

"That would be wonderful publicity," she replied, "for *me*!"

Asked to divulge her age in February 1961, Zsa Zsa refused, "on the grounds that it might incriminate my mother."

In September 1961, Zsa Zsa met Mickey Mantle "and that other guy"—Roger Maris. She vaguely knew of their race to break Babe Ruth's single-season home run record. An attractive socialite came in and Zsa Zsa noticed Mantle studying her. "Don't bother," said Zsa Zsa. "I know her. She's not as young as you think. She'll hit sixty before you do."

When Janet Leigh heard about Zsa Zsa's meeting Mantle and Maris, she said, "Oh my God, that's like a man sitting between Marilyn Monroe and Elizabeth Taylor!"

But lest you think Zsa Zsa knew anything *else* about baseball, she was once asked to throw out the first ball at a Dodgers game and tossed it into center field.

After her third divorce, Zsa Zsa was asked if she planned to marry again. She gave a one-word reply: "Always." She kept her word and tied the knot six more times.

Eva was working on a movie and marveled at the way she was treated. "I was given a huge trailer, and when I asked someone for a cup of tea, they asked if I wanted black or green. I never knew tea came in colors."

One evening, Zsa Zsa arrived at a dinner accompanied by Saul Brown, whose son was then Eva Gabor's husband, her fourth of five. Zsa Zsa loved the notion that if she married her date, the elder Brown, she'd become her sister's mother-in-law.

On another night, she noticed a bevy of waiters hovering over one diner. "Who is that unattractive man?" she asked. Told it was J. Paul Getty, the oil billionaire, Zsa Zsa brightened: "What a beautiful man!"

Bob Hope was shooting a film in Middlesex, England, and Zsa Zsa wanted to send him a postcard. She addressed it, but paused after writing "Middle . . ." to ask, "How do you spell 'sex'?"

Zsa Zsa met Mitzi Newhouse, the wife of publishing magnate Sam Newhouse, who was wearing a twenty-two-carat ring. Zsa Zsa later joked, "Twenty-two carats? I get rings that size from my *ex*-husbands." She didn't know that Newhouse would become richer than all her husbands combined.

Zsa Zsa's dream was to star on Broadway, then marry a star, then marry a millionaire, and finally marry a government official who would make her the wife of an "Excellency."

"But I did that exactly in reverse," she said. "My first husband was an 'Excellency.' Then I married Conrad Hilton, then the star, George Sanders, and now I'm an actress. Next I may become a chorus girl."

Soon after her marriage to Dick Brown, Eva announced she didn't want to be referred to as "Eva Brown," lest she be confused with Hitler's mistress.

When Zsa Zsa's ghostwritten autobiography was finished, her coauthor suggested his credit read: "As whispered to Gerold Frank."

Zsa Zsa met Lord Louis Mountbatten, First Earl of Burma, and later told friends how much she liked "that Earl fellow from Bermuda."

At a party a few nights later, my parents spoke with a woman who said, "Zsa's Zsa's got talent. But it's up here," she added, pointing to her temple.

"If it's up there," said my mother, "then it's been moved."

Then the woman speculated on Zsa Zsa's age.

"Easy," replied my mother. "Like a tree, you can guess her age by the number of rings."

When Eva saw Pearl Bailey on Broadway in *Hello, Dolly!*, Pearlie Mae, as she was called, introduced Eva after the curtain call and said, "I'm really the fourth Gabor sister, the one they don't talk about."

Eva was hired to do commercials for pipe tobacco. The ads were prominently displayed in the New York subway system, and she was taken there to see them—the first time she'd ever been to the subway.

After Zsa Zsa and Herbert Hunter split up, Eva spotted Hunter with another woman and told Zsa Zsa, whose only reaction was to ask, "Was she prettier than me?" Eva told her no, of course not, but later told a friend the other woman was indeed prettier. "That little fib? My gift to Zsa Zsa."

In early January 1964, Eva and her husband Dick Brown were robbed of jewelry and cash at gunpoint in their room at the Racquet Club in Miami Beach. The gunmen then demanded her husband go to the hotel's vault to get her diamond ring. While he was downstairs, she kept talking to the gunmen so they wouldn't shoot. "I never had such a lousy audience," she said later.

Finally her husband, who didn't alert hotel security, returned with the ring. Eva later recalled a thief saying, "He must really love you."

After the thieves left, she ran down to the lobby screaming "Help! Robbery!" She saw a tall, handsome man smiling at her. "What're you laughing at, you halfwit?" she yelled.

"I'm not a halfwit, I'm a half*back*," replied the New York Giants' Frank Gifford.

She wondered where the thieves had seen her large diamond ring in public, then realized she'd signed lots of autographs in Miami. "Never again will I do that," she said. "It gives people the chance to appraise the ring on the autograph hand."

In June 1966, Zsa Zsa was in Europe filming *Arrivederci, Baby!* with Tony Curtis. During a break in the shooting, he noticed her diamond-studded hand reaching into a diamond-studded purse and pulling out two pills. Then she asked a production assistant, "Can you please bring me a glass of champagne?"

In 1968, Zsa Zsa was the first guest to win on Minnesota Fats's *Celebrity Billiards* TV show. "It was easy," she said. "I just dazzled 'em!"

That fall, Zsa Zsa, just back from her homeland, said she'd spoken freely in Hungary against the Russians. "They could do nothing to me," she explained. "And if they arrested me and sent me to Siberia, I'd soon become the commandant's mistress."

In 1970, Zsa Zsa lunched with Doubleday executives and discussed her new book, which ended with a quote from playboy Porfirio Rubirosa. He was the Dominican diplomat who'd married Doris Duke *and* Barbara Hutton, two of the richest women in the world, as well as Trujillo's daughter and two French actresses. He'd also reportedly had relationships with Marilyn Monroe, Judy Garland, Joan Crawford, Veronica Lake, Kim Novak, and Eva Peron.

"Rubi was special," she recalled. "After all, two of his ex-wives are now on Broadway: Danielle Darrieux and me." My father asked Zsa Zsa when she'd been Mrs. Rubirosa. "Don't get technical, Lenny," she replied.

In 1970, a large amount of Zsa Zsa's jewelry was reported stolen from a famous New York hotel. A few months later, she returned to the hotel to dine at the restaurant, where she told her ex-husband George Sanders that she appreciated the extra security the hotel had put on this time around.

No one at the hotel had told her the additional police were there to guard President Nixon and Prime Minister Golda Meir of Israel.

GRETA GARBO

(1905–1990)

One afternoon around April 1989, I headed to Shirley MacLaine's apartment to conduct a radio interview. As I approached the building, I spotted Greta Garbo emerging behind her trademark sunglasses. MacLaine told me, "Oh yes, 'Mrs. Brown' is my neighbor."

After the interview, I rushed to a nearby phone booth to tell my wife I'd spotted *the* most enigmatic actress of them all. As I was chatting, I turned around and there she was behind me, waiting to use the phone. Two sightings in one hour!

In June 1934, an unusual list was passed around some of New York's most popular nightspots. Patrons were asked to name the people whose demise would make worldwide headlines, and the results were Hitler, Mussolini, Gandhi, Lindbergh, FDR, the Prince of Wales, King George V—and Greta Garbo.

In 1936, producer-agent Leland Hayward, who would produce legendary films like *Mr. Roberts*, *Call Me Madam*, and *The Sound of Music*, married actress Margaret Sullavan. "Before we marry, I want to make one thing clear," he said. "Never will I leave you, except for Greta Garbo."

The bride-to-be replied: "Me too!" (She would be Hayward's third of five wives, none of whom was Garbo.)

In April 1939, in Hawaii, Garbo came aboard a yacht called *The Ranger*, winner of America's Cup in 1937 and owned by a Vanderbilt. She met a young crew member who told her his last name was Johansson. "You must be Swedish," said Garbo. "Yes, ma'am," he replied.

"Don't call me 'ma'am,'" she said. "We're both from Sweden. So call me Greta."

In October 1939, her movie *Ninotchka* premiered in Hollywood. Director Ernst Lubitsch described her role before shooting began: "The American sees her dressed in a simple Russian hat and a plain-looking trench coat. She's like millions of other Russian women. He looks at her and is pleased by what he sees."

"But *why* is he so pleased? Why does he stop her?" asked the director's friend.

"Come on," replied Lubitsch. "She's *Garbo!*"

Early in 1941, MGM bought the rights to the story of Marie Curie, intending to cast Garbo as the greatest woman scientist. The story was written by Curie's daughter, no less. Several of Hollywood's top screenwriters failed to write an acceptable treatment for a screenplay; none could come up with an explanation for why a woman as beautiful as Garbo would ever study physics.

Garbo was more famous for her wish for privacy than for her movies. She refused to give autographs. At a friend's party in 1941, everyone signed the menu as a memento of the evening. She signed "XX." She had her fortune told at another party, but only after donning a floppy hat, so as not to be recognized.

In July 1944, Garbo was living in Los Angeles next door to a retired businessman. Ever since she had moved in, he'd hoped to meet or even get a glimpse of her, to no avail. Then he was named the local war bond salesman.

One night, a burglar broke into her home and ran off with a mink coat. She screamed and slid down a drainpipe, landing painfully on her ankle. Her neighbor called an ambulance, then carried her inside her home. Later he said, "I not only got to hold Greta Garbo in my arms—I also sold her a war bond!"

In December of the same year, Garbo was offered the lead part in *The Cross and the Arrow* but turned it down because the thirty-five-year-old character had a seventeen-year-old son. They offered to make the boy her stepson, but Garbo, then thirty-nine, rejected that idea, too.

In April 1945, Garbo met the Duke of Marlborough, a cousin of Sir Winston Churchill. Though young-looking and handsome, he told her he was a grandfather. Then he asked, "Miss Garbo, which one of your films took place in Paris?"

Garbo, who hated discussing her career, curtly replied, "Lord Marlborough, I will forget you're a grandfather if you forget my pictures."

Garbo was asked why she never returned to movies after 1941's *Two-Faced Woman.* "I looked down from my window the other day," she replied, "and saw Selznick filming *Portrait of Jenny.* It all seemed so silly."

Garbo attended a screening of Jean Cocteau's *Beauty and the Beast,* and at the end of the movie, when the frightening beast turns into the handsome prince, Garbo complained loudly: "Oh no! I want the nice beast back!"

Everything about her was mysterious, including her love life. For instance, playwright Ferenc Molnár (whose play *Liliom* was the basis for the musical *Carousel*) dined at an Italian restaurant in New York. In a booth nearby, he saw Garbo with a man, engrossed in an animated conversation.

"Do you think that's her boyfriend?" asked a friend at Molnár's table. "No," he replied. "From their furious hand movements over the table, I'd say they're discussing business—probably real estate. Lovers' hands touch only *under* the table."

In 1955, a doctor was in her elevator and as soon as he entered, she pulled down her hat to cover her face, too late to escape recognition. The next day, their roles were reversed; he pulled down *his* hat in the same way, even going one better by pulling his coat up over his face. She laughed, and it led to a friendship.

Clarence Brown directed Garbo in *Conquest*, with Charles Boyer as Napoleon and she as his mistress Maria Walewska, the Polish noblewoman. On days when scenes of Napoleon mistreating her were scheduled, Garbo would arrive on the set and greet Boyer coldly. But when love scenes were scheduled, she greeted Boyer with an embrace.

A reporter asked a friend of Garbo's for an interview. "Seriously?" asked the friend. "Louis B. Mayer paid her two million dollars and she wouldn't talk to *him*! Why should she speak to you?"

Invoking her pseudonym, Sir John Gielgud said to her, "Isn't it time to stop this 'Mrs. Harriet Brown' nonsense? Can't I just call you 'Harriet'?"At a lunch aboard a yacht on the Riviera, impresario Sol Hurok noticed a familiar face he couldn't place. When he overheard a man addressing her as "Greta," he knew, and approached her.

"Ahh," said Hurok, "the voice of Anna Karenina!"

"Maybe once," she sighed, "years ago. But now it's a clown's voice speaking."

She rejected an offer to do a film for Jean Cocteau, explaining: "Producers want me to do all those things I've done before, so moviegoers would be able to say I no longer can do them."

A New York florist, thinking she recognized her, kept addressing her as "Miss Dietrich." Later, outside, Garbo giggled to a friend: "She must not have seen my legs."

SIR JOHN GIELGUD

(1904–2000)

One of the greatest classical actors of the twentieth century, he's regarded as the foremost Hamlet of his era. His memorable movies include *Julius Caesar, Richard III, Romeo and Juliet, Plenty*, and *Gandhi*. He was knighted in 1953. Younger audiences know him as Hobson the butler from *Arthur* and its sequel. Hobson's line "I'll alert the media," delivered with heavy-lidded disdain, has become part of the language.

When Gielgud played Romeo for the first time, in 1924, he'd learned the trick of weeping real tears on cue. One night he heard that Dame Edith Evans was in the audience, so he poured out an unusual amount. Later on, backstage, he asked her opinion of that tragic scene.

"John," she told the young man, "when you learn to cry *less* onstage, the audience will cry more."

In April 1941, with England fending off nightly German air attacks, Gielgud toured the provinces performing benefits for the war effort, including his greatest role, Hamlet. After the final curtain, he auctioned off the rarest commodity in England at that time: a bucket of onions.

While flying to entertain the troops, Gielgud's Royal Air Force plane was attacked by anti-aircraft fire. While flack surrounded the aircraft and the other passengers cowered, Gielgud calmly completed the London *Times'* crossword puzzle—wearing white gloves!

In 1949, Gielgud was directing the London production of Tennessee Williams's *The Glass Menagerie* with three respected Americans in the cast: Helen Hayes, Frances Heflin, and Phillip Brown. Before rehearsals, he addressed the cast, but swallowed some words at the end of sentences.

Finally, Helen Hayes said, "John, what did you say?"

"I only said you Americans have to be sure not to swallow your words."

He directed and starred in a play and was visited backstage by friends impressed by the way the other actors remained motionless while Gielgud spoke. "How'd you do that?" they asked.

"Easily," replied Gielgud. "If anyone moved while I was speaking, I'd *kill* them!"

Richard Burton played Hamlet, and on opening night learned that Gielgud was in the audience. Apprehensive about getting approval from Gielgud, he kept thinking about it during his performance. Later Gielgud said simply, "Fine. You were fine, Richard. Now where should we dine?"

On the day he was knighted, there was a rush for tickets to *Venice Preserv'd*, in which Gielgud was performing. To prolonged cheers, Gielgud stepped from the wings and said his first lines as a knight of the realm: "I am not the wretch that thou beholdest here."

In January 1959, Marlene Dietrich saw Gielgud in *The Ages of Man*, his one-man show on Broadway. She noticed the French Legion of Honor in his lapel. Backstage, Dietrich, also a winner of the honor for wartime service to France while in exile, told him that few people in America know how to sew the ribbon on properly.

She knew how, so the next morning, Dietrich arrived unannounced at Gielgud's apartment carrying a needle, thread, and the thin red ribbon from Cartier designed for the Legion of Honor. While Gielgud breakfasted, Dietrich dutifully sat with him at his table, sewing the red ribbon on each of his dozen jackets.

After one performance in London, Gielgud felt he hadn't been especially good. He told the stage manager he'd not permit any visitors afterward. Then word came that the famed Russian actress Maria Ouspenskaya had been in the audience and wanted to visit. Of course he welcomed her. "I'm afraid I gave a bad performance tonight," he told her.

"You are right," she replied. Then walked out.

Early in 1960, Gielgud warned young actors, "Never play to one member of the audience, no matter who. It would diminish the performance. When I starred in *Musical Chairs*, I spotted Noël Coward in the sixth row. So I addressed my first six punch lines directly to him," he recalled. "When it came time for my seventh, Coward's seat was empty. He'd walked out."

Gielgud once said, "An actor's job onstage is half shame, half glory. Shame when you're conscious of making a public exhibition of yourself; glory when you completely forget yourself in your role."

A woman approached Gielgud and said, "Sir Gielgud, I loved you in Edward Albee's *Tiny Alice*."

A friend whispered, "It's 'Sir John,' not 'Sir Gielgud.'"

"I don't know him that well," the woman explained.

During his starring run in *Ivanov* on Broadway, Gielgud and costar Vivien Leigh endured a delay in the curtain time. A couple had purchased three seats and brought along their pet chimpanzee. Over their objections, the odd trio was escorted out. At least two of them objected, anyway.

Jack Hawkins, best known for leading the commandos in *The Bridge on the River Kwai*, told Peter O'Toole that Gielgud had once directed him in *Hamlet*. It was performed at Elsinore, Denmark—the setting of the play—right before the war. Gielgud made Hawkins play the ghost as well. "It was awful," laughed Hawkins. "Maybe that's why Denmark remained neutral."

O'Toole grinned and replied, "It *really* must have been awful, Jack, to confuse you about history. Actually, Sweden was the neutral country."

In his eulogy for his friend Sir Noël Coward in November, 1973, Gielgud quoted Coward: "The world has treated me very well. But then, I haven't treated *it* so badly, either."

SIR ALEC GUINNESS

(1914–2000)

His generation produced many thespian knights of the realm: Gielgud, Richardson, Redgrave, Mills, and Olivier. When I interviewed him extensively around 1980, he was at ease and forthright. His films of note included *Kind Hearts and Coronets, Our Man in Havana, The Horse's Mouth, Tunes of Glory, The Man in the White Suit, The Ladykillers, The Lavender Hill Mob*, and *The Bridge on the River Kwai*, for which he won an Oscar.

He once conducted an experiment after an opening night, deciding to ignore the reviews until weeks later. "It didn't work," he said. "You can't help hearing about them."

He toured the provinces in a play by Samuel and Bella Spewak, who also wrote the book for the smash Cole Porter musical *Kiss Me, Kate*. This one surely had lower expectations, since it took place inside an anthill. "The actors love it," said Guinness. "We can have a picnic without leaving the stage."

When his housekeeper heard he'd be knighted in 1961, she burst into tears, saying, "They should've made you a duke." I asked Guinness about that day. "You march slowly down the aisle in Westminster Abbey," he said, "and I remember staring at the huge bum ahead of me on line, belonging to some banker from Bristol, and wondering what on earth *he'd* ever done to get such an honor."

He once listened to a friend describe the investiture of another eminent actor who said that his greatest fear was having the queen mispronounce his name. Sure enough, she did. "That couldn't have been his greatest fear," said Guinness. "Anyone getting knighted is terrified of being hit on your ears as Her Majesty swings that heavy sword between your shoulders."

Guinness told me he'd been sent a script by director David Lean, "involving a prison camp in a steamy jungle, and women with bananas and luggage on their heads. It seemed like a bother." Then he carefully read the script for *The Bridge on the River Kwai*, agreed to play Colonel Nicholson, and won the Oscar. "Thank goodness," he said.

He played T. E. Lawrence onstage in *Ross* (1960), but had the role of Arab prince Faisal in *Lawrence of Arabia* (1962). Lawrence, who was about five foot three, was played by then-unknown Peter O'Toole, nearly a foot taller than Lawrence and eighteen years younger than Guinness.

"That's a British actor for you," said a friend of Guinness's, referring to his willingness to take a supporting role in the movie. "But he knows his new part is a great one, too. *That's* a British actor for you, too."

While Guinness was performing in *Ross*, an American tourist walked to the footlights and snapped a flash photo. Guinness stepped out of character and said, "Madame, if you do that again, I will have you escorted out." She ignored him and snapped another photo. True to his word, Guinness got her ejected. She sued. He won.

Lawrence of Arabia was filmed in Jordan, which prompted Guinness to say, "One sets off in the theater as an ambitious youth, never realizing the journey may end in a dust storm in some remote corner of the world."

He accepted one movie role because his character would be hanged. "I'd died eleven times in films up to then," he said, "but never by hanging."

His son Matthew toured with the Comédie-Française, and in each city, the younger Guinness received long ovations. He wired his father: "Success disproportionate to talent. Plan change of vocations at end of tour."

Guinness's first screen kiss came from Yvonne De Carlo, in 1953's *The Captain's Paradise*. It wasn't until 1962's *Damn the Defiant* that he got his second kiss. Asked about the nine-year lapse between kisses, he explained, "Someone booed and hissed at the screening of that first kiss. It was my wife."

In *The Captain's Paradise* he portrayed a sea captain with two wives, played by Celia Johnson and Yvonne De Carlo. In the American version, De Carlo portrayed his mistress, not his other wife. The producers explained that American audiences could tolerate infidelity more than bigamy.

In 1963, he was introduced to an African diplomat and gave the perfunctory greeting, "I hope your stay in London will be a long and enjoyable one."

"A *long* visit?" replied the diplomat. "I hope not. I'm here in exile."

At the height of the popularity of the Twist in 1963, Sybil Burton asked Guinness if he'd ever tried it. "Only once," he replied. "With Sophia Loren in Segovia. I thought that would be a good way to begin—and end it."

In 1964, Guinness played the Welsh poet Dylan Thomas on Broadway. Guinness had known Thomas and recalled, "He never accepted flattery, nor refused a drink."

Actress Cathleen Nesbitt came backstage after a performance of *Dylan*. They'd been friends since 1938, when she played Queen Gertrude to his Hamlet. When they kissed, some of his nose putty rubbed off onto her hair. "I don't mind," she said. "It's something for me to remember your performance."

He refused a lucrative offer to do a TV commercial for a liquor brand. "I'm flattered," he said, "but most people would think I've become a has-been."

While on Broadway, he refused to make any commitment to a future role. "When a working actor signs for another play, he becomes bored and anxious to get on to the next."

He refused to have his effigy displayed in Madame Tussaud's wax museum. "I'm afraid that someday I'd be melted down."

Guinness once advised young actors, "Dress so people can't tell if you're the son of a laborer or a duke."

HELEN HAYES

(1900–1993)

everal actresses have been called "The First Lady of the American Theater," among them Ethel Barrymore and Katherine Cornell. But the unofficial title is usually associated with Helen Hayes, whose career began on Broadway in 1912, a month after the *Titanic* sank, and lasted until 1986—an incredible ninety-eight shows, in addition to movies and TV appearances.

On September 7, 1943, she wrote a guest column for The Lyons Den that provided some rare insights into the craft of acting. "I have a pet theory on acting," she wrote. "An actress stores up experiences the way a squirrel tucks away nuts, filing them away for future use. Usually, this hoarding is unconscious.

"These stored-up experiences don't have to be your own. One may be a vivid line in a book. Another may be the look on an old lady's picture in a tabloid. They sink deep into your mind, often lie there half-remembered or even forgotten. But they're all there when you need them, shining and vivid and crystal clear in the Pandora's Box of your subconscious."

Her son James MacArthur left Harvard in 1959 to pursue acting (his most famous role, "Danno" Williams on *Hawaii Five-O*, would come nine years later). He'd taken an aptitude test that said he'd make a fine architect. "So I took it again," he said, "only this time I made every mistake possible on the test. The result: 'Actor.'"

In June 1959, Hayes became a member of the Troupers, an organization benefiting the children of needy theater people. She was sent an application in the form of a questionnaire.

"Name?" "Helen Hayes." "Connection to the Theater?" "Actress." "Where are you employed?" "The Helen Hayes Theater."

An autograph seeker said, "I know you: Ethel Hayes." "No, sorry," replied the actress. "I'm Helen Merman."

When she became a grandmother in May 1960, she beamed, of course, and spoke of the baby. "He's beautiful," she said, "and looking at him I realized how much I've lied over the years telling my friends how pretty *their* grandchildren are."

In February 1961, she met the great actress Dame Edith Evans at Sardi's and asked her what brought her to New York. Looking a bit sheepish, Dame Edith said, "I'm doing a TV version of the role *you* created in *Time Remembered*." It was then that Hayes gave her shortest but best performance: she smiled and looked genuinely pleased.

At a luncheon at Sardi's, a woman sat next to her and marveled: "Helen Hayes! In person! You've always been a dream to me, and here you are. You're human!"

"Listen," replied Hayes, "I'm here, I feel lousy, and I've got a terrible cold. You can't get more human than that."

A young actress came to Helen Hayes for advice: "What do you do when you've won a role, read the script, signed the contract, and then realize the play is lousy?"

"You go to rehearsals," she replied, "and try to suggest changes, then go out of town with it in previews. Then, if the out-of-town critics pan the show, say to yourself: 'What do they know in Philadelphia?'"

In December 1965, Ruth Gordon, celebrating her fiftieth year in the theater, denied she was a born actress. "Helen Hayes is the only born actress I know. From the moment she first stepped on a stage as a child, everyone knew Helen Hayes would be a star."

When Rodgers and Hammerstein produced *Happy Birthday*, they installed special bathroom plumbing in Hayes's dressing room. In reciprocation she put up a plaque: "The Rodgers & Hammerstein Memorial Seat."

CHARLTON HESTON

(1923–2008)

Born in Wilmette, a Chicago suburb, Heston studied acting at Northwestern University under legendary teacher Alvina Krause, whose students included Richard Benjamin, Paula Prentiss, Warren Beatty, and playwright George Furth.

Rock Hudson (then still Roy Scherer) got his start as an actor at New Trier High in nearby Winnetka, Illinois. He tried out for the lead in the annual school play, but lost to a classmate, Heston. "Right then and there," he said, "I should've known that one day he'd part the Red Sea."

Kirk Douglas once told me an actor is lucky if he or she is defined by one role. Heston, of course, had several defining roles: Moses in *The Ten Commandments*, the title role in *Ben-Hur*, and George Taylor in the *Planet of the Apes* movies.

He claimed there was only one reason he got cast in *Ben-Hur*: "I'm one of only two actors in Hollywood who knew how to drive a chariot," he explained. "The other was Francis X. Bushman, who played the role of Messala back in the 1925 version, but he was seventy-three at the time."

My father and younger brother Douglas were on the set of *Ben-Hur* near Rome in 1958, and Heston gave them a chariot ride. Douglas, then eleven, said Heston was the best chariot driver he'd ever seen.

Living in New York in 1956, Heston, not surprisingly, was stuck in noontime traffic. "I could get God to part the Red Sea easier than getting through this mess," he said.

In *The Ten Commandments*, Heston rehearsed in the Sinai desert, in full view of fifty thousand extras. In his next film, *Touch of Evil*, he rehearsed with Orson Welles in the tiny compartment of a trailer.

Heston costarred in one of the greatest westerns of all time, *The Big Country*, as Steve Leach, the tough head wrangler on a sprawling Texas ranch. One day on the set, he was asked about his versatility. "Yes, I have range," he said. "I can play Shakespeare better than Gary Cooper and a cowboy better than Sir Laurence Olivier."

Paddy Chayefsky, the great screenwriter, took his mother to *The Ten Commandments*. In the scene where Moses leaves the Burning Bush and wanders across the desert, there was a shot of Yvonne De Carlo, as Moses's wife Sephora. "She was an unhappy woman," said Mrs. Chayefsky. "Moses was never home."

Heston was offered a starring role in *Let's Make Love* opposite Marilyn Monroe in February 1960, but turned it down for a role on Broadway in *The Tumbler*. Mel Brooks asked him why he did that. "I wanted to be directed by Laurence Olivier," Heston replied. "And then, I'm an actor and wanted to know what it's like to start projecting an emotion and to sustain it for two and a half hours. In Hollywood, there's no such chance." The play ran for five performances.

In June 1964, I was in Rome with my father and we headed to the Forum. I couldn't resist the temptation to say I hoped a funny thing would happen to us on our way. And it did—we saw Heston shooting *The Agony and the Ecstasy*, in which he played Michelangelo.

Heston said, "He lived at the right time in history. Today, if they were building the Sistine Chapel, the Vatican probably would've used wallpaper."

In November 1967, Heston was elected to a third term as president of the Screen Actors Guild, but disavowed any future political aspiration. "But if the president ever needs someone with a long beard who can arrange to have the Red Sea parted for him," he said, "I'd consider a cabinet appointment."

Douglas Fairbanks Jr.'s daughter Melissa was in Sunday school one morning when her teacher asked who'd stood on Mount Sinai and received the Ten Commandments. Melissa raised her hand and replied, "Charlton Heston."

At a New York restaurant, patrons at two tables spotted Heston and asked him over to say grace over their meal.

Major Dundee, a Heston western, had a cost overrun, so he took the unusual step of returning some of his fee to the studio. "Won't this set a precedent?" he was asked. "No," said Heston. "It won't even set a precedent for *me*!"

In 1974, Heston wore a false nose to play Cardinal Richelieu in *The Three Musketeers*. He explained, "Richelieu is the first historical figure I've played who had a nose larger than mine."

He said that during the shooting, "When I looked at Raquel Welch and Faye Dunaway, I almost forgot my Cardinal vows."

Heston and Raquel Welch were to meet Queen Elizabeth on the red carpet at the London premiere of *The Three Musketeers*. Heston was nervous, but Welch said, *"She's* the one who should be nervous, Chuck. After all, you played Moses. You've argued with God."

WILLIAM HOLDEN

(1918–1981)

Watching the marvelous 2014 movie *The Railway Man*, I couldn't help think of *The Bridge on the River Kwai*, since both dealt with British POWs used as slave laborers building a railway through some of the world's thickest jungles during World War II.

In the earlier movie, Holden gave one of his greatest performances as the only American prisoner in the camp.

One of the premier leading men of the 1940s and '50s, Holden was born William Franklin Beadle in tiny O'Fallon, Illinois. In 1939, he starred in the film version of Clifford Odets's *Golden Boy*, in the part created on Broadway by John Garfield. He did his own negotiating for that role, earning $50 a week.

When Kirk Douglas turned down the lead in *Stalag 17*, Holden got the role, for which he won the Oscar in 1953. His other iconic films include *Sunset Boulevard, Sabrina, The Bridges at Toko-Ri, The Country Girl, The Wild Bunch, Network,* and *The Counterfeit Traitor,* one of the best true stories about World War II.

Holden spent much time in Africa, where he was a leader in conservation. He didn't come through New York often, but he and my father spent several weeks together in March 1957 in the steamy jungles of what was then Ceylon (today Sri Lanka), the remote site of the filming of *The Bridge on the River Kwai*.

Every time Turner Classic Movies shows the movie, I stay tuned for the short "making of" film afterward. There, atop one of the small trolleys going back and forth along the tracks over the river, I see my father, shirtless, in shorts, with his familiar hat, gathering anecdotes and having the time of his life.

The cameras for the movie had to be brought all the way from Los Angeles carefully wrapped in newspapers for padding (no bubble wrap back then). It was a long, arduous shoot in the dense jungle, made even more difficult by the cacophony of chirping birds just before the cameras rolled. Director David Lean solved the bird problem by firing a gun a moment before calling "Action!"

My father (left) and William Holden (right) on the set of *The Bridge on the River Kwai*, in what was then Ceylon, now Sri-Lanka.

Producer Sam Spiegel, a gourmet, brought in his own French chef for his cast, along with a water-purifying system and extensive indoor plumbing. My father's journey there had begun months before and a world away at the Colony Restaurant in New York, when he joined Spiegel and Holden at lunch. They invited him to come to Ceylon and blow up the bridge, the climax of the film.

My father had never willfully destroyed anything in his life, but a few months later, in the scene in which Holden's and Alec Guinness's characters are both killed, my father was the one who pushed the plunger in the sloping hills overlooking the river.

The most famous bridge in movie history was constructed with thirty thousand cubic feet of timber, hauled through the jungle. The 57-year-old train, which plunged into the river at the movie's end, had to be cut in half for transport and re-welded after their journey deep into the jungle.

An expert from the International Chemical Industries in London had trekked to the site to prepare the dynamite. He quickly noticed the cast and crew giving him a wide berth.

The temperature was close to 110 degrees, the humidity high. Spiegel hired sixteen elephants to clear brush so workmen could build miles of roads to the location, then lay railway tracks.

Holden had built a makeshift zoo, comprised of stray animals he'd come across near the set: a cat, a dog, two parrots, an owl, and a monkey. The owl was found before it could fly, and took a liking to Guinness, who, before feeding it every day with an eyedropper, would say, "Come on, here's Mum!"

A legend in those days was that you could have a suit tailored in Hong Kong overnight at a fraction of the cost a Western tailor would charge. So with two days off, Holden flew to Hong Kong and bought several fifty-dollar knockoffs of his expensive Italian suit. Back in the steamy jungle, Holden showed one off to his friends. He learned that you get what you pay for. When someone noticed a thread sticking up, he pulled on it, and the entire arm of the jacket peeled away.

On his way home from the set, Holden held a press conference on a stopover in Tokyo. He praised Japanese women as far more sociable, and far less arrogant, than American women. Just then, his wife, actress Brenda Marshall, walked in. "Uh-oh," he said, "here comes the exception!"

Whenever the actor would meet a fan who disliked his newest movie, he'd reimburse them for the price they'd paid for a ticket. "It's a good policy," he explained, "and besides, it's a legitimate business expense."

In 1962, Holden negotiated a lucrative profit-sharing deal for *The Counterfeit Traitor*. Holden said, "Nowadays, it's as important for an actor to attend business school as the Actors Studio."

In June 1964, while he was filming *The Seventh Dawn*, Holden was invited to a dinner in Malaya. The main course was a stew made from a freshly killed thirty-foot python. Holden declined a bowl of the steaming meal, tactfully saying he was a vegetarian. Then he was asked when he'd started being a vegetarian. Unable to fib any longer, he confessed, "When I peeked into the kitchen and saw the main course fighting for its life."

In 1968, Holden teamed with Ernest Borgnine in Sam Peckinpah's gritty western *The Wild Bunch*, filmed in a hot, bug-infested *pueblo* in Mexico. Holden asked, "Ernie, how come we don't get to kiss the girl anymore, or drink martinis in penthouses?" Borgnine, possibly thinking the same thing, sighed and replied, "Bill, it's because a long time ago, the industry ran out of those kind of pictures for guys like you and me."

CELESTE HOLM

(1917–2012)

A native New Yorker, she was the sensation of Broadway in 1943, winning the Tony Award for *Oklahoma!*, one of the theater's landmark musicals. She also won the 1947 Best Supporting Actress Oscar for *Gentleman's Agreement* and had a fifty-year career in films and on television. She starred in William Saroyan's classic *The Time of Your Life*, *A Letter to Three Wives*, *All About Eve*, and *Three Men and a Baby*.

The night she opened on Broadway in *Oklahoma!*, Twentieth Century Fox production chief Darryl Zanuck and his wife were in the audience. When she sang "I Can't Say No," he whispered to his wife, "This show will run longer than World War II and she'll be a huge star."

One frigid night in December 1944, Holm stood outside in midtown and couldn't get a cab. Just then a *Daily News* truck stopped on the corner for a red light. "Mister, I'm freezing," she said to the driver. "Can't you give me a lift home? I live downtown."

"Sorry," said the driver. "What nerve to ask me to go in the opposite direction! Who do you think you are?"

He drove off too quickly for the shivering actress to point to the side of the truck, which carried a huge picture of her face, touting her musical *Bloomer Girl*.

In December 1947, she played a brief return engagement as Ado Annie, the role she had originated in *Oklahoma!* four years earlier. No member of the original cast was still there. "It's the nightmare all actors have," she said, "suddenly finding that you're onstage, delivering your lines to strangers."

That same month, she received a gold card from the stagehands' union, designating her as an honorary member. It permitted her to move a prop onstage without bringing on a strike.

When she signed for *Gentlemen's Agreement*, she wrote to screenwriter Moss Hart expressing her delight. Except for one line. The editor in the story advises the reporter to change his name from Schuyler to Phil, "because 'Schuyler' is an awful name. I wouldn't

Celeste Holm and my father at the Stork Club, 1945.

call a dog 'Schuyler.'" At the time she was married to Schuyler Dunning.

After *Gentleman's Agreement*, Spyros Skouras, head of Twentieth Century Fox, said, "It would be like stopping Niagara Falls to stop her from becoming a star." Then the studio suspended her for refusing a minor part in *Sitting Pretty*.

She returned to New York in June 1949 after a tour entertaining troops in France, Morocco, Italy, and Greece, and met Supreme Court Justice William O. Douglas. He told her he was headed to the same countries. "I hope you get as many laughs as I did," she said.

That same year, she played a French nun in the movie *Come to the Stable*. She was offered French lessons by the studio. "I don't need any," she explained. "I was educated in Paris. But there *is* a scene where I'm supposed to play tennis."

Early in 1950, Holm dined with the Duke and Duchess of Windsor at the Stork Club, and the duke told her he was leaving the next day for Mexico "for a shooting trip." "Good luck with your shooting," she replied. "Whoever it is!"

When she starred on Broadway in *Oklahoma!* and then *Bloomer Girl*, two faithful bobbysoxers would stand outside her dressing room after every performance, running errands for her, hailing a taxi when it rained, etc. By the time she returned to Broadway in *Affairs of State* in 1950, her two doting fans had become Broadway angels—they owned a piece of the show.

In January 1952, she walked from her hotel to the theater where she starred in O'Neill's *Anna Christie*, and said the walk to the theater on opening night "is the loneliest in the world. You're completely on your own and nobody in the world can help you."

In June of that year, she performed in Las Vegas and took a turn at the gambling tables. "I promised myself I'd quit when I'd come out ahead," she said. She won thirty-five cents. Pearl Bailey told her, "Here in Las Vegas, when people say eight to five, they're not talking about the correct time."

One afternoon in October 1953, Holm tried on a new and revealing gown in a Hollywood shop, but refused to buy it. "When I come into a room," she later explained, "I'd rather people ask 'Who is she?' than wear something which will have them asking, 'Who does she think she is?'"

Later that year, she explained that "an actress is someone who pretends to be someone else only because she's uncertain who she herself is."

Early in 1954, she was being wooed by an Italian diplomat and another statesman from a different country. "If nothing else," she observed, "this is a great way to improve one's language skills."

"There is no such thing as a captive audience," she said in 1954. "The only captive audience is an inmate or a baby in a carriage."

James C. Petrillo, head of the musicians' union, was a germophobe who always touched his pinky to outstretched hands. Yet he gave Holm a vigorous handshake when they met. "People often think we blondes are inherently cleaner," she surmised.

"It's an advantage to be a blonde," she continued. "A blonde can say almost anything, even the silliest things, and nobody minds."

She arrived late at a dinner party and explained, "My young son and I took a bubble bath together." Oscar Levant was there, and asked her, "Have you made a down payment yet for his psychoanalyst?"

She turned down an offer to do a five-night-a-week TV show, saying, "I don't know anyone *I'd* like to visit that often."

In September 1952, she was swimming on a beach when a policeman came by. "People are complaining about the brevity of your suit," said the policeman. "My suit?" she asked. "It's not very brief." "I know," said the policeman. "*That's* the complaint!"

One of her Norwegian relatives visited her in Hollywood. His knowledge of English was limited, but he asked Holm the meaning of the phrase *gilding the lily*. She explained: "If you see Marilyn Monroe in a bathing suit that would be a lily. But if you see her in a *wet* bathing suit, that would be gilding the lily."

Onstage with Robert Preston in *His and Hers*, they kissed and he accidentally cut her lip. At intermission she told him, "Robert, in the theater, you're supposed to shoot blanks."

AL JOLSON

(1886–1950)

In the years prior to television, Jolson was Hollywood's top all-around entertainer—in vaudeville, recordings, movies, and radio. After George Jessel, who'd played the role onstage, rejected the part, Jolson starred in the first talking feature film, *The Jazz Singer*, in 1927. While Jolson's trademark blackface performances, singing about his mammy from Alabammy, are today rightly judged an offensive relic of Hollywood's racist past, that was only a part of his legacy. "The World's Greatest Entertainer" made only sixteen films, but the Lithuanian-born Asa Yoelsen, the son of a cantor, left an indelible mark. His most famous line was the first he ever spoke on-screen: "You ain't heard nothin' yet."

Warner Bros. wasn't prepared financially for the overnight sensation *The Jazz Singer* caused at the box office so paid him in stock, the value of which zoomed after the film was released.

He'd come a long way from St. Mary's Industrial School for Boys, in Baltimore, where he was sent after his mother died in 1895—the same institution where young Babe Ruth had been nurtured.

He was the first American entertainer to perform for the troops in World War II, and entertained more soldiers than anyone save Bob Hope. When he returned home from a tour of bases in Iceland and Greenland, he didn't bother to check into his Manhattan hotel, nor even to take off his uniform. Instead, Jolson headed straight for the Stork Club, found my father, and angrily greeted him: "So! 'With the *exception* of Bob Hope,' eh?" He'd read that line in *Stars and Stripes*, the soldiers' newspaper, which carried The Lyons Den.

In August 1937, Jolson dined at the home of studio boss Jack Warner and was asked what he'd like for his main dish. Before hearing the choices, he said he'd like some ham. "But we keep a kosher home," Warner said. "Oh, I forgot," replied Jolson. "You just give *contracts* to hams."

In April 1938, Jolson was married to actress Ruby Keeler and promised her he'd stop spending so much time at the Santa Anita racetrack. The next day, she asked him how far they lived from Jack Benny's home. "Oh, about eight furlongs," he replied.

The next year, when a rumor spread that Jolson had died, the phone in his hotel suite rang. Jolson told his manager, "Tell them I have no comment."

Jolson was asked about fans' adulation. "When the crowd loves you," he said, "*bathe* in it!"

While entertaining near the front, his troupe came under an air attack. Racing for cover, Jolson saw a machine gun on the ground, picked it up, and fired at the planes, the way George C. Scott would do with his pistol in *Patton* twenty-eight years later.

"Are you crazy?" yelled an officer. "Get inside!"

"I promise you," replied Jolson, racing for cover, "that when the smoke clears, you'll see six dead Nazis falling from the sky."

Such was his stardom that after he punched theater mogul Lee Schubert during a heated dispute, Schubert said, "I won't hire him again—until I need him."

Another dispute with Schubert ended up in court, but Jolson settled. He peeled off two thousand dollars outside and gave it to the opposing attorney, saying, "The only reason I settled is because I don't like getting up early for a trial."

After another tour of the troops, he again headed straight for the Stork Club. Proprietor Sherman Billingsley gave him the top table, table 50, and tore up the "Reserved" sign placed there for a then-obscure senator from Missouri, Harry S. Truman.

Jolson constantly had the need to mention his fortune to stimulate his ego. His money was the proof he must be great. One summer, Jolson went to the racetrack at Saratoga, New York, with Alfred Gwynne Vanderbilt to see the tycoon's horse, Air Flame, race. The multimillionaire bet five dollars. Jolson bet four thousand dollars. The horse, which went off at odds of fifteen to one, won.

Jessel once made a test of Jolson's ability to bring his money into any conversation. "Jolie," said Jessel, "it's raining in Minnesota."

Sure enough, Jolson replied, "Think that'll affect the cotton crop there? I got a hundred Gs tied up in cotton futures."

Then Jessel introduced Jolson to a man named Kinney.

"Is it 'Kinney' or 'McKinney'?" Jolson asked. "'Cause 'McKinney' happens to be the name of a teller at a bank where I got six million."

Only once did Jolson permit a testimonial dinner to be given for him. He'd brought his twenty-one-year-old bride with him, "just to show her how I work an audience. She's too young to have seen me."

The speech he gave and the songs he sang that night, when he'd been considered a washed-up vestige of another time in Hollywood, revived his career, and he was soon performing in front of a new generation of fans.

"That's a pretty daughter you have," said a waiter to him in a Hollywood restaurant.

"That's not my daughter," Jolson replied. "She's too young to be my daughter. This is my wife."

At his own expense, he flew to Korea in 1950 to perform for the troops; after ignoring his doctor's orders and performing forty-two times in just sixteen days, he returned home and died soon afterward.

BURT LANCASTER

(1913–1994)

For my money, the only actor who should be mentioned in the same breath with Kirk Douglas among postwar action and drama stars is New Yorker Burt Lancaster. Trained as an acrobat, he burst onto the scene in *The Killers*, adapted from an Ernest Hemingway story. No supporting or small roles before stardom: he was top billed in his first film, opposite Ava Gardner. He starred in every one of his seventy-six films, the consummate movie star.

When he starred in *Kiss the Blood off My Hands* in 1948, New York's Capitol Theater had to stop displaying life-size cutout posters of the actor. The first two were carried off by bobbysoxers and the third was smeared with lipstick kisses.

1954's *Apache* was the first time he didn't get to kiss his costar, in that case Jean Peters. Apaches didn't kiss.

That year, he directed and starred in *The Kentuckian*, and was asked what it was like to handle both tasks. "I feel like I'm in a race and can't run until I hear the gun go off—and I'm firing the gun!"

In *Sweet Smell of Success*, Lancaster played a Broadway columnist with a heart of stone: vicious and conniving. When it hit theaters in 1957, my friends kidded me, saying it showed how all columnists were scoundrels. But Lancaster said, "No, I just played a heel who happened to be a columnist."

James Hill, one of Lancaster's producing partners, was dating Rita Hayworth in November 1957. He took Hayworth's younger daughter Yasmin to play with Lancaster's children but quickly noticed that the children weren't playing together and asked why. Billy Lancaster explained, "How can we play games with her if she insists on being called 'Princess'?" Yasmin's father was Prince Aly Khan.

Lancaster's hobby was photography. He took a photo of Hill, who wanted Lancaster to inscribe it. Mindful of Hill's imminent marriage to Hayworth, Lancaster wrote: "To Husband Number Five." The marriage lasted two years, seven months.

In *Separate Tables*, Lancaster starred with Hayworth. Their love scenes took two days to shoot. Deborah Kerr costarred, and when

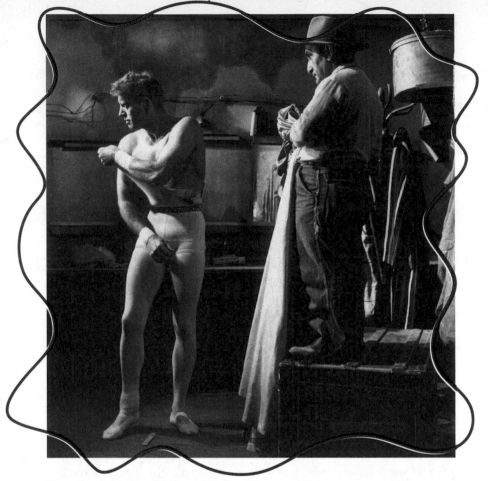

Burt Lancaster and Johnny Puleo, *Trapeze*, Paris, 1955.
Photograph by Sam Shaw.

Hayworth said she was exhausted, Kerr replied: *"Two days?* In *From Here to Eternity*, Burt and I took *two weeks* for that love scene on the beach."

"I know," replied Hayworth, "I saw the movie. But at least you two had the ocean breezes on that beach to cool you off."

Lancaster starred with Audrey Hepburn in *The Unforgiven*, a picturesque western. It was filmed in Durango, Mexico, an ideal site, until winds began carrying the sounds of nearby radios miles across the bowl-shaped valley. The sounds interfered with the shooting, so producer Hill purchased time on the local radio station, guaranteeing two hours of silence.

Lancaster won the Best Actor Academy Award for *Elmer Gantry*. His costar, Shirley Jones, won Best Supporting Actress, and in presenting it to her, Lancaster referred to the flimsy slip she wore in the film. She replied, "I never knew so little could go so far."

Early in 1957, Frank Sinatra, one of whose nicknames was "The Skinny One from Hoboken," expressed his admiration for Lancaster. "What do you admire the most?" he was asked. "His weight," replied Sinatra.

Like his friend and frequent costar Kirk Douglas, Lancaster became an independent producer, and explained why. He'd starred in *From Here to Eternity* on a loan-out to another studio and was paid just forty-eight thousand dollars for the demanding role, a pittance even then. What galled him was that the producer who'd had him under contract and loaned him out collected three hundred thousand.

When Lancaster was in Italy playing the Sicilian prince in *The Leopard*, director Luchino Visconti doubted Lancaster's background as an acrobat. The next morning, Lancaster walked onto the set on his hands.

In 1964, while he was filming *The Train*, as a laborer trying to save precious artworks from the Nazis, one scene called for him to tumble down a three-hundred-foot hill. To no one's surprise, Lancaster eschewed the use of a stuntman and did the dangerous tumble himself.

Afterward, he was asked why he took that risk. He shrugged and gave the classic daredevil's answer: "Because it's there."

Poor Robert Mitchum. He was the only movie star mistaken for both Kirk Douglas *and* Burt Lancaster. In March 1964, a fan approached Mitchum, addressed him as "Mr. Lancaster," and asked for an autograph. As had happened when he was mistaken for Douglas, Mitchum signed an obscene suggestion, only this time, he added: "Burt Lancaster."

Lancaster met Marc Chagall in France while filming *Trapeze* in 1955. Twelve years later, Chagall heard that Lancaster's Hollywood home had been partially destroyed by fire, including some Chagalls. Lancaster received a lithograph from Chagall inscribed: "To lessen your misfortune." (It turned out the paintings hadn't been destroyed after all.)

A few weeks later, Lancaster was in New York visiting the art galleries along Madison Avenue. He winced describing the day, years before, when the playwright Clifford Odets had shown him canvases Odets was buying for under a hundred dollars apiece. "I told him that cliché which I'll never use again: 'My kid can paint better than that.'" He explained that the paintings were by a then-unknown Paul Klee and now were worth tens of thousands of dollars.

In 1968, Lancaster was the title player in an odd movie called *The Swimmer*, which featured the first score written by Marvin Hamlisch and the first film appearance of Joan Rivers. The story, about a man determined to swim (uninvited) across his neighborhood by way of all its backyard swimming pools, was written by John Cheever, who told Lancaster he'd been offered a cameo in the movie but turned it down.

"Why?" asked Lancaster. "It would've been fun."

"Because," replied Cheever, "I didn't want my grandchildren to see my screen debut as a drunk asleep at a pool."

Lancaster seemed to have a knack for being in the right place at the right time for historical events. While filming *Scorpio*, he was living in the Watergate Apartments on the night of the infamous break-in in 1972. And he was filming in Israel the next year when the 1973 war broke out.

"If I play Moses in my next film," he said, "I plan to ask God what he has in store for me."

ANGELA LANSBURY

(1925–)

She came here in 1940, among the last groups of children to leave London, then being ravaged by the Luftwaffe. It was her brother-in-law Peter Ustinov, then in uniform making information films for the war effort, who arranged her escape.

Gaslight, in 1944, won her stardom and a Best Supporting Actress Oscar nomination. Other films, especially *The Harvey Girls* and *The Picture of Dorian Gray*, which earned her a second Oscar nomination, assured her an enduring screen career. As the heavy-handed Mrs. Iselin in the original *The Manchurian Candidate*, Lansbury earned a third Supporting Actress nomination.

Lucille Ball had been considered for the part of Mrs. Iselin, but director John Frankenheimer insisted on Lansbury, though she was just three years older than Lawrence Harvey, playing her brainwashed son.

Lansbury won stardom on TV as Jessica Fletcher in twelve seasons of *Murder, She Wrote* and on Broadway in *Mame, Dear World, Sweeney Todd*, and revivals of *Gypsy* and *Blithe Spirit*.

In 2000 she capped her career as an honoree of the Kennedy Center Honors.

She was asked how she got over losing three Oscars. "Each time, I comforted my husband," she replied.

Lansbury, then starring in *Mame*, attended a party in New York for the Duke and Duchess of Windsor after the premiere of the documentary *A King's Story*. She was presented to the duchess, who said, "You have such a wonderful show." Lansbury replied, "I hear your story is wonderful, too."

"Yes," said the duchess, "but ours is a little sadder."

In October 1966, the Actors Studio held a supper party honoring Lansbury, who told the attendees she wasn't a member of the studio. New York mayor John Lindsay, a huge supporter of Broadway, who'd made a cameo walk-on in a show or two, as well as in a movie, then said, "Actors Studio: Please send her a membership form. And a second one to *me*!"

In December 1966, an elite Manhattan prep school ordered her son to cut his long hair "or else." She chose "or else" and took him out of that school.

In March 1973, she was performing in a tribute to Stephen Sondheim when her earrings fell off. Lansbury picked them up and, before reattaching them, said to the audience, "Diamonds? What are they compared to a good performance?"

PETER LAWFORD

(1923–1984)

The suave, handsome English actor was best known for three things: the television version of *The Thin Man*, his membership in Sinatra's "Rat Pack," and being JFK's brother-in-law after he married Patricia Kennedy, the first of his four wives.

An MGM contract player during Hollywood's Golden Age, Lawford was one of the stars in the famous "More Stars Than There Are in Heaven" photo—the largest gathering of movie stars ever photographed. His memorable films were *Good News*, *Easter Parade*, *Little Women*, *Exodus*, the original *Ocean's 11*, and *The Longest Day*, in which he had a cameo.

When Phil Silvers was starring on Broadway in *Do Re Mi* in 1961, Lawford came backstage. Lawford mentioned that he and his Rat Pack pals had dined at the White House with Lawford's brother-in-law, JFK. Silvers was silent until Lawford said, "I was having a sandwich at the Stage Delicatessen when Irving, the waiter, said . . ."

Silvers interrupted. "Irving? You know Irving the waiter? You name-dropper, you!"

While his brother-in-law was in the White House, Lawford enjoyed a de facto exemption from a review by one movie critic: Arthur Schlesinger Jr., JFK's aide. He'd been given permission to review movies for *Show* magazine—with the proviso that he not review any film with Lawford.

In May 1962, Lawford and his wife, Pat, gave a party for JFK in Beverly Hills. The Secret Service had to vet every guest. An actress phoned to accept the invitation and then, the day of the party, asked if she could bring her beau. It was too late for him to be cleared by the Secret Service, so the request was denied, and the actress didn't attend. Her boyfriend was Cliff Robertson, who would portray JFK the following year in *PT 109*.

When Lawford's youngest child was born, JFK sent a letter that read: "Welcome to the newest member of the clan. Your entrance is timely as we need a new left end on the touch football team. Here's hoping that you do not acquire the political assets of your parents, the prolific qualities of your Godfather, Attorney General Kennedy, or the problems of your uncle."

In 1974, Lawford signed to play the head of M G M in a TV movie called *The Phantom of Hollywood*. He'd made his debut at M G M, in 1938's *Lord Jeff*, back when studio bosses controlled actor's lives and careers. Lawford was asked how the business had changed over the years.

"These days," he replied, "a studio head has just two main duties: buying new scripts and selling old props."

VIVIEN LEIGH

(1913–1967)

Born Vivian May Hartley, she won an Oscar for playing Scarlett O'Hara in *Gone with the Wind*, and another for playing Blanche DuBois in *A Streetcar Named Desire*. The British actress also won a Tony for *Tovarich* and was married to Laurence Olivier from 1940 to 1960.

In 1948, she starred in *Anna Karenina*, and one scene had her bouncing a boy on her lap. In 1961, Jeremy Spenser, who had played the boy, worked with her again in *The Roman Spring of Mrs. Stone*. By then twenty-four, he was the right age for that scene—a seduction.

During a 1948 tour of Australia, Olivier and Leigh were invited to a glass factory outside Sydney to see a troupe of itinerant actors hired to entertain workers on their lunch hour. The leading actor had adapted Molière's works into a one-hour show.

What they saw astonished them. The lead actor impressed them so much they brought him to London. Forty-five films and twenty-eight years later, Peter Finch became the first actor to win an Oscar posthumously, as Howard Beale, the news anchor in *Network*.

William Wyler offered Leigh a role in *Wuthering Heights* in 1939, but not the role of Cathy; that went to Merle Oberon. It was a supporting part, which Leigh rejected. "You'll never have such an important role as this one," Wyler warned.

A few days later she won *the* most coveted role in movie history: Scarlett O'Hara in *Gone with the Wind*.

A delegation representing the Soviet film industry was visiting New York and spotted Leigh at a nearby table in Sardi's. All three told her she was their favorite star. "What about Elizabeth Taylor or Marilyn Monroe?" asked Leigh. "Nothing special," they said.

Joanne Woodward, the Oscar-winning actress who was born in Thomasville, Georgia, recalled watching the premiere of *Gone with the Wind* in Atlanta in 1939. She was nine, and what impressed her most were the diamond and emerald earrings Vivien Leigh wore. When Woodward starred in *Rachel, Rachel*, her husband, Paul

Marlon Brando and Vivien Leigh, *A Streetcar Named Desire*,
Los Angeles, 1951. Photograph by Sam Shaw.

Newman, who directed the film, presented her with an identical
set of earrings.

Early in 1966, Sir Michael Redgrave took Leigh to the Old Vic production of *Love for Love*, which starred Olivier and featured Redgrave's younger daughter Lynn. As the curtain descended, Leigh
said, "I'll applaud for Lynn if you clap for Larry."

On July 5, 1967, Vivien Leigh told Edward Albee she'd memorized
the lines from his new play *A Delicate Balance*, and was prepared to
star in it on Broadway. "But I don't understand any of it," she said.
Three days later she died of tuberculosis.

SHIRLEY MACLAINE

(1934–)

Before she became a star, MacLaine worked as both an understudy and a standby. Asked the difference, she explained: "A standby hopes the star will get sick. But an understudy hopes she'll never recover."

The story of an understudy who goes on for the lead and becomes an even bigger star is a cliché. But it happened to Shirley MacLaine. In 1954, she was in the chorus of *The Pajama Game* and the understudy for the star, Carol Haney. One night Haney took ill. Hollywood producer Hal Wallis was there, and he offered MacLaine a movie contract.

Before she signed, the show's producer advised, "Stick here, kid. You know what always happens to all those girls who go out to Hollywood, hoping to make it big in the movies. You never hear of them again." She signed.

In 1963, Billy Wilder said she'd become "infected with that one-take 'Rat Pack' all-play-and-no-work nonsense, until she worked for me in *The Apartment*."

After starring in *Woman Times Seven*, MacLaine sent each of her seven male costars a photo with the same inscription: "The other six couldn't compare to you."

In June 1967, she was asked about her ten-year-old daughter, Stephanie, going into show business. "I wouldn't mind," she said, "but right now, all she wants to be is a horseback-riding ballerina-veterinarian."

She once joked about the idea of playing opposite her younger brother, Warren Beatty, "just to see what those other girls were raving about." Later she explained, "I had to say *something*. And besides, don't you think Warren's too old for me?"

JAYNE MANSFIELD

(1933–1967)

Born Vera Jane Palmer, she came along at the height of Marilyn Monroe's fame, but unlike Monroe, Jayne Mansfield had a Broadway résumé. She even won a Theater World Award for her work in *Will Success Spoil Rock Hunter?* It would be her only Broadway appearance, but it made her a star.

Before her horrifying death at just thirty-three in a Louisiana car crash, she starred in twenty-five movies. Like Monroe, to whom she was frequently compared, for obvious reasons, she posed for *Playboy*, but several things distinguished them. Mansfield was a college-educated wife and mother, spoke five languages, and would stop at nothing to have her picture taken. Monroe, though the most photographed woman of her time, had an official photographer, Sam Shaw, and many of her photos were from professional work sessions. Mansfield, on the other hand, allowed herself to be photographed almost anywhere.

She visited Grossinger's resort and submitted to an experiment with a hypnotist. Using a technique called hypnotic regression, he tried to bring her back to the age of six. While hypnotized, she recalled that even at that age, she was being chased—by a seven-year-old boy named Tommy.

At a New York hotel, a cameraman once asked if he could photograph her. "You don't have to ask my permission to take my picture," she replied. "By now, I'm public domain."

After posing for another photographer, she called her agent and asked him to get the picture killed for publication.

"When did you pose for it?" he asked.

"Five minutes ago," she replied. "In fact, I'm still in the studio."

"Then if you didn't like it, why'd you pose for it?" was his next question.

"Oh, you know how I am," said Mansfield. "I always do whatever a photographer tells me to do."

At a charity concert, everyone expected to see her simply posing. But she surprised the audience by stepping into the orchestra pit, picking up a violin, and playing two pieces flawlessly.

Jayne Mansfield

A director in Hollywood lunched one day with Ethel Barrymore and conveyed the news that Mansfield, seeking an important role in a new movie, threatened to retire if she didn't land it.

"Retire?" asked Barrymore. "Retire? Retire from *what*?"

While filming *The Girl Can't Help It*, she entered the studio commissary trailing her mink coat on the floor. "I know it's dragging," she said, "but I'm just trying to show I don't care about money or material things."

FREDRIC MARCH

(1897–1975)

orn Ernest Frederick McIntyre Bickel, March was one of the most enduring actors of his time, with an impressive résumé starting with silent films in 1921. He won two Best Actor Oscars, in 1932 for *Dr. Jekyll and Mr. Hyde* and in 1947 for *The Best Years of Our Lives.*

March was never able to keep anniversary gifts a secret from his wife, actress Florence Eldridge. He bought her a car one year, but the dealer spoiled the surprise by sending the registration to her a week before the anniversary. The next year he ordered some gowns. Her couturier phoned her to come for a fitting a week before the big day. Another year, he returned by ship from England. She was at the pier to greet him, and he told friends to keep her away from customs because he'd brought a surprise. He almost got away with it. As they were leaving the pier, the customs appraiser walked by and said, "You sure got a bargain, Mr. March. That necklace is worth a lot more than fifteen hundred dollars."

Disdaining actors who tried to experience the lives of their characters before filming, he quoted advice from Lionel Barrymore: "You don't have to sit on a hot stove before pretending to do so."

March costarred in *The Young Doctors*, in which he delivered the line, "Look, I'm only a doctor. After all, I'm not playing God." He followed that by starring on Broadway in *Gideon*—playing God.

When March got the part in *Gideon*, his agent got another client, Burgess Meredith, a part in another play, *Kicks & Co.*, playing the devil. Thus the agent collected ten percent commissions from both "God" and "the devil."

He left *Gideon* before his contract was up in order to star with Sophia Loren in Italy and Greece in *The Condemned of Altona.* Alas, leaving the play wasn't considered "an act of God," so he had to buy out the contract.

March played Alexander's father, Philip of Macedon, in *Alexander the Great.* He was to be stabbed by an actor named Peter Wygard, who seemed overly eager. The actor lunged at March, who slowly picked himself up and said, "Listen, kid—suppress your talent."

MARY MARTIN

(1913–1990)

Texas native Mary Martin debuted on Broadway in 1938's *Leave It to Me* before heading to Hollywood to make some routine musicals. Back on Broadway, she would become one of the great musical stars of all time.

One Touch of Venus, with Martin in the title role, ran for 567 performances. Another great role was Ensign Nellie Forbush in *South Pacific*, which ran for four and a half years. She electrified the country in the title role of *Peter Pan*, on Broadway and in a live telecast, part of millions of Americans' childhoods. Then she created the role of Baroness Maria von Trapp on Broadway in *The Sound of Music*, which ran for 1,443 performances.

When she was starring on Broadway in *South Pacific*, Myron McCormick, playing one of the sailors, did a nightly belly roll with his huge tattoo wiggling. "Whenever you have to do something that's even a little risqué," Martin advised, "just close your eyes and look to the heavens. The audience will think you don't know what you're doing."

During the run of *South Pacific* there was a water shortage in New York. One of the most famous scenes had Ensign Forbush showering while singing "I'm Gonna Wash That Man Right Out of My Hair." The producers rejected using a dry formula, since it made no sense in a show set on an island. But on the day designated Water Saving Day, Martin compromised by showering in club soda.

Cast members tanned under sunlamps every day to appear as if they were stationed on a sunny Pacific Island. Martin's husband, Richard Halliday, joined them, "so people wouldn't think we'd taken separate vacations."

In June 1954, Martin ended her long run in *South Pacific*. Producer Leland Hayward presented her with a diamond bracelet onstage. The next day, Mrs. Oscar Hammerstein II said she and Mrs. Richard Rodgers also deserved diamond bracelets.

"When you can sing 'Wonderful Guy' the way Mary does," said Haywad, "I'll buy you a bracelet."

After she left the show, her son, Larry Hagman, joined the London cast, playing one of the Seabees. He later became an enormous TV star as J. R. Ewing on *Dallas*.

At the White House signing ceremony for the National Foundation on the Arts and the Humanities Act, on September 29, 1965, President Johnson gave two signing pens to producer David Merrick. "One for you, and please give the second one to Mary Martin," said LBJ.

In the program of every show in which Mary Martin ever starred, the name "Sue Yeager" appeared. The mysterious name belonged to a childhood friend back in Texas. If the name wasn't in the playbill, Martin was sure to mention it onstage. The only other actor I know of who did anything similar was Karl Malden, born Mladen Sekulovich; he made sure to call a nonspeaking character by that name in many of his movies.

Martin and her husband bought an estate in the Brazilian jungle as a retreat. Then the Brazilian government announced a decision that proved a windfall. The new capital, Brasilia, would be built nearby, thus skyrocketing the value of their land.

At the 1960 Tony Awards, she arrived in a stunning gown, and won for playing Maria von Trapp in *The Sound of Music*. Her gown was so impressive that someone remarked, "She must've known in advance she'd win. *No one* shows up dressed like that to go home a loser."

Later that year, Martin received a cable from Australian prime minister Robert Menzies, saying he was a big fan and wanted to see her in *The Sound of Music*. But when he arrived in New York, Actors' Equity was on strike. So Martin invited the prime minister and his wife to her home for dinner, where she performed the songs from the show.

A few weeks later, Menzies returned for the UN General Assembly. By this time the strike had ended. When Menzies invited Martin and her husband to hear him speak to the delegates, Martin reminded him that the speech was on a Wednesday, matinee day.

"Why not let your understudy go on?" he suggested.

"Why not let *your* understudy, the deputy prime minister, give the speech, and come see me?" she replied.

He saw her perform the next night.

In early December 1960, she did a second TV version of *Peter Pan*. Soon after she began receiving fan mail addressed to "Peter Pan, Never-Never Land."

In August 1962, she and her husband went to the Stratford Festival in Ontario to see Christopher Plummer in *Cyrano de Bergerac*. Because of a clerk's error, however, there were no hotel reservations. But the festival officials quickly found accommodations. They set up cots in a spacious, air-conditioned locale, complete with a bathroom and a kitchenette. It was the most secure room in town: the Stratford Bank.

JAMES MASON

(1909–1984)

Born in Yorkshire, England, Mason was a classical actor, equally adept at lead, supporting, and character roles. Among his 155 movies were 20,000 *Leagues Under the Sea, Journey to the Center of the Earth*, and the first remake of *A Star Is Born*. He was a spy in *5 Fingers*, Brutus in *Julius Caesar*, and Professor Humbert Humbert in *Lolita*. In *The Desert Fox*, Mason spoke with his familiar, condescending English accent as General Erwin Rommel. Then, two years later, cast again as Rommel in *The Desert Rats*, he spoke with a German accent!

Mason was considered for the role of James Bond in a 1958 teleplay that was never produced. Illness forced him to abandon plans to portray the pompous, intimidating Harvard Law professor Charles Kingsfield in *The Paper Chase*, a part for which John Houseman won an Oscar. Mason was also the original choice for Victor Komarofsky in *Doctor Zhivago*, but the role eventually went to Rod Steiger.

One of Mason's lesser-known parts was the title role in "The Love Story of Napoleon," on the classic TV series *Omnibus* in 1953. His wife Pamela portrayed Josephine. That show was hosted by Alistair Cooke, later the host of PBS's *Masterpiece Theater*. Ironically, Cooke and Mason had been classmates at Cambridge, where Cooke, directing the class play, rejected Mason for a role, even suggesting Mason return to studying architecture.

In 1946, Mason agreed to star as Paganini in *The Magic Bow*. While the screenplay was being written, he prepared by buying an expensive violin, then hiring a teacher and learning the complex fingering for the music. After twelve lessons and practice for hours after each one, the screenplay arrived. Mason read it, then sent a three-word note to the producer: "No thank you." Stewart Granger played the role.

In 1951, the Masons gave a party for my father at their home in Beverly Hills. A lifelong New Yorker, my father had never learned to drive, so he took a taxi, which dropped him off and drove away. The house was locked and deserted, since, unbeknownst to my father, the Masons had recently moved and forgotten to tell him. He began walking back to his hotel. He turned his collar up, "to look furtive," he wrote, hoping that the Beverly Hills police, known for detaining pedestrians at night, would stop him.

But no policeman was to be found, and an hour later, he arrived at his hotel and called the Masons, who sent a car. When he finally arrived at the party, Mason announced: "Here's our guest of honor, Leonard Lyons. Famous columnist. Read by millions. Big connections. Knows everybody. But he literally couldn't get himself arrested."

ADOLPHE MENJOU

(1890–1963)

*Y*ou may not know his name, but if you've seen any of Menjou's movies, you'll recognize the suave, always nattily attired character actor with a crisp, staccato delivery and thin mustache. He was voted Best Dressed Man in America *nine* times. His films of note include *Paths of Glory, Dancing in the Dark, State of the Union, You Were Never Lovelier*, and the original *A Star Is Born*.

Menjou was an archconservative and a "friendly" witness during the infamous House Un-American Activities Committee hearings. While his reactionary beliefs probably didn't cost him any work—149 movie roles speak to that—they didn't win him many friends, either.

In addition to his legendary dust-ups with Katherine Hepburn, he once clashed with Spencer Tracy, his costar in *State of the Union*. But the argument wasn't about politics. Menjou called Tracy "uncouth," then added the worst insult he could conjure up: "And besides," he snarled, "you wear eighty-five-dollar suits!"

Menjou reintroduced plus-fours, those old-fashioned trousers extending just four inches below the knees, when he played golf. A manufacturer offered to send him samples, but Menjou replied testily, "I have nine tailors and *never* wear ready-made clothes!"

Menjou made radio broadcasts to the troops during World War II in eight languages: French, Spanish, Italian, English, German, Russian, Greek, and Mandarin.

He often claimed his right-wing political beliefs cost him roles, but one director known for his liberal leanings hired him, probably just to cast him as a communist.

Menjou once got a private tour of the living quarters of the Roosevelt White House while the First Family was away at Hyde Park. He was shown Eleanor Roosevelt's bedroom, and while the guide wasn't looking, he pulled out his card, scribbled a short message on the back, and placed it on her pillow. It read: "Eleanor: Bet you never expected to find *me* here! Adolphe Menjou."

ROBERT MITCHUM

(1917–1997)

Of the nearly nine hundred actors I've interviewed in forty-four years, none was more difficult to talk to than Robert Mitchum, with the possible exception of Robert De Niro, who's always uncomfortable in an interview. Those trademark droopy eyes behind large black glasses and that almost disdainful demeanor (captured so well by the late mimic Frank Gorshin) evoked someone who just didn't care.

By 1976, when I interviewed him, he'd amassed one of the most impressive résumés of all the major postwar stars. Consider the original *Cape Fear*, *The Night of the Hunter*, *Heaven Knows, Mr. Allison*, the TV epic *The Winds of War*, *Midway*, *The Big Sleep*, and *Ryan's Daughter*. He was one of Hollywood's greatest stars.

In July 1945, Mitchum was inducted into the army, but unlike most recruits, he found basic training easy. He'd just starred in *The Story of G.I. Joe*, for which he'd undergone seven grueling weeks of army combat training, unaware he'd soon need it for the real thing.

In 1953, he starred in *Angel Face*, whose director, Otto Preminger, told him on the first day of shooting, "Bob, I'd just like one thing understood between us from the very beginning. I'm very intense and hot tempered at times, and sometimes I say mean things to my actors. But five minutes later, everything on my set is quiet, I'm in charge, and everyone's forgotten the whole thing."

Mitchum quickly responded, "I'm glad we understand each other, Otto. Because I'm bad tempered at times too. And when anyone says something rude like that to me, I promptly flatten him. But five minutes later, I, too, have forgotten everything."

There was no trouble on the set.

Mitchum was in Monte Carlo and appeared on local TV with French actors who did all the talking. Finally, the announcer asked Mitchum to say a word in French. Mitchum said, "Cognac."

Mitchum was in Kenya in 1964 shooting *Mister Moses* with Carroll Baker. She suspected that Susie, a female on the set, had a crush on Mitchum, because after Baker filmed a love scene with him, Susie never let her get close to him again. Susie was an elephant.

In Spain three years later, Mitchum was asked the difference between working for two colorful directors, Otto Preminger and John Huston.

"Simple," he replied. "Otto is bald. John has hair."

Another director, Sir David Lean, worked with Mitchum on *Ryan's Daughter* in 1969. On a day off from shooting in Ireland, Lean showed Mitchum photos of his collection of one-hundred-year-old pressed flowers. Mitchum seemed unimpressed, saying, "You roll 'em. I'll smoke 'em."

An MGM executive asked Mitchum if he had a message for his friends and fans back home. "Tell 'em I'm alive, shooting a movie, and drinking," he replied.

DAVID NIVEN

(1910–1983)

*I*n his 93 films, Niven exuded a special prewar aura of elegance and charm, nowadays a long-gone quality. That made him one of the most popular movie stars of his era, in films like the original *Wuthering Heights, Around the World in 80 Days, 55 Days at Peking,* and *The Pink Panther.* He was one of several James Bonds in the ill-fated, little-seen 1967 original version of *Casino Royale.*

Niven's other films of note include *The Guns of Navarone, Magnificent Doll, Separate Tables,* and *The Sea Wolves.*

Who will ever forget his brilliant ad lib as a presenter at the 1974 Oscars? Just after a streaker had run across the stage, Niven, who'd been about to introduce Elizabeth Taylor, didn't miss a beat: "That was almost bound to happen. Isn't it fascinating to think that probably the only laugh that man will ever get is by stripping off and showing his shortcomings?" It brought down the house.

Long before Niven thought of becoming an actor, he came to New York and phoned a friend, but dialed the wrong number. Intrigued by the woman who answered, he gave her his name and suggested they meet. "I'll be at the corner of 58th and Madison," he said. "I'll be in a gray suit with a red carnation."

"If you don't think I'm attractive" he continued, "keep walking."

The woman agreed and at the appointed hour, Niven arrived and waited. A woman walked by and said: "Hello, Mr. Niven" but kept walking. Then a second did the same. *Fifteen* women greeted him by name, but kept walking. They were obviously friends of the woman on the phone. She might've been one of them. He never found out, for none of the women stopped!

Niven arrived in Hollywood in 1934. Among early bit parts, he played a slave, uncredited, in the Claudette Colbert version of *Cleopatra.*

When he was making *The Prisoner of Zenda* in 1937, he was still so broke he sold his autopsy rights to three hospitals. When his brother heard about that, he secretly bought those rights back and

Producer Charles K.Feldman, David Niven, and John Shepherd on the set of *Casino Royale*, London, 1967. Photograph by Sam Shaw.

presented them to him on a certificate Christmas morning—a most unlikely stocking stuffer.

In September 1939, Niven was under contract to Sam Goldwyn, who'd spotted him in a nonspeaking role in *Mutiny on the Bounty* in 1935. Goldwyn discouraged his actors from appearing on the radio, lest it somehow diminish their box-office appeal. To accomplish this, Goldwyn demanded 50 percent of all his contract players' radio earnings. Undeterred, Niven appeared on the Bing Crosby show, and was paid $750 and given a wheel of cheese from one of the sponsors. He then sliced the cheese in half and put it on Goldwyn's desk with $375.

On November 11, 1939, Niven became the only British star in Hollywood to return to England to fight in World War II. He sailed aboard the Italian liner S.S. *Rex*. En route, he phoned his friend John Perona, owner of El Morocco, to assure him that "to date, everything is all right." Perona, an Italian by birth, assured the actor, "I know the captain of the *Rex*. I know a lot of ships' captains, in fact."

"That's fine," Niven replied, no doubt scanning the horizon nervously, "but do you also know any U-boat captains?"

Back in London, Niven headed straight to his men's club, a custom of the day. There he met an old member, in a scene that evokes *Around the World in 80 Days.*

"Been away?" the man asked.

"Yes, to America," Niven replied.

"I've been there," the old man said. "Rio de Janeiro is a beautiful city."

"No, that's in South America," replied Niven. "I've been in North America."

"Oh," came the reply. "They say Saskatchewan is beautiful."

"No, I've been working in Hollywood," Niven said.

"Actor, eh?" replied the old gentleman. "Boy, that William Powell. What a cad!"

He became a star with 1939's *Wuthering Heights*, but by October, Niven was in the army stationed in the Midlands of England, far from Hollywood, training his regiment—men who needed a lift in their morale.

"Boys," Niven said, "I know you miss home and your loved ones, but our cause is just. We all have to make sacrifices. Look at me. This week, I'd be in Hollywood, dining on Monday with Paulette Goddard, Tuesday with Rosalind Russell, Wednesday with Hedy Lamarr, Thursday Ann Sheridan, and Friday Ginger Rogers."

By this time Sam Goldwyn had developed a deep affection for Niven. Goldwyn said, "If he could cut my heart out, he'd find 'Gratitude' written on it."

In January 1941, during the Blitz of London, Niven took American journalist Quentin Reynolds to his club Boodles, which lay in rubble. Niven picked through the debris and came across an early-nineteenth-century chair, tipped over but otherwise intact. He dusted it off, saying, "Beau Brummell himself sat in this chair nearly every day of his life. What a pity. He was such a one for neatness."

Despite nightly bombings by the Luftwaffe, Niven was given permission to appear in a government-sponsored film called *The Way Ahead*. (Peter Ustinov did as well, along with James Donald, later to costar in *The Bridge on the River Kwai*.)

Niven wrote to his agent in Hollywood and his studio, RKO: "Filming's going well despite the Blitz. If you want your share of what's owed you, come on over and get it." He would later partici-pate in the landings in Normandy on D-Day, June 6, 1944.

In March 1950, Niven returned to London after months away and went straight to his other club, White's, which he had joined soon after graduating from Sandhurst, England's West Point. There he met an old army officer, retired for many years, the type who prob-ably lived in the club's easy chairs.

"I say, old boy," said the old soldier, twirling his large white mus-tache. "Where've you been?"

"Hollywood," the actor replied. "Making pictures."

"Really?" said the old gentleman. "Tell me, which do you prefer when you make a picture, oils or watercolors? And do we have a gar-rison in this place called Hollywood?"

I interviewed Niven in 1972, in connection with one of his four books, *The Moon's a Balloon*, about his tumultuous early life. He told me a useful tip for any writer: "The hardest thing about writing is applying the seat of the pants to the seat of the chair."

Niven died in 1983, the same day as Raymond Massey, best known for playing Abraham Lincoln in *Abe Lincoln in Illinois*. He and Niven had costarred in *The Prisoner of Zenda* and *A Matter of Life and Death*.

PETER O'TOOLE

(1932–2013)

Although it wasn't his first screen appearance, the image of Peter O'Toole in a close-up atop a speeding thirties motorcycle, wearing goggles, headed to a fatal crash in *Lawrence of Arabia*, is how most audiences first saw him. After other stars, including Marlon Brando and Albert Finney, balked at signing a long-term contract with the film's producer, Sam Spiegel, O'Toole agreed and became an instant international star.

O'Toole studied at the Royal Academy of Dramatic Arts and debuted on-screen in *Kidnapped* in 1960. His other movies of note include *The Lion in Winter*, *Becket*, *Lord Jim*, and *My Favorite Year*, the latter built around his incredible performance spoofing a drunken Errol Flynn.

O'Toole holds a record not likely to be broken: most Oscar nominations as a leading actor with no wins. He was nominated eight times. He did receive an honorary Oscar in 2000.

In October 1962, O'Toole brought his father, a licensed English bookmaker, to a preview of *Lawrence of Arabia*. His father's take on the epic? "I can handicap horses all right, but not camels."

One of O'Toole's most underrated roles was in *Night of the Generals*, as a Nazi general with obsessions for art and murdering prostitutes. To research the role, he visited the hotel where Hitler stayed during his only visit to Paris in 1940. Dominic, the same bartender who'd served bottled water to Hitler, could still be found behind the bar. Later, O'Toole visited the spot where six generals involved in the failed 1944 plot to kill Hitler were executed.

Though he appeared in sixty-six films and twenty-seven TV shows, the stage was his first love. "I only do films for money," he said. "I look at other actors with their cars and agents and masses of secretaries and wonder what it's all about. Fame? What's fame except a few bob and an entrée?"

Asked to name history's most famous general, he picked an unusual choice, an Air Force Reserve brigadier general: Jimmy Stewart.

Producer Joseph E. Levine signed O'Toole for a movie called *The*

Peter O' Toole and Ursula Andress, *What's New Pussycat?*, Paris, 1964. Photograph by Larry Shaw.

Ski Bum, but O'Toole had to postpone that commitment in order to star in *The Lion in Winter*, which became one of his most famous roles. When the movie was completed, a special print was prepared to show Levine. The gag opening showed O'Toole, dressed as Henry II, wearing a pair of skis.

When he was a young street actor, he'd perform Shakespeare in London's Russell Square, relying on the generosity of passersby. "I didn't mind the street noises," he recalled, "except the honking of the taxis. I knew they were taking people to the theater to see actors getting paid for doing the same thing as I was giving out for free."

Headed to New York to publicize *Goodbye, Mr. Chips*, O'Toole learned that he would be arriving on Election Day, when the bars would be closed. "Marvelous!" was O'Toole's surprising reply, followed by a request: "Please have the bloke who meets me at the airport bring a bottle so I can drink a toast to Election Day."

O'Toole loved New York, especially Downey's Irish Bar and Grill and the still-popular P. J. Clarke's. When my father told him Downey's had been sold, O'Toole gasped. "Sold? 'Tis like a dagger to my heart. I love those places, where eloquent strangers discuss the meaning of the world."

He insisted his children be born in Dublin, though his wife, Siân Phillips, was a fervent Welsh nationalist who spoke only Welsh until she was seventeen. Just before each delivery, Mrs. O'Toole sang "Sosban Fach" ("Little Saucepan"), the unofficial Welsh anthem, and when the children were growing up, she spoke to them in Welsh. That forced O'Toole to learn that language as well.

When O'Toole told the Queen Mother that he'd bet on her horse the day before but lost, she said, "Mine generally do."

In early January 1963, O'Toole shared drinks at P. J. Clarke's with two other great actors, Jason Robards Jr. and Martin Gable. At one point, Gable, who stood five foot four, thought O'Toole had insulted him, and whisked off his glasses. O'Toole, who stood six foot three, immediately donned his.

In March of that year, my father was in London, where, in exchange for a tour of New York he had given O'Toole, the actor guided him around, even though my father had visited London often.

They went to the Salisbury pub on St. Martin's Lane, built in 1805. "This pub is a way of life to so many of us," O'Toole said. "It's my office. I get my phone calls and messages here. It's my bank, and sometimes, I even sleep upstairs. This was Dylan Thomas's favorite pub, and here Brendan Behan poured ale over his head."

O'Toole then showed my father the unheated cold-water building where he lived when he arrived from Ireland. It was the same building where Thomas had lived years before. "Twelve and six a week," he said—about two dollars.

Later in 1963, he and Richard Burton had wardrobe and makeup tests for *Becket*. O'Toole, exuberant at the prospect of working with Burton, walked into the test shot and kissed Burton lustily on both cheeks. Then, before the retake was filmed, Burton said, "Peter, let's just settle for a medieval handshake this time."

Elizabeth Taylor's son Michael Wilding Jr. wanted to be an actor, so, trying to discourage him, stepfather Richard Burton took him to the set of *Becket* to show how tedious filming could be. At the end of the day, Burton asked Michael if he still wanted to be an actor.

"Oh, yes," the boy replied. "When I grow up, I want to be exactly like Peter O'Toole."

In 1963, O'Toole received an offer to star in *Lord Jim*. Producer-director-screenwriter Richard Brooks refused to send him the script, lest it somehow fall into others' hands. So O'Toole wrangled a free two-week trip to New York by offering to read ten pages a day in front of Brooks. The filmmaker agreed. O'Toole arrived from London just as Brooks and his wife, the actress Jean Simmons, were headed out for dinner. "Just a moment, dear," Brooks said to his wife. "Peter is going to read the first ten pages."

Two hours later, O'Toole had read the entire script aloud for Brooks, who signed him.

In February 1964, O'Toole was in Cambodia filming *Lord Jim* with Eli Wallach. Wallach's role called for him to shoot several scenes riding an elephant, which swayed to and fro constantly. O'Toole, who had had to ride a camel continually in *Lawrence of Arabia*, yelled up to Wallach: "Hey, Eli! If you need some motion sickness pills, I have a few left." Years later, O'Toole told me the camels in *Lawrence of Arabia* were "disgusting animals."

When my father assured O'Toole that Burton's *Hamlet* on Broadway was praiseworthy, O'Toole said he'd wire Burton: "I've heard the reports that your 'Hamlet' was well received, but I'm still convinced mine was better."

O'Toole was asked why Charlton Heston and not he was cast as God in *The Bible*.

"He's got too many teeth," replied O'Toole. "He grows a new tooth every year."

GREGORY PECK

(1916–2003)

I once did a long radio interview with Gregory Peck. Did Hollywood ever have a more heroic, dignified, elegant hero? He was that way in real life, too. It was when telephone answering machines came into wide use, and as I often did after interviewing stars, I asked him to record a message. Ten years later, I had another interview with Peck scheduled, but I needed to push it back an hour. I left a message at his hotel, asking him to confirm the change. Then I inserted his old message on my machine so that when he called, he heard his own voice, politely asking the caller to leave a message! He must've laughed for five minutes, and finally said, referring to the famous impressionist, "Rich Little, eat your heart out!"

Peck told me that one day when he was a child, in his hometown of La Jolla, California, he saw a troupe of actors in a parade. One of them was Ethel Barrymore, whom he'd seen in some of her fifteen silent films. He was struck by the makeup the actors wore, and his curiosity eventually led him to the stage and finally to screen immortality.

His professional career began in 1940, when the famed Barter Theater in Virginia was holding auditions. Actress Dorothy Stickney was a judge. Five hundred aspirants showed up. Each was allowed only one minute, and the winners were to be given a summer job. Only one was chosen by Stickney: Gregory Peck.

Spellbound was one of Peck's early starring roles. Hitchcock had bought the rights to the novel *The House of Dr. Edwards*, set in an asylum, without having read it. Just before the opening scene, Hitchcock told Peck and costar Ingrid Bergman how he wanted them to play it. Then he turned to the twenty extras who were playing the roles of asylum patients and said, "The rest of you behave just as you normally would."

Before Peck became a star, he took a date to the Stork Club. He wanted to sit in the famed Cub Room, reserved for VIPs, but the maître d' told him all the tables were taken and they'd have to wait.

My parents with Gregory Peck (right) on the set of *On the Beach*, Australia, 1959.

"But Greg," said his date, "tell 'em who you are." Peck then said something wise for a young man: "If I have to tell 'em," he replied, "then I ain't."

In the summer of 1947, Peck met Spencer Tracy on vacation, and they reminisced about their beginnings. "What did you do before acting?" asked Tracy. "My family wanted me to become a doctor," replied Peck, "but when I began appearing in plays at school I abandoned that. Then I drove a truck for an oil company, came to New York, and worked as a guide at the 1939 World's Fair and as an usher at Radio City before getting my break."

"I was a bum," Tracy recalled. Then they began laughing at their enormous good fortune, which had propelled them to the top of their lucrative profession. Finally Tracy stopped laughing, looked at Peck in mock seriousness, and said, "Boy, Greg, ain't this a racket?"

Later that year, Jimmy Durante compared his own film career to Peck's and said, "The only difference between us is fifty million women."

One night in 1949, just after Sidney Kingsley's successful play *Detective Story* opened on Broadway, Kingsley and his wife, former MGM star Madge Evans, took playwright Irwin Shaw and his wife to the Stork Club to celebrate. They talked about the bit players in Kingsley's play and analyzed their work. Shaw then said one of the bit players in his own play *Sons and Soldiers* had told him he knew little about casting.

"After all," said the actor, "you turned down an unknown Marlon Brando for a role."

"That's true," Shaw replied, "but I chose another unknown instead: Gregory Peck."

In *Moby Dick*, Peck played the peg-legged Captain Ahab. One critic said, "He looked like Lincoln, only shot in the leg."

The Big Country was Peck's first attempt at coproducing a film in which he starred. "I'm well prepared," he said, "because I'm a worrier by nature. But there's a big difference between an actor's worries and a producer's. As an actor, I worry about the work I did today. But as a producer, I worry about the work to do tomorrow."

He and coproducer-director William Wyler had their differences, especially over the size of the cattle. Peck told me that the herd looked too small; Wyler thought it looked too large.

When filming was completed, Peck said, "My acting in this movie cost me only five months of my life, but the producing part of it cost me fifteen years."

SIDNEY POITIER

(1927–)

idney Poitier's Academy Award–winning performance in *Lilies of the Field* was a groundbreaking event, since he was the first African American to win Best Actor. Hattie McDaniel had been the first African American to win an Oscar, in 1939, for Best Supporting Actress in *Gone with the Wind* (while forced to sit in the rear of the theater during the ceremony), but no black actor in the intervening years was even nominated.

Born prematurely in Miami while his Bahamian parents were visiting, Poitier spent his first few months there before going to the Bahamas, where he was raised. Later, he moved to New York and joined the American Negro Theater. Poitier's memorable films include *Cry the Beloved Country*, *The Defiant Ones*, *In the Heat of the Night*, *The Slender Thread*, *To Sir, with Love*, and a little-known film I strongly recommend, *Shoot to Kill*, in which he plays an FBI agent pursing a fugitive through the rough terrain of the Pacific Northwest. He also played one of the Harlem Globetrotters in *Go, Man, Go!* and Justice Thurgood Marshall in a riveting TV movie, *Separate but Equal*.

Poitier is one of five major stars to date who've portrayed Nelson Mandela. He did it in a TV movie in 1997; the others are Danny Glover, Dennis Haysbert, Morgan Freeman, and, most recently Idris Elba.

When *No Way Out* played in Nassau, Bahamas, Poitier took his mother. When the scene came where costar Richard Widmark pistol-whips Poitier's character, she arose and shouted at the screen, "Hit 'im back, son. Hit 'im back!"

His friend Harry Belafonte is just nine days younger. When they began acting around 1945, on those nights when Belafonte had to help his father, a tenement superintendent, dispose of the garbage, his roles were played by Poitier. A producer came one night intending to see Belafonte, but saw Poitier instead and signed him for a movie.

In 1960, they agreed to star in movies coproduced by each other's

Sidney Poitier with Anna Magnani and my father, July 24, 1959.

companies. In addition, each agreed to give the other a Bentley and contribute to the other's favorite charity.

Poitier's brother-in-law for a time was Archie Moore, the light-heavyweight champion of the world, who had an incredible twenty-eight-year career. He fought heavyweight champs Ezzard Charles, Rocky Marciano, and Muhammad Ali. As his ring career began to wane, Moore, also known as "The Mongoose," won the role of the escaped slave Jim in *The Adventures of Huckleberry Finn*.

But he wasn't satisfied. In October 1961, Moore announced he wanted to join the cast of the Broadway show *Purlie Victorious*. When he heard that, Poitier said, "If Archie steps out on the stage that night you'll soon see me in the ring at Madison Square Garden."

When Poitier starred in *A Raisin in the Sun* in 1961, the only person who didn't like his character was his mother, who explained, "He spoke disrespectfully to women."

Early in June 1962, Poitier and his wife attended a white-tie dinner at the Kennedy White House, after which he said, "For me, it was the icing on a cake that took thirty years to bake."

Poitier's Oscar arrived at his New York apartment at an inopportune time. He was in the shower when the delivery man rang the doorbell. Poitier sat there in a towel contemplating the statuette and realized the last time he'd seen it, he was in white tie and tails.

A few weeks later, Poitier and Paul Newman sat in adjacent booths at Downey's, the New York Irish bar. They greeted each other and said they'd voted for each other for the Oscar.

In November 1967, Poitier was shooting a film called *For Love of Ivy*. One scene called for a backdrop of Forty-Second Street near Times Square, but they had to move the location elsewhere; four of the theater marquees displayed the names of Poitier movies.

TYRONE POWER

(1914–1958)

orn in Cincinnati, Power came to the profession by blood; his great-grandfather had been a renowned Irish actor and co-median of the same name in the mid-nineteenth century. He was related to Laurence Olivier and the stage director Tyrone Guthrie. His father, Tyrone Power Sr., acted on Broadway from 1899 until dying in his son's arms of a heart attack in 1931. Power would meet the same fate twenty-seven years later.

What set him apart from other handsome leading men in Hollywood was that he came from the stage and could really act. He could do westerns, costume dramas, and romances, starring in *Blood and Sand, Suez, The Mark of Zorro, Jesse James, The Sun Also Rises, Alexander's Ragtime Band, Witness for the Prosecution*, and *A Yank in the R.A.F.*, to name a few.

Power served in the Marine Corps and during basic training, referred to his rifle as a "gun." For that infraction of marine tradition, he had to write "A rifle is not a gun" three hundred times and sleep with his rifle. For a month.

Commissioned as a second lieutenant, he filled out a form that asked his life's ambition. "Uncertain," he wrote.

In 1948, Power was filming *Nightmare Alley* and lunched at the Fox commissary while still in costume: a tattered shirt, dirt-stained cap, and grimy suit. A studio executive greeted him, "Hi, Ty. Are you working these days?"

In May 1949, Power was filming *The Black Rose* in French-controlled Morocco. He asked a French general if there were any Americans in the French Foreign Legion.

"Only a few," replied the general. "Mostly poets."

On January 27, 1949, Power married Linda Christian, the Mexican-born actress (née Blanca Rosa Welter) who starred in *Green Dolphin Street* and *The Moment of Truth*. She was the first Bond girl. Not in the movies, but on live TV in a 1954 episode of *Climax*: "Casino Royale." It aired October 21, 1954, with Barry Nelson (later the pilot in *Airport*) as the first 007.

Power was in New York during a heat wave. The air-conditioning in his hotel failed, so he called the manager and asked him to send up some fans. The manager obliged, sending up two thrilled teenagers with autograph books and pens at the ready.

Just before the cameras rolled for an important scene in the 1950 movie *American Guerrilla in the Philippines*, director Fritz Lang distributed props to the cast, to be carried in a massive retreat from advancing Japanese troops. He noticed his star had yet to pick up the props and asked: "Ty, what are you carrying?"

"Just the plot, Fritz, just the plot," came the reply.

In 1955, he was in a wonderful John Ford biographical film, *The Long Gray Line*, about a longtime West Point employee who mentors several generations of cadets. Maureen O'Hara was his leading lady. Soon after he finished that movie, Power was lunching in New York with some friends when a young woman came over, spotted an empty chair, sat down, and counted to sixty. Then she rose and said, "Sorry for the intrusion, but I just wanted to be able to say I once had Tyrone Power to myself for a minute."

Power told of a young actor who took pride in a small role he'd landed in a production of *Hamlet*. The part was Osric. He told another actor about it, but the other actor said he'd never heard of that play and wondered what it was about.

"Well," said the first actor, "there's this guy named Osric . . ."

Gene Kelly took his daughter to see the Broadway comedy *Who Was That Lady I Saw You With?* Power spotted them from another aisle, too far away to greet them at intermission. Afterward, they met for dinner and Power asked Kelly, "Who was that lady I saw you with at *Who Was That Lady I Saw You With?*"

When I met him on the set of Hemingway's *The Sun Also Rises* in Pamplona, Spain, in 1956, he seemed the picture of health. But just two years later, while filming a sword fight sequence with George Sanders in *Solomon and Sheba*, he collapsed and died of a heart attack at forty-seven. Yul Brynner took over his last role.

ANTHONY QUINN

(1915–2001)

No actor in Hollywood history played characters of as many diverse ethnicities as Anthony Quinn (Antonio Rodolfo Quinn Oaxaca). From Eufemio Zapata in *Viva Zapata!* to Paul Gauguin in *Lust for Life*, both of which won him Best Supporting Actor Oscars, to the Bedouin Auda abu Tayi in *Lawrence of Arabia*; from Ukrainian archbishop Kiril Lakota in *The Shoes of the Fisherman* to the title character in *Zorba the Greek* and another Greek in *The Guns of Navarone*; from the Italian strongman Zampano in *La Strada* to Native Americans in *Seminole* and *Yellow Hand* and an Inuit in *The Savage Innocents*, no role was beyond his reach.

In 1952, MGM was contemplating a movie about the life of Jim Thorpe, the Sac and Fox Indian and Olympic gold medalist. Thorpe wanted Spencer Tracy to portray him, but the studio didn't want a huge star, preferring to make the movie more about race relations. They suggested a younger actor named Anthony Quinn. "What? A Mexican to play me?" said Thorpe. "Never." Burt Lancaster eventually portrayed Thorpe at Warner Bros., one of his most memorable roles.

In 1960, while filming *The Savage Innocents*, Quinn explained why he found playing an Inuit such an attractive challenge. "They have the real secret of living," he explained. "They don't judge you merely by how big your igloo is."

He replaced Marlon Brando on Broadway in *A Streetcar Named Desire* as Stanley Kowalski, opposite the great actress and acting coach Uta Hagen's Blanche DuBois. One night, as the rape scene began, the lights failed to dim on cue. Quinn, staying in character, began to doff his clothes, causing his costar to scream: "Stop! Stop! Lights! Lights!"

In November 1961, Quinn was in training for the movie version of *Requiem for a Heavyweight* and jogged five miles a day through New York's Central Park. One day he asked his costar, Jackie Gleason, to accompany him. The rotund Gleason declined, of course,

Anthony Quinn, *The Visit*, Rome, 1963. Photograph by Sam Shaw.

saying, "I want to make certain I'll always be the only heavyweight on this movie set."

It took ninety minutes in the makeup chair each morning to transform Quinn's looks into those of a veteran boxer. His stand-in was Abie Bain, one of the great Jewish fighters, who also had a minor role in the film. The veteran middleweight had a record of 67–31–7 and was later enshrined in the New Jersey Boxing Hall of Fame. He boasted to Quinn that he needed only five minutes in the makeup chair. Quinn replied, "Yes, but it took you fourteen years to get *your* face right for this role."

Quinn was an accomplished painter and owned a prized art collection. One of his most valuable paintings was acquired inadvertently. He'd gone to an art gallery with Greta Garbo, who'd just bought Quinn's house. Garbo purchased eight paintings, then told Quinn: "Now *you* buy one." So he did—a Renoir. It took him five years to pay for it.

Asked the difference between acting onstage and in movies, Quinn said, "It's like switching from painting in watercolors to oils."

One of Quinn's most memorable roles came in Sir David Lean's epic *Lawrence of Arabia* in 1962. Quinn had to live in a tent in Jordan for seven months, with all his possessions stored in one trunk. He quickly got accustomed to that life. Quinn then returned to New York and the six-story town house where he, his wife, and their many children were living. "After living in a tent," he said, "I can't stand a place where you have to go upstairs to find a handkerchief. That's why I put our home on the market."

He filmed *Atilla* and *La Strada* simultaneously; one in the morning and the other at night, an almost impossible feat. "In the first film, I did lots of my own stunts," he told me, "and got really carried away with the role; often on a stretcher."

In 1968, Quinn portrayed a pope in *The Shoes of the Fisherman*. During the filming, fiery Italian actress Anna Magnani visited the set. "I'd like to be a man for a while," she told Quinn, "so that I could have the honor of portraying the pope like you." "And I'd like to be a woman for a while," replied Quinn, "so that I could have the honor of playing opposite Anthony Quinn, like *you*." They would costar in *The Secret of Santa Vittoria* the next year.

Quinn's title role in *Zorba the Greek* is his most famous. One night at a Greek nightclub in New York, he asked permission to dance with the wife of a patron. The husband granted permission and added, "But only if you give me equal time." So when he finished dancing with the woman, Quinn did the Greek handkerchief dance—with her husband.

JASON ROBARDS JR.

(1922–2000)

ontrary to some biographies that say he was aboard a warship at sea that fateful day, when I spoke to Jason Robards Jr. in 1991, he confirmed that he was indeed at Pearl Harbor on Sunday, December 7, 1941. He was underground in a bunker working the radio, calling out distress signals: "THIS IS NOT A DRILL!"

The son of an actor with the same name, he far eclipsed his father's fame. The first time I saw him onstage, it was in the witty comedy *A Thousand Clowns* as a disenchanted TV writer, a role he successfully re-created on screen.

Robards won two Academy Awards for Best Supporting Actor in successive years, for *All the President's Men*, as *Washington Post* executive editor Ben Bradlee, whom he resembled, and for *Julia*, as the writer Dashiell Hammett. He played other historical figures like Sheriff Pat Garrett, Howard Hughes, and three presidents: Lincoln, FDR, and Grant.

Soon after he became an actor, Robards met producer John Golden. "How old are you?" Golden asked the young actor. "I'm twenty-six," Robards replied. "What took you so long?" Golden said. "Your father was a star at twenty-one!"

He started with an off-off-Broadway troupe, the Crosstown Players, putting on free shows at the Twenty-Third Street YMCA. They performed Shaw's last play, *Buoyant Billions*, and were somehow able to lure in a drama critic, who promptly fell asleep. Robards assured the audience: "Better to have a sleeping critic than no critic at all."

He auditioned for *Mr. Roberts*, with Henry Fonda, but director Joshua Logan, normally a keen spotter of untapped talent, turned Robards down, thinking the skinny actor looked nothing like a real navy man. Roberts told Logan he'd been a radio operator at Pearl Harbor during the attack and had survived the sinking of the U.S.S. *Northampton* and later a kamikaze attack on the U.S.S. *Nashville*. The *Northampton* was later awarded six battle stars.

"Very impressive," replied Logan, "but I don't need six battle stars on you. I need more pounds."

Ironically, Robards would later portray Admiral Husband Kimmel, in charge of naval operations at Pearl Harbor, in *Tora! Tora! Tora!* The day they re-created the attack, codirector Richard Fleischer invited Robards to the set, saying, "You have a free day today, but come anyway; you'll see what you missed that Sunday morning."

While Robards was in O'Neill's *Long Day's Journey into Night* on Broadway, he was invited by the Shakespeare Festival Theater in Stratford, Ontario, to play Hotspur in *Henry IV, Part I* the following season. Robards wanted a copy of the play as soon as possible, but all the bookstores were closed for the weekend. Fredric March, the star of the show, said, "Look at the bookcase on the set." Sure enough, there was a copy.

At a dinner one night Robards met comedian Stubby Kaye, who said, "It's an honor to meet such a great dramatic actor. All we comics get to do is wear sloppy clothes and holler." "Same goes for us dramatic actors," said Robards.

When he starred in Lillian Hellman's *Toys in the Attic* on Broadway in 1960, a young aspiring actor asked him for a good teacher. "The best teacher I know," replied Robards, "is there every night: the audience."

Robards, who battled alcoholism for years, played a reformed drunk in *The Iceman Cometh*, an alcoholic in *Long Day's Journey into Night*, and the drunken writer in *The Disenchanted*. After he played a ne'er-do-well in *Toys in the Attic*, he said, "My success comes from being adept at playing failures."

Robards told me we shared the same dream, playing Major League baseball: he for the old New York Giants, me for the Boston Red Sox. "Whenever March comes," he said, "my mind goes to Florida and I want to be trying out." Tell me about it!

When his son, future actor Sam Robards, was born in 1961, Robards and his then-wife, Lauren Bacall, gave the baby the middle name Prideaux. A congratulatory telegram from Groucho Marx said his father's name was Sam, too, but his grandparents could never have afforded such a fancy middle name.

When Robards and costar Irene Worth left *Toys in the Attic* to do movie roles, the third star, Maureen Stapleton, sighed: "Working with them was wonderful; they were saints. But I guess those saints have gone marchin' *out*!"

In March 1963, Robards's father was acting strangely. "All day long, he plays a ukulele and sings into a tape recorder," said Robards's mother. "And all he does is sing old, long-forgotten songs—songs he's learned since 1892. He says he wants to be sure you know these lost songs."

Once he'd finished his taping, Robards Sr. died of a heart attack at seventy.

In February 1966, Twentieth Century Fox released *The St. Valentine's Day Massacre*, starring Robards as Al Capone, mastermind of the slaughter. The studio used fifteen thousand bullets to reenact the massacre. Robards received $37,500 a week for that role—about a day's take for Capone's operations during his time.

In March 1974, the Yankees were about to move to Shea Stadium for two years while Yankee Stadium was being renovated. "Makes no difference where you play," said Robards. "Whenever a batter steps up to the plate, that fence looks a mile away."

MICKEY ROONEY

(1920–2014)

He had the longest career in Hollywood history, with an astonishing 338 credits in films and TV, spanning eighty-nine years! He even conquered Broadway in *Sugar Babies* and *The Will Rogers Follies*. When you add in innumerable vaudeville and radio appearances, his was a career unmatched by any other.

Rooney was the biggest star of the Depression, making fifteen Andy Hardy movies. Other films of note include *Manhattan Melodrama*, playing Clark Gable's character as a boy—the movie John Dillinger watched just before F B I agents gunned him down outside Chicago's still-standing Biograph Theater. He costarred in *Captains Courageous* and *Boys Town*, both with Spencer Tracy; with Elizabeth Taylor, in her film debut, 1944's *National Velvet*; with his Andy Hardy costar, Judy Garland, in *Babes in Arms*; with William Holden in *The Bridges at Toko-Ri*; and in many, many more.

He could've started a baseball team with only his wives: eight of them, including Ava Gardner.

In June 1949 Joe Yule, Mickey's father, was performing on the road in *Finian's Rainbow*, but said he wanted to get to his son's latest wedding (to Martha Vickers, his third wife) "before Mickey gets another divorce." That marriage didn't last three years.

In 1954, Rooney had his own TV show, opposite his friend Jackie Gleason's. Nevertheless, he assisted Gleason in choosing new chorus girls for Gleason's program. "He has a good eye," explained the Great One. "After all, he married Ava Gardner." Rooney's show lasted just thirty-three episodes—one season.

In *The Bold and the Brave* in 1956, Rooney starred with French actress Nicole Maurey. She asked him to explain something Bing Crosby had said about her: "She's a combination of Marlene Dietrich, Rita Hayworth, and the farmer's daughter." She didn't understand that final reference.

Rooney said, "Let me put it this way: freely translated from the French, it means 'Ooh la la!'"

In May 1963, Rooney was costarring in *It's a Mad, Mad, Mad, Mad*

World and his studio biography referred to him as "an actor, golfer, swimmer, tennis player, composer, director, producer, and he plays every instrument." Costar Buddy Hackett asked, "So, Mickey, what do you do in your spare time?"

"I explain to all my ex-wives' lawyers why I can't keep up with so many alimony payments," Rooney replied.

In June of that year, he was sued by author Roger Kahn, who later wrote *The Boys of Summer*. He'd begun work ghostwriting Rooney's autobiography, but after hours of interviews and a hundred thousand words written, Rooney abandoned the project, saying, "I'm no Sandburg." The title of the book was supposed to be *Sue Me*.

Rooney said he got into show business "when I was so young, I learned how to bow before learning how to walk."

He and Gardner remained cordial after their divorce. When he phoned her in Spain, he asked if she had any message for his children. "Yes," she replied. "Tell them to go see my latest movie, *55 Days at Peking*."

In May 1967, Rooney was filming *The Extraordinary Seaman* in Mexico and hated the ten-week shooting schedule. "Never again on extended location for me," he said. "In Los Angeles, I get homesick just going to the supermarket."

ROSALIND RUSSELL

(1907–1976)

Born in Waterbury, Connecticut, in 1907, one of seven children, Rosalind Russell got her start as a model, then worked in stock and regional theater before finally landing on Broadway—albeit for only twelve performances—in *Garrick Gaieties* in 1930. That company included a young Imogene Coca, twenty years before becoming a television comedy icon as Sid Caesar's costar.

Russell's movie debut came in a small part in *Evelyn Prentice*, which starred William Powell and Myrna Loy, two of Hollywood's reigning stars of that era. She worked constantly through the thirties and starred in *The Women*, one of the best films of 1939, Hollywood's greatest year. Other memorable films included *His Girl Friday*, *My Sister Eileen*, *Sister Kenny*, and *Auntie Mame*. Unlike most studio contract players, she returned to Broadway, in *Wonderful Town* and *Auntie Mame*.

When Russell opened on Broadway in *Wonderful Town* in 1953, she got rave reviews. In fact, Brooks Atkinson, the *New York Times* critic, wrote: "I'm for Rosalind Russell for President!"

Along with *Auntie Mame*, *Wonderful Town* was surely Russell's signature Broadway performance. Soon after it opened, someone discovered that one of the chorus girls was just seventeen. When her mother saw the strapless gown her daughter wore in the finale, she asked Russell if the girl wasn't too young to wear such a gown. "If the gown stays up," replied the star, "then she's old enough."

She signed a huge contract with Decca Records to make the album of the show, with a fee only matched by Bing Crosby. "I'm no singer like he is," she said, "but when it comes to business, I'm right there with him."

After he spent a summer at camp in upstate New York, her eleven-year-old son Lance posted a photo of himself on the backstage bulletin board, holding a snake. He inscribed it: "Dear Mom, this is my favorite snake." Beneath it, his mother wrote: "Dear Cast, I work reasonably hard in this show. For *this*?"

When she starred in the movie version of *My Sister Eileen*, she

From left to right: my father, Rosalind Russel, Ethel Merman, and Frederick Brisson at the Stork Club.

insisted that the young actress Janet Blair get costar billing. She explained, "Years ago at MGM, they wanted to give me costar billing, but the star wouldn't permit it. I swore that if I ever was in such a spot, I'd offer costar billing." Blair got the billing.

In 1955, she was filming a movie in which a moose was supposed to surprise her by raising its head through some bulrushes. The only moose on the West Coast was at the San Diego Zoo, and it took months to convince zoo officials the animal wouldn't be harmed.

Forty technicians set up the lights and cameras. Sure enough, the moose poked its head through the rushes. But that wouldn't have scared anyone, since during the night, the moose had shed its antlers and now looked like just a fat deer.

During the run of *Auntie Mame* on Broadway, she often had visitors like Eleanor Roosevelt come backstage. When former president and Mrs. Truman came backstage, the cast kept their distance. Finally Truman said, "Hi, everybody. My name is Harry Truman. Doesn't anyone want to meet me?"

In November 1956, Columbia Pictures had a wrap party after the shooting of *Auntie Mame*. Russell wore a gown from the movie and told studio head Harry Cohn she wanted to keep her wardrobe. Cohn, who'd been expecting such a request, knew the gowns' worth and said, "The gowns cost twenty-one hundred dollars." "Fine," she replied, and wrote out a check. "And now," she said: "I wore my own fur coat in that movie for twenty-one days, at a hundred dollars per day." Cohn took out his checkbook and wrote her a check—for twenty-one hundred dollars.

For the movie version of *Auntie Mame*, Russell became a strawberry blonde. During a break in the filming, she met her husband at the Los Angeles airport. As she approached, he failed to recognize her. "Now I know he's been faithful to me," she said later. "I tried to pick him up, but he didn't flirt back."

She and her husband owned land in Madera County, California, for ten years as an investment. Then they sold it. Eight years later, gold was discovered there—$150 million worth.

In 1960, she was hospitalized and given a sedative. A nurse came into the room, noticed the dried-out flowers, which had arrived days before, and was going to discard them. Semiconscious, Russell said, "Please don't throw those away." When the sedative wore off, she found a get-well card hidden among the flowers. It came from heiress Barbara Hutton. Inside the envelope was also a large gold and diamond bracelet.

In April 1966, she was flying to St. Louis to attend a premiere of *The Trouble with Angels* when the captain announced, "If you look to your right, you'll see the Grand Canyon. On your left, there's Boulder Dam." Ms. Russell, who was a fearful flier, then sent a note up to the cockpit: "Never mind looking to your right or left. Please just look straight ahead. I'll feel much safer."

Two years later, she attended a birthday party for Johnny Carson. Invitations contained several objects each guest was required to provide for a scavenger hunt. Hers were a set of brass knuckles and a Great Dane. Unable to convince the local police precinct to supply her with a real set of the illegal weapon, she simply painted her husband's knuckles gold. She also used him to satisfy the other requirement, explaining that his ancestors were Danish.

By 1970, she'd begun writing screenplays under the pseudonym "C. A. McKnight," which was her mother's maiden name. A columnist at the *Charlotte Observer* noticed this and wrote a column using as his byline "Rosalind Russell."

PETER SELLERS

(1925–1980)

I n the fall of 1979, Peter Sellers came to New York to promote *The Pink Panther Strikes Again*, in which he reprised his character of Chief Inspector Clouseau. Staying in character, complete with trench coat and intentionally rotten French accent, he visited the Fifty-Second Street police station and met many of the cops working that shift. I interviewed him for WPIX-TV and he continued to stay in character. Hilarious!

Later that day, I did a radio interview with Sellers and was warned not to wear anything green or face a certain direction, among other warnings about his unique set of idiosyncrasies and superstitions. To ensure a usable interview I brought along fellow critic James

Jefferey Lyons interviewing Pete Sellers, in character as Inspector Clouseau, West 52nd St., New York.

Delson, one of the few Americans who happened to know all of Sellers's comedy bits from *The Goon Show*, the British radio series that made him famous. We talked for two hours, during which he recorded my telephone answering message as the voices of John Lennon and Winston Churchill.

For his movie *A Talent for Loving*, the British-born Sellers had to learn a Tennessee accent, so he studied the recorded speeches of former vice presidential candidate and senator Estes Kefauver, a native of Madisonville, Tennessee.

Sellers thought producer J. Arthur Rank had underpaid him for years. But his contract with Rank was ironclad. Sellers played a hunter in a movie and made himself up to look like Rank, an avid hunter. Rank was enraged, and fired Sellers. End of contract.

Sellers got a break early in his career by using his amazing talents as a mimic. He called a London radio station and pretended to be Laurence Olivier and John Gielgud. He "recommended" the station hire a young guy named Peter Sellers—and got the job.

OMAR SHARIF

(1932–2015)

*L*awrence of Arabia brought him international acclaim, as did his title role in *Doctor Zhivago*. He was the male lead in *Funny Girl*, which helped launch costar Barbra Streisand, and was superb in *The Night of the Generals*. The only Egyptian-born international movie star, Sharif was born Michel Chalhoub, the son of a lumber merchant in Alexandria.

Educated there at Victoria College, where he studied languages—he spoke at least six—he also studied at the University of Cairo. One of the young students, whom he served as a prefect, or mentor, was King Hussein of Jordan. It was thus Sharif's responsibility to punish Hussein and other underclassmen for infractions.

"That's why," he explained, "whenever the king came to see us filming *Lawrence of Arabia* in the desert in Jordan, he always greeted me by saying, "Hello, Captain.'"

International audiences first saw him as a tiny speck on the horizon, slowly riding his camel toward Peter O'Toole. When Sharif came to my set at WNBC for an interview, he confirmed what O'Toole had told me a few years before, describing the camels as "disgusting." The scene had to be reshot several times; each time the crew had to smooth over a quarter mile of sand that had been littered by the camel's calling cards. But it turned out to be one of the most famous sequences in that classic film.

In June 1964, I accompanied my father to London, where we visited the set of *The Yellow Rolls-Royce*, an anthology film in which Sharif starred in one segment opposite Ingrid Bergman. The movie dealt with several owners of the titular luxury car.

Sharif said that afternoon that he couldn't wait to return to New York for the world bridge team championships. He was a member of the Egyptian team and a world-class contract bridge player. He even cowrote a syndicated bridge column with the great bridge player, teacher, and author Charles Goren.

Sharif spoke of the earlier rounds in the competition, in which his team was eliminated. "Ridiculous," he sighed. "We beat England and other big nations but lost to Jamaica and Bermuda. Absurd!"

Sharif's kiss with Ingrid Bergman in *The Yellow Rolls-Royce* marked his first love scene in an American film. But for him, such a romantic milestone was nothing new; Sharif had been the first Egyptian actor to kiss a woman in an Egyptian-made film. He later married that actress, Faten Hamama.

In *Funny Girl*, Sharif played Nicky Arnstein, the Jewish gambler, con man, and husband of entertainer Fanny Brice. Producer Ray Stark took a chance by casting an Arab but joked, "I was a little worried when he arrived on the set that first day on a camel he'd rented, but then when he asked for time off on Yom Kippur, I knew we'd be all right."

Stark used an unorthodox tactic to promote the film. He announced that the ads would read simply: "Barbra and Omar."

A woman seated nearby in Sardi's persuaded Sharif to autograph a playing card by saying, "I want to be able to tell my friends I got some diamonds from Omar Sharif—even if it was only a seven of diamonds."

Sharif was at the chemin de fer table at a casino when he was approached by Amy Vanderbilt, the etiquette author. She recognized him, then decided to violate her own rules of proper behavior about speaking to strangers. Later, after she'd nervously introduced herself, she explained, "Occasionally, after a certain age, it's okay to speak to strangers, especially if they look like Omar Sharif."

BARBARA STANWYCK

(1907–1990)

Brooklyn-born, she was one of Hollywood's greatest stars. When she was four, her mother was killed falling off a streetcar, and a few weeks later her father disappeared while building the Panama Canal. Unlike other actresses who changed their names, she would've been perfect using her real name: Ruby Stevens.

Stanwyck was discovered by Mrs. Henry B. Harris, who'd spotted her in a Broadway chorus line. She signed the young actress for *The Noose*. Mrs. Harris was the widow of a successful producer who perished on the *Titanic*. She was the last survivor to leave the ship, then took over his theatrical interests. Forty-one years later, her discovery, Barbara Stanwyck, starred in *Titanic*.

Stanwyck starred in the first movie to play Radio City Music Hall, *The Bitter Tea of General Yen*, in 1933. Her other films of note include *Union Pacific*, *Golden Boy*, *The Lady Eve*, *Stella Dallas*, *Meet John Doe*, and one of the greatest film noir thrillers, *Double Indemnity*. A four-time Oscar nominee, she was presented with an honorary Academy Award in 1982.

In 1942, Stanwyck wanted to star in a movie based on a story by famed stripper-actress Gypsy Rose Lee, but her movie star husband at the time objected. "The first things we'll have to strip from Barbara," said the producer, "are Robert Taylor's arms."

When she was a young actress, producer David Belasco told her she had talent, but didn't know how to walk. "You should walk like a beautiful young woman," he said. "Go to the zoo and study the lions, tigers, and especially the panthers. Watch how they walk."

"After a week," Stanwyck recalled, "I learned. So whenever I'm in town, I pay a visit to the zoo—as a refresher course."

From 1965 to 1969, she starred in the ABC western *The Big Valley*. On the set, she noticed costar Peter Breck rolling a coin over his knuckles again and again. She said, "You try that when the cameras are rolling and I'll start fidgeting with my girdle." He stopped.

GLORIA SWANSON

(1899–1983)

She was one of the great stars of the silent era, her screen career enduring from 1914 through *Airport 1975*. She married six times and was Oscar nominated three times, including for *Sunset Boulevard*, a film whose story reflected her own career.

Henry Fonda spotted Swanson at a faraway table at Sardi's one night and said, "That's Gloria Swanson. I don't know her, but I'd like to make a movie with her someday." At the same time, Swanson spotted Fonda and said the same thing. It would never happen, alas.

In June 1950, Swanson lunched at a midtown restaurant where a stranger kept staring. Finally she asked her friend if she knew who he was. "Oh, that's the man some gossip columnists said you plan to marry," replied her friend. "Don't you want to meet him?"

"No," replied Swanson. "He probably hasn't heard our 'engagement' is over."

In *Sunset Boulevard*, a clip from her silent film, *Queen Kelly*, is shown. The clip wasn't chosen at random. Swanson lost her investment in that 1929 movie—eight hundred thousand dollars.

She had her own radio show in 1951 and a critic said she talked too much. "I didn't get out of silent pictures until I was nearly thirty," she said, "so I'm catching up."

In July 1957, Swanson bought a home in Paris. She visited one of the cathedrals there and met the archbishop, who complimented her on her career. "That career is now ended," Swanson replied. "After all, I'll be sixty soon."

"Sixty? That's nothing," replied the archbishop, raising his arms and looking up at the ceiling.

"Sixty may not be old for a cathedral, but it's old for an actress," she replied.

In June 1965, Swanson was discussing her autobiography. A friend suggested she be frank about her relationship with Ambassador Joseph P. Kennedy. "I'll discuss it, all right," she replied. "The chapter will be called 'And Then I Met Joseph P. Kennedy,' and it'll be followed by eighteen blank pages."

Gloria Swanson and my father.

It was no secret that Swanson was the longtime mistress of Kennedy, who'd bought his way into several studios. When the Roxy
Theater in New York was being demolished, *Life* magazine asked
Swanson for any photos of herself at movie premieres there. She
brought up some old trunks and rummaged through scores of old
photos. She also came across a letter written in 1925 by an eight-
year-old boy, thanking her for toys she'd sent. The letter was signed,
"John F. Kennedy."

To elderly fans who'd tell her they loved her when they were children, Swanson, a star at fifteen, would always say, "My mother's still alive and still has all her teeth."

I was with my father in Paris in June 1964 when we met Gloria Swanson at the famous restaurant Maxim's. She recalled her first talking picture, 1929's *The Trespasser*. There was a gap in the story, so director Edmund Goulding asked her to sing, a talent she lacked. Goulding then began to whistle a tune, over and over. Finally Swanson called a friend, who summoned a violinist to listen in and write down the notes. Then singer-actress Elsie Janis was commissioned to write lyrics to the tune. It was called "Love, Your Magic Spell Is Everywhere" and was later a hit for Peggy Lee.

Swanson once spotted her husband flirting with another actress at a party. She put a smudge of her lipstick on a handkerchief, folded it, and put it in his pocket, saying, "Why don't you escort her home? She looks tired." He did, and later she confronted him about the lipstick-stained handkerchief. To her surprise, he confessed he'd been unfaithful but reminded his wife she'd urged him to take the actress home. They divorced.

ELIZABETH TAYLOR

(1932–2011)

British-born Elizabeth Taylor was arguably the most publicized actress of all time, even more than Marilyn Monroe, because Taylor had a much longer career and was married eight times (including twice to Richard Burton) to Monroe's three.

She was in front of the cameras for most of her life. Her debut was *There's One Born Every Minute* in 1942, in which she was billed eighth. *National Velvet* made her a star in 1944, and she made the difficult leap into adolescence in *The Courage of Lassie*, then *Life with Father*. Other early roles include *Little Women*, *A Place in the Sun*, the sword-and-sandal epic *Quo Vadis*, and *Ivanhoe*.

By the time she did *Giant*, *Raintree County*, and *Cat on a Hot Tin Roof*, Taylor was one of Hollywood's greatest stars. Subsequent performances, especially the title role in *Cleopatra* and her Oscar-winning turns in *Butterfield 8* and *Who's Afraid of Virginia Woolf?*, made her a screen immortal.

Taylor married her third husband, flamboyant producer-showman Mike Todd, in 1957. A few weeks later, Todd bought her "a little something every woman should have"—a new Rolls-Royce. Then he arranged with her favorite beauty salon to have a bottle of chilled champagne there for her "in case she gets thirsty."

Todd opened his movie *Around the World in 80 Days* in Chicago, buying adjacent theaters for maximum exposure. He renamed the theaters "His" and "Hers."

"I'll bet mine's the dirty one," she said.

The Todds sailed from New York to England on the *Queen Elizabeth* in 1957. At dinner with the captain, Taylor said, "I like this ship. Can't you cruise around a bit?"

In July, their entourage returned to New York aboard the luxurious French liner S.S. *Liberté*. A dockside photographer noticed the port side of the ship seemed to rise suddenly in the Hudson River.

"Oh, that's probably because Taylor and Todd have finished unloading their bags," another photographer explained. "I counted sixty bags, boxes, and crates."

When she went to the hospital in August 1957 to give birth to her third child, Todd had all the hospital furniture removed from the room and brought in Louis XIV furniture. Also a Renoir, a Hals, a Pissarro, and a Monet for the four walls. Todd said, "I should've sent Liz a fifth painting, for the ceiling."

The birth of the baby brought a gift from her husband, a diamond bracelet, and a telegram: "Congratulations from Cartier of Paris."

The next day, Taylor was paid a visit by Rex Harrison and his then-wife, Kay Kendall. They found her on her stomach, a position the doctor prescribed, sipping champagne through a straw.

When the Russians launched the first satellite, Sputnik, in December 1957, director Billy Wilder and his wife studied a life-size photo of it, and she said, "It's not even as large as the diamond Todd gave Taylor."

On August 4, 1960, Taylor landed the title role in *Cleopatra*. Director Joseph Mankiewicz said, "If Elizabeth didn't look like Elizabeth Taylor looks, people would say she's a wonderful actress."

Little did anyone know the production would become legendary for incredible delays, cost overruns, and the most publicized breakup of a marriage of the century.

The rabbi who performed her wedding to Eddie Fisher spoke of the Arthur Miller–Marilyn Monroe divorce: "I didn't marry the Millers," he said. "My marriages never break up."

Her marriage to Fisher didn't last five years,

Such was her fame that when a class at a New York City public school held a contest to name the two baby hamsters recently born there, the winning entry was "Taylor and Burton."

As endless production interruptions and cost overruns on *Cleopatra* mounted, a studio executive compared a Marilyn Monroe movie to an Elizabeth Taylor epic. "With Marilyn, you can't get a film started. With Taylor, you can't get it completed."

The most lavish scene in *Cleopatra* was her arrival in Rome. Thousands of extras were used, with giant sets and lavish costumes. My mother said of that scene, "Fox could've saved fifteen million bucks right there if Cleopatra had just sneaked into town."

In April 1963, Burton and Taylor were in Paris to attend the premiere of *Lawrence of Arabia*. Alexandre, Paris's foremost hairdresser, spent three hours on Taylor's coiffure, giving her an Egyptian hairdo. Producer Sam Spiegel said to the stylist, "Put a little sand in her hair, to remind audiences of *Lawrence of Arabia*."

My father interviewing Rock Hudson (front) and
Elizabeth Taylor (back) on the set of *Giant*, 1956.

In August 1963, Burton welcomed visitors to his trailer while he
was filming *Becket*. There they found Taylor bending over a sink,
cleaning her diamonds. "Don't mind her," said Burton. "She's doing her washing."

A few days later, a couple went to see *Cleopatra* and on the way
out, a vendor hawked a souvenir program to them, not realizing who

the woman was. "No, thanks, I know her well," said Debbie Reynolds, whose storybook marriage to Eddie Fisher had been broken up by Taylor.

Throughout the long press coverage of the Burton-Taylor romance on the set of *Cleopatra*, Sybil Burton, a formidable actress herself, maintained her dignity. She turned down a substantial role in a movie lest her name be exploited. "I won't let Elizabeth make a star out of me," she said.

Producer Walter Wanger wrote a book called *My Life with Cleopatra*, in which he revealed why the film couldn't be made in London. He included three years of British weather charts to prove Taylor's health couldn't stand the dampness.

Yves Saint Laurent received some dresses he'd made for Taylor that needed alterations. He didn't mind that—what he *did* mind was that the clothes arrived in a Christian Dior box.

Taylor took Sam Spiegel to see Burton in *Hamlet* on Broadway in 1964. Just before the curtain, he received an international call and had to leave. He returned forty minutes later.

The next night, she accompanied Spiegel again, and at the forty-minute mark whispered to Spiegel, "This is where you came in last night. You're excused."

Linda March played Ophelia to Burton's Hamlet, and her death scene came in the fourth act. At intermission Taylor, who every night waited in Burton's dressing room, sent the young actress a note: "Come up and have a drink with me when you're dead."

So intense was the publicity around the Burtons that the Regency Hotel on Park Avenue hired extra security. Actor Emlyn Williams and his wife had been invited to dinner in their suite. After security interrogated them, Williams asked, "Would you like to blindfold me, so I won't see their room number?"

The Sandpiper was released in late June 1965. In the film, a young actor played Taylor's son. Her own boy had been proposed for the part, but she rejected that suggestion, citing her own movie debut in *There's One Born Every Minute*, when she was just ten. "It's not that I had a terrible childhood," she explained. "It's that I didn't have *any* childhood!"

She played an unmarried mother in that movie, and if you look closely, you'll see flesh-colored tape on her ring finger concealing her wedding ring, which she'd refused to remove.

When Mike Nichols directed the movie version of *Who's Afraid of*

Virginia Woolf?, Taylor was transformed into a boozy, middle-aged, foul-mouthed shrew. Nichols said, "I feel like I've just painted a mustache on the Mona Lisa."

Before a command performance in London, a call came from Stanley Donen in New York. Despite the fact that Donen directed *Singin' in the Rain*, *Funny Face*, *Two for the Road*, and *Damn Yankees*, among many other films, Burton didn't recognize his name.

Taylor said, "I'd guess I'd better take the call. After all, I was once engaged to Stanley."

After Franco Zeffirelli directed them in *The Taming of the Shrew*, the Burtons gave him a gold cigarette case inscribed: "Thanks from the Shrew and the Tamer."

Burton hadn't watched any of his films since *Look Back in Anger*, in 1959. But he did watch *The Sandpiper* just to see how she performed. "When my scenes came up, I just turned away," he said.

In February 1972, Taylor celebrated her fortieth birthday. Burton gave her a heart-shaped diamond pendant and invited a large group of friends to join them in Budapest, where he was filming. Although they'd heard that the gem had already been purchased, jewelry companies from around the world sent representatives to the set, in case she disliked the gift and wanted a replacement.

In December of that year she asked the producer of *Under Milk Wood* to move her name below the title, since she had a small part and didn't want to disrespect Burton and costar Peter O'Toole. The producer refused.

While Burton was filming *Anne of the Thousand Days* in England, he took over the local inn, including its pub. When Taylor told him she was coming to visit, he had a new chandelier brought in from London for their room. It arrived by chartered helicopter.

In May 1970, Burton bought a $125,000 mink for Taylor, having already given her the Krupp diamond and the Peregrina pearl, among other jewels. "She's just as excited over a gift which cost a million dollars as one costing thirty-two dollars, both of which I've given her," he said. Right.

When Taylor visited the set of her husband's movie *Villain*, in November 1970, she wandered off and he couldn't find her. When Burton asked the crew if they'd seen her, one said, "Can you describe her?"

ROBERT TAYLOR

(1911–1969)

*I*f ever a man was born to be a movie star, it was Robert Taylor. And if ever there was a career unfulfilled, it was Robert Taylor's. He was a chain-smoker who died of lung cancer when he was only fifty-seven.

Born with the unglamorous name of Spangler Arlington Bruch in tiny Filley, Nebraska (population 174 in the 2010 census), the son of a farmer-doctor, he became a big MGM star and was married to Barbara Stanwyck from 1939 to 1952.

Taylor was very controversial during the Red Scare years, for his congressional testimony led to the blacklisting of actor Howard Da Silva (the bartender in *The Lost Weekend*) and others.

Taylor's memorable films include *Magnificent Obsession*, *Camille*, *Quo Vadis*, *Ivanhoe*, *The Last Hunt*, and *D-Day, the Sixth of June*. He also had a popular TV series called *The Detectives* from 1959 to 1962 and hosted *Death Valley Days* from 1966 to 1969, after Ronald Reagan left to run for governor of California.

In 1940, Taylor was on a train to New York. At the stopover in Chicago, a porter recognized the star and said, "Look at this watch, Mr. Taylor." The actor admired it, and noticed that instead of numbers, the watch spelled out "R-O-B-E-R-T-T-A-Y-L-O-R."

"That's amazing," said Taylor, undoing his own watchband as if expecting an exchange. "That's so thoughtful of you. Thank you very much for this gift."

"Who said I'm giving it to you?" replied the porter. "I'm also Robert Taylor."

Taylor lunched with Spencer Tracy in the MGM commissary and explained why he'd turned down the second lead in *Northwest Passage* with Tracy.

"Spence," said Taylor, "I want you to understand that I've worked fifteen years to become a star."

"Funny thing," replied Tracy. "I worked fifteen years to become an *actor*." The role went to Robert Young.

In April 1942, Taylor had completed filming *Her Cardboard Lover* and went right into his next role for MGM in *Stand By for Action*. On an off day, he went with his agent to see studio boss Louis B. Mayer about a salary increase. "Why don't you go in by yourself?" Taylor's agent suggested. "He doesn't like agents but likes you a lot." Taylor agreed and went in alone.

Mayer listened to Taylor's request and said, "You know, ever since you came here to MGM, I've taken a liking to you. I never had a son, and you've become a son to me. And so I'm speaking to you not as Mayer to Taylor but father to son when I say you can't have a raise."

Outside, Taylor said, "I didn't get the raise, but I think I just gained a second father."

In February 1945, Taylor brought his wife, Barbara Stanwyck, to the Stork Club and told the headwaiter, "We want to see celebrities."

"You and your wife are the number-one celebrities here tonight," he was assured.

"No," replied Taylor, "we mean senators. People like that. Those are the *real* celebrities."

In April 1952, an MGM producer, Armand Deutsch, told the actor, known for his perfect profile, "I wish I could look like you and be a leading man." Taylor reminded him, "You're wrong to feel that way. You, after all, can go on looking the way you look forever. Someday, my looks will fade."

SPENCER TRACY

(1900–1967)

Unlike the leading man type popular in his day, he wasn't tall, dark, or handsome. Tracy's acting ability and incredible range made us think the real-life characters he portrayed looked like him, not the other way around.

When his wife saw his first screen test, she wrote to her sister, "Spencer doesn't photograph very well. I'm afraid we'll have to forget about his being in talking pictures." Tracy would star in sixty-seven of them.

His advice to actors was, "Learn your lines and don't bump into the furniture."

Tracy knew his lines in a slew of classics and one often overlooked film: *Bad Day at Black Rock*, in which he plays a one-armed man who comes to a dusty New Mexico hamlet and winds up fighting a gang of murderous thugs led by Lee Marvin and Ernest Borgnine.

In 1930, Tracy starred in a play called *The Last Mile*. The non-speaking role of a reporter was played by Dore Schary, whose big moment was to nod as Tracy's character passed by, whereupon Tracy would ignore him. Twenty-one years later, Schary became president of MGM, Tracy's home studio. "If I'd have known that reporter would someday be my boss," Tracy said, "I'd have nodded back."

In one scene during 1957's *The Old Man and the Sea*, the script called for him to munch on raw tuna. But Tracy didn't care for tuna, so marinated herring was flown in from the Hillcrest Country Club in Beverly Hills.

In 1956, when he heard that Grace Kelly was marrying Prince Rainier of Monaco, Tracy said, "What some people will do to get their picture on a postage stamp!"

Tracy wore makeup on-screen only twice. "I decided a long time ago," he explained, "that there isn't much you can do with a face like mine but wear it!"

In July 1963, Tracy suffered from a respiratory attack, but reached the hospital in time to be treated. His life was saved by Katherine Hepburn's foresight. He'd had a similar attack the day before, and his doctor mentioned that in such an emergency, the local fire department would have an oxygen tank. Hepburn, daughter of a doctor, immediately had four tanks and masks installed: three in his home and one in his car. That attack came while he was in the car.

In November 1963 Tracy noticed a persistent rattle in his expensive car. It took five visits to his garage before the noise was finally traced and eliminated. Somehow, a soft drink bottle had been hidden deep inside one of the doors. Inside the bottle was a note: "So you bought this car, you rich S.O.B."

Tracy made a speech at a party celebrating a friend's sixtieth birthday. He welcomed the guest of honor to the Sixty Club, then noticed Frank Sinatra, who was only forty-nine, in the audience. "Hey, Frank," said Tracy, "what're you doing here? It's not enough to *look* sixty. You have to *be* sixty."

Originally cast in *The Cincinnati Kid*, Tracy asked the studio not to costar one of those Method people: "I'm no good at playing a teapot," he said. Edward G. Robinson ended up playing the role opposite Steve McQueen.

ELI WALLACH

(1915–2014)

The genial, talented character actor who lived nearly a century began acting at twelve, portraying a sixty-five-year-old man. "I was the only man that age with bubble gum stuck in his beard," he recalled.

For my money, his finest performance was as the grizzled Mexican bandito in *The Magnificent Seven*, one of the greatest westerns of all time. I used to see him on the number 5 Riverside Drive bus, and as it snaked up the long, winding avenue along the Hudson, I'd greet him in a loud voice with his lines from the movie:

"You came back? To a place like *this?!*" Or, "If God hadn't wanted them shorn, he would not have made them sheep!" He'd playfully respond by giving me a Calvera-like scowl, his right upper lip curled menacingly.

Wallach began acting professionally during the Depression and said his parents "figured if I was out of work, I might as well be an actor. An actor out of work still retains a degree of social acceptance."

After he opened on Broadway in Shaw's *Major Barbara* in November 1956, Wallach went to Sardi's to await the reviews. "Facing an opening night audience is like fighting the heavyweight champ," he said. "In the first round, you spar. Then you start hitting harder, and by the final curtain, you've got to have them licked. And not by a decision—only knockouts count."

"I prefer stage acting to working in films," he said. "Onstage, you just keep going until the play's over. But in movies, it's two minutes of work, then stop. It's like having a love affair with constant interruptions."

Wallach's costar in *Major Barbara* was the show's director, Charles Laughton, who asked Wallach to make the postcurtain appeal for support during Actors Fund week. "He told me he would've felt odd doing the appeal," said Wallach, "because his character denounces poverty. So how could he ask the audience for money?"

In January 1958, his wife, actress Anne Jackson, recalled that while on tour, her suspicions were aroused when she read that Wal-

Eli Wallach in rehearsal for Tennessee Williams's play *Camino Real*, New York, 1953. Photograph by Sam Shaw.

lach was seen with another lady. "My mother taught me to hold on to a man with open hands," she said. "But I called Eli anyway. He said the other lady was from the Actors Studio, and he liked her like a sister. Marilyn Monroe? A 'sister'?"

When Wallach was set to play Albert Anastasia, the ruthless mobster who headed the infamous Murder, Inc., he visited the chambers of Judge Samuel Leibowitz, who'd defended Anastasia against other charges. Leibowitz told Wallach why actors make bad jurors:

"Actors can't be objective. They project themselves into the situation and find justification for the defendant."

In *The Chairs*, Wallach's character jumped out a window. In "Albert Anastasia: His Life and Death," an episode of the TV series *Climax!*, Wallach's character again met a violent end, gunned down in a barber chair at the Park Sheraton Hotel.

"An actor doesn't mind being killed," said Wallach, "so long as it's not in the first scene."

Wallach's father, Abraham, a Polish immigrant, was concerned about the kinds of roles his son played. Wallach was a drunken pug in *Major Barbara*, a vengeful Sicilian in *Baby Doll*, a scheming seducer in *The Rose Tattoo*, and a murderous gangster in the Anastasia teleplay. Then he played Stalin's secretary in TV's *Playhouse 90*.

"Yes, Eli, it's a respectable role at last," said his father, "but look who the secretary's boss is!"

Wallach once missed a performance on Broadway and his understudy did well. "When that happens," said Wallach the next day, "when you're back out there you feel like Rip Van Winkle."

Wallach received a cable from London inviting him to star in a production there of the play *Once More with Feeling*. "We will have that great international star Robert Morley as director," it read. The cable was signed: "Robert Morley."

In 1960, Wallach played his most memorable role, Calvera the bandit leader in *The Magnificent Seven*. Nowadays, a Latino actor would surely have been offered that part first. But stretching his craft to unforeseen limits, he was brilliant. The next time it's shown on TCM, note the detail, the nuance, the body language—a perfect performance. At the end of the movie, Yul Brynner, the leader of the seven gunfighters hired by local villagers, outdraws Calvera.

Watching the movie, Wallach's children told him they always thought their father was faster on the draw. "How could you lose to Brynner?" his son wanted to know.

Wallach costarred in *The Misfits*, which marked the screen farewells of both Marilyn Monroe and Clark Gable. Wallach gained the distinction of becoming the only man who could say he cut in on Clark Gable to dance with Marilyn Monroe. He became her favorite dancing partner after that. In one scene, he had to appear out of breath, so, being a true Method actor, just before the scene was shot, Wallach did forty-seven push-ups.

Four decades before *Dancing with the Stars*, Arthur Murray had a popular TV dance contest show and asked Wallach to compete. It would be an Apache dance, which simulates violent confrontations between a pimp and a prostitute. Ever the Method actor, in the run-through, he slapped his partner, ballerina Sono Osato; after a second rehearsal, she quit and their appearance was canceled.

In April 1962, Wallach played a professional crapshooter on an episode of the classic series *Naked City*. He ran a $156 stake up to $16,000. A few weeks later, he was in Las Vegas and the casino pit boss, who'd seen the episode, challenged him to play for real. When the $156 plummeted to $80, he quit, saying, "Winning that much only happens on TV."

In *How the West Was Won*, Wallach was again cast as a bandit. This outlaw was an American, a swaggering criminal named Charlie Gant who at one point threatens the two young sons of U.S. Marshal George Peppard.

"*Again* as a bandit?" asked his son Peter when he saw the movie.

"Yes," replied Wallach. "Only this time I'm a very important bad man because the West couldn't be won until I was killed!"

Wallach's son worked for months making a stained-glass window at school for his parents. But as his teacher began to hang it on a wall, it slipped and crashed to the ground. Wallach tried to console his son, explaining that the great Michelangelo searched six months for the proper stone for a statue before finally finding it.

"But Dad," replied the boy, "this took me *seven* months."

Mrs. John Steinbeck visited Wallach on the set of *The Tiger Makes Out*. They had been schoolmates at the University of Texas, and she brought him an old program for the drama club's production of *Hay Fever*. She was listed as the star, and the stage crew was Eli Wallach and John B. Connally—the future secretary of the navy, governor of Texas, secretary of the treasury, presidential hopeful, and passenger in JFK's limousine that terrible day in Dallas.

In September 1963, Wallach was filming *Kisses for My President*. Before signing on for another role for Walt Disney, he asked his daughter Roberta, "Should I play a jewel thief who strikes Hayley Mills? What will people say?" "Tough on them," she replied.

Wallach costarred in *Lord Jim*. He arrived at the film's premiere in a limousine, went inside to be photographed, left by a side door, and slid into the same limousine to make his opening night curtain in *Luv*.

A few months later, there was a water shortage in New York. At one point in *Luv* Wallach's character dove off a bridge into water. That night, he became the first actor to dive into ginger ale.

One scene in *The Tiger Makes Out* required a night shoot on New York railroad tracks, which necessitated permission from the train company. The crew had to wrap by 6 a.m., in time for the morning rush. They finished with a few minutes to spare.

"A helluva way to run a movie," said a railroad executive.

In the mid-1960s, Wallach and his wife visited Arthur, the most popular discotheque in New York, owned by Sybil Burton. Yelling above the din, Wallach said, "It's like being stuck in the Lincoln Tunnel with every horn going nonstop."

Wallach was sent a script for a movie with Kirk Douglas called *A Lovely Way to Die*. Wallach's proposed character was a lawyer called Arkansas Fredericks. He rejected it, and the producer said they'd rewrite his role. The only revision made was to change the character's name to "Tennessee." Wallach signed on.

In September 1973, after he opened on Broadway in a revival of *Waltz of the Toreadors*, Wallach said that as far as he was concerned, the play was "new, good, and fresh, and I only wish those same adjectives applied to me."

Eli Wallach was once asked how he and his wife managed to make the demands of competing careers in the same profession work. "Easy," he replied. "We never go after the same role."

JOHN WAYNE

(1907–1979)

I met John Wayne twice: first at the 1968 Republican National Convention, which I was covering for Westinghouse Broadcasting, and later when director Howard Hawks died. He seemed in person exactly as he appeared on-screen. He didn't come to New York often, but when I mentioned The Lyons Den, Duke said he'd met my father and read the column in an L.A. paper. Of course, he was an actor, so I'll never be sure.

In October 1953, Wayne was a silent backer of a play called *Flareout*. "That way," he explained, "if it's a hit, there'll be plenty of time for me to take bows, but if it flops, I don't want people to call me a sucker." Neither happened. The play never made it to Broadway.

The Conqueror, which featured Wayne in absurd makeup as Genghis Kahn, was one of his worst films. Before production began, Wayne was asked if he'd met his costar, Pedro Armendáriz. "Of *course* I know him," he replied. "We fought Indians together in *Fort Apache*."

Jeffrey Hunter costarred with Wayne in *The Searchers*, considered one of the most authentic-looking westerns ever made. "I knew I'd been given a major role," said Hunter, "when the prop department gave me as much blank ammunition as John Wayne."

Wayne had advised Kirk Douglas not to take the part of Vincent van Gogh in *Lust for Life*, suggesting that he stick to action roles. Luckily, Douglas ignored him and gave an Oscar-nominated performance. "How's that movie doing?" asked Wayne one day early in 1957. When told it had just won Douglas a film critics' prize for best actor of the year, Wayne snapped, "That's not what I asked. How's it doing at the *box office*, not on some critics' desks."

Wayne directed *The Alamo* and frequently had to give orders to the extras, most of whom were Mexican. It seemed odd that he'd need a translator, since his three wives were all Latina. He explained that his Spanish was limited because he often ignored all three.

Director Billy Wilder was lamenting movie stars' exorbitant salaries. Wayne was being paid $750,000 per movie, or in today's money, $5.67 million. Wayne told Wilder he wanted to work with him. "Pay

John Wayne, *The Comancheros*, Los Angeles, 1961.
Photograph by Sam Shaw.

me whatever you think I'm worth," said the actor. "Forty-seven dollars," replied Wilder.

In 1961, Wayne filmed one of his most entertaining movies, *Hatari!*, in Tanzania. Wayne, portraying a big-game hunter, noticed that most of the real-life hunters on the set, rather than wearing pith helmets and khaki safari jackets and pants, wore T-shirts, blue jeans, and sneakers. "Take away the scenery and the animals around us," Wayne joked, "and this looks like a class at the Actors Studio."

In 1962's *The Longest Day*, Wayne, then fifty-five, portrayed Lieutenant Colonel Benjamin Vandervoort, who jumped with his men into Normandy on D-Day. When he saw the film in October 1962, Vandervoort gave Wayne a mixed review: "I never looked that old," he said. "I was twenty-seven then and no soldier moved about the way Wayne did. The fact is, I was really scared."

In 1966, Kirk Douglas was costarring with Wayne in *The War Wagon*, which Wayne produced. Douglas's character wore only one black glove, and he explained, "I'm economizing. This way, I only need makeup for one hand. I'm saving John Wayne money."

While filming that movie, Wayne said, "I feel the public likes my cowboy and soldier characters because they have simple, basic reactions. They look at somebody they love like they love 'em and somebody they hate like they hate 'em. That's a message that nobody has to try and figure out."

In one scene of Danny Thomas's TV special *Block Party*, a show demonstrating friendship among people of varied backgrounds, Thomas asked a group of Native Americans what would make them happy.

"Easy," replied one. "Just give us five minutes alone with John Wayne."

Wayne finally won his Oscar for *True Grit*, as an aging frontier lawman who wears a patch over one eye. When he returned from the ceremonies to the set of his current movie, a western called *Rio Lobo*, everyone was wearing an eye patch. Including Wayne's horse. And the sixteen-foot replica of his Oscar.

Before he became a TV icon as Wyatt Earp, Hugh O'Brian was a highly decorated marine, the youngest drill sergeant in the history of the Corps. When Wayne was nominated for an Oscar for *True Grit*, O'Brian announced he was rooting for the Duke. O'Brian, who would costar in Wayne's last movie, *The Shootist*, in 1976, explained that while he was in marine boot camp, he was slated to compete in a boxing match. Wayne visited the camp and noticed that O'Brian's opponent was much taller and heavier.

"What rules are you guys going to use?" asked Wayne. "Marquess of Queensberry or mine?" The fighters agreed on Wayne's rules—one round, no time limit.

The lighter and faster O'Brian then kept retreating in the ring until his lumbering opponent, in much poorer condition, collapsed.

Early in 1971, insult comic Don Rickles met Wayne and said, "I loved you in *Cimarron*." "But I wasn't in that movie," said Wayne. "Too bad," replied Rickles. "That was a great movie."

Later that year, director Peter Bogdanovich bought a pair of blue jeans once worn by Wayne in one of his westerns. "Wearing those John Wayne–worn jeans on the set of one of my movies," he explained, "gives me a sense of greater authority."

PART
III

They Made

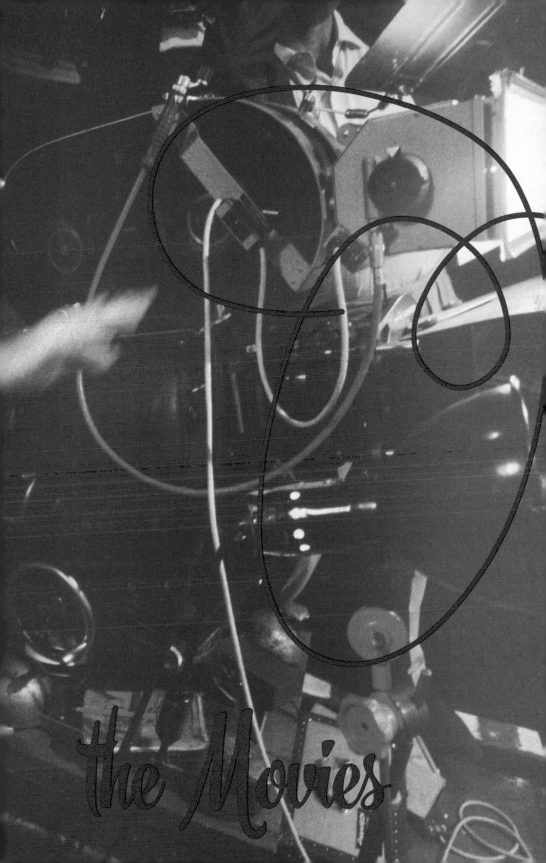

the Movies

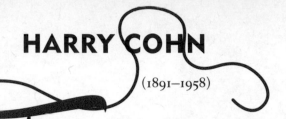

HARRY COHN

(1891–1958)

The quintessential Hollywood studio mogul, ruling his studio with an iron fist and smoking a thick cigar, Harry Cohn founded Columbia Pictures with his brother Jack. It was their 1934 movie *It Happened One Night*—winner of the Oscars for Best Picture, Director (Frank Capra), Actor (Clark Gable), Actress (Claudette Colbert), and Screenplay (Robert Riskin)—that took the second-rate studio off Poverty Row.

In February 1939, Groucho Marx, no friend of Cohn's, went to a film and when the opening frame of the credits came on, reading "Columbia Pictures Presents," he said in a loud voice, "This drags, don't you think?"

Nine days later, director Rouben Mamoulian, then working on the screen version of Clifford Odets's *Golden Boy*, was summoned with two of the screenwriters to Cohn's office to discuss the script. Cohn listened patiently to the story they outlined, then suggested one scene be altered.

"But that's dramatically impossible," Mamoulian protested. Cohn persisted. Then Mamoulian said, "Give me one reason why that scene should be changed."

"I'll give you one reason," Cohn replied. "The reason is: *I'm the president of Columbia Pictures!*"

At a later meeting, Mamoulian, undaunted, asked Cohn not to judge the movie "by the box-office standards all you producers are accustomed to. Please," he continued, "look ahead. Be perspicacious, Mr. Cohn."

"No!" replied the mogul. "For two reasons: first, I don't agree with you, and second, I don't know what 'perspicacious' means."

The following March, one of Cohn's assistants suggested he make a movie based on Homer's *Odyssey*. Cohn expressed interest and told a staff writer to prepare a synopsis. A few days later, the writer delivered it.

Cohn began reading it, then looked up and said, "Saaay, there's an awful lot about Greece in this."

In March 1942, Cohn read the completed screenplay of a comedy he planned to produce. Although it was well written, he expressed dissatisfaction. "We're living in a historic age now," he explained to the screenwriter, "and I want you to get that element into the script."

"But Mr. Cohn," the writer protested, "this is just a funny movie. When the customers see it, they'll say, 'That was a funny picture.'"

"When the customers see this," replied Cohn, "I want them to say, 'This is a funny picture—and what a history lesson!'"

In February 1943, he met Alfred Hitchcock and said, "I've been told you never see movies, not even your own."

"That's right," replied Hitchcock.

Cohn asked, "Then where do your ideas come from?"

In September 1947, Cohn drove with Orson Welles to a preview screening of Welles's *The Lady from Shanghai*, which Welles directed and in which he starred with his wife, Rita Hayworth.

"Tell me, Orson," Cohn asked, "Who is the world's *second* greatest actor? I'm looking to cast him in *All the King's Men*."

Welles replied, "I don't know who's second." Cohn chose Broderick Crawford, who won the Oscar as a Huey Long–type character.

Cohn carried a gold cigarette case inscribed to him from one of his stars: "The greatest president since Lincoln."

Cohn's father had a tailor shop near a police station in New York. The police commissioner, Teddy Roosevelt, would drop in periodically after keeping tabs on the honesty of the cops. "That's where I learned that everyone can be bought," Cohn recalled years later.

He used that lesson in the way he ran his studio. When Garson Kanin insisted that he alone would direct the movie version of his play *Born Yesterday*, Cohn snarled, "Everything's for sale. Name a price." Figuring Cohn would never agree, Kanin said, "One million dollars."

"It's a deal," said Cohn. George Cukor directed.

When other studios were reluctant to buy *From Here to Eternity*, Cohn told aides, "Don't anyone tell me not to buy it, because I just did." Frank Sinatra's Oscar for the film resurrected his career, and Oscars also went to director Fred Zinnemann, supporting actress Donna Reed, and four others. And it won Best Picture.

When Cohn's son was born, he called all his assistants into his office, told them the news, then poured drinks from a bottle of one-hundred-year-old brandy. One of his aides then offered this toast: "May the boy grow up to be just as great a man as his father."

Cohn glared at him and said, "Whaddya have against my kid?!"

When Cohn took a vacation in France, his office cabled, "Hope you're enjoying your vacation—as much as we are."

Cohn outlasted the Warner brothers, Darryl F. Zanuck at Fox, Bill Goetz at Universal, and Adolph Zukor at Paramount. He was the last of the Hollywood moguls to remain in power.

GEORGE CUKOR

(1899–1983)

He was one of Hollywood's greatest directors during its Golden Age, especially noted for his films starring Katherine Hepburn, including *The Philadelphia Story* and the Tracy-Hepburn classics *Keeper of the Flame*, *Pat and Mike*, and *Adam's Rib*. He directed the second (and by far the best) version of *A Star Is Born* and *My Fair Lady*, for which he won an Oscar as Best Director.

A Hollywood producer suggested to Cukor that the cost of making a romantic movie could be greatly reduced if the studios used real-life couples such as Robert Wagner and Natalie Wood, Robert Taylor and Barbara Stanwyck, or Tony Curtis and Janet Leigh.

"Not true," said Cukor. "I've always found that shooting a romantic scene with a real-life married couple always requires plenty of rehearsal time."

One afternoon, Bella Spewack, the Broadway and Hollywood writer who cowrote, with her husband Sam, *Weekend at the Waldorf*—a remake of *Grand Hotel*—and many others, was taken to a set where Cukor was directing Greta Garbo, whom Spewack had always wanted to meet. They shook hands, and Garbo noticed Spewack staring at her feet.

"They're big, aren't they?" asked Garbo.

When Cukor was inducted into the Army Signal Corps, the sergeant handling his paperwork didn't recognize him and said, "Private, you made a mistake. You put down three thousand dollars as your weekly salary. That must be your annual salary, or what you got in a week when you sold your home." Cukor politely informed him that yes, that *was* his weekly salary.

Private Cukor was assigned to direct films for the army. One included a general who was nervous working for the famed director. He walked into the scene while Cukor, seated in a director's chair, watched. Just then an aide interrupted, saying, "Private Cukor, don't you know that when a general walks in, you have to stand?"

"Now listen, you," said Cukor. "This war isn't going to last forever. So go away!"

In March 1943, Cukor was filming an army service short. One of the actors he used was named Jack Effrat, who, when he auditioned, was wearing his Phi Beta Kappa key, awarded by Ohio State University, from which he had graduated cum laude. Cukor made sure he put it out of sight. The short film was about soldiers being drafted despite subnormal IQs.

Cukor once directed a play starring Louis Calhern and Ann Andrews. At one performance, both actors forgot their lines. Cukor, standing offstage, was so frustrated, he tossed the script onstage and yelled, "Here, you go—find the next lines!"

Cukor, known as a "women's director" for having worked so often with a wide variety of actresses, believed women could withstand physical punishment better than men. In fight scenes he directed, for example, actresses would say, "When you kick me, make it real." But actors said, "Isn't there some way of parrying the blow?" He also said actresses were more daring. Joan Crawford, for example, learned a Chopin étude overnight.

In February 1944, Cukor received a copy of *The Razor's Edge* from its author, W. Somerset Maugham, who'd sent copies around Hollywood hoping for a movie deal. Cukor found one paragraph disturbing. It concerned the desire to learn Greek and Latin. He thought the words sounded familiar and wrote Maugham, saying he'd heard Orson Welles say those words verbatim.

Maugham wrote back, upset at the suggestion of plagiarism. Unconvinced, Cukor then asked Welles, who said yes, he *had* indeed said those words—which he'd lifted from Maugham.

In August 1948, Cukor was in London directing Spencer Tracy and Deborah Kerr in *Edward, My Son*. One of the locations was the London suburb of Chiswick, where a large group of neighbors watched the moviemaking. As a scene was about to be filmed, an assistant director shouted, "Quiet, everybody!" Everyone fell silent, except for an elderly lady in a house nearby.

"I said quiet!" yelled the assistant director.

"This is *my* house, and I'll talk as much as I like," said the lady. "By the way, young man, 'please' would help."

Spencer Tracy then stepped forward, smiled, bowed, and in a gentle voice said, "Please, ma'am. Please, for *my* sake?"

"With pleasure, Mr. Tracy," replied the woman. "Now shoot!"

In 1950, Cukor was directing Hepburn and Tracy in *Pat and Mike*. In one scene, Hepburn, playing a golf champion, sank a twenty-foot putt. "Cut!" said Cukor. "Well done, Kate," he told her. "But you're supposed to *miss* that one. Do it again, please."

In December 1972, Cukor posed for a photo for *Mademoiselle* magazine to accompany a story on *Travels with My Aunt*. It gave him the chance to ask the photographer a question dozens of stars had asked him: "Which is *my* good side?"

FEDERICO FELLINI

(1920–1993)

He is without a doubt the most important postwar Italian director, whose innovative movies still influence cinema around the world.

On a flight from Rome to Paris in 1954, Fellini sat next to an American journalist who, like any good newspaperman, engaged Fellini in conversation. Fellini said he was en route to Hollywood to receive the Directors' Guild Award for his movie *La Strada*, which starred Anthony Quinn and Fellini's wife, Giulietta Masina.

Fellini showed the journalist the remarks he'd prepared. "May I suggest some changes?" replied the journalist, who was far more experienced in public speaking and speechwriting. Fellini agreed, and the journalist rewrote the speech so that Fellini would appear modest and gracious about his less renowned colleagues in Italy. That journalist was my father.

When Fellini's classic 8½—one of the great surrealistic films of all time—came out in 1963, both Fellini's and star Marcello Mastroianni's wives were suspicious that the lead character, a director bored with his wife and mistress, was based on their husbands. Fellini and Mastroianni each assured his wife that the film was about the other man.

Fellini's next picture, *Juliet of the Spirits*, was in color, a medium he didn't especially like. "Color and movement conflict," he explained to my father over lunch in Rome. "Move the camera and the values of the lights change. It's like an embrace underwater."

Unlike some directors, Fellini didn't mind visitors to his sets. "My set is like a piazza during a revolution," he said. Making movies was an escape for him. "Lawyers are not permitted to bother me, businessmen don't disturb me," he said. "I can be as nervous and as upset as I want to. The people say, understandingly, 'He is doing a movie.'"

Fellini didn't even inquire as to the nationality of the actors he'd hired for his new movie. "When I shoot a film," he said, "it's like the Tower of Babel."

When he went to see *Oh! Calcutta!*, the all-nude show on Broadway, he shrugged: "So what else is new?"

"I direct," he said, "because I cannot do other things."

CECIL B. DEMILLE

(1881–1959)

His career stretched from 1914's *The Squaw Man*, Hollywood's first feature film, with Dustin Farnum (after whom Dustin Hoffman was named), to 1958's *The Buccaneer*, with Yul Brynner. Best known for his two versions of *The Ten Commandments*, DeMille also produced and directed the 1934 version of *Cleopatra*, *Samson and Delilah*, and *The Greatest Show on Earth*. DeMille played a pivotal part in the founding of Hollywood. Flagstaff, Arizona, had been chosen as the location for *The Squaw Man*, but when he arrived, he reported it unsuitable. "Found another place which will do," he wired his partner, Jesse Lasky. "A place called 'Hollywood.' Can rent a barn for $75 a month."

Lasky agreed, adding, "But take it on a month-to-month basis."

Thus the film industry in Hollywood was born. Incidentally, he played the role of a faro dealer in that film, to save two dollars on production costs.

DeMille found the will of an ancestor, Anthony DeMille, who left to a son the land which now is almost half of lower Manhattan.

After he completed shooting the 1923 version of *The Ten Commandments*, Paramount fired DeMille for cost overruns. When the film made millions, he was rehired.

By 1927, his name as a movie producer and director had become so well known, his version of *The King of Kings* was advertised as "Cecil B. DeMille's *The King of Kings*, with a Talented Cast of 10,000!"

While preparing to produce *The Greatest Show on Earth*, DeMille questioned circus owner John Ringling North about every detail of North's business, including North's investments in oil wells, and bought one. In December 1949, it brought in a gusher, as they say.

While shooting that film, DeMille was shocked by Betty Hutton's frequent use of off-color language. "Couldn't you just once say 'shucks' instead?" he asked the star. She agreed. Soon after, while climbing a rope ladder for a trapeze stunt, she slipped and blurted out "Shucks!" Then she looked down at DeMille and said, "It just hasn't got that sting."

The film won the Oscars for Best Picture and Best Story. The next day, Hutton sent DeMille a four-foot statue made of orchids, in the shape of an Oscar.

In 1950, DeMille played himself in the reunion scene with Gloria Swanson in *Sunset Boulevard*. He asked the director, Billy Wilder, for instructions.

Wilder, who'd been a child in Vienna when DeMille's reputation was established, was in awe, so he replied, "Play the scene your own way. You're the master."

"No, I'll play the scene *your* way," replied DeMille. "After all, I'll be acting out ideas which are yours as director." Then he added, "Frankly, Billy, just between us, there are very few directors who can act."

"And just between us," replied Wilder, "there are very few directors who know how to direct."

When his "performance" playing himself was reviewed favorably, DeMille sent the reviews to the head of Paramount with a two-word message attached: "At liberty."

When DeMille turned seventy in 1951, he received birthday greetings from all over the world. But most of them came from California civic groups and real estate interests who prospered from his having chosen Hollywood as the best location for moviemaking.

His favorite card read, "Best wishes from the San Fernando Funeral Home."

As his reputation for producing and directing huge movies with thousands of people grew, DeMille said, "We no longer hire just extras. We now hire whole tribes.'

In 1955, while filming part of his remake of *The Ten Commandments* on location in Egypt, DeMille's assistant directors took orders from him, but instead of saying "Yes, sir," or the punch line of the famous joke, "Ready when you are, C.B.," instead they said, "Thy will be done."

Lionel Hampton, the jazz vibraphonist, visited the set and said to DeMille, "The Ten Commandments? Pops, which one are you going to plug?"

He threw himself entirely into whatever production he was currently making. During the shooting of *The Ten Commandments*, he was asked to comment on some unrelated event and replied, "If it didn't happen in the time of Moses, I know nothing about it."

Halfway through the production he said, "I've finished shooting the ten plagues: frogs, hail, and all the rest. Now I'll get even busier; I'm preparing to part the Red Sea."

DeMille's father, Henry Churchill DeMille, had been a playwright, among other things. After a play he'd written became a hit, *Harper's* magazine paid him a thousand dollars to write an article called "The Ten Rules for Writing a Play." After a while, however, he returned the check, saying, "I was afraid that, after reciting the ten rules, I'd be held to them."

When Mario del Monaco was cast opposite Risë Stevens in the Metropolitan Opera's production of *Samson and Delilah*, he was asked if he really thought Samson wore leopard skins.

"No, I'm not sure," replied the tenor, "but Victor Mature wore them in DeMille's movie, and when it comes to the Bible, I'll take DeMille's word for it."

For *The Ten Commandments*, Yul Brynner worked for half his usual fee, explaining, "Gambling on DeMille is like betting on a one-horse race."

JOHN HUSTON

(1906–1987)

John Huston was one of the most colorful, quotable, interesting men in Hollywood. With his long, spindly cigar and casual safari attire, he looked like the ideal hunting companion for his contemporary Ernest Hemingway. They were cut from the same cloth.

Huston won directing and screenwriting Oscars for *The Treasure of the Sierra Madre*, for which his father, Walter, won an Oscar for Best Supporting Actor. His résumé also includes the film noir classic *The Maltese Falcon*, *Prizzi's Honor* (for which daughter Anjelica won a Best Supporting Actress Oscar), the cult favorite *Beat the Devil*, *Moby Dick*, and *The Misfits*. Huston was as interesting an actor as he was a director. His most bizarre role, perhaps, was as one of several James Bonds in the original *Casino Royale*.

In 1946, he was directing Jean-Paul Sartre's *No Exit* on Broadway. Huston and Claude Dauphin, the star of the play, waited to be interviewed. "I'm sure our interviewer will mention Sartre's existentialism," Huston told the actor, "so I'll ask the interviewer if he understands existentialism. If he says he doesn't, I'll explain it to him. But if he says he does, I'll ask him to explain it to *us*!"

In July 1947, Huston and his then-wife, actress Evelyn Keyes, gave a party to celebrate their wedding anniversary. Louis Calhern, then filming *Arch of Triumph* with Ingrid Bergman, said Huston seemed a little nervous because of all the names he tried to remember. "When I was leaving," Calhern recalled, "John said, 'Goodnight, Mr. Brown.'"

"Did that disturb you?" Calhern was asked.

"A bit," he replied, "especially since when I arrived he greeted me by saying, 'Welcome, Mr. Smith.'"

In August 1951, Huston was in the Congo filming *The African Queen* with Humphrey Bogart and Katherine Hepburn. Also there were Bogie's wife Lauren Bacall and coscreenwriter Peter Viertel. Soon after they arrived, they hired a guide to take them for a canoe ride. An hour later, they heard drums signaling. A bit fearful, Huston asked their guide what the drums were saying.

John Huston, *Casino Royale*, London, 1967. Photograph by Sam Shaw.

"'Americans coming. Raise prices,'" he replied.

In Paris shooting *Moulin Rouge* in 1952, Huston reminisced, "Although I won the Academy Award and am proud of movies which the critics were good enough to praise, I'll probably go down in history solely for directing *The Asphalt Jungle*, because it was the first important role for Marilyn Monroe."

He read that Monroe had purchased the classical music manuscripts from the estate of Max Reinhardt, who directed *A Midsummer Night's Dream*. Huston thought Monroe was becoming interested in cultural matters, so he sent her a book about the evolution of the fugue in eighteenth-century music. She returned it with a note: "Thanks, John, but I think I'll wait for the movie version."

Huston gambled on horses, cards, dice, and people. He was a devoted collector of Incan sculpture. When he and Evelyn Keyes were divorced, Huston proposed a toss of a coin, winner takes the entire collection. She agreed. He tossed. She won.

While making *Moulin Rouge*, Huston learned that a curious man would frequently find out where the next day's shooting was scheduled and rent a room overlooking the set. It was Picasso.

In March 1957, while filming *A Farewell to Arms*, Huston recalled visiting opium dens in Bangkok and India. He'd stretch out on the assigned bunk and puff on the pipes given him, but was unaffected by the drug. On return visits, he puffed his own cigars.

"I liked smoking a cigar in a Thai opium den," Huston said. "I enjoyed the scenery."

In 1961, the news came that Arthur Miller and Marilyn Monroe had split. Huston, who directed her in *The Asphalt Jungle* and *The Misfits*, said, "Marilyn tries too hard to prove herself a sex symbol." But her friend Susan Strasberg, actress and daughter of Monroe's acting teacher Lee Strasberg, disagreed, saying, "John Huston is an authority on filmmaking and big-game hunting. And that's all."

In 1964, he was filming *The Bible* and would often phone friends from the set, beginning with "Hello. I'm calling you from the Garden of Eden."

DAVID O. SELZNICK

(1902–1965)

*G*one with the Wind was Selznick's crowning achievement. His résumé, unmatched by that of any other producer in Hollywood's Golden Age, also includes *King Kong, Dinner at Eight, Rebecca, Duel in the Sun, Spellbound*, and *David Copperfield*.

His father, Lewis J. Selznick, was one of Hollywood's founders as a silent film distributor. In May 1915, his father was on the lot and heard a loud commotion outside. Rushing to investigate, he was told the RMS *Lusitania* had been sunk.

"Oh, is *that* all," said the elder Selznick. "I thought one of my actresses had walked off a set."

Against the advice of friends, the older Selznick produced a silent version of *The Prisoner of Zenda* in 1922 with Ramon Novarro, one of the biggest stars of that time. It flopped and he went bankrupt. His son, however, loved the project and produced a sound version in 1937 with Ronald Colman, which was a big hit.

In August 1942, Selznick told my father he'd kept all the screen tests of actresses vying for the most coveted role in movie history: Scarlett O'Hara in *Gone with the Wind*. While the film was still in production, Jean Arthur, who'd been one of the aspirants, asked for the footage of her test.

Selznick dutifully sent it over. The next day she said she'd burned the footage. Selznick said hers was a copy. History was preserved.

In 1943, Selznick was feuding with Charles Lederer, who cowrote *The Front Page, His Girl Friday*, and *The Spirit of St. Louis*, among other screenplays. Lederer, a noted practical joker, sent Selznick a ten-foot fishing pole attached to a note: "Dear Mr. Selznick: This is the pole with which I wouldn't touch you."

In July 1944, Selznick's production *Since You Went Away* opened. It was a wartime drama of life on the home front. The night of the opening, Selznick ordered the manager of the theater to oil every seat. "I don't want any squeaking seats heard at the wrong moments," he explained. But oil was a scarce commodity during the war, so the manager oiled only the seats in Selznick's row and the rows just in front of and behind his. Selznick never heard a squeak.

Soon after it opened, Selznick sent a telegram to a Paramount sales executive suggesting cuts in the film before its national release. The telegram ran fifteen pages. The executive's reply: "FILM LENGTH OK STOP SUGGEST YOU MAKE CUTS TO FUTURE WIRES STOP"

Selznick faced criticism of the film's 130-minute running time, unusual for those days. (The DVD version runs 177 minutes.) Unconvinced by that telegram from Paramount, Selznick persisted, and asked MGM studio head Nicholas Schenck for advice. "How long should the film be?" he asked the movie mogul.

"How long is it good?" came the reply.

Selznick and some friends drove to inspect property they hoped to buy for a studio site. They stopped at an ice cream stand on the way and paid twenty cents per cone. Selznick thought that was overpriced and argued with the vendor for ten minutes. Then they drove to the lot, which they were told would cost $3 million. "I'll take it!" said Selznick.

The next day the realtor called, saying the property had already been sold to Columbia Pictures boss Harry Cohn, who'd left ten minutes before Selznick's arrival—the ten minutes Selznick had spent arguing over the cost of a twenty-cent ice cream cone.

Selznick was in New York and went to an art gallery, accompanied by someone he considered an art expert. A painting was brought out; Selznick admired it and said he was interested in buying it. "What do you think?" he asked his companion. "I don't like it. It's ugly," came the reply. Selznick thanked the dealer and they left.

The "expert" was Selznick's eleven-year-old son. The painting was by Vincent van Gogh.

Early in 1948, Selznick was riding in a friend's car and the friend showed off his new gizmo: a wireless telephone connected to the car's antenna. "Go ahead," said the friend. "Call a friend." Selznick did; he called the actress Jennifer Jones—in Switzerland.

Selznick produced *Portrait of Jenny* in 1948, starring the aforementioned Jennifer Jones, Joseph Cotten, and Ethel Barrymore. One scene was shot in New York's Sheep Meadow, where Selznick hired fifteen sheep and a sheepdog. Soon the sheep were running around at will, with the dog paying no attention. Its owner explained that though it was a sheepdog, it had never seen a sheep before and had no herding instincts.

Selznick produced the second movie version of Hemingway's *A Farewell to Arms*. Some of it was filmed in an Italian resort town on Lake Maggiore. Like the famous Trevi Fountain in Rome, the lake, too, has a legend that if visitors toss a coin in, they'll return someday. The stars of the movie, Rock Hudson and Jennifer Jones, dutifully obliged, but the director, Charles Vidor, refused. "I know why," said Selznick. "You're afraid that if you return, it would only be because you had to shoot retakes."

Early in 1956, an agent was victimized by someone in Paris who sold him an exclusive option of the movie rights to all of Alexander Dumas's stories. Since Dumas died in 1870, those stories had, of course, been in the public domain for decades. The agent contacted Selznick, offering to sell him the Dumas rights. Selznick cabled back: "SORRY, NO SALE. SUGGEST YOU GET THE SAME MAN TO SELL YOU EXCLUSIVE MOVIE RIGHTS TO THE BIBLE, THEN APPROACH CECIL B. DEMILLE."

In November 1957, Selznick explained how he cast the most coveted role in movie history. He'd taken a train from New York to Los Angeles and for most of the trip was seated next to a lady with a thick southern drawl. When they arrived, he said, "You've done me a great favor. You've helped me cast the star of my movie, *Gone with the Wind*. I couldn't understand a word of your southern talk, so I'm giving the role to an Englishwoman, Vivien Leigh."

One of the more memorable Selznick memos wasn't written by the producer. An aide discovered he'd miscalculated figures regarding production costs on a movie. Selznick was gone for the day, so the aide left the following note: "Dear Mr. Selznick. In reference to your memo of tomorrow . . ."

Selznick cast Elaine Stritch, the actress-singer, for a role in *A Farewell to Arms*, and explained how she won the part: "A young man of great integrity and taste saw you perform," he said. "My son."

In March 1958, *Life* magazine published a collection of Selznick's numerous memos from the filming of *A Farewell to Arms*. They later became part of a book called, appropriately, *Memo from David O. Selznick*. Nearly five decades before the advent of texting, he was so prodigious a memo writer, he had his secretary accompany him to the airport so she could jot down memos until the last minute. In fact, as he boarded the plane he shouted to her: "Period. Very truly yours."

Alfred Hitchcock once expressed skepticism about the results of polls. He cited the example of one that asked the primary reason moviegoers were eager to see *Rebecca*. The poll was conducted along the long lines of ticket buyers outside Radio City Music Hall. Ninety-one percent of those polled said they'd come because it was a Selznick film.

SAM SHAW

(1912–1999)

He was one of the great professional photographers of his time, Marilyn Monroe's official photographer as well as a globe-trotting photojournalist. It was his photo of Marilyn on that subway grating that appeared worldwide and led to Joe DiMaggio's divorcing her. Shaw also shot the famous photo of Marlon Brando in a ripped T-shirt in *A Streetcar Named Desire*. He coproduced five films, including *Paris Blues*, with Paul Newman; *Husbands*, with his good friend John Cassavetes; and *A Woman Under the Influence*, directed by Cassavetes and starring Cassavetes's wife, Gena Rowlands.

Shaw was in Spain with Frank Sinatra during the filming of *The Pride and the Passion*, in which Sinatra played the leader of Spanish rebels fighting Napoleon, lugging an enormous cannon across the Iberian peninsula.

Since actors have to report to movie sets at dawn, Sinatra, used to staying up until 4 a.m., had to adjust his living schedule. Shaw told him the best way to fall asleep was to read a boring book. In an English-language bookstore in Madrid, Shaw found the perfect book and sent it to Sinatra: a book on meteorology. But Sinatra found it fascinating and stayed up all night reading. Shaw then bought a book on acoustics. That too piqued Sinatra's interest, and he became something of an expert. Shaw gave up.

At fourteen, Shaw's daughter Edith was elected president of the student body. She told her father, "I don't understand why you criticize Eisenhower. I tell you, being a president is a tough job."

One gray afternoon, Shaw was photographing young Marilyn Monroe in Brooklyn while showing her the historic buildings. A sudden storm erupted and they were drenched. Shaw remembered he had friends who lived in a townhouse nearby, so they sought shelter there.

The friends, Mr. and Mrs. Norman Rosten, welcomed Shaw and his "model, Marilyn." Shaw never said her last name and they didn't recognize her. When Monroe mentioned her interest in acting, they

Sam Shaw and Audrey Hepburn, Paris, 1957.

told her they had friends in the theater and could help. Rosten then gave her a book of his poems, which he'd dedicated to his daughter. Monroe never forgot that pleasant afternoon, became friendly with Rosten as her stardom grew, and remembered their daughter in her will.

Shaw took Monroe to the Metropolitan Museum on her first visit to New York. She studied the drawings of tortured dreams by Goya and told Shaw, "Sam, this man Goya understands me and I understand him. Those are *my* dreams."

While on a visit to the Prado Museum in Madrid, Shaw convinced the curator that a Goya painting was being hung upside down.

Shaw was on the set of *The Dirty Dozen*, one of whom was played by his friend and producing partner, John Cassavetes. Shaw had a football, and during a break in a scene, tossed it to costar Jim Brown. The great football player let the ball bounce off his chest, however, saying, "Only for money." A few days later, he announced his retirement from the NFL to become a full-time movie actor.

LEE STRASBERG

(1902–1982)

Born Israel Lee Strasberg in Ukraine, he was the most influential acting teacher in the world, whose students included Al Pacino, Ellen Burstyn, Paul Newman, Lee J. Cobb, and Marilyn Monroe and whose Theater Institute and Actors Studios in New York and Los Angeles continue to teach beginners and seasoned professionals alike.

In 1969, my late brother Warren, an Obie Award–winning producer, helped set up the Lee Strasberg Theater Institute and convinced me to study there for two years, attending night classes taught by Lee's son John. We did "sense memory" exercises, gingerly sipping from imaginary teacups, and spoke about ourselves extemporaneously in front of fellow students. Once a week, Lee lectured everyone at a studio in Carnegie Hall. It was great training for a long TV career I had no idea would begin the next year.

Lee espoused the Stanislavsky "Method" of acting, in which the actor calls on memories—real or conceived—to bring depth to a portrayal. He defied the adage that "those who can't do, teach." Just look at his amazing, underplayed performance as Meyer Lansky–inspired Mafia boss Hyman Roth in *The Godfather Part II* in 1974. He could teach *and* do.

In 1950 his daughter, future actress Susan Strasberg, was eleven and made her debut on a TV show. Her father asked her what sort of actress she thought she was. "I can play an old-looking nine-year-old or a young-looking thirteen-year-old," she replied.

Strasberg routinely gave actors only five minutes to impress him at auditions. "That's all you need," he said. "I usually can tell after the first *minute*."

Hermione Gingold was about to become a naturalized American citizen. The costar of *Gigi* said, "I know I'll pass the test. I'll go to the Actors Studio and have Lee Strasberg teach me the most dramatic way to recite the Gettysburg Address."

An actress was doing a scene from *Romeo and Juliet* and Strasberg questioned her technique. He went into great detail and had

Lee Strasberg at his home in New York City, mid-1950's, with self-por-
trait by Marilyn Monroe in frame. Photograph by Sam Shaw.

her do the scene several times. Peter Ustinov was watching and asked, "Shouldn't somebody get that poor girl a lawyer?"

The actress didn't need one: her name was Geraldine Page.

When Joe Louis visited the Actors Studio, Strasberg told him, "Acting can be compared to an iceberg, champ. Onstage, you see only the top eighth. Here, you see below the surface."

Strasberg directed Sidney Kingsley's *Men in White* on Broadway, in which a character said, "I'm filled up with this—up to here," pointing to his throat. At a rehearsal the actor instead pointed to his heart.

"Your throat!" said Strasberg. "Point to your *throat*!"

"I know, Lee," the actor replied. "But so far, I feel it only up to here."

When he spoke with his daughter about her prospects for marriage, she asked, "What if I marry a bad actor?" "That'd be fine," he replied. "I can always turn him into a director."

His second wife, Paula, a former stage actress, became the personal coach and confidante of Marilyn Monroe. In 1968, two years after Paula died, a young Venezuelan-born actress named Anna Mizrahi auditioned for membership in the Actors Studio, doing a scene from *Rain*, the old Joan Crawford movie.

Strasberg wasn't impressed by the choice of material or her performance and flunked her. She kept coming back, eventually winning a lifetime membership of sorts, as was fitting for Strasberg's third wife.

At their wedding, he hesitated before cutting the cake. "Lee, it's just a cake," she said, "not an acting exercise. You don't need to be motivated."

In February 1970, he directed Salome Jens in three one-act plays written by Shelley Winters. In one scene, Jens had to use one of Winters's three Oscar statuettes and worried about dropping it. "Don't worry," said Strasberg. "Here at the studio, we've won forty-two Oscars."

That same month, Strasberg was teaching a class at Actors Studio West in Los Angeles. A parking lot attendant snuck in and audited the class. Strasberg noticed this and, admiring his audacity, admitted him. The next day Laurence Olivier drove into the lot, and the attendant greeted him, "Lord Olivier, as of today, you and I are fellow actors!"

Strasberg's wife Anna was considering a role that called for nudity. Although Lee's students often did such scenes, he urged her not to. "There's no need," he told her. "A good actress goes only *emotionally* nude." She accepted a role in a children's play instead.

On a trip to Argentina, a reporter asked why there was so much publicity about Argentina's beef industry but so little about its actors. Strasberg replied, "When you pay as much attention to the theater down here as you do to your cattle, then your actors will get the recognition they deserve."

Strasberg's class performed Irwin Shaw's *A Medal for Jerusalem*. The rest of the studio served as observers. When the teacher asked for their comments, Sylvia Miles, an Oscar nominee for *Midnight Cowboy* and *Farewell, My Lovely*, said, "In the restaurant scene the waiters reminded me of those at the Russian Tea Room." Strasberg smiled, for good reason. The "waiters" had been coached by Dimitri, maître d' at the Russian Tea Room.

In October 1970, Strasberg celebrated his fiftieth year as a teacher and occasional performer. His younger son was then sixteen months old. "With him, I'm no longer a teacher. I watch and learn. When my son feels like laughing, he laughs. When he feels like crying, he cries. We needn't explore his motivations."

MIKE TODD

(1909–1958)

To describe Mike Todd as a man who lived life to the fullest is to redefine understatement. He was a visionary producer to whom money seemed a mere detail, an inconvenience, and who crammed more living into his forty-nine years than most people do who live twice as long.

He was born Avrom Hirsch Goldbogen in Minneapolis, the youngest of nine children of an immigrant Polish rabbi. He worked as a shoe salesman and a soda jerk, and after his family moved to Chicago, as a barker at the Chicago Century of Progress Exposition in 1933, where he produced a show. Then he moved to Hollywood, where his construction company soundproofed studios.

At the 1939 New York World's Fair, Todd produced *The Hot Mikado*. City greeter and World's Fair president Grover Whalen asked him if it bore an official seal of approval, which of course it didn't. So he made a giant replica of the seal and simply attached it to the huge banner.

Todd produced seventeen shows on Broadway, including *Something for the Boys*, starring Ethel Merman. *Something for the Boys* had a mediocre second act, so he rang up the curtain late, knowing the first-night critics would have to leave to make their deadlines and thus would write their reviews based only on Act I.

One night in 1943, it was announced that Merman's understudy, future star Betty Garrett, would perform in her place. Todd knew that the patrons would be offered refunds, so he quickly signaled for "The Star-Spangled Banner" to play. Everyone rose, then the curtain went up and the show began. No refunds.

Todd once approached the playwrights Sam and Bella Spewack for rights to their show *Man Bites Dog*, sight unseen. "So what?" he said. "I never read *Hamlet*, but my production was a hit."

About *Michael Todd's Peep Show*, a hit Broadway revue in 1950, one critic said, "What it lacks on paper, it makes up for in bare skin."

While filming *Around the World in 80 Days*—the only feature film he'd produce—Todd hired the population of an entire Spanish

Producer Mike Todd and Frank Sinatra, on the set of *Around the World in 80 Days*, Los Angeles, 1956. Photograph by Sam Shaw.

pueblo as extras. When the scenes were finished, he took great pride watching them line up for paychecks, reminding others on the set that not so long ago, during the Depression, he'd been on just such a line after a day's work as a Chicago street paver.

Todd filmed in 112 locations around the world and put all his own money into that movie. "I've made and lost fortunes, but I've never been poor," he said. "Being poor is a state of mind; being *broke* is a temporary situation."

No one had ever seen anything like *Around the World in 80 Days*, with an array of twenty-four cameos and worldwide anticipation. Tens of thousands of extras and nearly seven thousand animals were used. "I'm not just confident about my movie," he beamed. "I'm *arrogant!*"

One of those cast in *Around the World in 80 Days* was British actor A. E. Matthews, whose first screen appearance had come in 1914. Matthews was then ninety, and asked Todd about his costume. "What's the period?" he asked. The action is set in 1895, Todd said. "Oh, then I can just wear my own suit," replied Matthews, showing Todd the jacket label, which read, "Made in 1895."

Todd threw a huge opening-night party at Madison Square Garden, but Sir Noël Coward, who had a cameo, refused to attend. "I suspect the sincerity of any invitation with a general release for me to sign, waiving all rights should it happen to put me on TV," he explained.

Sir Cedric Hardwick, one of the stars, was seated atop an elephant without being strapped in. Todd had shouted for elephants before Hardwick was secured. After enduring an endless series of lurches, he looked at the elephant and said, "If I were an American citizen, this would've been enough to make me vote Democrat."

Todd wasn't flawless in his predictions. He saw a Broadway-bound musical in New Haven and scoffed, "No girls. No gags. No chance." *Oklahoma!* ran for five years and to date has been revived four times.

When Todd was honored in his hometown of Bloomington, Minnesota, he used extra nails to attach a "Todd Avenue" sign to a streetlamp. "I want to make sure they don't take the sign down as soon as I leave town."

He noticed the presence of then–U.S. Senator Hubert Humphrey and said, "Here in this room, we have two local boys who made good. One can grow up to become president someday.

The other can grow up to marry Elizabeth Taylor—not only *can*, but did!"

As a boy, he'd gotten his haircuts at the Moler Barber College (which still exists) for only five cents. The world-famous impresario returned for another haircut for the same price, and tipped the student barber twenty dollars. Of course he did this for a reason: national media and hometown newspapers covered the trimming.

Todd gave Gypsy Rose Lee, the famed stripper and author, a gold cigarette lighter, and saw her forget it on a table at Lindy's restaurant. So the next day he sent her a huge painting with a note: "Let's see you leave *this* on a table at Lindy's."

When Todd arrived for a business conference at Harry Cohn's office at Columbia Pictures, he put his feet up on Cohn's desk. "Take your shoes off my desk," roared Cohn. Todd obliged, removing his shoes, but then placed his stocking feet on the desk. "And take your feet off my desk, too!" Cohn yelled. Todd put his shoes back on and walked out. United Artists, instead of Columbia, got the lucrative distribution rights to *Around the World in 80 Days*.

During their honeymoon at Cannes, Todd explained Elizabeth Taylor's absence at dinner. "She's upstairs crying," he said. "I bought her a [twenty-nine-carat] ring, and nobody noticed it, so she's crying."

With Taylor expecting their child, he said, "Today is my day for humility, real humility." Then he entered his Rolls-Royce, saying: "See? No chauffeur. I drive this car myself. *That's* humility!"

Besides his movie, Todd's legacy was a film process he devised and named after himself: Todd-AO, which united several projectors into one. "Just make certain the picture comes out of one hole," he told the technicians.

When Todd moved his offices to 1700 Broadway, his press agent tried to have the building renamed after his client. Todd even used stationery with that name. But it wasn't until 1966, eight years after Todd's death, that the building was referred to in the newspapers as the Mike Todd Building.

It was an announcement that the building was being torn down.

ANDY WARHOL

(1928–1987)

Pittsburgh native Andrej Varhola Jr., the son of Slovakian immigrants, changed the way the world looks at ordinary objects and was at the center of the Pop Art movement of the sixties and early seventies. His silk-screen paintings of everyday items like Campbell's soup cans and portraits of icons like Marilyn Monroe are today worth tens of millions. His idiosyncratic movies, including one of a man sleeping for five hours, opened new doors of cinematic experimentation. He was a true visionary. He and his troupe of actors and models were at the center of the pop culture of their time.

When the absence of an art pavilion at the 1964 World's Fair in New York was noted, several patrons offered a solution: have ten artists display their works on the walls of the New York State pavilion. Warhol submitted a montage of the FBI's thirteen most-wanted men, but fair director Robert Moses rejected it. So Warhol painted a second canvas, featuring forty-five images of one man's smiling face: Robert Moses.

When the Canadian Pop Art Exhibition was going to display some Warhol works, customs officials deemed the sculptures of Campbell's soup cartons dutiable merchandise, not art. Today they're worth a fortune. Instead, Warhol shipped sculptures to the exhibit: of electric chairs. The officials had no problem with that.

Another of Warhol's underground movies was called *Poor Little Rich Girl*, dealing with a young jobless woman in bed who reads, smokes, makes coffee, and talks with friends.

It grossed $164.

In September 1966, Warhol was asked to make a cameo appearance in an off-off-Broadway play called *The Gas Heart*. He made it clear, however, that he would be unable to recite lines, so he sat atop a ladder in his trademark sunglasses while his lines were recited by one of his film prodigies, Ingrid Superstar.

Early the following year, for another underground movie, Warhol filled a Greenwich Village restaurant with nude patrons. Just before his cameras rolled, however, he realized he'd created a problem: no one had anywhere to carry cash to pay for the meal.

A month later, he came to a party with his current star, six-foot-tall International Velvet, on his arm. There he met comedian Milt Kamen, whose date stood about five feet. "International Velvet," Kamen said, "meet Domestic Cotton."

Warhol and his favorite "superstar" (a word he coined), Viva, attended a party after a performance by the Metropolitan Opera. One bejeweled lady told the offbeat-looking couple, "You're more fun than we are." Viva replied, "We're supposed to be."

Glamour magazine asked several notables their IQs. Jill St. John claimed 162. Famed heart surgeon Dr. Denton Cooley said 135; writer Jacqueline Susann said 128. Truman Capote claimed his was 185. Warhol said his was 84.

Warhol sent a new TV as a birthday gift to an actor friend with a signed card. "His signature is worth more than the TV," the actor said.

Warhol's portraits of Chairman Mao sold at a London art gallery for huge sums, and he explained the advantages of using the communist leader as a subject: "I'm sure he'd refuse a model's fee."

WILLIAM WYLER
(1902–1981)

Not to be confused with Billy Wilder, William Wyler had a forty-five-year career. He had no cinematic signature; he could handle any genre and tell wonderful stories. His best films include *Dead End* (from the stage play written by my godfather, Sidney Kingsley), which helped make Humphrey Bogart a star; *The Westerner*; *Detective Story* (again from a Kingsley play), with Kirk Douglas; and two sweeping epics: *The Big Country* and *Ben-Hur*.

Wyler was a meticulous director, ordering many retakes, long after the actors were convinced he'd gotten several perfect ones. When he was directing *Friendly Persuasion*, one scene required an embrace between Gary Cooper and Dorothy McGuire. After the first try, Wyler called, "Cut! Gary, don't you think you've held Dorothy in your arms too long?"

"Well, gosh, Willie," replied Cooper, "that's true, but then again, I don't smoke or drink."

When Wyler was in Paris preparing *How to Steal a Million*, he stood in front of the Ritz hotel during a storm, trying to get a cab. A driver noticed Wyler's predicament and offered him a lift. The director accepted, then told his benefactor, "Oh, I know you. You're the pianist who made his comeback at Carnegie Hall last month."

"No," the man replied. "I'm a pianist all right, but I'm Arthur Rubinstein. I don't make comebacks!"

"The last time I made anything in Paris," Wyler recalled, "was when I manufactured shirts in a factory. And making shirts isn't so different from making movies."

When Wyler was about to leave his native Alsace for America, his mother gave him a prayer book to keep up his Jewish traditions. Soon after his arrival in Hollywood, he found himself jobless and penniless, and went to a local synagogue, prayer book in hand. He opened it and found a hundred-dollar bill inside, which helped him get on his feet.

In 1953, Wyler was hired to direct *Roman Holiday*, which made

Audrey Hepburn an international star and won her a Best Actress Oscar. Paramount insisted it be filmed on the lot, where Wyler was assured Roman locations would be faithfully reproduced.

"How can you faithfully reproduce the Coliseum?" Wyler replied. "No Rome? Find another director." The movie was filmed magnificently in Rome.

The movie brought so many tourists to Italy that the Italian government awarded Wyler its prestigious Star of Solidarity, Second Class. The Paramount executive who'd wanted to shoot on the back lot? He was honored as well, but his was the Star of Solidarity, *First* Class!

Wyler dined with René Clair, the French director, who noticed Wyler's empty lapel. "You mean you haven't been awarded the Legion of Honor?" asked Clair. Wyler was soon informed that he would be so honored, after which the French consul in Los Angeles gave him a party.

"Why did I win this?" asked Wyler.

"I have no idea," the diplomat replied.

DARRYL F. ZANUCK

(1902–1979)

I f ever a Hollywood studio head were chosen out of Central Casting, he'd look like Darryl F. Zanuck. Born in Wahoo, Nebraska, the three-time Oscar winner wasn't just a cigar-chomping executive seated behind a huge desk. He was a producer and writer and one of the most important figures in the history of the studio system. From his days making the first movie starring Rin-Tin-Tin, the famous German shepherd found on a World War I battlefield, to his Oscars for *How Green Was My Valley*, *Gentleman's Agreement*, and *All About Eve*, Zanuck was a giant. He also produced the star-studded epic *The Longest Day*, among the best movies about World War II. Its budget was reportedly bigger than the cost of the D-Day invasion itself, twenty years earlier.

Zanuck produced or was executive producer of 227 films from 1925 to 1973. They include *The Public Enemy*, *The Grapes of Wrath*, *Tobacco Road*, *The Razor's Edge*, *Twelve O'Clock High*, *Viva Zapata!*, *The Snows of Kilimanjaro*, and *Tora! Tora! Tora!*

In June 1941, Hollywood was busy making war pictures. But before the cameras rolled on *A Yank in the R.A.F.*, starring Tyrone Power, Zanuck, seeking to make the film as accurate as possible, phoned Lord Beaverbrook, the British media baron, asking for suggestions.

"Just keep it as funny as possible," replied Beaverbrook.

In October 1942, Zanuck was the guest of honor at a luncheon on the Fox lot on the eve of his relinquishing all outside interests to devote his full time to the army. He was asked how he had felt accompanying a squad of commandos in a raid along the coast of France.

"When those German bombs were falling, and machine gun bullets came close, I thought, Zanuck, you're the head of a big movie studio. You have a lot of people working for you. You have a wonderful wife and swell kids. You even have French tutors for your children. So what in hell are you doing here?"

In September 1950, Fox was promoting *All About Eve*, and memos between Zanuck and writer-director Joe Mankiewicz were made public. Zanuck had disapproved about one casting decision in the

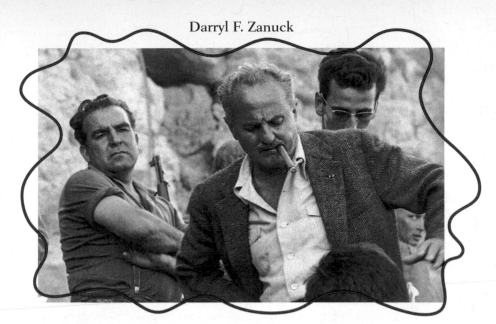

Producer Darryl Zanuck and Paul Anka, *The Longest Day*, France, 1961. Photograph by Sam Shaw.

film, saying the woman couldn't act. "You're right," Mankiewicz wrote back. "But there is nothing you nor I could do that will prevent Marilyn Monroe from becoming a big star."

Orson Welles was cast as a character based on defense attorney Clarence Darrow in *Compulsion*, a fictional account of the Leopold and Loeb murder trial. Zanuck reflected on Darrow's decision to have the case of the young, rich Chicago men tried by a judge, rather than a jury. "That cost me an extra twenty thousand dollars," he said. "Because with a jury, you only have to pay twelve extras to sit in the box. But with only a judge, I'll need to pay 170 extras to fill the courtroom."

In 1963, my father was in Paris and visited Fouquet's, one of that city's fanciest restaurants. Always working, even thousands of miles from home, he table-hopped and chatted with Red Buttons, who'd won the supporting Oscar for *Sayonara*. In another part of the restaurant he ran into Zanuck, who was casting *The Longest Day*. My father recommended Buttons, a former GI, and led Zanuck to Buttons's table. Zanuck offered the role of a paratrooper whose chute gets caught in a steeple, just as the church bells begin to clang. Then he asked Buttons if he'd read Cornelius Ryan's book.

"No," replied Buttons, "but I was in the original cast." Zanuck signed him.

ADOLF ZUKOR

(1873–1976)

He was the founder of Paramount and remained in power for decades, overseeing the studio until 1959 and remaining there for years after.

In 1952, Hollywood was still looking over its shoulder at the new medium of television. In that year, things began to change. The novelty of TV was wearing off. "We went through that phase in movies, too," recalled Zukor. "In the first years, we advertised no stars, no stories. We just opened our theaters and the customers poured in. Then the novelty wore off, and we had to give them stars and good stories. The same's true of TV now."

To lure customers back to movie theaters, Hollywood moved to wide-screen formats like CinemaScope, Cinerama, VistaVision, Todd-AO, Super Panavision, and Superscope, as well as 3-D. Zukor had been an innovator for years, so when the studio was hesitant to buy new 3-D cameras, he suggested they look in the warehouse. There they found 3-D cameras he'd bought in 1933 and used to film *Sangaree*, one of the first movies in that format.

He rejected an advertising campaign for a Mae West movie that referred to it as "lusty entertainment." "It sounds dirty," he said. "But Mr. Zukor," an aide protested, "'lust' comes from the German word 'lustig,' which means lively, joyous." "That may be," replied Zukor. "But if you look at a photo of Mae West, 'lusty entertainment' still sounds dirty."

After the premiere of *The Five Pennies*, the Danny Kaye movie, Zukor said, "I can remember when that was the price of admission, not the title of a movie."

It was Zukor who first put actresses' names in lights above the title. He did it for Mary Pickford, America's Sweetheart. He took her and her mother to dinner at a hotel across the street from a theater showing her new film. When the lights on the marquee came on and they saw Pickford's name light up, they wept.

In 1960, Zukor studied the long shooting schedule for *One-Eyed Jacks*, which Marlon Brando starred in and directed. "It took the same amount of time to make this movie," said Zukor, "as it took the pioneers to settle eight western states."

The following year, Zukor, then eighty-eight, was asked the secret of longevity. "Three rules," he said. "Never dwell on the past. Always take a nap after lunch. And the most important rule: don't go into the movie business."

By January 1966, Zukor was the chairman emeritus of Paramount, celebrating his ninety-third birthday. He posed for publicity shots being kissed by Natalie Wood. After several shots, the photographers called, "Just one more, please."

"Why just *one* more?" replied Zukor, pointing to his cheek for Wood. "Take more. *Many* more!"

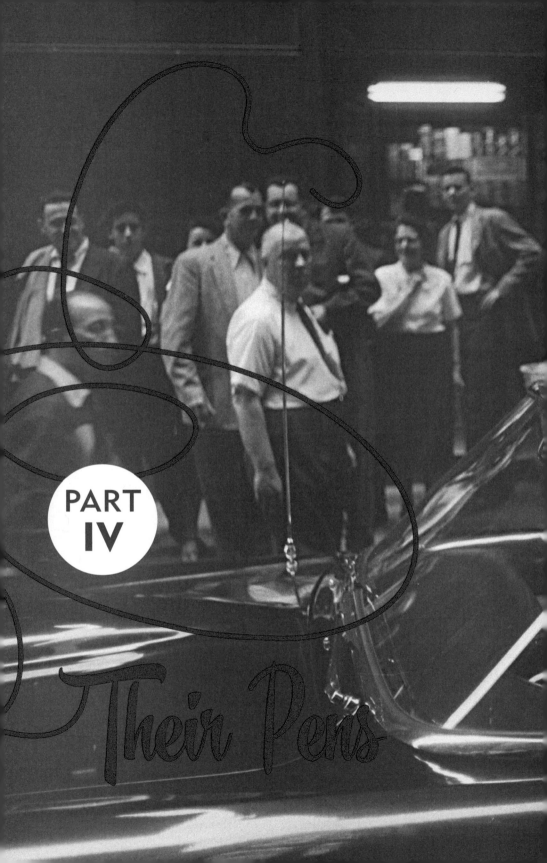

PART
IV

Their Pens

Were Mightier

DASHIELL HAMMETT

(1894–1961)

When Gertrude Stein made her first visit to Hollywood, she asked to meet just two people: Charlie Chaplin and Dashiell Hammett, creator of Sam Spade, the epitome of the hard-boiled detective. Hammett's characters came out of his early work as a private investigator for the storied Pinkerton Detective Agency, beginning in 1915.

After *The Maltese Falcon* became a hit novel, he moved to Hollywood and worked at Paramount as a screenwriter. *The Thin Man*'s Nick Charles, played so suavely by William Powell, was one of his most beloved characters.

By May 1940, Hammett had announced he wasn't writing any more "Thin Man" stories. His newest book, *There Was a Young Man*, he said, would be published by Random House. It was about a man who'd fathered seventeen children. When he added that there were three murders in it, his former publisher, Alfred A. Knopf, reminded Hammett that *he* had the rights to any future Hammett mysteries. Hammett resolved that dilemma by solving the murders halfway though, thus freeing him to have it published by the rival house.

In September 1942, when he was forty-eight and prematurely gray, Hammett, who'd been a sergeant in World War I and been gassed, was initially deemed too thin to serve in World War II. He told the doctor he'd been deemed underweight in the last war but was allowed to serve, and the doctor accepted him, adding, "Just be sure you're not underweight for the *next* war."

Hammett told the army brass he wanted to go to the European theater to fight Nazis. Instead, they sent him to the Aleutians to write radio scripts. The Alaskan weather didn't bother Hammett, oddly. "In the winter, there's snow up to your waist. In the summer, there's mud up to your waist," he said.

To pass the time, he and other GIs built a radio station and broadcast jazz recordings after midnight. The army picked up the broadcasts and suspected they were from a Japanese radio station but could never locate the source.

In the fall of 1945, he told friends he planned to return to the Aleutians someday. "You're the only ex-GI who's ever said that," said a friend.

"That's because all the other guys were walking in the mud with their heads down, afraid of tripping. I walked with my head *up* and saw the magnificent beauty there," he replied.

Hammett once signed a contract for a screenplay, writing the terms on the back of a menu at New York's "21" restaurant. When a sequel was proposed, he asked the producer to provide another menu to compose the new contract.

He was jailed for contempt of court during the postwar Red Scare years for refusing to name the contributors to his Civil Rights Congress bail fund. Assigned to a federal prison, Hammett was sent to work in the prison library, where his books were on the shelves and other inmates would debate him on the technicalities of the crimes in his novels.

In 1957, Peter Lawford and Phyllis Kirk starred in the popular TV series *The Thin Man*. Hammett's name did not appear in the credits, incredibly. After he was blacklisted, he'd had to sell the rights to all his characters to remain solvent.

JAMES JOYCE

(1882–1941)

Joyce's book *Finnegans Wake*, published in 1939, not only confused the critics but drove copy editors mad. Joyce read the proofs, made the corrections, and cabled the corrected version. "That word on page 155 is still misspelled," he wrote. "You spell it: 'Semperexcommunicambiembisumers.' Well, that's wrong. Correct it to: 'Semperexcommunicambiambisumers.'"

Joyce feared thunder and lighting. When his wife persuaded him to take a vacation, he consulted all the charts and records and learned that in Amsterdam, thunderstorms are rarer than in any other city in Europe. So in July 1939, he went there, but after only one day lightning hit the steeple of the church across the street from his hotel.

John O'Hara and Thornton Wilder were in the Stork Club and Wilder asked O'Hara whether he'd read *Finnegans Wake*. "Only the first page," O'Hara confessed, "because I couldn't understand any of it." Wilder then called for a menu, and on its back wrote the first page of Joyce's book, explaining and translating each word all from memory, including such phrases as "mishe mishe to tauftauf thuartpeatrick," "green since devlinsfirst loved livvy," and "sosie sesthers wroth with twone nathandjoe."

In January 1941, Joyce was in occupied France but refused to come to America because he feared traveling on ships. An American visitor saw him in Paris, where Joyce gave him a piano recital, after which his wife got him into a cab. "I'd like to write a book" was her parting message to the American visitor. "It'll be called 'How to Live Twenty Years with a Genius.'" Then, as the cab pulled away, she stuck her head out the window and yelled, "So-called!"

When *Ulysses* was finally cleared by American censors, in 1933, Morris Ernst, the lawyer who had fought for the right to send the controversial book through the U.S. mail, went to Paris and delivered Joyce his first royalty check—for ten thousand dollars. By then, Joyce was nearly blind. He held up the check close to his eyes and was asked what he planned to do with the money.

"Get his eyes fixed," said a friend. "So he'd have to read his own book, which contains words like 'nitshnykopfgoknob,' 'yetagahain,' and 'solongapatom.'"

Producer Collier Young was discussing future projects with William Saroyan and questioned the efficacy of producing films based on difficult-to-understand writers like Joyce and Gertrude Stein. "Bill," said Young, "I like sentences to have a subject and a predicate." Saroyan sighed and said, "That's the attitude which has been holding back literature for five thousand years."

Over lunch in 1960, Groucho Marx asked Brendan Behan if he understood *Finnegans Wake*. Behan sang the Irish song from which Joyce took the title, but said he didn't understand it either. Then he recalled discussing *Ulysses* with Mrs. Joyce, in particular Molly Bloom's soliloquy, the longest sentence ever written in English.

Mrs. Joyce said, "It only proved that he really knew nothing about women."

Groucho is mentioned on page eight of *Finnegans Wake*: "This is the three lipoleum boyne grouching down in the living ditch." When he learned about that, Groucho said, "There's no reason why I shouldn't appear in *Finnegans Wake*. I'm certainly as bewildered about life as Joyce. If Joyce saw us in *I'll Say She Is*, he saw three fellows putting on our act to an indifferent world."

LEONARD LYONS

(1906–1976)

O n his radio show in May 1951, his rival, Walter Winchell, said it was funny that my father risked contempt of court for refusing to reveal his sources for items about the Rosenbergs, the atom bomb spies.

My father hit back: "'Funny' is the word Winchell used. I wonder if Walter would find it as 'funny' if the Senate Crime Investigating Committee were to subpoena him to disclose the full details of how Lepke [Louis "Lepke" Buchalter, the notorious gangster] happened to surrender to *him,* or the sources of *his* sympathetic stories about Frank Costello [another mafioso]."

Late on the evening of May 30, 1940, my father was in a taxicab accident en route to the Stork Club. Cars of that era had no seat belts, so when the door of the cab flew open, he was flung clear. His right hand was slightly injured, but somehow, he pecked out a column. Unable to make his rounds of nightclubs, he pored over inscriptions and personal letters in his library, a literary treasure trove, for the next column.

George S. Kaufman's *You Can't Take It With You* (revived recently on Broadway for the fifth time) had the inscription, "For Sylvia and Leonard Lyons—without whom every line of this play was written." From Dorothy Parker, who'd seen my oldest brother, then five and a half, in the bathtub: "To George Martin Lyons, with deep respect." Another writer sent a book enclosing ten dollars he owed. Other inscriptions quoted were from John O'Hara and William Saroyan. It made for a very unusual column.

He had sources everywhere. For example, financier Bernard Baruch, an advisor to seven presidents, gave a party for Winston Churchill that was officially off the record. The next day, my father had a complete record of Churchill's remarks.

When he was ten, in 1916, he worked as a telephone message boy at Goodwin's drugstore on Rivington Street on New York's Lower East Side. His job was to go to people's apartments and tell them there was a call for them at the only phone in the neighborhood: in the drugstore. For that, he received two cents per call—a pittance today, of course, but back then, only three cents away from enough for a ticket to the local movie theater.

He went to City College ("The Poor Man's Harvard") at night to study accounting, and finished second in his class at the newly formed St. John's Law School. Twenty-five years later, he was admitted to practice before the Supreme Court of the United States, where five of the justices—a majority—waved to him as he took the oath, much to the astonishment of lawyers waiting to plead their cases.

On February 20, 1939, the German-American Bund, consisting of American-born Nazis, rallied at Madison Square Garden. During the many haranguing speeches from Hitler zealots, his name was mentioned as a prominent New York journalist proud of his Jewish faith. Boos cascaded from the rafters. When he learned of that two days later, it made him proud. *Very* proud!

In July 1945, he flew to Germany with the First Army Press Corps and then drove up to the Berghof in Berchtesgaden, Hitler's retreat in the Bavarian Alps. Several color movies of Hitler were filmed there. My father shot a few feet of his own color home movies: urinating on those ugly swastikas (sorry for the redundancy) outside the building and on Hitler's rug.

He also swiped several items, including a silver tray with an eagle, swastika, and the initials "A.H." on it. We'd later use it to serve the most kosher food imaginable: stuffed derma, kreplach dumplings, and gefilte fish. A dinner guest at our home noticed the initials and tried to claim it as his own: Alfred Hitchcock. My father also took one of those old-fashioned prewar phones from Hitler's desk, marked "Eva," and a doorknob.

My father had a special place for that doorknob: he gave it to Jennie Grossinger, the beloved proprietor of Grossinger's, the world-famous resort in New York's Catskill Mountains. She affixed the doorknob to the door leading into the largest kosher dining room in the world.

My father went deep-sea fishing off the Florida coast with FBI director J. Edgar Hoover. "We'd cruised happily through the gentle channel and the day promised to be ideal—until we reached the Gulf Stream," he wrote. "Then, every time I became seasick, Hoover caught a fish—five in all. Hoover would've caught more if I'd eaten a bigger breakfast. We turned for home only after the boss G-Man became ill."

In May 1951, he was called to appear before federal judge John C. Knox under subpoena from the defense attorney for Ethel Rosenberg, the accused atom bomb spy. It was the trial of the most sensational case of espionage in American history.

Defense attorney Emanuel Bloch read aloud to the court all the stories my father had written about the case. Then Bloch asked my father his source, knowing full well he'd refuse to reveal it, as that would violate the first rule of journalism.

While the judge deliberated over the weekend whether to make my father a guest of the government—by ordering him held in jail unless he revealed his sources—two of my father's wealthiest friends, producer-songwriter Billy Rose and Albert D. Lasker, the founder of modern advertising, offered to put up bail. Sherman Billingsley, owner of the Stork Club, and Leo Lindy offered to make him the best-fed inmate in history. Olivia de Havilland, possibly still in her altruistic Melanie mode from *Gone with the Wind*, offered to deliver those meals.

Broadway stars Ethel Merman, Vivian Blaine, Gertrude Lawrence, and Celeste Holm offered to serenade him at midnight across the street from the jail. (Merman's voice alone might've knocked down the jail's walls.) Even William Boyd, TV's Hopalong Cassidy, offered to come to the jail "with guns a-blazin'" and have his horse Topper pull down the bars!

Judge Knox wisely decided that sentencing my father to jail would have irreparable repercussions for American journalism. No sources were revealed.

Late in 1952, he appeared in *Jigsaw*, starring Franchot Tone and Tone's ex-wife Jean Wallace. The scene had to be reshot four times because in between takes, the former spouses kept arguing. One critic wrote, "Portraying himself, Leonard Lyons was unconvincing."

On four successive nights in June 1957, my father ran into actress June Havoc. On the first night, at Sardi's, he introduced her to Governor Joe Foss of South Dakota. The next night, again in Sardi's, he introduced her to New York governor W. Averell Harriman. The third night brought another governor from another state: Robert Meyner of New Jersey. Finally, at the Oak Room at the Plaza, she got to meet Governor Abraham Ribicoff of Connecticut. "You're not a name-dropper," she said. "You're a *governor*-dropper."

When Nixon's "Enemies List" was revealed, my father was disappointed at not being included, saying he'd rather have been on that list than nominated for the Pulitzer Prize (which he was). Nevertheless, he and Nixon had a cordial, if restrained, relationship. One night, Nixon invited my father to his table and introduced him to his companion, a former governor and senator from South Carolina.

"Mr. Lyons used to practice law," Nixon told his friend.

"So did I," James Byrnes replied. "No longer. Because I had to quit private practice when I became an associate justice on the Supreme Court." Byrnes had also been secretary of state—one of the few Americans to serve in all three branches of government.

In December 1955, my father wrote a full column about my younger brother Douglas's first day as a Cub Scout. All the fathers of the newly formed troop were asked to accompany their sons on an outing to the woods adjacent to Palisades Amusement Park in New Jersey. Most of the other fathers knew how to cook. My father, who'd run away from Fresh Air Fund summer camp twice to get back to the hot city tenement where he lived, could just as soon construct a computer.

The fathers were told to bring hamburger meat for a cookout. He complied, sticking it in a *New York Post* envelope. Then it came time to start a fire.

"My son turned his innocent eyes to me and held out two stones," he wrote. "I remembered that in one drawer at home, I have twenty-two lighters—French, British, Swiss, Japanese, American—gold, silver-plated, and one even has a tiny watch embedded; lighters, with inscriptions from Tallulah Bankhead, Johnny Ray [a popular singer of the day], London's Westbury Hotel, El Morocco and The Little Club. I rubbed the stones and finally got a fire going."

Douglas lasted one day. He quit after his pocket was picked.

Back in his element out on the town a few nights later, my father asked Bertrand Russell, the British philosopher, if he was willing to die for his beliefs. "Of course not," he replied. "I could be wrong."

My father never took a music lesson, but played the piano and harmonica by ear. He'd eavesdrop on one of his sisters' piano lessons, then play what she'd played. "I play the piano in El Morocco's Champagne Room," he wrote, "when Arthur Rubinstein or Vladimir Horowitz are there—just to see them shudder." And in a fancy nightclub in Cannes, he played his harmonica, given to him by concert harmonica maestro Larry Adler, "just so the French know what 'My Old Kentucky Home' sounds like."

In January 1960, Jackie Gleason was lunching with his agent at the Four Seasons as my father made his midday rounds. He joined them for coffee. Just then a woman walked by and said, "Oh! That's Leonard Lyons," then stared blankly at Gleason, one of the biggest stars in show business. Gleason glared at her, then said to his agent, "Get me back on TV *now!*"

Early in July 1961, my father and younger brother Douglas lunched at the Beverly Hills Hotel. Seated with his family at a nearby table was Richard Nixon. Even though he knew my father was a staunch Democrat, Nixon sent strolling musicians to their table and had them play "The Sidewalks of New York."

Nixon said his older daughter, Patricia, was beginning to date and needed her parents' permission. "That's a tough decision for a parent to make," said Nixon. "Tougher than what to do about Cuba."

On June 14, 1962, my father was to perform in the parents' show before my school graduation from the Fieldston School in the Bronx. As the only parent with professional "acting" experience, he took no chances. He decided to do a parody of "I've Grown Accustomed to Her Face," from *My Fair Lady*, talking his way through the song the way Rex Harrison did on Broadway and in the subsequent movie.

Now, my father being my father, he went directly to the source: Fritz Loewe, composer of that classic. Not entirely satisfied with Loewe's lyrics, he then sought Frank Loesser, who wrote *Guys and Dolls* and *The Most Happy Fella*. The result?

> *I've grown accustomed to his grades*
> *He kicks a football like a pro*
> *But how often I explain*
> *I want an educated brain—*
> *In science . . . in math . . . my mounting wrath*
> *Was second nature to me now*
> *Like breathing in and breathing out*
> *I tried to tell him his athletics*
> *Only put me in a sweat*
> *That one English honors' cheers, accustomed to my fears . . .*
> *Accustomed to his grades.*

But he wasn't done. For good measure, he sought out Richard Rodgers and Alan Jay Lerner, who were lunching together. Lerner had written the original lyrics, no less. They, too, approved.

Despite the endorsement from four Pulitzer Prize–winning song-writers, incredibly, the amateur parents' committee members were less than enthusiastic! They were miffed when, due to my father's hours, he skipped a rehearsal. "It doesn't fit," he was told.

He got his revenge the next day, however, by printing this story. I recently posted the story on our class website, demanding to know whose parents voted against my father. So far, no one has fessed up.

At the opening of *Funny Girl*, on March 22, 1964, when Sidney Chaplin, playing the gambler–con man Nicky Arnstein, came on-stage the man next to my father whispered, "He was a racketeer."

"Nonsense," replied my father, "he was only a charming rascal."

"I ought to know," said former U.S. attorney, New York governor, and two-time presidential candidate Thomas E. Dewey. "I prose-cuted him."

My father took Randolph Churchill, son of Winston Churchill, to El Morocco. "There's Gene Tunney," said my father. "How'd you like to be in a clinch with Gene Tunney?"

"I'd like that," replied Churchill. "Where is she now?"

"No, it's Gene Tunney, the former heavyweight champion."

"Oh," replied Churchill. "I thought you said Gene *Tierney*."

My father was at LaGuardia Airport, en route to Boston to speak at a UN function. Two women were traveling with him. Another woman recognized him, saying, "I know you from the photo at the top of your column." She didn't recognize the women with him: Luise Rainer, a two-time Academy Award winner . . . and Eleanor Roosevelt!

In December 1955, a troupe of performers traveled to Russia to perform *Porgy and Bess*; my father and Truman Capote accompa-nied them as "group historians." The first day there, my father met a young American journalist who spoke fluent Russian. She served as his guide, rather than one provided by the Soviets.

Capote, who had no love for my father, was jealous of his having an American guide. In fact, in my father's hotel room, Capote com-plained, talking directly into the chandelier, suspecting the room was bugged, which indeed it was. The Ministry of Culture took in-terest as well, until my father explained to Capote in a loud voice so the Soviets could hear him clearly, "My interest in this young woman is purely amorous."

That woman, incidentally, was Priscilla Johnson, who trans-lated the writings of Svetlana Alliluyeva, Stalin's daughter, and later, Marina Oswald. She is, in fact, the only person ever to interview both Marina's husband, Lee Harvey Oswald, and President Kennedy.

One night in mid-January 1969, just before he would lose his job, a man said to my father, "Now that I'll be free, I may just go around with you on your nightclub tour." It was LBJ.

That October, my younger brother Douglas accompanied our father on his rounds. At P. J. Clarke's, a friend called them over and immediately he asked my brother, who'd just graduated from Berkeley, why he didn't cut his long hair. "Mr. Ford, when I testified in front of Senator Phil Hart's subcommittee opposing capital punishment, I trimmed my hair a bit, but I assure you, it was clean and neat—as it is tonight," Douglas replied.

Later, my father asked him how he knew the man's name, as they hadn't been formally introduced.

"Pop, you said his first name: Edsel," said Douglas.

In early December 1969, my brothers and I gave our parents a surprise thirty-fifth wedding anniversary party. Sammy Cahn, who wrote songs like "High Hopes" and "Love and Marriage," wrote a welcome song to the tune of Rodgers and Hart's "The Lady Is a Tramp":

> *I'd say this party is richly endowed*
> *I've never faced such a fabulous crowd*
> *The guests of honor I'm sure must be proud*
> *'Cause each one of you's a champ*
> *You think the* New York Post *is terrif*
> *Then thank owner Dorothy Schiff*
> *She's cute. Got loot*
> *Just beware should her little foot stamp*
> *But still the lady's a champ.*

The rest of the song rhymed every guest, from Supreme Court Justice William O. Douglas to Betty Comden and Adolph Green, Mary Hemingway, and John Steinbeck. Then Ethel Merman, Broadway's greatest musical star, arose and sang a tribute song, including these lyrics:

> *He walks alone; eleven thirty each night he's at Sardi's*
> *After twenty-three parties*
> *When it's half after two, he's not half through*

Then Comden and Green sang a song, and my mother joined Sammy Cahn in a parody of "The Man That I Marry."

One summer in Paris, my father visited France's naval headquarters. He had his movie camera, but encountered no problem with security. Later that day, a friend took him to a fashion show at a department store. There he *was* stopped and had his camera confiscated.

NORMAN MAILER

(1923–2007)

One August night in 1960, Shelley Winters was in Downey's, the bar that was an actors' hangout, and recalled Mailer coaching her for her first important screen role, *A Place in the Sun*. Mailer told her which pages of the Theodore Dreiser source book to read in order to form her characterization. He never thought she'd get the part or survive in Hollywood. She did. Her two Oscars proved that.

Mailer was interviewed for a book on Marilyn Monroe. Most writers usually asked, "How could a genius like Arthur Miller fall for a dumb blonde like Marilyn?" But Mailer's reaction was "Why would a wonderful girl like Marilyn marry a second-rater like Arthur Miller?"

In January 1969, Mailer lunched at the Algonquin and said he'd finally finished his movie *Maidstone*. He'd edited it down to three hours. It had originally run forty-five hours, "and it took me a week to watch it," he said.

In his quixotic campaign for mayor of New York, teamed with columnist Jimmy Breslin, Mailer said, "I'm running on many platforms—from black power to Irish self-righteousness."

In September 1969, he was aboard a small boat in Provincetown harbor. Suddenly a whale moved into the area, showing only its huge back above the water. Mailer said the danger didn't worry him: "I just kept thinking this would be a wonderful way for a novelist to die."

In May 1971, Mailer was considering revising his play *The Deer Park* to add an orgy scene onstage. He ultimately rejected that suggestion, which had come from a producer, saying, "I want the audience to pay attention to the words."

Before debating a women's liberation group, he said, "Dear Lord, at least give me a tie."

He somehow dominated Gore Vidal on *The Dick Cavett Show*. Vidal, who won most of his debates, said, "It was like being in a cage with a tiger."

Late one night, Mailer called my father at home. He was calling for legal advice, remembering that before he began writing The Lyons Den, my father had practiced law. Mailer had just stabbed his wife and wanted legal advice. He referred to my father as "the three a.m. lawyer."

ARTHUR MILLER

(1915–2005)

He was one of America's great postwar dramatists, with *All My Sons, The Crucible, Death of a Salesman, A View from the Bridge*, and *After the Fall*, among the most important American plays ever written. Miller won a Pulitzer Prize and two Tony Awards; his commentaries on vital social issues revolutionized American drama. He also wrote the screenplay for *The Misfits*.

A few weeks after *Death of a Salesman* opened to rave reviews, Miller found a sealed envelope in an unused desk drawer where it had been lying for several years. On the face of the envelope he'd written the name of an abandoned project: *Death of the Salesman*.

Soon after Miller and Marilyn Monroe married, they bought a three-hundred-acre retreat in Roxbury, Connecticut. It would be Monroe's first real home after a turbulent childhood in foster homes and two failed marriages. Miller filled in a lake and planted two thousand trees, and they hired the greatest architect in the world—Frank Lloyd Wright—to design the house. Before it could be built, however, Wright died and the Millers divorced.

In January 1958, *A View from the Bridge* premiered in London. Monroe planned to wear a red satin off-the-shoulder sheath gown to the event, but a friend advised against it. "The theater will be filled with intellectuals," she explained, "so you should wear black."

"You have to wear black for intellectuals?" Monroe asked. "Well, my husband Arthur is an intellectual. And he likes this dress." She wore it.

In May of that year, Miller was inducted into the National Institute of Arts and Letters. John Mason Brown, the critic and author, was one of the presenters and later said, "Seeing Mrs. Miller in the audience gave a new dimension to the speeches. If you didn't care to listen, you could always look."

Not surprisingly, Miller was a voracious reader: "I'm sure I'm the only person who read *War and Peace* standing in a crowded New York City subway."

A Russian theater delegation visited New York in September

Arthur Miller and Marilyn Monroe, New York City, 1957.
Photograph by Sam Shaw.

1959 and was entertained at the home of Lee Strasberg. The act-
ing teacher had been asked to invite Tennessee Williams, Thornton
Wilder, and Arthur Miller. Miller accepted the invitation and asked,
"Do you think they'd mind if I brought my wife?"

Miller went with his wife to Philadelphia to receive an award and
made a speech at the annual dinner of the American Friends of Hebrew University. He began writing his speech on the train. Monroe
observed him write and said, "Look. Just like Abraham Lincoln writing the Gettysburg Address!"

"I was not a good student," Miller recalled. "I went to elementary
school in Harlem where, if you spoke to your neighbor, the teacher
would grab both of you by the hair and bang your heads together.
That was the level of instruction."

During the Depression, Miller wanted to buy a bicycle: "I went
to the bank and took out my savings—twelve dollars—and I bought
that bike. The next day, the government closed all the banks. That

was the smartest financial move I ever made." The bike was stolen the following week.

Miller was invited by the Soviet Union to attend a Stanislavsky festival. He replied, "I'll attend when you pay me the royalties you owe me."

In November 1964, Harold Clurman was directing Miller's *Incident at Vichy*. Miller interrupted him when he was speaking to an actor. Clurman cut him off, saying, "You do the writing. I'll do the directing!"

EDWARD R. MURROW

(1908–1965)

E dward R. Murrow created and defined broadcast journalism. In an age when newspapers and newsreels were the primary news source, radio began to intrude. Murrow's "This . . . is London" broadcasts during the German Blitz of 1940 riveted millions of American listeners and became the standard for concise reporting.

He later transferred those talents to television, where his *See It Now* (a successor to his *Hear It Now* radio show) forged the way for today's 60 *Minutes*, *Nightline*, 20/20 and other shows. It was his exposure of the paranoid bullying tactics of Joseph McCarthy, the junior senator from Wisconsin, that led to McCarthy's downfall.

Shortly before his death in 1946, H. G. Wells, author of *The War of the Worlds*, *The Time Machine*, *The Invisible Man*, and *The Island of Dr. Moreau*, spoke with Murrow about the dawn of the nuclear age. He said, "I refuse to regard the destruction of this minor planet as a major catastrophe."

In October 1950, Murrow visited his hometown in North Carolina, where a friend offered him a deal in a business whereby Murrow would be his own boss. By then a CBS vice president, Murrow declined, explaining, "A long time ago, I learned that when you're your own boss, you're working for a man who really isn't concerned about your welfare."

In November 1954, there were rumors afloat that Murrow would soon leave CBS. In denying them, Murrow said, "As my father, a locomotive engineer, put it, I'm still on the rails and on the payroll. I have no intention of leaving and no appetite to do so, unless the air force develops their rocket to the moon."

By March 1955, television had entered millions of homes and was beginning to eclipse radio as the primary mass medium. Murrow, however, was still appearing on both, and on his radio show expressed his views on various subjects. Robert E. Sherwood, the playwright and former Roosevelt speechwriter, called Murrow and told him he agreed with the views he expressed on the radio.

Murrow was elated. "In these times," he said, "what a novel and refreshing thing it is to get a reaction from a radio show!"

In December 1955, my family and I appeared on *Person to Person*, Murrow's other TV show. Although he disliked doing a non-news program, it was very popular and profitable for CBS. It helped pay the bills for the news shows.

We heard Murrow's voice coming out of a speaker in our apartment, which had been torn apart by a score of technicians. A thick group of heavy black wires snaked around every corner. On our terrace overlooking Central Park, an antenna was aimed south, toward the Empire State Building, and synced up with another antenna there—1950s technology.

My father explained to Murrow his daily routine and showed Murrow his collection of books inscribed with drawings and dedications from artists and presidents, and told stories about them.

As soon as our fifteen minutes (of fame?) were over, we heard Murrow saying to Kim Novak in Chicago, "Kim, we can see you but we can't hear you. We may switch back to the Lyonses." Out came the basketball, more books, whatever we could ad-lib on that scripted show, which gave half hours only to former presidents. Finally her audio returned.

In May 1956, Murrow was in Israel, deep in the Negev Desert, interviewing Prime Minister David Ben-Gurion for *See It Now*. When the show ended, Ben-Gurion said, "You'd have had a much better show if you and your crew had arrived thirty-five hundred years ago. Down there," he said, gesturing, "not many miles away, is Mount Sinai, where Moses received the Ten Commandments. What a TV interview *that* would've made!"

When Murrow left CBS to head the Unites States Information Agency, his partner and coproducer, Fred Friendly, assured him there'd "always be a door for you here at CBS." Soon after that, CBS moved its headquarters from Madison Avenue to Sixth Avenue. Sure enough, leaning next to a large screen in the viewing theater in the new headquarters was Murrow's old door, with his name on it.

The producers of *Person to Person* once asked Murrow if he would ever consent to be the sole guest on the program.

"I'd never let you people into my home," he replied.

CLIFFORD ODETS
(1906–1963)

lifford Odets changed the American theater. His *Waiting for Lefty* and *Awake and Sing* sounded the protests of the Depression years. Odets wrote with poetic beauty. Instead of anger and nastiness he wrote with hope. That's why his plays endure.

Odets, who was my older brother Warren's godfather, began as an actor with a minor part in *my* godfather Sidney Kingsley's Pulitzer Prize–winning play *Men in White* in 1933. The cast included Elia Kazan, Luther Adler, and the acting teacher Sanford Meisner.

Years later, Odets and Kingsley reminisced about the play and Kingsley recalled one actor adding an extra line opening night: "Say, what are we, Boy Scouts?" Odets admitted he was that actor.

Odets was an explosive actor. He'd strike his head against a wall, bang his fist on a piano, or hurl a billiard ball at a wall. The acting teacher Stella Adler (sister of the aforementioned Luther) would have none of this.

"Clifford," she warned, "if you become a great actor, no one will ever speak to you."

He boasted that he could write a Broadway hit whenever he wanted to and did, twice, with *Golden Boy* and *The Country Girl*, both of which became memorable films.

"An American playwright shouldn't be afraid of being corny," he said. "Corn is part of American art. If an artist isn't a bit corny, then he's imitative of the Old World."

Early on, he bought paintings by Utrillo, Soutine, Modigliani, and Klee. Had he held on to them, they'd have been worth millions, but he lost many in a divorce settlement.

In May 1938, Odets's father was preparing a catalog advertising the mattresses he sold in his Philadelphia store. He turned to his son to create a phrase that would entice people to buy his restful products. His son wrote, "Civilization Harasses People."

One night, Odets and his wife Luise Rainer went with my parents to several nightclubs. At one, she asked for a pencil and drew a heart with an arrow though it. Inside the heart, she wrote, "L.R.-C.O."

Billy Rose (left), my father, and Clifford Odets (right).

Two weeks later, they filed for a divorce.

Odets wrote my father from London a little more than a year before World War II: "This town's got me dizzy. The cars go on the left side of the street, the steering wheels are on the wrong side of the cars. The only thing I'm sure of is that the U.S.A. is on the right side of the Atlantic."

In 1939, Odets said he'd been talking with Sinclair Lewis about acting in a two-man show, highlighting the different Americas they represented: Odets from Jewish ancestry, born in Philadelphia and then moving to New York; Lewis descended from pioneers, born in tiny Sauk Centre, Minnesota.

The show was never produced, because Odets insisted on playing the midwesterner.

In going through his old photos a few months before his divorce became final in January 1940, Odets found a picture of himself and his wife taken at their home on Long Island. A third person had been cut out of the photo, a neighbor summering there that year: Albert Einstein.

When the producers of an anti-Nazi movie approached Odets with an offer to return to acting, John Garfield, who'd starred in

Odets's *Awake and Sing* and *Golden Boy*, advised, "We leave the writing to you. You leave the acting to us."

Odets's play *Night Music* was criticized because its style seemed too similar to William Saroyan's. The writing style of Saroyan's *The Time of Your Life* was also criticized because it was too much like Odets's. Odets then received another offer to return to acting, in the title role of a new show called *The White-Haired Boy*—based on the career of William Saroyan.

In September 1942, Odets was working on a screenplay about the life of George Gershwin, *Rhapsody in Blue*, which would star Robert Alda (father of Alan). He would dine late, go home from the studio lot, read the papers, and go to bed. When local gossip columns reported he'd been dating the sultry Hedy Lamarr, Odets sighed. "Oh, boy," he said. "How I envy myself."

In 1955, Odets wrote a screenplay for a movie about the movie industry called *The Big Knife*, which starred Jack Palance and Ida Lupino. The studio asked Odets to suggest some quotes to use in the ads. He submitted only one: "Better than *On the Waterfront*."

In December of that year, Odets received three expensive pipes with a cryptic note: "In appreciation for what you have done for H.M.G." Odets didn't know anyone with those initials, so he checked the store where the pipes had been purchased.

The gift was from Her Majesty's Government, in return for work he'd done on a British wartime documentary for which he had refused payment.

He described certain actresses merely as "runaways. They all ran away from home to come to New York and act," he said. "The fact that you're an actress may make you run away from home. But the fact that you ran away from home doesn't make you an actress."

When Sammy Davis Jr.'s musical version of *Golden Boy* was being prepared for Broadway in 1960, the producer finally got the last page of the script from Odets, adapted from his straight play. It read, "THE END."

In 1961, Odets was living on the same block in Los Angeles as violinist Jascha Heifetz. They dined together every other week, exchanging lists of ideal dinner conversationalists. But they realized this was a bad idea; Heifetz listed film executives while Odets listed musicians.

As he lay dying in August 1963, Odets clasped his friend Lee Strasberg and asked, "Can you give me one word for God?"

EUGENE O'NEILL

(1888–1953)

Every summer when I take the Cross Sound Ferry from Orient Point, New York, to New London, Connecticut, en route to see my beloved Boston Red Sox, I pause at a huge rock on the Connecticut side with a metal sculpture of a little boy sitting atop it. Next to it is a photo of a young Eugene O'Neill, seated on that rock in 1893. It was erected to mark the centennial of his birth. Though born in a New York hotel room (today the building is a Starbucks, a block north of Times Square) he spent his boyhood summers in New London.

Today O'Neill's works like *Ah, Wilderness!*, *Anna Christie*, *Desire Under the Elms*, *The Hairy Ape*, and *Long Day's Journey into Night* are among the most performed American dramas. *The Iceman Cometh* returned to Broadway recently, for the fourth time. O'Neill won three Pulitzer Prizes and the 1936 Nobel Prize.

A visitor to O'Neill's home was told by his host to come into the bedroom. "I want to show you something I'm proud of," said O'Neill. He rummaged through drawers, pushing aside his Pulitzer Prizes for *Strange Interlude*, *Beyond the Horizon*, and *Anna Christie*. "Oh, here it is," he said, pulling out a certificate from a local sailing club proclaiming his status as an able-bodied seaman.

In the months after World War II, there was a shortage of white shirts to dress the troops. O'Neill was unaffected, however. In France in 1932, he had bought a lifetime supply of shirts and suits.

When *The Iceman Cometh* opened, John Mason Brown, critic for the *Saturday Review*, decried its four-hour length. But he was furious when his magazine cut fifty-three lines from his review.

Although written in 1941, *Long Day's Journey into Night* wasn't performed until November 1956, three years after his death. It was one of the plays he'd stored in the attic. The Theater Guild wanted to produce it, but O'Neill told them, "I'm not interested in having my plays produced anymore." Nor would he permit revivals of his other plays. "In these times," he said, "the minds of men are too confused to think."

A friend told him she'd enjoyed *The Iceman Cometh*. "But frankly, I thought it was too long."

"Tell me," replied O'Neill, "when you eat at a restaurant and have wonderful food, do you complain that the service had taken too long?"

O'Neill didn't permit cuts in his plays, some of which ran four hours or more. When one producer begged him to cut twenty minutes of *The Iceman Cometh*, O'Neill defiantly threatened to write another hour of dialogue.

He did, however, agree to shorten *Ah, Wilderness!* during its out-of-town tryouts—he eliminated the intermission between the third and fourth acts.

When O'Neill met fellow playwright S. N. Behrman, who wrote twenty-six plays and twenty-eight screenplays, they agreed they had lost interest in the theater. But when they asked each other's immediate plans, both said they were working on new plays.

O'Neill never attended a performance of any of his plays until one night in December 1946, when he was persuaded to see *The Iceman Cometh*.

At one point O'Neill noticed the woman sitting next to him lean forward to hear a pivotal part of the dialogue. Later, he said, "I knew it was well done because that woman next to me never leaned back."

Long Day's Journey into Night was autobiographical, and he used "Tyrone" as the family name for all the characters. The O'Neills had been ruling chieftains of County Tyrone in ancient Ireland. When *All God's Chillun Got Wings*, about an interracial marriage, opened, starring Paul Robeson, O'Neill received a threatening letter from the Ku Klux Klan. He returned it after writing on the bottom, "Go to Hell!" and signed it, "Gene Tyrone O'Neill."

Jimmy Durante once took his father to a long O'Neill play, after which the elder Durante said, "Talk, talk, talk. Allatime talk."

E. G. Marshall starred in the 1946 original production of *The Iceman Cometh*. He bought a copy of O'Neill's collected works, wrote an inscription to himself on the flyleaf, and signed it "Eugene O'Neill." Then he showed it to the author, who added, "This is a genuine forgery," and signed it.

O'Neill's last words were "Born in a hotel, and dammit, died in a hotel."

DOROTHY PARKER
(1893–1967)

In an age when few women writers reached prominence, Dorothy Parker was a successful author, screenwriter, poet, and oft-quoted wit. She's best remembered for being a charter member of the legendary Algonquin Round Table, the daily lunch that gathered the wittiest writers in New York at the famous old hotel.

Her Hollywood years with her actor-writer husband, Alan Campbell, were her most productive. They wrote the screenplay for the original *A Star Is Born*, earning an Oscar nomination. She also worked on *The Little Foxes*, published short stories and poems, and covered the Spanish Civil War. A victim of the Hollywood blacklist, she kept writing and today is revered as one of the great American writers.

She finally agreed to visit a friend who'd been continually telling her how cute her three-year-old son was. As soon as Parker arrived, the child began bawling. He finally settled down and began building a tower with his blocks. Then the mother went into the kitchen, accidentally knocking it over. This, of course, initiated another tantrum. Exasperated, Parker said to the boy, "Listen, you little shit! That's life."

Actress Lucille Watson, who had been in the movie *Watch on the Rhine*, said to Parker, "I hear so much about your beautiful farm in Pennsylvania. What can you tell me about it?'

Parker's response was succinct: "Want it?"

Then Watson asked her about her one-liners. "Is there one for which you're most famous?"

"Yes," sighed Parker. ""Men seldom make passes at girls who wear glasses.'"

Watson nodded, then said, "Go on . . ."

Parker went to the circus and saw the star attraction, Gargantua the gorilla and his bride, Toto. After watching the two tossing food at each other, Parker said of the "newlyweds," "I give it six months."

Her husband was commissioned in the Army Air Corps and trained at a flight school in Miami. On graduation day, Parker wired him from New York, saying she'd fly down to attend the ceremonies. When she didn't arrive, he learned her flight had been grounded en route, but the airline didn't know where. He wired her in New York and it was forwarded to her in Raleigh. Then came a telegram from Parker using four words to explain her whereabouts: "Nothing could be finer . . ."

Asked about people attributing witty remarks to her, she said, "I guess *I* started it."

In October 1946, she learned her friend Lillian Hellman was writing a "prequel" to *The Little Foxes* and asked Parker to come up with a title. Parker wired: "Call it 'Part One.'"

In 1950, she remarried her ex-husband, from whom she'd been divorced for three years. She surveyed the guests at their second wedding ceremony and said, "People who haven't spoken to each other in years are here. Starting with the bride and groom!"

During the period of Hollywood blacklisting, two government men arrived to question her about alleged communist affiliations. Her two dogs were romping around the living room, ignoring her commands to stay. When one of the agents asked about her influence on suspicious committees, she replied, "Influence? *My* influence? See for yourself. Look at my dogs. I can't even influence *them*!"

S. J. PERELMAN

(1904–1979)

One New Year's Eve, my wife and I were invited to Woody Allen's party for two hundred of his "intimate" friends. He greeted us in black tie and sneakers. One of the guests, standing quietly in a corner, was S. J. Perelman, one of America's great men of letters.

Perelman frequently wrote pieces for *The New Yorker*, as well as books and screenplays. He wrote two Marx Brothers films, *Monkey Business* and *Horse Feathers*, and won the Best Adapted Screenplay Oscar for *Around the World in 80 Days*.

In December 1946, Perelman and caricaturist Al Hirschfeld decided to take a round-the-world cruise. Hirschfeld was famous for his beard, while Perelman was clean-shaven. Every day, Hirschfeld would clip a little off his beard, while Perelman stopped shaving. By the time they reached Paris and presented their passports, Hirschfeld was clean-shaven, Perelman bearded.

In April 1959, Perelman was asked his age. "I'm fifty-four," he said proudly, then added, "but I can pass for a man of seventy-five." When asked about his financial status, he said, "Let's put it this way: if a beautiful young woman were to use my name at Cartier, she'd find it meaningless." Asked about working as a freelance writer, he said, "It's about halfway between an unemployed actor and a pensioner."

In June 1964, he inscribed a copy of his book *The Rising Gorge*, "Before they made Sid Perelman, they broke the mold."

Three years later, he was in Asia looking for a white Siamese gibbon. He'd been painting his barn in Pennsylvania and noticed that its width was just enough for a white Siamese gibbon to swing.

"I looked up at the heavens for a sign," he said, "and the good Lord answered: 'Holiday.'" So off he went, writing an article for *Holiday* magazine.

En route, he stopped in London and toured Scotland Yard. Perelman asked his guide if he'd noticed any sorts of patterns in criminals.

"Yes," the inspector replied. "Brown-eyed men are often bigamists."

NEIL SIMON

(1927–)

e is *the* most successful playwright since Shakespeare, with more hits on Broadway than anyone has written or in all likelihood *will* ever write. Oscar winner George Kennedy starred in a production of *The Odd Couple* and told me, "Simon writes words meant for actors with a rhythm which precedes the punch line. The actor can easily build up to it."

Simon was a member of the legendary writing team for Sid Caesar's various shows, along with Larry Gelbart (later to create the TV series *M*A*S*H*), Carl Reiner, Mel Brooks, and later, Woody Allen. A Murderer's Row of comedy writers!

Based on the Broadway success of *Barefoot in the Park*, which ran for 1,530 performances over four years, Simon's agent Irving "Swifty" Lazar signed a deal with Paramount: six hundred thousand dollars for the movie rights to Simon's next play. Simon hadn't written a word. Paramount got their money's worth: the play was called *The Odd Couple*.

When it opened in 1965 and quickly became Broadway's hottest ticket, Harry Truman sent a message that he was anxious to get tickets. "The trouble is," Simon said, "if I get 'em for Truman, I'd have to get them for *every* former president."

In June 1967, the movie version was filming in New York. Simon marveled at the huge expense of making a movie, and sighed, "This one all started when I heard two men arguing over pot roast."

Simon based *The Odd Couple* on his brother Danny and his friend Ray Gruber. The real-life postscript of the show came when Gruber reconciled with his wife, but Neil Simon was barred from their home.

In one scene in *Promises, Promises*, the hero stands outside Madison Square Garden, unable to enter. Eventually a doorman tells him, "The Knicks lost in double overtime." Red Holtzman, the Knicks' coach, was in the audience opening night and sent Simon a note: "Can't you change that line to 'The Knicks *won* in double overtime'?"

Early in 1966, with the arrival of critics on TV, Simon was asked about the new custom of allowing critics to attend previews.

"Oh, I don't mind," he replied, with tongue in cheek. "Pretty soon, they'll be looking over my shoulder while I'm writing!"

In January 1972, Simon was given the Cue Entertainer of the Year award. Accepting his plaque, Simon said, "I think they really voted for Neil *Diamond* and contacted me by mistake. Or else Diamond was busy."

In the play *The Prisoner of Second Avenue*, the character later played by Peter Falk in the movie adaptation mentions a deceased psychiatrist called Dr. Pike. A real-life Dr. Pike insisted his name be eliminated from the script, so Simon changed the name of the character to Dr. Carp.

Simon was asked if he was the sole investor in his plays because he wanted complete control. "No," he replied. "I do it just out of greed."

"I've got no ambitions to write drama," he said. "Strangers meeting me for the first time are usually disappointed because they think being a comedy writer, I'll be funny. The truth is, I can't tell a joke. I prefer to put my gags down on paper."

Lou Jacobi and Jack Gilford were starring on Broadway in *The Odd Couple*. Before one performance, they made New Year's resolutions. "I'll try to get Simon to write a play for me," said Gilford. "If not a play, then a sketch. If not a sketch, then an act. If not an act, then a scene. And if not a scene, then a memo!"

Jacobi's resolution? "To stop taking roles away from Paul Newman."

GERTRUDE STEIN

(1874–1946)

When she was at Radcliffe, Stein studied under philosopher William James. Her final exam was given on a lovely spring day. In no mood to be stuck indoors, she wrote on her test, "Dear Professor James, I'm sorry but I do not feel like an examination paper in Philosophy."

"I understand," he wrote on a card—and gave her an A.

There were many who didn't understand her writings, but her work made her world famous. In Woody Allen's magnificent *Midnight in Paris*, Kathy Bates captures her persona. That movie showed her apartment in Paris as a gathering spot for artists and writers.

In 1936, Charlie Chaplin told Stein about his new movie, *Modern Times*. He related the story and acted out some scenes. She listened carefully, then said only, "Oh. It's a comedy."

In the fall of 1939, Stein was anxious to return to America, but she'd been warned that her arrival wouldn't be front-page news because of the outbreak of the war. Her previous return on July 22, 1934, had been relegated to the middle of the papers because that day John Dillinger, "Public Enemy Number One," had been shot and killed by Melvin Purvis of the FBI in an alley outside Chicago's Biograph Theater.

Best known for her line "Rose is a rose is a rose is a rose," she suggested her publisher release a cheap edition of her writings. His telegram replied: "Sorry sorry sorry. No sale is no sale is no sale."

In July 1940, France had been occupied by the Nazis for two months. Stein, who'd been left alone by the Germans, sent her publisher in New York the manuscript for her next novel. Vichy French censors didn't even bother to read it. Once they saw the byline, they knew it would be useless to translate and try to decipher her complex writings.

A day before Hitler declared war on the United States, Stein was cloistered in an old house in an unoccupied area of France. She and Alice Toklas avoided arrest by the Gestapo because a friendly policeman had given them identification papers good for four years, then persuaded them to move to the country. The Nazis were occasional visitors to Stein's apartment on the Rue Christine and took her silverware and linen, ignoring her paintings by Picasso and others.

Toklas shared Stein's love of Paris, saying, "Living in Paris you become your true self or you disintegrate."

Someone asked Stein why she got so much free publicity. "Because I have such a small public," she replied.

During the twenties, Pablo Picasso was visiting Stein at her salon in Paris. He'd written a poem, thinking he could translate his artistic talents from one medium to another. Picasso read it to Stein. All she said was, "Pablo, go home and paint."

Stein's brother Leo then took Picasso into another room. He locked the door and demanded, "Pablo. What makes you paint the way you do?" When Picasso emerged from the room, he complained to Miss Stein, "Leo asks things he has no right to know."

A few years after Stein died, in 1946, Hemingway took my father on a tour of the city of his youth. My father suggested they visit Toklas. "No, I don't like her," Hemingway said. "She was so cruel to Gertrude, particularly at the end." But Thornton Wilder explained, "Alice was merely the dragon protecting the treasure."

The last time my father saw Toklas, he asked her if there was anything she wanted from America.

"Yes," she replied. "A plumber. Send me a plumber!"

He'd met Toklas in Paris in 1945, just after V-E day. She told him she was born in Seattle and moved to Paris because "Paris is the Seattle of Europe."

When she toured the country lecturing, she never permitted anyone to introduce her. "An introduction," she said, "would be silly. Besides, everybody knows who I am. That's why they came."

In December 1970, New York's Museum of Modern Art had an exhibit of Stein's Picasso collection. My father had seen them just after the war when she invited him to visit. The collection included a painting resembling Cézanne's *Three Oranges*. She had owned the original Cézanne, but her brother Leo had quarreled with her and taken it away with him. Picasso heard about the incident and consoled Stein by painting a copy of the Cézanne.

GORE VIDAL

(1925–2012)

He was perhaps the most acerbic, witty writer of his generation, a brilliant debater and wise observer of the world situation whose writings are still relevant.

After the 1956 Democratic convention named Adlai Stevenson and Estes Kefauver as the party's presidential ticket, Vidal reflected on being related to two senators who'd been considered possible vice presidential nominees: Senator Albert Gore Sr. of Tennessee and Senator John F. Kennedy of Massachusetts. He advised them how to get over their disappointment: "When you get up in the morning, look in the mirror and try to name the vice presidents in order. See how far you get."

Vidal wrote a teleplay about his grandfather, Senator Thomas Gore of Oklahoma, the only blind senator in U.S. history. "I wrote a small role for myself in it," he said, "but as I kept rewriting, my role kept getting bigger. I must be out of my mind, because I can't act!" The title role of *The Indestructible Mr. Gore* was played by William Shatner.

In April 1960, Vidal announced he planned to run for Congress, admitting he thought himself "only a two-hit playwright" (referring to *Visit to a Small Planet* and *The Best Man*). He ran, helped in the campaign by friends Eleanor Roosevelt and Paul Newman, and won more votes than any Democrat in a Republican district. But he lost, and called his campaign "a victorious defeat."

When she learned of the election results, Lillian Gish told Vidal, "I'm sorry you lost, but don't feel badly. We already have many good congressmen, but so few good playwrights."

In December 1961, Vidal was asked to be the godfather to the daughter of Paul Newman and Joanne Woodward. It was the fourth time he had been so honored. "Always a godfather," he said, "never a god."

In June 1962, Vidal lunched with Tennessee Williams and they discussed their writing. Williams said, "Gore, I write with my heart, and you write with your head. The two of us together would make a fine writer."

When his racy book *Myra Breckenridge* was published, Vidal loved to see people sneaking looks at the daring tome in bookstores. His father, a retired general, called him after reading it, sighed, and said, "Gore, I hope you haven't made a mistake writing this."

Vidal said he tried to avoid people who discuss the weight they've recently lost. "I have a theory," he said, "that Nature assigned a constant amount of weight in the world, just to keep the grass down. Someone loses, another gains. It's 'Vidal's Law of Constant Weight.'"

In August 1966, Vidal was working on the screenplay for *Is Paris Burning?* but got little cooperation from the French government, since officials were reluctant to remind the world they were conquered by the Germans in just forty-three days.

Vidal retaliated by writing a mock script in which the French gave a party in 1940 and invited the Germans to send their troops into France for a visit.

His play *Weekend*, which opened early in 1968, criticized President Johnson. At intermission during a preview, one patron walked up the aisle muttering, "That Gore Vidal must be the nastiest person in the world." She was accompanied by a Secret Service agent, since it was Lynda Byrd Johnson. The play closed after twenty-one performances.

In December 1968, Vidal received a letter from "The Office of the President-Elect, Richard M. Nixon," whom Vidal loathed. The letter inside bore only the date, "Mr. G. Vidal, Barrytown, NY," and Nixon's signature.

Vidal wondered, "Could it be that the thirty-seventh president of the U.S. has *nothing* to write to me?"

Among several homes, he had an apartment on the Avenue Foch in Paris. That apartment had been occupied over the years by Sophia Loren, the Paul Newmans, the Gregory Pecks, William Holden, and Kim Novak. The elderly landlady was asked where she went when the apartment was rented out. "I have a room next to the kitchen," she replied, "and an island in the Mediterranean."

Vidal, distantly related to the Bouvier family through his stepfather's remarriage to Jacqueline Bouvier Kennedy's mother, was asked about Senators Robert and Ted Kennedy. "The future looks bright for them," he replied, "if not so bright for the country."

Late in 1967, Vidal was again named a godfather to the child of some friends, then learned they'd been married only a few months. "I almost became an illegitimate godfather," he said.

After he'd moved to Italy in 1967, Vidal dined aboard the yacht of a wealthy friend off the coast of Sardinia. When told that the owner of the vessel flew the Panamanian flag, Vidal challenged him: "I'll give you ten thousand dollars if you can whistle just one bar of the national anthem of Panama."

Vidal boarded a flight in Frankfurt bound for New York. Also aboard was future New York senator Pat Moynihan. They began speculating on who'd get top billing if the plane went down.

"You'd be the lead story in the *Harvard Crimson*," Vidal speculated, "while I'd be headlined in *The New York Review of Books*." Their conversation became moot when the flight stopped in London and the Rolling Stones boarded.

In November 1966, Vidal discussed the movie adaptation of his Broadway hit *The Best Man*. Someone had proposed Ronald Reagan for a leading role. "I don't consider him believable as a viable national candidate," said Vidal.

Vidal met a New York hostess who said she'd like him to paint her portrait, because she admired his portraits of many of her friends. "You have me confused with the artist Vidal-Quadras," he corrected her. A few weeks later, they met again and she said, "I'd love to see your famed palace in Tangier."

"Wrong again," said Vidal. "That's Yves Vidal who lives in that palace." Then, sure they'd meet again and she'd confuse him with Vidal Sassoon, he said, "But I'd love to cut your hair sometime."

In May 1970, his new play was *Drawing Room Comedy*, which he announced was being produced under strict terms: no rewriting or attending any rehearsals. "I want to be treated as if I were the best of dramatists—that is, dead."

It never made it to Broadway.

THORNTON WILDER

(1897–1975)

*T*he Skin of Our Teeth and Our Town are two of the finest American plays, continually performed. In many high schools, the novel *The Bridge of San Luis Rey* is required reading. Wilder was a three-time Pulitzer Prize winner. Ruth Gordon won the Tony Award for her performance in his play *The Matchmaker*, which turned into the musical *Hello, Dolly!* Both came from his earlier play *The Merchant of Yonkers*.

Even before *Our Town* was completed, producer-director Jed Harris got a look at the unfinished longhand manuscript. He tore it from the author's pad and brought it to actor Frank Craven, who would originate the role of the Stage Manager. Harris said he could cancel the actor's contract if Craven didn't think it was the finest role he'd ever been offered. Craven agreed with Harris, ignoring Hollywood friends who'd advised him to stay in California. When the play won the Pulitzer Prize, Craven wired them: "You see the advantages of *NOT* reading a completed script!"

Wilder was always a stickler for facts, and checked each detail of *Our Town*. One, however, slipped through, and he learned about it only after the show had run for eight and a half months on Broadway and went on tour. One line reads, "May 7, 1901—a Friday."

In Boston, someone called out, "No! That was a Tuesday!" And so it was.

After Wilder starred in a special performance of *Our Town*, he confided he'd made two other errors in the script. One referred to string beans in May—out of season—and the other concerned the longitude and latitude of the fictitious Grover's Corners, New Hampshire. The coordinates he gave in the play placed the town somewhere in Antarctica.

The Soviet government refused to allow *Our Town* to play in the USSR, believing it was "too much in praise of capitalism."

John Beal acted in two productions of *Our Town*, in which actors planted in the audience ask questions of those onstage. One night a paying customer, unaware that the questioners were plants, called out, "What do you think of the Republican Party today?"

Thornton Wilder (center) with my father (right) at
Circle in the Square Theater, New York, October 2, 1952.

Beal responded from the stage, "This play is set in 1901. My character can't comment on the politics of today."

One night my father took Wilder on his nightclub rounds. It was a dreary evening, with not much copy for the column. Wilder then quoted a line from his play *The Matchmaker*, in which a lady makes her first visit to the Harmonia Gardens and says, "To think this is going on in hundreds of places in New York every night, while I sit at home darning stockings."

Wilder's friend Gertrude Stein, who influenced his writing, hosted him in Paris and asked him how she could become rich. He pointed to the paintings she'd purchased years before from young, unknown artists: a Picasso for twenty-five dollars, and a Matisse for a hundred dollars.

Wilder destroyed all unfinished works lest others complete them after his death, saying, "The wastebasket is the writer's best friend."

TENNESSEE WILLIAMS

(1911–1983)

One of the most acclaimed playwrights of the twentieth century, Tennessee Williams wrote such plays as *The Glass Menagerie*, *A Streetcar Named Desire*, *Cat on a Hot Tin Roof*, *Sweet Bird of Youth*, and *Night of the Iguana*, which flourished on Broadway and regional theaters and continue to do so today. Many have been turned into memorable films.

Before he came to New York for the first time, young Thomas Lanier "Tennessee" Williams had only seen three plays: *Ghosts*, *Hedda Gabler*, and *The Barretts of Wimpole Street*. But by then he'd already written eight full-length plays and twelve one-acts.

In September 1950, when Warner Bros. was preparing its publicity campaign for the screen version of *The Glass Menagerie*, a studio executive told Williams he didn't like the title, and suggested that *The Gentleman Caller* would've been an easier title to promote.

"That's what I called it when I first tried to sell it as a screenplay," he replied, explaining that when no one seemed interested, he changed the title and adapted the screenplay for Broadway, where it ran for fifteen months.

All of Williams's characters were based on real people, often his family members. His first hit was *The Glass Menagerie*, in which his mother was the basis for the mother character. When she saw Laurette Taylor's portrayal, she had only one comment: "Her accent is poor."

Late in 1952, William Inge invited Williams to a preview of the movie version of Inge's *Come Back, Little Sheba*. Williams arrived at the screening with Eli Wallach, costar of his hit *The Rose Tattoo*. But at the door a young woman with a clipboard and a list of invitees stopped them. "Where are you from?" she asked. "From Mississippi," replied Williams, born in Columbus, Mississippi.

When she refused to let him enter, Wallach said, "Let's go, Tennessee."

"You mean you're Tennessee Williams?" the astonished girl asked. "Why didn't you *say* so?"

Tennessee Williams, New York, 1975. Photograph by Sam Shaw.

"You asked where I was from, not who I am," he replied.

In April 1955, Williams was at work on *Orpheus Descending*. It was a rewrite of *Battle of the Angels*, which had been produced in Boston in 1940.

"No man ever wrote for the theater with less foreknowledge of it," he said. "My conversion to the theater arrived as mysteriously as those impulses which center the flesh at puberty."

He knew his old play had to be rewritten. It had come into conflict with local censors, and in the closing scene, the smoke pots onstage went wrong and the smoke hit the audience. "I remember all the little ladies with black velvet ribbons about their throats, gasping for breath." The play closed immediately.

One of Williams's unproduced plays was called *Stairs to the Roof*, about a shoe store clerk who sets off on a rocket to colonize a new star. The bizarre idea came to him while he was working as a clerk for the International Shoe Company. For several weeks, he forgot to deliver a fifty-thousand-dollar order to his employer, who finally told him, "Williams, I'm only keeping you on here out of curiosity. I want to see what you'll do next in life. Just what *will* you do next?"

During the run of *Period of Adjustment* in 1960, Williams lamented the fact that he'd soon turn fifty and called that "the old age of youth." "No, Tennessee," replied costar James Daly. "Consider yourself about to enter the youth of old age."

Williams went to see the 1950 movie version of *The Glass Menagerie*, which starred Gertrude Lawrence in the role created on the stage by Laurette Taylor. Asked to compare the two performances, Williams said, "I was in Rome one time and saw a Madonna and Child by Raphael, then another painting with the same name by Botticelli. Same subject. Different artists. Both classic."

In September 1955, Williams arrived in Paris and, as usual, checked into a small hotel, because he disliked meeting people who recognized him. In the lobby he met William Faulkner, there for the same reason.

When asked if there were any messages in his plays, he said, "I have no messages. I'm only interested in the hearts of people. Not their minds."

One day in March 1961, Williams lunched with friends discussing knighthoods. "I'd love to be named a knight," he mused, "if only to be called—just once—'Sir Tennessee.'"

Later that year he announced that he'd stopped going to his

psychiatrist, explaining, "He was meddling too much in my private life."

That fall, he and William Inge went to see Harold Pinter's play *The Caretaker*. Walking out of the theater, Williams said, "Well, Bill . . . should we give up?"

Williams explained the disadvantage of his fame. People recognized him everywhere, making it impossible for him to learn about their true nature, as he once could. "I'm going to shave my mustache, change my name back to 'Tom,' and enjoy some anonymity," he said.

When a friend told him she knew everything about someone, Williams corrected her: "Nobody knows everything about anybody."

A stranger recognized Williams on a New York street and said, "I like your plays, Mr. Williams. They're obscure and demented." "So am I," he replied.

A director asked him to write a play for Lincoln Center's new theater in 1962. "My plays are a bit far out," Williams warned. The director assured him it'd be all right. "But how do you know I'm not insane?" replied Williams. "What has sanity got to do with writing?" the director replied. "We just want your play."

Williams and Arthur Miller once drafted an angry letter to a critic who'd written that he believed some of their dialogue was written by Elia Kazan, who'd directed both *A Streetcar Named Desire* and *Death of a Salesman*. Budd Schulberg joined the table and said that the critic had made the same charge about his Kazan-directed screenplay for *On the Waterfront*. "Save space for my signature," he added.

Shelley Winters, who starred in *The Night of the Iguana*, later starred in a revival of *Three Sisters*, occasionally ad-libbing dialogue. "Can you imagine," she asked Williams, "*me* rewriting Chekhov?" "You used to do that to my play every night," replied Williams.

Winters then asked Williams, "What do you think when you hear about your plays being performed all over the world?" Williams replied, "Just the royalties. *Royalties!*"

He offered to write a play for Greta Garbo and she agreed, with one condition: "Just don't make me a man and don't make me a woman." The play was never written.

In April 1972, Williams was to give a speech honoring Charlie Chaplin, but when he arrived at the stage door, the guard didn't recognize him. "But this is Tennessee Williams," the guard was told. A blank stare ensued. Someone nearby who'd seen what was happening said, "This is Tennessee Ernie Ford." "Why didn't you say so?" asked the guard, letting him pass.

Asked to compare his plays to others', he declined. "I don't believe in competition. I only judge my work against my other work. Rivalry, not money, is the root of all evil."

PART
V

Larger

GEORGE ABBOTT

(1887–1995)

One of my earliest memories is attending the ticker-tape parade welcoming General Douglas MacArthur back from Korea on April 20, 1951, just nine days after President Truman fired him for disobeying orders. Although I was only six, I remember our perfect view from a building on Wall Street and everyone tossing confetti—except one tall, elegant gentleman. He was Broadway's greatest producer, George Abbott. Then sixty-four, Abbott, who would live to be 107, was tossing fliers advertising his current Broadway shows out the window. Always the producer. Of forty-five plays!

His first Broadway appearance was in *The Misleading Lady*, in November 1913. After acting in a few plays, he began writing and directing as well. And he never stopped.

Abbott told an Actors Studio cast member that in one scene, his character was to walk across the stage and say his line. "That's fine," said the actor, an obvious student of the Method, "but what's my motivation?"

"Your job," replied Abbott.

When an actor died, his friend asked Abbott to produce a copy of the actor's last contract. "Some day, he may be disinterred, and people will know what he did," said the friend. Abbott obliged and delivered the contract, but first boosted the late actor's salary by three hundred dollars a week.

An actress once told Abbott she was quitting the business to devote herself to marriage and motherhood. "I often think," the producer said, "that marriage is an institution designed to absorb every bad actress."

Actors always addressed him as "Mr. Abbott," even if they'd worked for him for years. Stanley Prager, who was an actor and later a TV director, told Abbott, "We're expecting a baby, and if it's a boy, we'll name him after you. He'll be called Mr. Abbott Prager."

Guests joked about Abbott's reputation for being extra-careful about his money. Actress Fran Warren, asked if she believed a magazine article calling Abbott a "penny-pinching millionaire," said, "I don't know. I didn't finish reading it. Mr. Abbott borrowed my copy."

An artist came to Abbott for advice. "I want to try my hand at writing a play," he said. "It's been coming along well, but I always seem to have trouble getting my characters offstage. What should I do?"

"Simple," replied Abbott. "Just have 'em say 'G'bye.'"

He was asked to speak at the Smithsonian Institution one year on October 31. "As for me being asked to speak in a museum on Halloween," he laughed, "feel free to draw your own conclusions."

In January 1974, Abbott, then eighty-six, was asked about how long he'd keep planning productions in advance. "At this point," he said, "I haven't planned any projects past ninety."

BERNARD BARUCH

(1870–1965)

Bernard Baruch was one of the most interesting men of his time. He was self-made, respected all over the world, and one of the wisest and most influential Americans in history.

By the time he was thirty, he'd made a fortune on Wall Street and bought a seat on the New York Stock Exchange. He served as an advisor to half a dozen presidents, starting with Woodrow Wilson. He loved to joke, "I gave them lots of advice, but none of them ever took it."

During World War I, Baruch, serving as chairman of the War Industries Board, received a visit from Broadway producer John Golden, who was upset that the theater had been placed on a list of unnecessary luxury items.

"The War Industries Board insists on including Broadway with perfumes and ice cream sodas," Golden protested. But that night, Golden attended the theater with President Wilson and Wilson's doctor, who'd taken away all the president's medications and instead prescribed frequent visits to the theater.

The next day, Golden phoned Baruch and told him about the president's new regimen. Broadway was quickly removed from the list of luxury items.

He had this bargaining advice: "Only act strong if you *are* strong. It's not enough to be right; you have to *look* right."

Although he lived in a twelve-room Fifth Avenue apartment and had a private box at Belmont racetrack, Baruch never bet more than two dollars on a horse, no matter the odds.

Two screenwriters wrote a biography about Baruch and wanted to send it to him for approval. Not knowing his address, they did know that in Washington, he always occupied the same park bench. So they addressed it to "Mr. Bernard Baruch, Park Bench, Number 1, Washington, D.C."

Three days later came the reply: "No!"

During the Second World War, Baruch was testifying before a legislative committee when an eager young lawyer asked, "Mr. Baruch, you're a very rich man, aren't you?" Baruch nodded and smiled.

"How much are you worth?" the lawyer continued. "One hundred million? Ten million? Only one million?"

"Young man," the frustrated Baruch replied, "the next time you say *only* a million, try *earning* a million."

Baruch defined being rich as "having one more dollar than you'll ever want to spend."

In New York he opened two "branch offices": a bench in Central Park and another a few feet away for private conferences.

Baruch attended a meeting in London of diplomats from countries leaning toward Soviet influence. "This isn't like a card game," he said. "Once you're in, there's no turning back. No second hands."

In December 1951, Baruch was invited to be the guest at a university event the following April. "I'm now eighty-one," he replied. "Long-term plans aren't wise for me to make. I suggest you contact me next March . . . "

On a sunny day in 1952, a friend called him at home and asked what he was doing. "I'm just looking out my window, overlooking Fifth Avenue in this magnificent city, recalling how I came here seventy years ago with no money, living in a two-room tenement. And I marvel at how wonderful America is," he replied.

Eleanor Roosevelt asked Baruch for advice on something. "My mind tells me one thing, but my heart tells me another," she said. "Always go with your heart," he advised. "If that turns out to be a mistake, you won't feel as badly."

Two financial writers asked Baruch about the future of the economy. "Don't worry," he said and pointed to their fancy hats. "As long as this country can manufacture such expensive hats, our economy will prosper."

On Baruch's desk stood a green cat made of china, a gift from his mother, who had told him, "The Lord won't forget you if you keep this on your desk."

Then his father pulled him aside and said, "Just the same, son, keep hustling."

When John L. Lewis, head of the United Mine Workers' Union, retired he posed on Baruch's famous park bench in Washington. "John," a friend warned him, "you're mistaken if you think just sitting on Baruch's famous bench makes you a statesman."

Former heavyweight champion Bob Fitzsimmons taught Baruch how to throw a punch, and he used that skill to flatten a cabdriver who'd insulted him. He was seventy-nine at the time. He continued to lift weights for six more years.

In 1960, Baruch turned ninety. His living legend status was solidified that same year when he began receiving mail addressed simply to "Baruch, U.S.A." Even at that age, he never stooped, continuing to stand erect in his six-foot-three-inch frame. He stood as erect as in his days playing baseball at City College of the City University of New York, where he hit a game-winning home run and suffered an ear injury that would forever affect his hearing. Today, Baruch College at CUNY bears his name.

GENERAL OF THE ARMY OMAR BRADLEY

(1893–1981)

One warm Friday afternoon in the spring of 1965, I was in my junior year at the University of Pennsylvania and headed home for a weekend in New York. At the track level of the Thirtieth Street Station, I remembered the exit in New York was at the front of the train. So I began walking ahead.

I noticed a figure off in the distance. Soon I saw his famous face: General of the Army Omar N. Bradley, commander of American forces on Omaha and Utah Beaches in Normandy, France, on D-Day, June 6, 1944.

He knew my father, so I introduced myself and we had a cordial chat. I'd give anything to recall what we discussed. I do recall his unassuming nature, given his place in the world—the reason he was known as the GI's General.

He was one of only five modern generals of the army with five stars. (The others: MacArthur, Eisenhower, Marshall, and Arnold.)

Late in the war, Bradley attended a ceremony in Belgium where General George S. Patton received the Croix de Guerre from a French general. Patton whispered to Bradley, "What do I do if he kisses me?"

Bradley replied, "Kiss him back—hard!"

As he led troops inland after the Normandy landings, the fighting was so close that Bradley was often awakened by the rumbling of tanks outside his quarters, not knowing whether they were German Panzers or American Shermans.

"So I went back to sleep," he told my father. "If my battle plans were working, they'd be our tanks. If not, I'd done my best and there'd be nothing else I could do."

Bradley attended a postwar party at which a colonel pointed to his own decorations and cynically said, "Any one of these, plus a nickel, can get me a ride on the New York City subway."

Bradley pointed to a Soviet ribbon he'd won and replied, "But *this* ribbon can get me a subway ride *without* a nickel in any *Moscow* subway."

In May 1948, Bradley gave a speech at the Waldorf. In the elevator taking him up to the banquet hall, four soldiers stepped inside as protection and drew their guns. Startled, Bradley said, "Put those things away. I'm scared of 'em."

In May 1953, Bradley was succeeded as chairman of the Joint Chiefs of Staff by Admiral Arthur W. Radford. The night the announcement was made, Bradley presented a plaque to Rosalind Russell for her performance in the movie *Never Wave at a WAC*. Afterward he announced, "This is the right time to let you know, as they say in your business, that I'm 'available and will travel.'"

Early in the Soviet-American cultural exchange program, when Bradley commanded American troops in Berlin, his counterpart was Marshal Ivan S. Konev. The marshal invited Bradley to a party where Bolshoi dancers performed, and Konev shrugged: "Oh, just a few girls from the glorious Red Army."

Then Bradley invited Konev to a party where the world-renowned violinist Jascha Heifetz performed.

"Oh, that's just one of our GIs," said Bradley.

Bradley addressed the 1960 U.S. Track and Field team, departing for the Rome Olympics. He stressed the importance of sportsmanship while striving for victory.

One of the track stars came late and asked a teammate what General Bradley had said.

"Oh, that we're to go over there and beat the hell out of those Russians—but nicely," said the teammate.

Prominent attorney Louis Nizer represented MGM in a long, bitter litigation. When he presented his huge bill for legal services, Bradley, a member of the MGM board of directors, examined it and said, "Holy mackerel! D-Day didn't cost this much!"

By 1966, Bradley was chairman of the Bulova Watch Company, and one perk was a chauffeured limousine. But the general, then seventy-two, put the car and driver at the disposal of the Bulova car pool while he walked thirty blocks to work and back each workday.

In October 1967, Bradley toured South Vietnam with a reporter for *Look* magazine. The reporter said, "General Bradley is amazing. If you don't watch him, he'll be carrying *your* bags. And he's always on time. Makes sense, I guess, since he headed the Bulova Watch Company."

PRESIDENT CHARLES DE GAULLE
(1890–1970)

The proud, tall, ramrod-straight symbol of resistance to German occupation during World War II, he was an inspiration to his imprisoned countrymen while in exile in London and became France's preeminent postwar leader.

Shortly after the liberation of France, de Gaulle met with President Roosevelt, who asked him in French, "What shall we talk about?"

"Anything but recognition of the new French government," said de Gaulle. "We are 'recognized.' The people of France recognize us. We are Frenchmen."

In September 1945 he had a long discussion with French deputies, who complained, "The Third Republic is heading for ruin." De Gaulle disagreed. "There have been 112 French governments in the past fifty years of the Third Republic. One more won't matter."

In February 1947, a British writer who'd known him before the war visited de Gaulle, then in temporary retirement. He urged him to return to run for election. "It will be perfectly all right if I don't," said de Gaulle, who knew better. "After all, if Joan of Arc hadn't been burned at the stake, she'd have married well. I'm already married."

De Gaulle was asked if he distrusted journalists. "That's true," he said. "Even the best journalists have a sadistic streak; they prefer to denounce liars rather than praise truth-tellers."

When a candidate for his cabinet was described as a "horror" by another minister, de Gaulle interceded. "There are so many people in the world to whom that description could apply," he said, "maybe *they* have a right to be represented in the government too."

Former French premier Pierre Mendès-France described de Gaulle in July 1960, comparing him to Alfred Hitchcock: "He loves suspense and adores enigmas."

On a visit to San Francisco, de Gaulle was served a glass of California wine. He took a sip and said disdainfully, "Didn't they know I never drink tea?"

In October 1961, a French politician reluctantly agreed to accept a government post he didn't really want, on the condition that he be granted a top rank in the Legion of Honor. De Gaulle said, "It's amazing how many people there are who will barter honor for honors."

In a heated discussion with de Gaulle, Prime Minister Pompidou kept repeating, "Mon Dieu. Mon Dieu. [My God. My God.]" De Gaulle interrupted: "You may call me 'General.'"

Madame de Gaulle made a visit to the Louvre and admired the Rubenses, the Tintorettos, the *Mona Lisa*, and some El Grecos. "Charles," she said later, "we need these for our home."

"I know," he replied. "But I'm so busy, how could I take even half an hour to paint?"

Soon after the Kennedy assassination, de Gaulle, who marched in the funeral procession up Pennsylvania Avenue, met with LBJ and gave him this advice: "For now, go nowhere. See no one until your hand has steadied the ship of state." During that visit, de Gaulle watched some television coverage, then wondered, "How is it possible to govern America properly when the government doesn't control television?"

In November 1966, he tried to have unions share responsibility with employers for running businesses more efficiently, explaining, "We live in a world where the organized imbeciles will always have the upper hand over the nonorganized intellectuals."

One Parisian asked another: "What do you think of de Gaulle?"

"There is no de Gaulle," replied the second Frenchman. "I'm an atheist."

"After I retire," de Gaulle said in 1969, "Frenchmen can enjoy the delights of anarchy."

SUPREME COURT JUSTICE WILLIAM O. DOUGLAS

(1898–1980)

ouglas served longer and wrote more opinions than any other justice. He was a staunch liberal whose view of the world and the law still inspire people today.

During his confirmation hearings before the Senate Judiciary Committee in 1939, one senator who opposed him thought the seat on the Supreme Court should be filled by a westerner "for regional balance." After all, the senator said, Douglas's last voting address had been New Haven, Connecticut, where he was teaching at Yale Law School. Then the senator added, "Besides, he cusses a lot," to which Douglas's sponsor, Idaho senator William Borah, replied, "That *alone* proves he's a westerner!" That and the fact that he was born in Maine Township, Minnesota, and grew up in Yakima, Washington. He was overwhelmingly confirmed, 62–4, taking the seat of Justice Louis Brandeis.

Among Douglas's most prized possessions was a clipping from Yakima's Republican newspaper. He had once worked for that paper as a young man before hopping a freight train to New York to study law. When the Securities and Exchange Commission was created in 1934 to be a regulator of Wall Street transactions, it was bitterly opposed by conservative Republicans. When Douglas was named one of its commissioners, the newspaper ran a streamer headline: "Yakima Is Not to Blame for This."

Soon after his confirmation, Douglas visited Professor Thomas Powell, his old constitutional law professor. "Don't forget, Bill," the teacher said to his former pupil, "I once laid down the law to *you*."

"And don't *you* forget," replied the newest member of the Supreme Court, "I now lay it down to *you!*"

A lawyer wanted to be admitted to practice before the Supreme Court. "I'd move for your admission," replied Douglas, "but I've never been admitted to practice here!"

Another lawyer addressed the court by saying simply "Gentlemen," rather than the customary, "If it please the Court."

"I'll settle for 'Gentleman,'" Douglas whispered to fellow justice Robert H. Jackson.

Justice William O. Douglas (center), with my parents at the Stork Club.

Some of Justice Douglas's former students were reminiscing about their old teacher. They recalled a time when they asked him about a point of law. "I could give you the correct answer now," he replied, "but you'd quickly forget it. Instead, go to the library and you'll find the proper textbook."

The teacher noticed their sly looks at one another. "I know what you're thinking," he laughed. "That I don't know the answer. Here's what I'll do: I'll write it down and show it to you when you return from the library." He did. They did. He was correct.

Douglas vacationed in remote locations in the far West, sometimes fifty miles from the nearest telephone—the farther away the better. During the summer of 1942, a forest ranger who had the nearest phone reported to Douglas that Washington was trying to reach him. Back then, phone connections were poor and communication had to be made via relays involving five people. The message from Washington was confidential, and all five had to pledge not to reveal that a special session of the Court was being held to decide the appeals of the convicted Nazi would-be saboteurs of Operation Pastorius.

In the summer of 1943, Douglas had a cabin in the Oregon wilderness and invited a wealthy friend from the East to join him there. "I'll bring my butler, too," said the friend. "That's how we do things in the East."

"No need," replied Douglas. "Out here, in my cabin, *I'm* the butler. That's how we do things in the West."

Back in Washington for the first Monday in October 1945, Douglas was driving through the outskirts of the city when a motorcycle cop pulled him over for speeding. Not recognizing him, the cop said, "What's the matter, pal, don't you know the law?" Douglas, who has participated in countless dissents during his time on the Supreme Court replied, "Officer, if that's a rhetorical question, I can get a lot of witnesses who'll agree with you!"

In late March 1947, snow covered the two-mile Alexandria, Virginia, paper route of young William O. Douglas Jr., making bicycle riding impossible. But the readers on the route received their newspapers anyway; the justice himself delivered them from his car.

In August 1948, Douglas was at his Oregon vacation cabin when a messenger arrived telling him he was wanted on the telephone. So Douglas mounted his horse, rode several miles to the general store, picked up the phone, and heard, "This is Harry Truman." The president then asked Douglas to be his running mate.

"I can't discuss this here," replied Douglas, eyeing the townspeople sitting within earshot around the cracker barrel. "I'll call you back." He found a car, drove to a hotel in Portland, locked himself in one of the rooms, and called the president to tell him he'd remain on the Court.

In June 1949, Douglas was in Chicago and attended a broadcast of *Don McNeill's Breakfast Club*, a popular network radio show that ran for thirty-five years. When he was called up to the stage, McNeill asked a woman in the audience to guess his profession:

"A truck driver?" she guessed.

On a flight to Israel, the captain told his copilot they had an associate justice of the U.S. Supreme Court on board. "Gee," replied the copilot, "I just signed a new lease on my apartment. There are some questions about it I'd have liked to ask him."

Justice Douglas addressed Israel's Institute of Technology in English, but ended with three sentences in Hebrew, translated as "Strength to Israel. Freedom to all. Peace to the world."

On the same trip, he gave the commencement address at the

American University in Beirut. He referred to his alma mater, Whitman College in Walla Walla, Washington, which got a laugh. Later he learned that city's odd name translates into Arabic as, "By God, By God."

At Lebanese customs, the agent asked if he was carrying out any caviar, which was prohibited. "I guess I forgot to get some," Justice Douglas joked. The guard took him aside and slipped him a can, saying, "Here. I took this off the previous passenger."

When his horse rolled over him in 1949, breaking seventeen ribs, a friend wired, asking about his condition. Douglas replied, "The horse will recover." Just before he left Yakima to recuperate in Tucson, Douglas was given a resolution from the Yakima Chamber of Commerce stating that all the publicity Yakima received made the Chamber "damned happy the accident took place here."

In late 1951, he visited India and set a record with his 250-mile trek through the Himalayas in just fourteen days—six days faster than local army officers. He crossed six mountain passes on foot, one 13,200 feet high, and made the rest of the long trek on horseback and yak.

Back in Washington, the Burmese ambassador watched a session of the Court and invited Douglas to visit his country. "Any special reason why I'm the one you invited?" asked Douglas. The ambassador explained that Douglas was internationally known not only as a distinguished jurist but also as an outdoorsman, conservationist, and explorer.

"We have a fifteen-thousand-foot mountain which has never been climbed," he continued. Douglas asked why no one had attempted to reach the summit. "Head hunters," the ambassador replied. "But I've made an arrangement with them about your head," he said. Soon afterward, Douglas announced his next trip would be to Burma (now Myanmar) to climb that mountain.

In November 1952, a friend, looking for Justice Douglas in New York, quickly found him at the Yale Club and explained, "I knew he'd either be there or Tibet."

In March 1953, a country doctor in a dusty town in Arizona was about to leave his office when a bearded, ill-clothed man entered. The doctor treated the man's foot injury. Then he began filling out the necessary forms: "Name?" "William O. Douglas." "Residence?" "Washington, D.C." "Occupation?" "This week, hunter. Other times, associate justice of the Supreme Court of the United States."

Winchell took a swipe in his column at Justice Douglas for postponing the execution of atomic spies Julius and Ethel Rosenberg. For good measure, he criticized my parents for naming my younger brother Douglas.

"Parents usually name their children after people they deem truly great," my father hit back in print. "We named our fourth son 'Douglas.' Winchell named his boy 'Walter Winchell Jr.'"

In 1955, Douglas went to climb the Elburz Mountains in Iran. He was accompanied by Josephine Black, daughter of Douglas's colleague Justice Hugo Black. She'd just graduated from college and her father's graduation gift was granting permission for her to accompany Douglas.

A New York cabdriver recognized Douglas and asked, "You're a wise man. Do you know what the phrase 'The past is prologue' really means?" Eager to hear the driver's answer, Douglas said he didn't know. "Well, Mr. Justice," the cabbie said, "All it means is 'You ain't seen nuthin' yet.'"

In January 1963, Irving R. Levine, NBC's courtly Moscow correspondent, was in the Soviet city of Tashkent and noticed a tall, slim man whose face and bearing looked familiar. He introduced himself: "Irving R. Levine, NBC News." The other man replied, "William O. Douglas, Supreme Court."

ABBA EBAN

(1915–2002)

Born Aubrey Solomon Meir Eban in Cape Town, South Africa and raised in London and Belfast, he studied at Cambridge and eventually became involved in the creation of the state of Israel in 1948. He served in the British army in Egypt and what was then Palestine. Fluent in ten languages, Eban served as vice president of the United Nations General Assembly and was a scholar and author of half a dozen books on the history of the Jewish people. Eban is surely Israel's greatest orator and foremost citizen never to become prime minister.

In April 1957, Eban asked my father if he'd visited any Arab countries on a recent trip.

"Yes," my father replied, "I was in Libya."

Eban expressed surprise, since those with Israeli travel stamps on their passports were usually barred entry. My father explained that on the Libyan visa form, under "Purpose of Visit," he put "Accompanying Sophia Loren"—Loren was in Libya to film *Legend of the Lost*.

Eban addressed students at the New School promising, "to do my best to answer or do my best to think of a way to evade the question."

Asked how Israel defeats the large armies of the enemies that surround it, he said, "We have a lesser talent for being pushed into the sea than we have for pushing others into the sand." He also decried the need to maintain the status quo in international relations: "A great danger to world peace lies in excessive normality."

Eban became Israel's ambassador to the UN at thirty-three, and said, "One of the advantages of such an early start is that it enables you to obtain seniority without the disadvantages of decrepitude."

After one of his speeches at the UN, Eban's wife remembered how different he was before they were married. She asked her father what he thought of the young man. "How can I tell?" her father replied. "He never says a word!"

Before departing his diplomatic post in New York, Eban said,

"Ambassadors cannot join a labor union; we're not considered workers, because we don't work with our hands. Furthermore, we ambassadors could never call a strike, because if *diplomats* were to go on strike, who would notice?"

Speaking again at the New School, Eban noticed familiar faces in the audience. "This proves," he told them, "that man doesn't always profit from experience."

In April 1959, he resigned as Israel's ambassador to Washington to return home and run for office. At a farewell dinner for him, he was heaped with high praise. He responded by saying, "As a diplomat, I used to disassociate myself from such praise. But now that I'm a politician, I can't afford to regard any praise of myself as excessive."

In November 1962, Eban was back in New York fund-raising for Israel's scientific research programs. He told a group of potential donors, "Science is not a sacred cow. Science is a horse. Don't worship it. *Feed* it!"

One day, after a meeting of diplomats in New York, Eban was mistakenly handed a smaller version of his black Homburg hat. It was American UN ambassador Adlai Stevenson's hat, stamped "A.E.S.," whereas Eban's was stamped "A.S.E." When the two diplomats exchanged their hats, Stevenson said, "I'm relieved. For a moment there I thought this job had given me a swollen head."

While speaking at Princeton, Eban noticed Albert Einstein sitting in the front row. Later, he asked the famous scientist why he'd come to hear a diplomat from such a small state.

"Big states don't need diplomats," said Einstein. "They have battleships. Small states need diplomats."

Eban replied, "Professor, you've taught me relativity in diplomacy: the smaller the state, the more interesting its diplomats."

By February 1964, Eban was Israel's deputy prime minister. He attended opening night of *What Makes Sammy Run?* and during the intermission, a woman asked him, "Mr. Deputy Prime Minister, do you still have that same sense of humor?"

"Yes," Eban replied, "only now I no longer laugh at jokes about vice presidents or deputies."

On a flight from Washington, D.C., to New York, Eban heard the flight attendant say over the PA, "Nice to have you aboard, Mr. Vice President." When she came down the aisle, he corrected her, saying he was the deputy prime minister of Israel, not the vice president. Then he noticed the man next to him: Richard Nixon.

In November 1967, Eban gave a speech before the UN Security Council. In a cab outside, his friend told Eban he'd spoken well, "but I don't think the average person could understand you."

Disagreeing, Eban asked the cabdriver if he'd heard the speech. "Yes, I did," came the reply. "I thought you spoke well, but I don't think the average person understood you."

After Israel won the Six Day War in June 1967, Eban paraphrased Churchill's famous 1940 speech about the RAF pilots after the Battle of Britain: "Never have so few owed so little to so many."

Eban was one of the world's greatest orators. He gave his first speech at Grossinger's resort before he realized he could be paid for speaking. He thought that a hundred dollars was too much and fifty too little. So he settled for seventy-five dollars.

Early in 1969, the UN Security Council adopted a resolution condemning Israel after a retaliatory raid on the Beirut airport. Eban, then Israel's foreign minister, was asked his reaction. "I'd rather have condemnation than condolences," he said.

In September 1969, Eban met A. B. "Happy" Chandler, the former governor of Kentucky, then baseball commissioner, who had been the first Democrat to declare his candidacy for the 1960 presidential election. Eban told him he was returning to Israel to campaign for prime minister.

"I wish I could send along some of our Kentucky voting machines," Chandler said. "They help remove from elections democracy's only disadvantage: doubt."

Eban liked to say there was a clear difference between a clever man and a wise man: "A clever man attempts to get out of a situation, which a wise man never got into in the first place."

Eban made a speech in New York against the orders of his doctor and wife, since he was suffering from laryngitis. "Anyone who disregards the advice of both his doctor *and* his wife isn't likely to be intimidated by the Arabs," he said.

PRESIDENT DWIGHT D. EISENHOWER

(1890–1969)

*E*arly in December 1942, The Lyons Den reported on the success of *Casablanca*, which my father described as "that timely thriller"—"timely" because it was released around the time of the Allied invasion of North Africa. Peter Lorre, who costarred, said, "Oh, sure, Ingrid Bergman and Humphrey Bogart were great, but the real stars of the film are Eisenhower and Patton."

In July 1943, Eisenhower adopted a wait-and-see style of maneuvering his troops in North Africa, anticipating a German mistake. Back in New York, Carl Sandburg was asked if such a tactic had ever been used in the Civil War. "General McClellan did just what Eisenhower is doing," he replied, adding, "but that irked Lincoln, who wrote him in a dispatch: 'My dear McClellan. If you don't want to use the Army, I should like to borrow it for a while.'" McClellan was subsequently removed from command. Not so Ike.

The date and location of the D-Day landings was one of the most closely guarded secrets of World War II. Besides Eisenhower and his top commanders, only one other person knew the scheduled date for the invasion: producer and theater owner J. Arthur Rank.

The weather for early June 1944 was unfavorable, and storms were forecast for June 5. Eisenhower had two contingency plans: one was to wait a day for the weather to clear, which it did, more or less, and the invasion began. But if June 6 had been stormy as well, Eisenhower needed a place to bivouac one hundred thousand troops. He came up with the idea of movie theaters "up the coast from Bristol to Dover."

He contacted Rank and told him of the plan, so that the movie theaters could begin preparations. Rank told his board of directors to get ready for a large influx of customers in all his theaters, but didn't reveal why.

In September 1944, Eisenhower secretly returned to Washington, bearing an unusual gift for a friend's daughter: a puppy born in his tent during the North African campaign. Her parents gladly accepted the puppy, then learned that their daughter would have to remain at home for two weeks, lest she tell her friends who'd given her the gift and risk revealing Eisenhower's presence stateside. That dog, incidentally, was later "introduced" to Fala, President Roosevelt's Scottie.

In January 1945, the Battle of the Bulge was being fought in Belgium—Hitler's last, desperate offensive. At first the battle wasn't going well for the Allies. That's when Eisenhower was paid a visit by Leon Henderson, the former head of the Office of Price Administration. Henderson told Eisenhower the press was beginning to criticize the general's leadership. "Leon," sighed Eisenhower, "mine is a profession often ruined by amateurs."

Early in 1945, rotund Henry Sherek, England's most colorful theatrical producer, was an aide to General Montgomery, but was injured and forced to return home. A few days later, his unmistakable form was seen walking on a London street when General Eisenhower's car passed by. The general noticed Sherek, stopped the car, rolled down the window, and asked, "You've left the army, Henry?"

"I was invalided out," replied Sherek.

"We'll just have to try to win this war without you," Eisenhower said, smiling, as his car drove off.

In March 1945, Eisenhower was aboard a British cruiser and asked the captain to bring the ship closer to shore. The captain obliged, but the ship ran aground, within range of German shore batteries. Several destroyers rushed to tug it back to deeper waters. Eisenhower, fearing the captain might be blamed, called Churchill to assume full responsibility, saying, "A soldier shouldn't try to do a sailor's job."

The following month, Eisenhower was inspecting the Buchenwald concentration camp in Poland and ordered that reporters and townspeople, including local officials, be escorted in to see the horrors.

As a reward for the difficult experience they underwent, Eisenhower gave the eighteen correspondents the "assimilated" rank of major general. But one viewer stood outside, refusing to accompany his commanding general into the crematoria. "I can't take it," explained General George S. Patton, supposedly the toughest general of them all.

On October 14, 1946, Eisenhower was asked if he would ever run for president. "No, thank you," he replied. "Remember what happened to Grant? He was a great general, but then he stepped into a different line of business."

At a party in Florida in 1947, he asked the host for "something tall, cold, and with lots of gin in it." "Meet my wife," replied his host.

In June 1948, Eisenhower was asked to confirm the report that after he gave the order to go on D-Day morning, he took a nap. "Of course," the general replied. "The plans were complete. What should I have done, unload a truck?" The man who asked the question was Sid Caesar.

Eisenhower was introduced to an elegant elderly lady named Frances Folsom Preston, who told Ike she'd lived in Washington for years. In what Eisenhower recalled as one of the most embarrassing moments of his life, he asked her where in Washington she'd lived.

"In the White House," replied Frances Folsom *Cleveland* Preston, the much younger wife of President Grover Cleveland and the only First Lady to live at 1600 Pennsylvania Avenue in two nonconsecutive terms.

Eisenhower had a reunion in May 1949 with an old correspondent, and they reminisced about all the nice people they'd met during the war. Finally Eisenhower said, "Wouldn't you like the war—without the shooting?"

The next month, fourteen other correspondents flew from Washington to France for the fifth anniversary of D-Day. Eisenhower saw them off. Just before takeoff, the general asked the pilot for a favor. "If, while you're flying over the Atlantic, you see storm clouds ahead, head into them and fly through. It'll remind them of the trip over the Channel on D-Day morning."

Senator John W. Bricker of Ohio, Dewey's running mate in 1944, flew over Germany with Eisenhower a few years after the war. Together they looked down on the ruined cities, filled with sprawling rubble and skeletons of bombed-out buildings. Bricker then turned to Eisenhower and asked, "Do you think anything like this could ever happen again?"

"If I thought it could happen again, I'd jump out of this plane—right now!" said Eisenhower.

It wasn't until August 1951 that Eisenhower returned to the beaches of Normandy, where photographers kept asking for different angles for their pictures. Finally, Eisenhower said to them, "Last time I was here, *I* was the boss."

Before he decided to seek the presidency, Eisenhower paid a visit to President Truman, who advised, "Go down to the Republican club and get yourself a lot of thick elephant skin for protection."

In 1962, with Eisenhower a year out of office, Truman would refer to him as "the most thin-skinned president in history."

The only Truman to support Eisenhower for president in 1952 was Truman Capote.

In March 1952, Eisenhower was still listed in the Pentagon directory under the acronym "SACEUR," which stood for "Supreme Allied Commander in Europe." Then he received a letter addressed only "CAPUS." Because there was a French writer named Camus, his staff wondered if the letter was intended for the writer, not the general. They traced the letter and learned that "CAPUS" stood for "Candidate for President of the United States."

Once he won the nomination, the oddest moment of Eisenhower's campaign came when his plane landed in Chicago. When the door opened, he looked at the mob waiting for him, and there, right up front, taking photos and hoping to meet him, was Joan Crawford.

Eisenhower and MacArthur had no love for one another. But in November 1952, just before election night, MacArthur offered to make a speech backing Eisenhower, on the condition that Eisenhower come see him at his apartment in the Waldorf Astoria. Eisenhower refused.

Eisenhower's favorite pastime was golf. Indeed, there was a joke told among Democrats that if World War III were to break out, Eisenhower would say to golfers ahead of him, "Do you mind if we play through?"

Bobby Jones, the Babe Ruth of golf, once played with Eisenhower and the general asked him the secret of his success. "Just before I swing," replied Jones, "I secretly say to myself, 'Please God, let me relax.'" Years later, when Jones was no longer able to play the game he loved, he sent his clubs to Eisenhower with a card that read, "Remember, please God, relax."

One day in March 1953, a Secret Service agent in the White House passed by President Eisenhower's study and was startled to see him lying on the floor flat on his back with his eyes shut. The agent started to call for help, but then saw the president stir. He learned that's the way Eisenhower liked to nap—a habit probably learned during the war.

In October 1953, the president played golf near a military base where he hit a ball into a gully away from the hole. He took an extra stroke but moaned, "This is an awful trap." The next day he hit the same kind of drive on that hole, but this time there was no gully. It had been filled in overnight.

In March 1954, an army friend was asked when he first got an inkling that the general was considering a run for the White House. "It came when he was asked to pose for a picture at a party," said the president's old friend. "He agreed, but put his drink down first."

Whenever an interesting guest would leave the White House, the president would immediately jot down his impressions, along with the guest's wife's and children's names. Then when that guest was scheduled to return, Eisenhower would pull out the card and study up on conversation points.

In August 1955, the president decorated Admiral Robert B. Carney, retiring chief of naval operations, with the Distinguished Service Medal. The two were photographed laughing. Later the admiral explained that just before Eisenhower pinned the medal to his stiffly starched shirt, he reminded the president that Admiral "Bull" Halsey, when awarding medals, would intentionally break the skin of the recipient, after whispering, "Let's see how brave you *really* are!"

In December 1956, Eisenhower ordered one of his Christmas gifts from Tiffany's. Walter Hoving, then head of the store, wondered whether it would be proper to send a bill to the president of the United States. He asked one of his veteran employees, who replied, "It's fine, sir. We sent a bill to Abraham Lincoln."

On their visit to Washington in 1958, Queen Elizabeth and Prince Philip welcomed the Eisenhowers at the British Embassy. As they were entering, a cockroach scampered by, much to the horror of the queen. "Don't worry," said the president. "Over at the White House, they're bigger and tougher."

When Mamie Eisenhower's mother, Elivera M. Doud, died in 1960, The Lyons Den ran the little-known story about the first time young Mamie told her mother of her intention to marry Eisenhower, a young second lieutenant from Kansas. "Mamie," her mother replied, "Ike's a nice boy, but he'll never have any money."

In May 1965, the twentieth anniversary of V-E Day, CBS aired a special report during which, via the Early Bird satellite, Eisenhower would reminisce with General Montgomery about that day. Don Hewitt, who would create 60 *Minutes* three years later, produced the show. During a run-through, Eisenhower told Hewitt he'd once bet Montgomery "five pounds the war would be over by December 1944. I paid up!"

Joan Miró, the Spanish surrealist, visited the White House and Eisenhower showed him one of his own paintings. Looking at the work done by the president, the artist thought a minute and used two carefully chosen words: "Very sensitive." Eisenhower, incidentally, was often suspected of painting by numbers.

When James Roosevelt was a congressman, he phoned President Eisenhower's secretary for permission to show his three sons the White House family quarters where he and his brothers had played two decades before. Eisenhower sent word he'd see the boys at 9 a.m. Then, for two hours, he talked to the boys about their education.

The boys later told their father that the president didn't have one piece of paper on his desk and the *New York Times* nearby hadn't been opened. Then they said, "He kept us there for two hours. Doesn't a president really have anything to do?"

For a time, my father co-chaired the Damon Runyon Cancer Fund. One day the fund received a contribution from Eisenhower accompanied by a note: "Please don't look at the amount. I've given as much as I can on a humble soldier's pay."

SUPREME COURT JUSTICE
FELIX FRANKFURTER

(1882–1965)

The immigrant son of a merchant in a family of rabbis, Frankfurter was a Phi Beta Kappa graduate of the City College of New York. After graduating from Harvard Law School he taught there, helped found the American Civil Liberties Union, and defended the condemned anarchists Sacco and Vanzetti.

He helped found the League of Nations and, urged by an earlier Jewish justice, Louis Brandeis, became involved in the Zionist movement for a Jewish state. He was an advisor to FDR, who asked him to find a successor on the Court after the death of Justice Benjamin Cardozo. When none could be found, FDR nominated *him*. He was confirmed just a few weeks before Brandeis left the Court.

Before he was confirmed, Frankfurter received a telegram from Harpo Marx, reading, "Tentative congratulations."

Frankfurter, the first nominee to testify in person before the Senate Judiciary Committee, was confirmed without dissent. He became a champion of judicial restraint.

Frankfurter's first opinion as a Supreme Court justice wasn't from the bench. It came at a party after the opening in Boston of a tryout of Sir Noël Coward's play, *Set to Music*. Coward told the justice, "I think it needs a new finish."

"I agree," said Frankfurter.

In London in October 1939, he received an honorary degree from Oxford and was also honored by prominent barristers. One said, "I'm delighted to speak at a dinner given to one of the five Supreme Court justices of America." The next one referred to the number of justices as six. Then Lord Chancellor Frederic Maugham said, "The previous speakers erred. There are seven members of the U.S. Supreme Court."

When it was Frankfurter's turn to speak, he corrected their mistakes, but he did it tactfully. "Actually, there are *nine* members of the Court," he explained. "Nine—the same as on your cricket teams."

A designer proposed making jackets for the justices, and Frankfurter joked about putting numbers on the back, like ballplayers.

In May 1942, Eleanor Roosevelt entertained groups of students with a weekly picnic. One girl assigned to supervise the picnic food told the First Lady, "We'd better order some more sausages; we're getting low." "The reminds me," replied Mrs. Roosevelt. "Our speaker today is Justice Frankfurter."

In December 1942, actress-screenwriter Ruth Gordon was set to marry director-writer Garson Kanin, and asked their friend Justice Frankfurter to perform the ceremony. "I'm afraid that's impossible," he said. "I'm a federal judge, and thus have no power to do that. Apparently marriage is not a federal offense."

Frankfurter asked lots of questions during lawyers' pleadings. An attorney was arguing an appeal and, as usual, Frankfurter kept interrupting. The elderly lawyer for the other side noticed this, and when his turn came, he began, "May it please the Court. You see I'm elderly, and stooped, with little energy or strength left. I will try to make my argument brief and because of my age, I ask one favor: that I not be interrupted for the first five minutes." Two minutes into his remarks, Frankfurter made his first interruption.

During his years teaching at Harvard Law, Frankfurter chose the best student to clerk for Justice Oliver Wendell Holmes. He'd invite the top four students in the class to a party—in those days the classes were all male—and invite four female students. He'd then ask the women to vote on which law student seemed smartest.

Pages sitting behind a curtain ran errands for the justices when the Court was in session. Frankfurter led all the jurists in errands. His pageboy got revenge by rubbing his shoes on the thick carpet whenever he was called, thus giving Frankfurter an electric shock when he would hand over a note to deliver.

An attorney was arguing before the Court and cited majority opinions in recent cases written by the justices. When he quoted an opinion written by Frankfurter, the justice interrupted him on a technicality, saying, "Counselor, that wasn't just *my* opinion. It is now the opinion of the Supreme Court of the United States."

"There are two ways for a man to become a rich lawyer," Frankfurter told some friends in 1950. "The first way is to marry a rich woman. The second way is to apply yourself diligently to the study and practice of every aspect of the law for 25 years—*then* marry a rich woman."

That same year, a lawyer who was arguing before the Court said, "I taught in the field of law in question for a number of years, and

I'm sure that what I say about it is correct." Just then Frankfurter interrupted and asked, "Where did you teach?" "At a law school which no longer exists," the attorney replied. "Why'd it close?" asked Frankfurter. The lawyer hesitated, then finally said, "The reason given was . . . the incompetence of its faculty."

Two years later, Phillip Hamburger, a longtime writer for *The New Yorker*, wanted Justice Frankfurter to perform his wedding ceremony. Like Ruth Gordon and Garson Kanin, he was told that a federal judge had no such power. The justice added, "And anyway, it's not right for a Frankfurter to marry a Hamburger."

In December 1952, Frankfurter was given a seventieth-birthday party at the home of fellow justice Robert H. Jackson. He was reminded of a statement he'd made saying Supreme Court justices should retire at seventy, so his colleagues began playfully making their good-byes. The following Monday, when he returned to the Court, the other justices asked, "Forget something? What're *you* doing here?"

In September 1959, Frankfurter attended a screening of *Anatomy of a Murder* with Garson Kanin. The judge in the film was played by Joseph Welch, the famed lawyer who had helped bring down Senator Joseph McCarthy five years earlier. Welch had been a student of Frankfurter's at Harvard. Frankfurter later affirmed "Judge" Welch's opinions in the film, but at the climax of the story, Frankfurter became indignant. The prosecutor, played by George C. Scott, questioned a witness played by Kathryn Grant and asked her if she'd been the slain man's mistress. She replied that she was his daughter. "That violates the first rule of cross-examination," said Frankfurter. "Never ask a question unless you know what the answer will be."

He also winced when one actor referred to "Chief Justice Holmes," since Holmes was never chief justice.

H.R.H. QUEEN ELIZABETH II

(1926–)

*J*ust after VE-Day, in May 1945, Princess Elizabeth asked her parents if she could mingle incognito with the revelers. King George VI and Queen Elizabeth reluctantly agreed, but cautioned her two security guards, "Whatever you do, don't take her to Piccadilly Circus. Anything can happen there." As soon as she left the palace grounds, Princess Elizabeth told the two security men, "Please take me to Piccadilly Circus."

In October 1946, a burglary was committed at a candy plant in Hoboken, New Jersey. Among the items reported stolen were five cases of Tootsie Rolls, which were to be shipped to Buckingham Palace to the "attention" of Princess Elizabeth.

When she was young, she was riding with her grandmother, Queen Mary, when the car stopped for a red light. A flower vendor tossed a corsage to her, saying, "Flowers for the little lady." The young girl replied, "But I'm a princess."

"Everybody knows that," Queen Mary explained, "but we're trying to bring you up to be a little lady."

When she read of Elizabeth's coronation in 1953, Greta Garbo, who played Queen Christina but abhorred publicity, said, "Oh, how wonderful it is *not* to be a queen!"

Johnnie Ray sang at a command performance, then showed the queen the cable from his parents, Elmer and Hazel, back in tiny Dallas, Oregon, saying how proud they were of their son for making it all the way to Buckingham Palace. "How charming," said Elizabeth. "Tell them *we* were here, too!"

During a trip to America in October 1957, the royal couple went to a football game. Later they stopped at a supermarket, where Philip asked one of the shoppers how much her husband earned and how much she spent on food.

"Now, may I ask *you* a question?" the woman said. "I noticed you've just walked ahead of the queen. Aren't you supposed to walk a step or two behind her?"

Philip replied, "We were chummy at the game today, so I'm sure she doesn't mind."

Woody Allen (left) and Raquel Welch (center) meet Queen Elizabeth at the Royal Film Performance of *Born Free* at the Odeon Theater in Leicester Square, London, 1966.

Comedian Alan King met the queen on a red carpet at a movie premiere. The queen extended her hand and said, "Nice to meet you, Mr. King."

"Likewise, Mrs. Queen," came the reply. Later he explained, "I didn't know her last name."

A friend of my father's visited London frequently. As soon as she'd check into her room, she'd casually tell the hotel operator to phone Buckingham Palace and ask to speak to the queen. Her second call was to Clarendon House, where she'd ask for the Queen Mother.

"I never get them on the phone, of course," she said, "but from then on I always get excellent service."

Princess Margaret's favorite London musical of 1961 was *West Side Story*. She saw it several times and finally she reserved five seats. As usual, the manager of Her Majesty's Theater waited on the sidewalk to greet the princess, who stepped from her car and told him, "Oh, I hope you don't mind. I've brought my sister."

The queen once met Mae West, the raunchy, flamboyant movie star. When the monarch offered the actress some sherry, West replied, "No, thanks. I don't drink, and frankly, I'm surprised you do."

When the queen knighted Michael Caine in 2000, he used his real name to honor his father, and she thus said, "Arise, Sir Maurice Mickelwhite." Caine told me that the queen, obviously not the most avid moviegoer, said, "I understand you've been doing this for quite some time." By that time, he'd appeared in eighty-four movies over forty-three years.

Ian McKellen told me that at his investiture in 1991, she asked a question you *never* ask an actor: "Are you working now?"

Peter Ustinov told me that when he got the news that he'd be knighted, it came with a questionnaire. "There were two boxes," the portly actor recalled. "One read, 'I can kneel,' since many of the honorees are elderly. The other read, 'I cannot kneel.' So I had to ring up Buckingham Palace and say, 'Please tell Her Majesty that I *can* kneel, all right. But then I can't get up again."

In October 1964, the queen had scheduled a trip to Canada, but before she left, she lunched with the Queen Mother, who noticed her daughter was ordering her third Scotch. "Libbet," said the Queen Mother, "aren't you scheduled to rule this afternoon?"

On a visit to New York, the royals received a ticker-tape parade, during which a Scotland Yard man said to an NYPD detective, "I'm worried about all this open space. What's your security?"

"This is my security," replied the detective, pulling out a rosary.

When Woody Allen met the queen on a red carpet, he recalled, "I knew I had only ten seconds, and I was deliberating whether in such a short time, I could try to sell her a mutual fund."

In 1966 and 1967, Francis Chichester circumnavigated the globe in a fifty-seven-foot craft, sailing 28,500 miles, alone, for 220 days. To mark the end of his voyage, the queen knighted him with the same sword used by the first Queen Elizabeth to knight the first Englishman to circumnavigate the globe, Sir Francis Drake, in 1580.

Duke Ellington was presented to the queen at the Leeds Music Festival, saying, "I'm sure the last time I was here was before you were born."

JENNIE GROSSINGER

(1892–1972)

We spent many happy summers at Grossinger's, the most famous, beloved resort in the Catskill Mountains, a hundred miles northwest of Manhattan. It had a lake, a championship golf course (still open), tennis, horseback riding, Olympic-size outdoor and indoor pools, a nightclub, and even an airport. It was three hundred acres of paradise.

At the Playhouse, young comedians like Buddy Hackett and Sam Levenson performed. One Labor Day weekend, Eddie Cantor brought out his protégé, a young singer named Eddie Fisher.

Many of the jokes told by the standup comics had punch lines in Yiddish, so we didn't get them, but I figured if the guys in Eddie Ashman's band laughed, the joke had to be hilarious. I only wish I'd been a few years older: I'd have seen a brilliant young comic named Melvin Kaminsky performing around the pool. Harry Grossinger fired him for "not being funny," as Kaminsky once told me—after he'd changed his name to Mel Brooks.

Boxing champs Rocky Marciano, Randy Turpin, and Ingemar Johansson trained at Grossinger's. Marciano, aware of the culinary delights of "the G," brought his own chef to his camp. Johansson, flush from defeating Floyd Patterson to win the heavyweight title, ate Grossinger's food—creamed chicken and cheesecake!—and then lost his crown in the first round of his rematch.

New York baseball players who didn't make the All-Star team had three days to relax there. New York governor Nelson Rockefeller often visited, along with other national politicians and Eleanor Roosevelt.

The face of the resort was Jennie Grossinger, called "The Jewish Eleanor Roosevelt" for her philanthropies and grace. If you'd come from the other side of the world and never heard of a Borscht Belt resort, meeting her would be life changing, such was her charisma.

Her family founded Grossinger's in 1912 as a small boardinghouse after moving up from the city. It grew to be internationally famous. There was even a Grossinger's-brand rye bread.

Jennie Grossinger (right) with Eleanor Roosevelt (left)
at her famous resort.

Former Olympian Eleanor Holm inaugurated the outdoor pool
by diving in from a helicopter. Florence Chadwick trained there before becoming the first person to swim the English Channel both
ways. She taught swimming there, and tennis immortals Lew Hoad,
Ken Rosewall, and Don Budge played exhibition matches on Grossinger's courts.

Eddie Fisher married Debbie Reynolds there. *This Is Your Life* did
a show on Jennie Grossinger. Lou Goldstein, the house comedian
and director of activities (the "tummler," in Yiddish) gained national
fame with his games of Simon Says, which he later played with famous athletes on ABC's *The Super Stars*.

The movie *Dirty Dancing*, its setting supposedly based on Grossinger's, didn't remotely re-create the lavish, luxurious landscape,
the plush rooms, or the friendly ambiance. You felt you were being
welcomed into the Grossinger family for the weekend, a week, or in
our case, a whole summer.

In August 1949, *Holiday* magazine featured a story on Grossinger's. "I remember this lot filled with cows," Jennie told the magazine. "Now it's filled with Cadillacs."

In 1950, George Jessel was invited to play in a charity softball game there on July 4, but declined. "I'm still recovering from the game I played there in 1940," he explained. "I hit a double and made it all the way to second base unaided. It was my first hit since *The Jazz Singer*."

In January 1951, Sonja Henie, the Olympic figure skating champion and movie star, entrusted the job of sharpening her skates to Grossinger's employee Eddie Peck. When she was booked to skate in Chicago, she summoned him. Peck then drove down to New York, took the overnight train, studied the delicate alignment on Henie's blades, honed the right one with three strokes—a matter of seconds—then took the train back to New York and drove up to Grossinger's.

Red Buttons did a weekend engagement at Grossinger's and said, "I'm surely the only comedian in show business who's played both Mount Fuji and the Catskills."

When Bobby Fischer was fourteen, in 1958, he won the U.S. Chess Championship and was slated to go to Russia to play the Soviet champion. He was known to refuse to wear a tie or jacket. On a visit to Grossinger's he tried to enter the dining room wearing a sweater. Maître d' Abe Friedman stopped him and asked, "If you're invited to a state dinner in Moscow next week, won't you wear a tie?"

Fischer replied, "Then I won't go."

In November 1959, Jennie received a doctor of humanities degree from Wilberforce University. "If only my truant officer could see me now," she sighed. She'd stayed home from grammar school to support her family with factory work. Years later, she had a private tutor to nurture her insatiable love of learning.

Grossinger's specialized in catering to singles; they were carefully seated together in the dining room. After Jennie saw the movie *Who's Afraid of Virginia Woolf?* she couldn't believe the snarling dialogue of the couples.

"Don't worry, Jennie," said a friend. "As long as they didn't meet at Grossinger's."

John Guare, the gifted playwright who wrote *Six Degrees of Separation*, *The House of Blue Leaves*, and the screenplay for *Atlantic City*, put it best when he met Jennie Grossinger: "It's like suddenly meeting Santa Claus—an institution I'd read about, seen photos of, admired, and somehow always doubted really could exist."

W. AVERELL HARRIMAN

(1891–1986)

If you've seen the classic western *Butch Cassidy and the Sundance Kid*, you'll remember the recurring joke showing George Furth, the wonderful actor-playwright, as Woodcock, the real-life brave mail clerk. He refused to open the train door for the infamous bandits. "I work for Mr. E. H. Harriman of the Union Pacific Railroad," he said in the summer of 1899. E. H. Harriman, the richest railroad baron of the nineteenth century, was the father of W. Averell Harriman, the diplomat, presidential advisor, wartime ambassador to Moscow, Truman's secretary of commerce, governor of New York, Vietnam peace negotiator, and presidential hopeful. No one held more pivotal positions.

When writer Quentin Reynolds asked Harriman to run for office in 1940, a friend asked, "On what side of the tracks was Harriman born?"

Reynolds replied, "Averell wasn't born on either side. He was born *on* the tracks!"

Harriman was given the dangerous post of ambassador to the Soviet Union during the darkest days of World War II, when the Nazis' terrifying Operation Barbarossa—the invasion of Russia—was in full force.

Ever the diplomat, Harriman arrived at his post and cabled his wife. Using diplomatic restraint, he described the fierce Russian winter: "Cool here."

When Roosevelt sent him to Cairo during the summer, he again cabled her: "Heat principal industry of Egypt." Then he was sent to the Gold Coast in southern Africa, which was even hotter. Back in Cairo, his next cable read, "Egypt delightful."

In 1942, when the war was going badly for the Allies, Harriman was sent on a mission. The trip included a twenty-four-hour flight on a clattering military aircraft, during which the tall Harriman sat knee to knee with a Frenchman of the same height. Throughout the flight, the only thing he said to the Frenchman—General Charles de Gaulle—was "We'll do better."

Ambassador Averell Harrimann (center), with my parents at WNBC studios during his campaign for governor, c. 1954.

As ambassador, he's seen in historic photos standing behind Roosevelt, Churchill, and Stalin at their summits in Tehran in 1943 and Yalta two years later. In 1946, he was asked by a reporter if he'd kept a diary of these momentous events.

"No," replied Harriman. "In this job, one has to make up one's mind whether you want to work or keep a diary."

Stalin invited Harriman to ride a prize horse that had performed at a cavalry show in Moscow. Stalin didn't tell him it was a circus horse. As soon as Harriman mounted, the horse dipped, pranced sideways, and knelt.

But Harriman couldn't be unseated, for he'd learned horsemanship as a young polo player in the Hamptons, playground of the superrich. Stalin, pleased by this impressive feat, gave the horse to Harriman.

In June 1948, Harriman was in Paris to help administer the European recovery plan. His official title was "United States Special Representative," but he considered changing the title, since its initials were U.S.S.R.

In August 1960, Harriman flew to the Congo on a fact-finding mission for Senator John F. Kennedy. When his party arrived at the ferry to cross the Congo River, en route to meet with Patrice Lamumba and Joseph Kasavubu, reporters following them were barred from the ferry, since they lacked permits. Harriman then "deputized" them, allowing them to board. Harriman received daily briefings of events in Washington as well as Yankee box scores, no easy task back then.

In August 1965, Doris Warner Vidor, daughter of one of the Warner brothers, rushed to the resort in Sun Valley, Idaho, when it opened. On arrival, she handed her car keys and a fifty-cent tip to the tall, slim, gray-haired man who was moving furniture around as guests arrived. He was dressed in work clothes, and carried Mrs. Vidor's bags.It was Harriman, helping his employees get everything ready for the resort—which he owned—on opening day.

Harriman leased an apartment in Paris, but to give it a touch of home, shipped paintings from New York. The paintings were by Picasso, van Gogh, and Cézanne.

When Harriman met Khrushchev, he asked the Soviet Premier when he'd hold free elections.

Khrushchev replied, "How can *you* talk to me of free elections when in the election for governor of New York it was you versus Nelson Rockefeller?"

Harriman lunched at Toots Shor's, where William Randolph Hearst III was brought over to meet him. The newspaper heir, then a junior at Harvard, expressed admiration for Harriman's speeches on Vietnam. Harriman pointed out to the young man that Hearst newspaper editorials criticized him for his views.

Then Harriman told his father, William Randolph Hearst Jr., "You would do well to let your son write your editorials." The father said, "He will—in time."

The superrich of his time had curious ways. When, for instance, Harriman arrived in Paris on a diplomatic mission, he informed embassy officials he carried no money. He was then given twenty dollars' worth of French francs. When he was about to return to New York a week later, Harriman still carried those bills.

Harriman went to the Louvre for a Gauguin exhibit. The guard asked him for the nominal two-franc admission fee, but the billionaire Harriman, who'd left his few francs in his hotel, had to leave. One of the paintings in the exhibit belonged to him.

One morning, Harriman arose and said to his wife, "I feel like a million bucks."

"Is *that* all?" she asked. "What happened to the rest of it?"

Peter Duchin was a famous society bandleader, just as his father Eddy was in his time. When Peter was thirteen, he spent the summer at the Harrimans' estate and received a fifty-cents-a-week allowance. Peter protested that it was insufficient.

"I'll take it up with Averell," said his father.

"If you call him in," said the boy, "I'll call in Toots Shor." Thus the meeting was held between the patrician billionaire diplomat and the bouncer turned restaurateur. Toots won the debate. Peter got a raise.

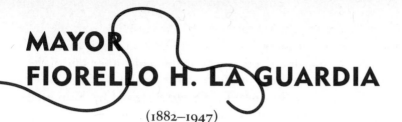

MAYOR FIORELLO H. LA GUARDIA
(1882–1947)

He was known as "The Little Flower," this diminutive native of New York's Greenwich Village, the son of an Italian father and an Italian-Jewish mother. A former congressman, he was the city's most colorful mayor (until Ed Koch), who famously read the Sunday comics on the radio to the city's children during a newspaper strike. He served three terms as mayor, from 1934 to 1945. Technically a Republican, he was a progressive New Dealer and a reformer who crossed party lines.

In June 1937, La Guardia attended a concert and was asked for his autograph. "Mine?" he asked, incredulously. "You want Brahms's."

During one reelection campaign, he met Paul Muni, the movie and stage star. Muni expressed his admiration, after which the mayor placed his hands on Muni's lapels as a sign of friendship. Later, Muni noticed that his jacket now bore a button reading "La Guardia for Mayor."

A group of executives came to City Hall to ask the mayor to extend daylight savings. They showed him complicated charts explaining the solar system, orbits of the moon, the meridian, etc. After a few minutes, the mayor pushed the charts away, saying, "First, let me tackle unemployment in the city. Then we'll see."

In 1940, David Rockefeller was an unpaid worker at City Hall. He occasionally manned the switchboard, but La Guardia put a stop to it. Callers would get the impression that the city was dominated by the wealthy if they heard, "Hello, City Hall. Rockefeller speaking. May I help you?"

Late in 1940, La Guardia met with three Soviet officials. Noticing their elegant attire compared with his old, frayed suit with baggy knees, he said, "Gentlemen, I represent the proletariat."

Asked why he didn't move to a swanky apartment, he replied, "I don't want to become accustomed to things I won't be able to afford once I leave office."

La Guardia was scheduled to meet with an official from the International Ladies' Garment Workers' Union who stood four foot eleven. When the mayor arrived, the policemen on either side of the hallway snapped to attention. Out of respect, so did the diminutive visitor. As the five-foot-two-inch La Guardia passed by, he patted the man on his head and said, "Hey, I'm taller than you!"

Too busy to attend a function at the American Jewish Congress one evening, La Guardia sent the City Council president, Newbold Morris, instead, along with a note that read: "I can't attend, so I'm sending this *schlmeil*."

In October 1941, Gene Autry made a rare visit to New York, to perform at the rodeo in Madison Square Garden, and asked to meet the mayor. La Guardia, with little interest in westerns, asked an Oklahoma-born friend, "Is this guy *really* a cowboy or just a Hollywood dude?" Assured that Autry, a native of Tioga, Texas, was the real deal, the mayor talked with him for an hour.

After La Guardia voted on Election Day, he went to the Central Park Zoo, listened to opera, and did nothing related to the election, explaining, "Election Day is not for politics."

Called on to conduct an orchestra at the Stage Door Canteen, where soldiers came to relax, he mounted the conductor's stand, turned his back to the orchestra, and conducted facing the soldiers.

During a bitter political fight, he dictated and signed a resignation letter. "This is how I feel," he said, then discarded it, saying, "Now I feel better."

While chairing a meeting on juvenile delinquency he confessed that when he was a boy, he spied a horse tied to a hitching post. He unhitched it, rode it for a while, then returned it.

"Mr. Mayor," said one member of the group, "are you saying you were once a horse thief?"

"No," replied La Guardia, "I'm saying I was once a boy."

In November 1944, actress Dolly Haas, wife of *New York Times* theatrical caricaturist Al Hirschfeld, wrote Mayor La Guardia praising him for his accomplishments, especially for building the George Washington Bridge. She even suggested a plaque be erected on the bridge praising him.

La Guardia wrote back thanking her, but telling her that the bridge had opened in 1931, when Jimmy Walker was mayor. "But you can always visit *my* Bronx Whitestone Bridge," he continued. "That's a really beautiful bridge, too."

In April 1942, former postmaster general James Farley appeared in a scene in *Pride of the Yankees*, and needed six takes before director Sam Wood was satisfied. When La Guardia, who'd been asked to appear as well, heard that he boasted that he could do better. His bit role took seven takes.

La Guardia confessed that he was not a fan of ballet. "When I sit at the ballet," he said, "I have a hard time keeping score. I just can't tell who's ahead."

In February 1945, La Guardia met a honeymooning couple on a flight between Washington and New York. They didn't know who he was but accepted his lift from the airport. They'd never seen a phone in a private car, much less one used to arrange for their luggage to be picked up by a policeman and delivered to their hotel.

"Clothing should not be the concern of honeymooners," he said.

In several of his radio broadcasts, La Guardia attacked Frank Costello, the gangster. Then he broadcast a Red Cross appeal, promising a signed thank-you letter to any donor, no matter how small the amount. Costello, who'd been listening and expecting another attack, sent a five-thousand-dollar donation. Sure enough, the letter came. The next day, La Guardia resumed attacking Costello on the air.

JUDGE SAMUEL L. LEIBOWITZ

(1893–1978)

When I was seven, my father took me to the chambers of Judge Samuel Leibowitz, in Brooklyn. He put me in a cell to scare me and make certain I'd live a life on the straight and narrow (as they used to say). There was a suspect in the cell with me for moment or two! It worked; my next arrest will be my first.

Little did I know I'd met a giant of the American legal profession and civil rights movement. Born Simon Leibovici in Romania, he arrived in America in 1900, earned a law degree, and began as a defense attorney handling high-profile cases.

On his first case as a defense lawyer, Leibowitz's client was accused of burglarizing a saloon, using a skeleton key that was entered into evidence by the prosecution. Leibowitz asked that the jurors be taken to the bar to see for themselves if the key could open the door. The prosecutor objected, the judge sustained the objection, and no such trip was made. In his summation, the young lawyer wondered why that key wasn't allowed to be tested before the jury.

The jury agreed with his suspicions, found reasonable doubt, and the defendant was acquitted. The skeleton key opened every door in the courthouse.

Leibowitz earned worldwide fame appealing the convictions of the Scottsboro Boys, nine African American youths from Alabama who were falsely accused of rape and sentenced to death by a white jury in 1931. A fiery Jewish defense lawyer from New York seemed to have little chance in the heart of Jim Crow country. But he worked on the case pro bono for four years, risking his life against the angry citizens of Decatur, Alabama, and exposing racial bias in jury selection.

Norris v. Alabama was a landmark Supreme Court decision, ensuring equal protection under the Fourteenth Amendment. When Leibowitz showed Chief Justice Charles Evans Hughes fraudulent jury selection records, the case was won and retrials conducted. The defendants were eventually exonerated, including Clarence Norris, the last surviving defendant, pardoned by Alabama governor George Wallace in 1976.

From left to right: Comedian Joe E. Lewis, *New York Times* writer William Lawrence, my father, Judge Samuel L. Leibowitz, and composer Frank Loesser.

Mrs. Leibowitz accompanied him during his long stays in Alabama in order to cook for him—she feared that otherwise he would be poisoned.

In February 1934, a Broadway play called *They Shall Not Die* opened, based on Leibowitz's defense of the Scottsboro Boys. Claude Rains, the great British character actor from *Casablanca*, played Leibowitz. He'd studied Leibowitz's mannerisms for weeks, copying his clothes and brusque speech. Rains even wore a ten-dollar knockoff of the diamond ring Leibowitz had been given by a grateful client named Al Capone.

Leibowitz went backstage afterward. Rains was hoping for praise for his portrayal, but Leibowitz simply held up Raines's cheap ring and put his alongside, saying, "Good copy!"

When Leibowitz surrendered Capone to the Brooklyn police, he displayed photos of the gangster's unmarked body.

"This is how I'm delivering the package," said Leibowitz. "I expect it to be returned in the same condition."

Bruno Richard Hauptmann, convicted of kidnapping and murdering the Lindbergh baby, had his chief lawyer, Edward "Death

House" Reilly, retain Leibowitz for Hauptmann's fruitless appeal. Reilly, an alcoholic, only visited his client briefly. He even sued the destitute Hauptmann for nonpayment and was eventually fired, winding up in a mental institution. When asked about his own sanity, Reilly said, "Am I crazy? Of course not! I hired Sam Leibowitz."

When he became a judge, Leibowitz handed out heavy sentences, especially to career criminals. In 1945, a Brooklyn mobster headed for trial was told if he didn't confess, he'd get tried by Leibowitz. A confession, however, would result in another judge deciding his sentence. He confessed.

In October 1947, three convicts were headed to Sing Sing prison. During the train ride the first said, "Judge Leibowitz gave me a two-and-a-half to five-year sentence. This will be his stepping-stone to City Hall. He'll be the next mayor of New York."

The second said, "You're wrong: he gave me five to ten years. That means he'll be the next governor."

The third convict then said, "You boys must be referring to future president Leibowitz. He sentenced me to twenty years to life."

During a robbery trial, the defendant was about to be sentenced. Suddenly his wife arose in the back of the courtroom and asked to speak to Judge Leibowitz. She told him he'd defended her husband twenty years before. "I can't recall that case," said Leibowitz. "How'd I do?"

"Your Honor," replied the wife, "if you hadn't been his lawyer and gotten an acquittal back then, today he'd just be coming *out* of jail instead of going *in*."

GENERAL OF THE ARMY DOUGLAS MACARTHUR

(1880–1964)

One of only five modern five-star generals, he was the son of a general who'd feuded with Secretary of War Taft and been removed from the rule of the Philippines. Douglas never forgot that. When the younger MacArthur finished first in his class at West Point, Taft, by then president, presented his diploma. Second Lieutenant Douglas received it, saluted Taft, then broke tradition. He walked over to his father and gave him the diploma.

Early in 1942, during the doomed defense of Corregidor, MacArthur was in his tent writing when a Japanese bullet whizzed by. He looked up and said, "Not yet. Not yet," and returned to writing.

His son Arthur, who was with his parents there, was just four during the siege. "That was the right age," his mother said. "If he'd been older, he'd have been frightened. When he heard the gunfire, he asked if the guns were ours. I told him they were, and he went back to sleep."

On March 11, 1942, the MacArthur family finally left Corregidor under orders from FDR, ahead of the approaching Japanese army. His sunset departure in a PT boat (where he uttered the famous words "I shall return") was one of the most heavily guarded secrets of the war.

A troupe of stars headed by Jack Benny and Carole Landis visited the troops in Australia and were directed to MacArthur's office. The general spotted three actresses on one sofa and Benny on the other. He sat down between the actresses and explained to Benny, "A general's prerogative, you know."

In February 1943, MacArthur was reminiscing with officers who'd served with him in the Philippines in 1927, during Prohibition back home, and recalled regulations banning liquor from all army posts. An officer reminded him that Prohibition applied to all U.S. territories, including the Philippines, and that he'd seen some soldiers drinking.

"Any soldier who comes halfway 'round the world just to wind up with a glass of buttermilk," MacArthur replied, snapping his fingers, "isn't worth *that!*"

After the war ended the Allied Advisory Commission met with MacArthur, who said, "Gentlemen, I am the supreme commander. *Supreme!* You are the Advisory Commission. In the next room, you'll find a large dictionary for use by any of you who do not understand the word 'advisory.' Good day, gentlemen."

In February 1946, just six months after the atomic bombs were dropped, a journalist in Tokyo asked MacArthur how the Red Cross might do an even better job in the event of another war. MacArthur said, "The next war won't last long enough for that."

Declaring himself out of the running for president in 1948, he said, "When my job in Japan is done, I'll head back to Tennessee, sit under a tree all day long, and throw rocks at anyone who talks politics."

When MacArthur visited the front in Korea in 1950, an aide was concerned that the general never wore a helmet and warned, "General, we just killed two snipers near here." MacArthur replied, "That's the proper thing to do."

Soon after he fired MacArthur for insubordination, Truman gave a tour of his library to Austria's foreign minister. One area had portraits of prominent military leaders from World War II. "All the admirals and generals are here," said Truman. "Here's Bradley, Marshall, King, Eisenhower, and . . ." arriving at MacArthur's portrait, the president said simply, "God."

After he left the army, MacArthur headed the Remington-Rand office machine corporation. Bob Hope called him "a typewriter salesman. But they had to hire him," the comedian continued. "He has more ribbons than they do."

His first wife, Louise Cromwell Brooks, later married British actor Lionel Atwill, who starred in seventy-five movies. As her ex-husband's fame grew, she said, "I traded in four stars for one star."

Soon after Truman fired MacArthur, my father lunched with him and mentioned General Billy Mitchel, depicted by Gary Cooper in *The Court Martial of Billy Mitchell*. Mitchell was a proponent of air warfare and, in 1924, predicted an air attack on Pearl Harbor by the Japanese. He was drummed out of the service in 1926 as a result.

MacArthur, then a Major General on that court, never revealed how he'd voted in the case. But at that luncheon, he praised Mitchell.

In July 1951, MacArthur and his second wife, Jean, saw the play *Gramercy Ghost* on Broadway and visited the stars backstage. One was Sarah Churchill, whose father, Winston, had publicly supported Truman's firing of MacArthur.

Nevertheless, the general said, "I think your father is the only hope for this world."

He went to a Giants game at the Polo Grounds and was seated behind first base. During the game a foul pop-up came near his box, pursued by first baseman Whitey Lockman, shortstop Alvin Dark, and catcher Wes Westrum. Everyone was looking skyward at the ball—some seeking to catch it, others trying to avoid it. Everyone except MacArthur, who, with the same steely-eyed disdain he'd shown for enemy fire on Corregidor, looked straight ahead.

By 1955, he was living in New York in the penthouse at the Waldorf Towers with his wife and son. One day he walked through the city's teeming costume jewelry district and, while waving at admirers, one said: "Look at the general. He's just turned seventy-five and not a gray hair on his head."

"That's easy when you've been a general," replied the other merchant. "But let him be in the ladies' bag business for twenty-five years!"

In November 1959, Truman said he'd had a wonderful dream the night before. "I dreamed I gave General MacArthur a direct order—and he obeyed!"

After MacArthur died, on April 5, 1964, his wife was asked what she hoped for their son. "I hope he becomes a good man, but not a genius," she replied. "Geniuses are lonely."

Seven years later, Mrs. MacArthur assembled a book called *MacArthur's Legacy*, a collection of his inspiring speeches. "Which one is your favorite?" she was asked. "The one in which he asked me to marry him," she replied.

DAVID MERRICK

(1911–2000)

George Abbott had the longest producing career in Broadway history, but Merrick was close behind: an astonishing eighty-five plays and musicals, many frequently revived. From 1943 to 1996, he ruled Broadway as the theater's most dynamic and controversial showman. Think of them as two giants of overlapping generations, like Astaire-Kelly or Crosby-Sinatra. Born in St. Louis, he eschewed a legal career and quickly made his mark on Broadway. He was full of bluster, but also able to spot talent and fill seats.

In 1958, tickets for his production of *The Entertainer* quickly sold out, but Merrick took out a huge ad nonetheless, just to see his name alongside Laurence Olivier's.

Merrick once phoned a columnist—not my father—and asked him for a quote about Merrick's new show. "Just make up any quote and put my name on the bottom," replied the columnist. Merrick chose "The greatest show since Time began."

In October 1960, Jackie Gleason, who starred in Merrick's production of *Take Me Along*, was feuding with him. For an exhibition golf match that Gleason played with Arnold Palmer, he had golf balls specially made—bearing Merrick's face.

Merrick always accepted a ten-dollar investment in his shows from Paul, the news dealer at Eighth Avenue and Forty-Fourth Street in the theater district. On the opening night of *Carnival*, Paul walked into Sardi's grinning, carrying the newspaper reviews, and said to Merrick, "Well, we've done it again."

Early in 1961, Merrick had four of his shows on one block of West Fourty-Fifth Street. A survey showed his first twenty productions averaged 75 percent favorable reviews. "That only shows that the critics were wrong 25 percent of the time," said Merrick.

In 1962, Merrick ran a huge newspaper ad for *Subways Are for Sleeping*. It featured glowing quotes from seven men with the same names as the seven newspaper drama critics. He'd hired limousines and treated them and their wives to orchestra seats at a preview. He also wrote the quotes attributed to these phony critics.

The *Herald Tribune* ran it in one edition before yanking it, but the stunt caused a sensation. (He'd been planning it for years but had to wait for Brooks Atkinson of the *Times* to retire, since he couldn't find another Brooks Atkinson.) Merrick called the group the David Merrick Fan Club and considered sending them again, but this time seated next to their namesakes.

Lest patrons doubt that two intelligent, successful people (played by Phyllis Newman and Orson Bean) would ever sleep in the New York City subway, he first blared an announcement over a loudspeaker: "This is a fantasy."

Then he ran an ad for *I Can Get It for You Wholesale* with a quote from Walter Kerr, below the heading "This is what the *real* Walter Kerr said."

The tables were turned on Merrick when the Strollers, an off-Broadway company, distributed handbills in front of his three Broadway shows with this quote: "'Better than *Tchin-Tchin*, *Stop the World—I Want to Get Off*, and *Oliver*. I wish I had a piece of it.'—David Merrick." Their Merrick was a Philadelphia postman.

"Whenever I feel blue," he said, "I cheer myself up by thinking up ads I know the *New York Times* would never run."

Backstage at *Carnival*, Merrick overheard chorus girls talking world affairs. "Okay, so the Russians put a man in space," said one. "Big deal. Can Mrs. Khrushchev do a high leg kick?"

When *I Can Get It for You Wholesale* moved to the Broadway Theater, Merrick didn't take down all of the signs from the previous occupant, *My Fair Lady*. Just above the name of his show, he left "World's Greatest Musical" intact.

After twice opening four shows in the same week, Merrick announced he'd be spacing out his openings, explaining, "My backers' laundry bills for their tuxedo shirts are soaring."

He said taunting drama critics was "all in good fun, all in the grand tradition of yelling at the umpire."

In October 1963, Merrick ceded his billing above the title of *Funny Girl* to his coproducer Ray Stark. The show had a potentially controversial nude scene in it and Merrick said to Stark, "This means if we run into trouble you'll be the first one headed to jail."

In 1964, Merrick won five Tony awards. Amazingly, two-thirds of the nominations were for shows he produced. "I guess I'm a monopolist at heart," he said.

As he began negotiations with Actors Equity, he distributed

postcards to the union representatives showing John Wilkes Booth shooting President Lincoln. "There you have it," said Merrick. "A founding member of Actors Equity, no doubt."

When Louis Armstrong finally got to see a performance of *Hello, Dolly!*, Merrick's biggest hit, he said, "Man, so *that's* what my song is about!"

Merrick dined at Sardi's with Arthur Cantor, a press agent considering directing his first show. "Why on earth would you want to do that?" asked Merrick. "Then you'd *have* to fraternize with actors."

In the Merrick-produced Anthony Newley musical *The Roar of the Greasepaint, the Smell of the Crowd*, one of the actors, Murray Tannenbaum, stood seven foot three. Merrick insisted he have an understudy and arranged tryouts for any actors at least six foot eleven. A line formed outside the stage entrance, and at the end stood a man who was only five foot nine: a college basketball coach looking to recruit the rejects.

This may have been the impetus for a plan Merrick considered: seating basketball players directly in front of opening-night critics for his show *Cactus Flower*.

In November 1965, Merrick toured bases in Vietnam and was asked if he was frightened. "I've faced forty Broadway openings. *Nothing* frightens me," he said.

"Each member of our troupe had sandbags around our sleeping areas and sentries. The thought struck me that I could often use such protection on West Forty-Fourth Street and Broadway."

When the N.Y. Critics' Circle voted *"Marat/Sade"* best play over his *"Philadelphia Here I Come,"* Merrick was initially depressed. Then he realized he'd produced both.

When a production of *Hello, Dolly!* had a huge gross in its opening week in Oklahoma City, the Otoe tribe gave Merrick the name Mun-Day-Ka-Me-Tah-Way, which means "Chief Collector of Wampum."

Merrick always kept a pair of tickets in reserve up until curtain time for whichever of his shows Jacqueline Kennedy Onassis had yet to see.

When *Hello, Dolly!* was slated to tour Russia, Merrick rejected the idea of having instant translation available at every seat via earphones. He feared that if communist audiences understood every word of dialogue, they might view the two young men in the story as underpaid toilers in a cellar, exploited by a corrupt capitalist involved in a scheming, decadent system of wife-buying.

Woody Allen, guest host on *The Tonight Show*, with David Merrick, New York City, 1967. Photograph by Sam Shaw.

In October 1967, Merrick was invited to the White House for a dinner honoring the king of Nepal. "They told me I'd be introduced as 'the King of Broadway,'" he said. "I'll tell the king my domain exceeds his in two respects: more people and more pollution."

George S. Kaufman, the Pulitzer Prize-winning playwright, told Merrick his daughter was determined to make a career in the theater. "That's wonderful," replied Merrick. "What's she doing?"

"She's starting at the bottom," replied Kaufman. "She's a producer."

In July 1967, Mae West, then seventy-five, called Merrick, saying she'd like to star in the movie version of *Hello, Dolly!* Merrick was intrigued, but the talks collapsed after West said she wanted to include three songs she'd written, a younger leading man for her, and to replace the waiter-dancers with her trademark musclemen.

Lauren Bacall advised a young actress to make demands of the producer for better working conditions. "If you don't ask, you don't get. Except for Merrick. You can ask but you won't *ever* get."

Merrick told Turner Catledge, executive editor of the *New York Times*, what "a fine, upstanding man you have in your Broadway critic, Clive Barnes." On the way out of the meeting, Merrick muttered, "That should get Barnes fired."

When he learned that a new musical version of *All About Eve* was planned with a villainous character based on him, he phoned the playwright and said, "If that character *isn't* based on me, I'll sue!"

As an owner of several shares of the *New York Times*, he attended the paper's annual stockholders' meeting every year. At one, he rose and said to publisher Arthur Sulzberger, "Forgive me for telling you how to run your business, but after all, your newspaper has for years been telling me how run mine."

A few days later, he was at the Friars Club luncheon honoring Barbra Streisand. Merrick, noted for his disdain for actors, sat next to a doctor who told the producer many of his patients were actors. "Oh, so you're a pediatrician," said Merrick.

The program for Merrick's *Child's Play* said, "David Merrick puts on plays, puts on musicals, puts on comedies, and puts on everyone and every *thing*."

When Ethel Merman took over the title role in *Hello, Dolly!* (a role originally created for her), Merrick said of her famous booming singing voice, "She's the only actress who can be heard both on Broadway and off-Broadway at the same time."

On June 16, 1970, there was a bomb scare at Merrick's midtown office. He remained calm throughout. "A bomb on Broadway? Big deal," he said. "Happens every season."

ARISTOTLE ONASSIS

(1906–1975)

He lived a lavish life, with multiple homes, a private Greek island called Skorpios, and his enormous yacht, the *Christina*, which my father and I visited in the harbor of Monte Carlo. She was a mere 325 feet long, with room to land a helicopter.

Onassis was born in a town now in Turkey called Karatas. After success in other businesses, he made his fortune in international shipping.

After he'd bought controlling interest in the casino in Monte Carlo, he spoke of a previous owner named Basil Zaharoff, known as the Merchant of Death, since he'd made his fortune in munitions.

"One night he gambled at the casino and lost five hundred thousand dollars," said Onassis. "The next night, he lost a million. The third night he was convinced it was a profitable business, so he bought the casino and let others lose their money."

In September 1958, several Greek shipping firms were indicted and faced civil suits from the American government. Their lawyers met in Washington with Attorney General William Rogers. After some talk, Onassis, who had decided it was no use fighting, called out, "Cut the baloney! What's the ransom?"

Invited to participate in New York's official St. Patrick's Day festivities, he signed the RSVP form "O'Nassis."

He once hosted oil tycoon J. Paul Getty on his yacht. As the billionaires were sunning themselves, Onassis said to Getty, "Paul, a hundred thousand dollars for your thoughts."

Early in 1966, Onassis gave a party aboard his yacht and invited impresario Sol Hurok. The lights were kept so low that Hurok could never see the face of his dinner partner, who kept silent during the meal. Only when she was leaving did Hurok realize it was Greta Garbo.

Onassis once told a friend that, despite his long-standing relationship with the tempestuous opera diva Maria Callas, he'd never marry again. "Pay no attention to that," said Callas. "After all, it's the woman who decides these matters."

The day after that item ran in The Lyons Den, Onassis married Jacqueline Kennedy.

He described Callas's talent as "a God-given gift of a whistle." Onassis advised her not to commit to perform at a specific place more than eighteen months in advance. "You should be like a guest conductor," he told her. "When you feel like it, you should call up the opera and say you're available."

In April 1967, a friend wondered why Onassis looked taller and he replied that it might be due to his having sold his interests in the casino in Monte Carlo. "I no longer have to bow to Prince Rainier," he explained. "My spine was beginning to curve after all the bows."

JACQUELINE KENNEDY ONASSIS

(1929–1994)

As First Lady, she traveled all over the world. In May 1961, she was headed to Paris and planned to bring Kenneth, her hairstylist. But the French ambassador pointed out that France might take this as a slight, since that country is the world's foremost fashion authority. So Mrs. Kennedy came up with a unique solution. Alexandre of Paris would style her hair, but to Kenneth's written instructions.

In 1961, she attended a Boston tryout performance of Noël Coward's *Sail Away*, and after the excitement in the theater about her arrival died down, everyone settled into their seats. Coward was seated just in front of her, and as the curtain rose, she leaned forward and whispered to him, "Isn't this exciting?"

When the show gave a benefit performance on Broadway, excerpts from the reviews of several critics who'd seen it were included in the fliers distributed at the performance. Then there was an additional quote: "I loved the show!" The critic's name and address appeared on the next line: "Mrs. John Fitzgerald Kennedy, 1600 Pennsylvania Avenue, Washington, D.C."

Later that year, she returned from another overseas trip and was greeted by an elderly White House usher with "Nice to see you back, Mrs. Eisenhower." Rather than correct him, she told a friend, "What a blur we all must seem to him."

One of Mrs. Kennedy's most famous television appearances was the guided tour of the White House she gave to CBS's Charles Collingwood in 1962. It introduced her to the nation, with her grace, soft voice, and elegance unmatched by almost any woman in the world.

After the program, JFK's press secretary, Pierre Salinger, phoned around to get some reaction. Then, after hearing nothing but raves about her presentation, he phoned her on the White House extension. His smile quickly changed to a serious expression, however, adding: "Oh, yes, sir. Yes, Mr. President. You were good, too."

When Mrs. Kennedy attended a performance of *A Funny Thing Happened on the Way to the Forum*, Zero Mostel knew she was in one of the first rows. So he ad-libbed a new lyric for one of the songs. After telling the Roman populace to go to their homes, he faced Mrs. Kennedy and said, "And you—go to the White House!"

In 1963, she and her sister-in-law Jean Kennedy Smith dropped by at a rehearsal of a comedy called *Children from Their Games*. (The cast included a young Gene Hackman.) Once the actors saw the two famous sisters, they began blowing their lines. The play ended up running for only four performances.

In June of that year, JFK hosted a meeting of labor leaders and stood on a White House chair to be seen. Then AFL head George Meany did the same. After he spoke to the group, Meany said, "Lucky Mrs. Kennedy isn't around. She'd have clobbered us both!"

In October 1964, a car with "NYP" (New York Press) plates stopped at a traffic light on Fifth Avenue just as she and a friend were crossing the street. She saw the plate and seemed to freeze, sure the journalists were about to take her picture. "Don't worry, Mrs. Kennedy," said a photographer from the front passenger seat. "We're just on our way to cover a collision somewhere."

In July 1965, she attended a play in London where, at intermission, the audience gathered near her seat just to stare at her. She kept her composure, yet said to her companion, "I guess I'll be living as a freak for the rest of my life."

In September 1966, she took her children to Hawaii, where they went to a party at a friend's home with a pool. When the party was over, she realized the children wanted to swim, but needed a signal to go in. She broke the ice by jumping into the pool fully clothed.

In September 1967, Caroline Kennedy was having a problem with "New Math." So Mrs. Kennedy asked a friend who was a prominent banker to try his hand at the ten homework problems. The next day at school, Caroline's teacher said the banker got six wrong.

After he retired from the New York Giants in 1962, quarterback Charlie Conerly returned home to Mississippi and opened a chain of shoe stores. When he heard about Jacqueline Kennedy's marriage to Aristotle Onassis, Conerly said, "The most amazing thing is her shoe size: 10-AA."

In September 1971, a friend of Maria Callas's invited her to the Kennedy Center for a performance that would also be attended by the former First Lady.

"What?" replied Callas indignantly. "I'd *never* be in the same room with *that* woman!"

ELEANOR ROOSEVELT

(1884–1980)

When she was eighteen, she taught gymnastics and dancing at the University Settlement on New York's Lower East Side, the same school my father attended as a boy a decade later. At an anniversary dinner there she revealed that when she was teaching, a young gentleman would escort her home each evening. Her students teasingly asked if he was her "fellah."

"Oh, no," replied the young Eleanor. "He's just my distant cousin Franklin."

With apologies to Michelle Obama, Eleanor Roosevelt is the most important, revered First Lady in American history. She spent her twelve years in the White House as her invalid husband's legs, eyes, and ears, traveling all over the world on his behalf. But she also established herself as a brilliant diplomat and humanitarian, and was the first U.S. delegate to the newly formed United Nations in 1945.

There is no portrait or sculpture of the First Lady taken from a life pose. The official White House painting was done from photographs. She refused to pose for two reasons: lack of interest and inability to stay put.

A New York cabdriver once recognized her in his rearview mirror and told her what he thought about the state of the country. She told FDR, and the next night he quoted the cabbie in his State of the Union address.

Wanting to avoid constant Secret Service protection, she went to the Library of Congress, where she learned that under the law she wasn't obliged to have it. She'd cite that law whenever agents turned up.

In June 1937, she signed a petition opposing government censorship of the arts. Then she attended a performance of *You Can't Take It With You* on Broadway. Producer Sam H. Harris had been told she'd be coming and ordered a last-minute change in the script. At one point, a character donned a mask and asked, "Guess who *this* is?" After several uncomplimentary guesses, the answer in the script was "Mrs. Roosevelt." Some other name was inserted and everyone—including Mrs. Roosevelt—laughed. But when she learned of the last-minute change, she returned another night unannounced—and laughed even harder!

She made the arrangements for a White House ball in 1937. She phoned society pianist Eddy Duchin, who'd been invited to play, and reminded him that the ball wouldn't start until 10 p.m. "I have one favor to ask of you," she said. "Of course," he replied. "It would be an honor, no matter what the favor might be."

"Before the ball," Mrs. Roosevelt replied, "we're having a family dinner downstairs. Will you join us?"

A few days later, Mrs. Roosevelt, hosting a tea for a women's group, was interrupted by a phone call. She returned to her guests and said, "A Mr. Gordon will soon be joining us. I hope he won't feel a bit awkward surrounded only by ladies." Mr. Gordon felt right at home. He was Max Gordon, producer of a hit stage play with an all-female cast, *The Women*.

April 1938 brought a meeting between Eleanor Roosevelt and the movie star Eleanor Powell. "Isn't it interesting," said Mrs. Roosevelt, "that we both have the same first name." "Yes, and we might've had the same *last* name, too, if I'd met one of those sons of yours a lot earlier," Powell replied.

When the Duke and Duchess of Windsor were scheduled to visit the United States, FDR's austere mother, Sara, told her son she disapproved of their controversial marriage. Eleanor disagreed, and urged the president to invite them to the White House. Finally FDR said, "This is *my* house, and I'll invite whomever I please."

One night the Roosevelts welcomed the humorous playwright George S. Kaufman to dinner. "Nice place you have here," he said, looking around the dining room of the White House. "The food is good, the service excellent, and if you get enough people to talk about this place, you could do some business."

"You're right," said the First Lady, "and the location's not so bad, either."

In July 1939, word reached Mrs. Roosevelt that Theodore Roosevelt's daughter Alice Roosevelt Longworth, no fan of FDR's, did a devastating imitation of the First Lady. Mrs. Roosevelt asked to see it, but Mrs. Longworth lost her nerve and instead did an imitation of Mrs. Calvin Coolidge.

November 1939 brought a visitor to the White House whom Mrs. Roosevelt introduced to the president. He reminded FDR about a campaign speech he'd made in 1932 wherein he said, "We have the key to the White House in our pocket." The president nodded, recalling that line.

"If you still have that key, Mr. President, please accept this, my new pick-proof lock," said the guest—Louis Segal, president of the Segal Lock Company.

That was the year FDR changed Thanksgiving to the next-to-last Thursday of November, rather than the last day, to give businesses more Christmas shopping days. A guest at the annual press dinner arrived carrying a firecracker, Easter egg, and Christmas stocking, "just to be prepared if any further changes are coming."

In January 1940, Mrs. Roosevelt hosted a party for the cast of the long-running Broadway play *Life with Father*. "Everybody sit where you'd like," she told her guests. "Just save a place for me somewhere."

In April 1940, she went to a Hollywood beauty parlor frequented by movie stars and was amused by the attendants prolonging their time working on her. Then she paid by check. Of course the owner of the parlor never cashed it. Instead, the check was framed and hung in a prominent position, to show the pampered clientele that Eleanor Roosevelt was the only *real* celebrity there.

When she was about to give a speech on the radio, the program's host, writer Clifton Fadiman, whispered that the previous guest had used up most of her allotted time, so she had only four minutes.

She nodded politely. Then the First Lady of the United States spoke extemporaneously and flawlessly—for twenty minutes.

By July 1940, FDR still hadn't formally announced his intention to run for a third term. Postmaster General James A. Farley, chairman of the Democratic National Committee, with his own aspirations, prodded FDR about whom he'd want to succeed him. "Only one person," replied the president. "Eleanor."

Just before King George VI and Queen Elizabeth came to visit the Roosevelts at the White House, Eleanor made a last-minute check of the bedroom assigned to the royal couple. To her horror, she saw that all the paintings on the wall depicted scenes from the Revolutionary War, and the bookshelves held a collection of histories of the conflict.

Thomas Mann, the German novelist and essayist, visited the

A signed photograph of my father and Eleanor Roosevelt.

White House and marveled after watching a group of underprivileged people talking with the First Lady about improving their situations. "It is wonderful to see this happening in a great democracy," Mann said.

Mrs. Roosevelt replied: "It *is* wonderful, but *anybody* would do this in my place."

In May, 1941, she became the first and still the only First Lady to take a ride in a fighter plane, when she visited the Tuskegee Airmen's base in Alabama.

Before Roosevelt announced he'd run for an unprecedented third term, there'd been speculation he might instead run for his previous office, governor of New York. But Mrs. Roosevelt put a stop to that. "When I leave the White House," she said, "I'm going to spend the rest of my life at Hyde Park, wearing a little lace cap, knitting all day long, and playing with my grandchildren."

Lord Beaverbrook, the British publishing magnate, paid a visit to the White House accompanying Prime Minister Winston Churchill. Mrs. Roosevelt told him that since his newspaper, the *London Standard*, had begun publishing her column My Day, she would henceforth address him as "Boss."

In February 1942, the cast of the Broadway play *Angel Street* was invited to dine at the White House. The play's producer, Shepard Traube, and his wife sat next to each other. The First Lady entered, spotted the Traubes, whom she knew, and said, "This White House is making many changes. But one thing remains the same: a husband and wife can never sit next to each other."

Planning to attend the Overseas Press Club's luncheon, she phoned for tickets. While she was talking, the secretary on the other end asked her to hold on for a minute, as another phone was ringing. Then the secretary realized that whomever was calling wasn't as important as the First Lady. She got back on the line and apologized.

"Not at all," laughed Mrs. Roosevelt. "Happens all the time."

In November 1942, Mrs. Roosevelt flew to England for a visit. Her Secret Service detail assigned her the name "Rover." She was trying to locate her son, Lieutenant Colonel Elliott Roosevelt. As her search began, the coded message from her security detail to those with a need to know was "Rover's Lost Her Pup." When she managed to elude reporters on that trip, one paper borrowed the title of the popular Hitchcock movie: "The First Lady Vanishes."

When an army captain was assigned to travel with her on a tour of the South Pacific in October 1943, his wife despaired for him. "I have no idea how he'll ever be able to keep up with her," she said.

When Dame May Whitty was headed to Washington for a preview of her movie *Madame Curie*, her press agent was told their drawing room compartment on the train had been accidentally double-booked and that another lady was occupying it. "Tell her to move," said the press rep. "The lady here is a Dame of the British Empire."

"Sorry," replied the porter, "but the lady inside is the First Dame of the United States."

In January 1943, Katherine Cornell, then Broadway's biggest star, and her husband, producer-director Guthrie McClintic, were overnight guests at the White House. Once they were settled in their quarters, he took a shower, then emerged wrapped in a towel. A knock came at the door. It was Mrs. Roosevelt, who said, "It's quite all right. Stay just as you are. It is only I."

Mrs. Roosevelt offered guests a guided tour of the private quarters of the White House. "There are plenty of grandchildren to go around as your guides," she said. "And later, I'll meet with you to correct any of their historical inaccuracies."

She told other guests the legend of the ghost of Lincoln.

"That item first appeared in Leonard Lyons's column," she laughed. "I want to know his sources."

The next day, my father responded to Mrs. Roosevelt in print. "How I get my stories, Mrs. Roosevelt, is a trade secret," he wrote. "But as one columnist to another, I'll tell you my sources if you tell me yours."

In 1944, she attended a preview performance on Broadway of a play called *But Not Goodbye*, which starred Harry Carey Sr., the old cowboy-movie star. Backstage afterward she told him, "I especially liked the way you sandpapered that boat. I've seen that done many times, and you did it properly. Franklin knows how to do that, among other things."

In June 1943, she and a companion went to see the Broadway show *The Doughgirls*. They were seated in the orchestra section near the stage, the same seats occupied the week before by the Duke and Duchess of Windsor. Before the second act, an usher said that if she liked, they could be escorted out just before the final curtain, so as not to have to wade through the crowd, just as the Windsors had done. "I'll stay," she said. "I'm enjoying the show and besides, I wouldn't want to disturb the actors."

A few days later, she took a round trip from Manhattan to Brooklyn by subway. A sailor and his girl sat across from her and stared. Finally, the sailor said, "Lady, did anyone ever tell you that you look like Eleanor Roosevelt?"

"Yes," she replied. "Especially because I *am* Mrs. Roosevelt." Then, for the rest of their ride, she discussed the philosophies of the war, the new world, postwar economics, etc. Leaving at Fourteenth Street, the sailor turned to her and said, "Lady, honestly, if anyone ever tries telling you that you look like Eleanor Roosevelt—believe them."

In mid-July 1943, she stopped off briefly in Reno, Nevada, where "quickie" divorces were the main attraction. A local reporter was careful to put her visit in perspective: "Don't worry," he wrote. "She's only passing through. She never stays in one place long enough to establish residence."

She had an appointment to meet Norman Cousins, editor of *The Saturday Review of Literature*, to share a train ride to a speaking engagement in upstate New York. "Let's meet at the information booth of Grand Central station," she suggested. She arrived early, so for five minutes, the First Lady of the United States stood alone, at the most famous meeting place in the land, two train tickets in hand.

When she visited Guadalcanal Island, the scene of one of the bloodiest battles of the Pacific, officers warned their marines to be done with their showers long before she arrived. Once on the island, however, she began walking in her customary fast gait and arrived much earlier than expected. Sure enough, several marines, unaware of her presence, left the showers and then, seeing her approach, quickly jumped back inside.

"Don't worry," she said. "I have sons, you know. Four of them."

In October 1944, the Duchess of Windsor was at a party where she overheard someone tell a cruel joke at the expense of Eleanor Roosevelt. She walked over to the man and said, "Excuse me. One of us must now leave."

Churchill couldn't believe she flew to the Pacific theater alone. "I didn't want to take up more than one seat on the plane," she explained. When she arrived at a naval base she carried a letter from FDR to Admiral William "Bull" Halsey, commander of U.S. naval forces in the South Pacific. It read, "Let her go anywhere she wants, so long as it doesn't interfere with the war effort."

When she visited Las Vegas, she did something even the nearby atomic bomb testing couldn't do: she brought the gambling tables to a halt. She told Beldon Katleman, the owner of the El Rancho Vegas hotel, that her son John had given her two quarters to bet in the slot machine. Unseen by Mrs. Roosevelt, he had his mechanic open the back of the machine and stand by with a finger on the lever. Thus she hit two jackpots.

On a transatlantic voyage on the S.S. *America*, she was invited to dine with the captain every night. "Only tonight," she said. "The rest of the voyage I want to dine with the other passengers. There are so many aboard I'd like to meet."

"The way I make a speech," Mrs. Roosevelt once said, "is to write out the beginning and then write out the end. Knowing how to begin and end is most important. Let the middle be flexible so you can make changes if you have to."

In March 1946, she was asked about rumors that she was considering a run for the Senate from New York. "It's not true," she said. "I'm sixty-two now. I've only got fifteen years of active life left." She was off by just a year.

In September 1948, she addressed an audience in Stuttgart, Germany, speaking in German. She hadn't spoken German since high school. "How did you brush up on your German?" a friend asked Mrs. Roosevelt, who was then serving as a delegate to the newly formed United Nations, completing the second volume of her autobiography, writing a daily column, and attending diplomatic luncheons.

"Easy," she replied. "I just hired a tutor and studied with him every day until I'd mastered my German."

Her trip had been prepared with two itineraries: one to Scandinavia, the other with visits to France and Germany. Her aides left it up to her to decide which one to accept. "I'll do both," she said. And did.

"The tragedy of our times," she said in March 1953, "is that our young people are being taught never to make a mistake; that mistakes are unforgivable. All great people have made mistakes. If you're afraid of making one, it means you'll stop functioning."

On her seventieth birthday, in 1954, she had a number of morning appointments, then appeared at several luncheon and tea meetings, made a number of campaign speeches, and attended a dinner in her honor. Then she rushed to a UN party, arriving there even before the dais guests from her own dinner!

"My husband said I'd never make a politician," she reminisced. "He said I lacked the one thing a politician needs: patience."

In March 1959 Alger Hiss, the former government official convicted of perjury in connection with accusations that he had been a Soviet spy, was serving a sentence in the federal penitentiary at Lewisburg, Pennsylvania. One day he asked another inmate to name the one American woman he thought had accomplished the most. "Eleanor Roosevelt," said the other prisoner, mobster Frank Costello.

PRESIDENT FRANKLIN DELANO ROOSEVELT

(1882–1945)

When Franklin and Eleanor Roosevelt honeymooned in London in 1905, they were given the royal suite at Brown's Hotel. The officials there had mistakenly thought it was to be occupied by President *Theodore* Roosevelt, Eleanor's uncle and Franklin's distant cousin.

Surely with an eye toward future campaigns, before the 1928 Democratic convention, FDR sent for all the newsreel shots of himself running for vice president in 1920 and studied each gesture he'd made. "To be a successful politician," he explained, "you have to be as professional about it as an actor. You have to know what every gesture is worth. I'm just studying my role."

Soon after her son was elected president in 1932, Roosevelt's strong-willed mother, Sara, was asked what it felt like. "For the life of me," she replied, "I cannot understand why he wants the job."

The day before his inauguration, FDR made the customary courtesy call to the outgoing president, Herbert Hoover. He told Hoover that he needn't return a courtesy call to Roosevelt the next day.

Hoover stared at FDR and coldly replied, "When you become president, you will learn that the president of the United States *never* calls on people." Five days later, on Supreme Court Justice Oliver Wendell Holmes's ninety-second birthday, FDR told his staff, "We're going to show Mr. Hoover that the president of the United States *does indeed* call on people," and he paid Holmes a courtesy visit.

Early in the new administration, two boys somehow eluded the guards and found their way upstairs to the president's study. They found FDR and asked for his autograph. But Roosevelt refused, saying, "You'd have had the autograph if you hadn't insulted the home of the president of the United States by sneaking in."

Late in 1937, Sara told a friend that whenever she was at Hyde Park and missed her son in Washington, she would go to a theater to watch him in newsreels.

After losing his battle to add several new justices to the Supreme

Court, thereby reducing the influence of the conservative wing, FDR was asked why he undertook such a hopeless fight. "It took 150 years for the country to gain respect for the Court," he explained, "and just a three-year battle to try to get the Court to respect the American people."

A newspaper syndicate arranged to publish some writings of FDR and reproduced an old photo showing him as a boy, standing next to Grover Cleveland, along with Cleveland's advice: "My dear little boy, I hope you never grow up to be president."

Early in 1940, actor Pat O'Brien was invited to FDR's birthday party. He mentioned this to the top electrician at MGM, who said that in 1933 the bank holding his mortgage repossessed his house. For fourteen months, he tried in vain to save his home. In desperation, he wrote to President Roosevelt, and within a month, federal officials arranged for him to get his house back. The electrician then gave O'Brien a gift for FDR: a photo of the house, once again his own.

A biographer asked FDR what his major was at Harvard. "Economics and international law," replied Roosevelt. "But both those have changed so much since then. Maybe I wasted my time."

FDR was a great admirer of Carl Sandburg, then working on his multivolume biography of Lincoln. The president wanted to be certain the Lincoln room in the White House really was his. So Sandburg came at the president's behest and entered the room. Recalling Lincoln's mentioning the view of the Potomac, he inspected the room while Roosevelt, seated nearby, feigned work on some papers and snuck looks at the famed historian. Finally, Sandburg nodded and said, "Yes, this was his room, Mr. President. Thank you. Good-bye."

In September 1940, Roosevelt gave a picnic at Hyde Park, and one guest, Katherine Hepburn, made an entrance worthy of a star. She piloted a seaplane from her home in Connecticut and landed on the Hudson River in front of the main house. She got out, saw FDR, yet still asked, "Is this the Roosevelts' place?"

Fala, the Scottie dog given to FDR by a cousin, was introduced to the world in The Lyons Den on November 18, 1940. The black puppy was prohibited entry to FDR's limousine en route to his third inauguration and parade, on March 4, 1941. Then he went missing, and was found later near a movie theater. Mary Eban, the president's longtime maid, asked him to forgive Fala. "They wouldn't let him attend the inauguration," she said, "so I guess he wanted to be first on line for the newsreel coverage."

Fala was named for an ancestor of FDR's, John Murray, a.k.a. "The Outlaw of Falahill." Roosevelt was quick to point out that Fala had only one "l" in his name. Russel Crouse, who cowrote the books for *Anything Goes* and, years later, *The Sound of Music*, remarked, "I've been telling that to everyone about my name. One 'l.' I often thought that this annoyance shouldn't happen to a dog. Now it has."

The president designed Fala's quarters on the Roosevelt yacht, making sketches, then blueprints for what he considered an ideal sandbox for a dog aboard a vessel. Pursuant to navy regulations, FDR submitted the plans to the naval architects, who passed on permanent additions to anything in the fleet. They approved, but made one addition: a small tree.

A Broadway producer asked the president's mother why she was opposed to a third term. "I also opposed a *first* term," she explained. "For the life of me, I cannot understand why Franklin *still* wants the job." She died in September 1941, three months to the day before Pearl Harbor.

My father had sources in the Roosevelt White House and often received exclusive stories on White House stationery. After the war, one of these sources told him Stalin would sometimes send FDR letters through normal mail, not diplomatic pouches. Oddly, the letters alternated in tone; a message of praise and gratitude for military support, followed by another letter full of insults. Then another thankful letter, followed by a tirade. The president was asked how he dealt with this.

"I wait until I receive the bad ones," replied FDR, "before I answer the good ones."

An American diplomat stationed in Latvia had to flee when the Soviets invaded in 1940. When he returned to Washington, he was summoned to the White House, where Roosevelt asked him what the first American thing he remembered seeing when he stepped on U.S. soil was.

"When I landed in San Francisco," the diplomat told FDR, "I saw a chauffeur wearing a Roosevelt button get out and open the door for the woman in the backseat. She got out and was wearing a Willkie button that read, 'Start packing, Eleanor. The Willkies are coming!' That's when I knew I was really home."

369

Just after Roosevelt defeated Wendell Willkie, the Republican candidate in the 1940 election, he declared that this third term would be his last.

"You shouldn't have said that, Mr. President," said one of his aides. "That statement will cost you a million votes—in 1944."

In late November 1940, a news cameraman arrived in Hyde Park to photograph the president. Before entering the room where FDR was to pose, he was suddenly stricken by the memory of the assassination scene in the Hitchcock movie *Foreign Correspondent*, in which the Dutch premier is shot by a pistol concealed inside a camera.

"I'm not a suspect," he told the surprised Secret Service agent outside the door, "but I think for everybody's protection, you should make sure everything's all right." And so, while the agents who hadn't requested it watched in fascination, he dismantled his camera, got the okay, and reassembled it.

In January 1941, Wendell Willkie flew to London after meeting with FDR. "On Inauguration Day," said FDR, "you'll probably be in some London pub, thinking how you'd rather be in Washington taking the oath of office. And I'll be here taking the oath, thinking how I'd like to be over *there* at some pub!"

Chief Justice Charles Evans Hughes had sworn in FDR as president in 1933 and 1937. Just before he administered the oath of office on January 20, 1941, he whispered to FDR, "Isn't this getting monotonous?"

My parents visited FDR at the White House and he told them that he was a sixteen-year-old student at the Groton prep school in Connecticut when the USS *Maine* was blown up in Havana, killing 395 sailors. The United States then declared war on Spain on April 25, 1898. That night, young Franklin and a friend, both ill with a fever, nevertheless decided to join up. They hid in a truck headed toward the army recruiting station. Both boys began complaining to each other about their fever. "Forget about it," said Roosevelt. "We're men now and have a man's job to do." An hour later, both complained of parched throats. "Let's forget about that too," said Franklin. "We'll act like men." But the "men" were caught, diagnosed with measles, and returned to school.

For more than fifty years, an American named Mrs. Post lived in Paris. In her youth, she had been a classmate of Sara Delano. In 1940 she was able to leave Nazi-occupied Paris and return home.

Back in New York that summer, she stopped and had tea with her old school friend.

"By the way, Sara," asked Mrs. Post, "I remember once you wrote me that you had a boy. What's become of him?"

"Franklin," replied the president's mother incredulously, "is the president of the United States."

There was a pause, and then Mrs. Post said, "Please don't be angry with me, Sara. Remember, I've lived abroad so long. And after all, can you tell me who the President of *France* is?"

By May 1941, America was inching closer to war. One prominent American, playwright Maxwell Anderson, who wrote *The Bad Seed* and many other plays and movies, had had a change of heart. He wrote FDR, "Mr. President. Shoot now! We can see the whites of their eyes!"

Later that spring, isolationists picketed the White House. When an aide offered to have them removed, FDR said, "Just let 'em picket. This is *my* house."

Three months before Pearl Harbor, FDR ordered a For Sale sign hung on the door of his town house in Manhattan. "Mr. President," a reporter asked him, "why didn't you do that the usual way, in the newspapers?"

"Because," replied the president, "eighty percent of your newspapers opposed my election and reelections. I don't think your papers reach the American people."

When he received Franco's ambassador after the end of the bloody Spanish Civil War, FDR discussed Loyalist prisoners and asked the diplomat to tell Franco about the mercy extended to all Confederate prisoners after the American Civil War. Franco ignored him.

FDR Jr. was asked if he'd ever run for president. "I won't," he said. "And besides, I was born on Campobello Island—that's in Canada!"

Browsing through a pile of old photographs, FDR found one of a baseball team. One of the players in the team photo was James A. Farley. FDR inscribed the picture to his friend, the former postmaster general: "To Jim Farley. In memory of your hair."

One day, Eleanor sent a note to FDR's secretary about a large bill awaiting payment, saying, "FDR will have a fit." The president replied, "Pay it. Have had fit."

In mid-March 1943, a freshman congressman put a direct question to the president: "How do you feel about a fourth term?" FDR noticed that the young Republican had a sandwich in one hand and an unfinished soda in the other, and asked, "How many bottles of soda pop have you had so far?"

"This is my first one, Mr. President," the bewildered congressman replied.

"Well, finish that one, then have another and then a third," replied the president. "*Then* come and tell me how you feel about having another."

In June 1943, an army-produced show called *Army Play by Play* was performed at Hyde Park for the Roosevelts and their guest, Queen Wilhelmina of the Netherlands, living in exile in America. One actor cautioned the rest of the cast not to squeeze FDR's hand when they met him, since he shakes thousands.

After five limp handshakes, FDR said, "What's the matter with you soldiers? Doesn't the army feed you enough?"

"Does the president *really* need so many bodyguards?" asked one actor. "Who'd attack him here in Hyde Park?" The Secret Service agent replied, "We're in Dutchess County," while never taking his eyes off FDR. "This is a Republican stronghold."

In July 1943, a young aide came to see FDR and announced his resignation because of limited access to the president. FDR replied, "When I was assistant secretary of the navy under Woodrow Wilson, I felt the same way. President Wilson called me in and said, 'In the Civil War, an aide came to see President Lincoln with the same complaint. Abe told him that in 1778, a young aide told President Washington the same thing.'

"Washington told that young man to get back to work. So did Lincoln. And that's what Wilson said to me. And that's what I'm telling you: get back to work." And so he did.

Eddie Cantor, the comic entertainer, accompanied FDR to Warm Springs, Georgia, the spa FDR created for fellow polio victims. Cantor marveled at the president's ability to remember the names of patients' family members. "How did you do that? Is it memory training?"

FDR laughed and said, "Not at all. Politician!"

Toward the end of the 1943 White House Correspondents' Dinner, FDR looked over the room and saw that many of the journalists had had a few. He took the microphone and said, "Tonight I'm concerned with the word 'humanity.' I think about humanity when

I awaken in the morning and when I go to sleep. And tonight, in the name of humanity, I'm announcing there will be no usual Friday press conference at the White House tomorrow."

At the Tehran summit in late 1943, Averell Harriman whispered bad news to FDR: railroad union leaders were threatening to strike. Stalin noticed him getting the report and when it was translated, he suggested, "Why not just liquidate them?"

In 1946, Roosevelt's bodyguard, Mike Reilly, revealed that at the Casablanca summit, he stood behind drapes while the President and General de Gaulle conferred. At one point, the argument became so heated that Reilly drew his pistol and stood there, ready, until the conference ended.

Back in Washington, FDR told his legal advisor, New York State judge Samuel Rosenman, "I met with Churchill and Chiang Kai-shek."

"That's nothing," replied the judge. "I met Frank Sinatra!"

FDR appointed James M. Landis to head the Office of Civil Defense. Landis favored flowery language on blackout signs: "Illumination Should Be Extinguished."

"You mean, 'Turn Lights Off'?" asked FDR. "Then *say* so!"

FDR gave Churchill a globe, and when it arrived at 10 Downing Street, the prime minister looked at it and said, "Humph! They say the globe he sent Stalin is bigger." It was.

An aide said he learned to keep memos to FDR short after he'd submitted a long, detailed treatise. When he asked the president if he'd read it, FDR replied, "Read it? I can't even *lift* it!"

Roosevelt was often asked about possible appointments to various positions for Herbert Hoover. Finally, FDR told press secretary Steve Early why he never named Hoover: "Confidentially, I don't like Hoover."

In February 1944, President Isaías Medina of Venezuela visited, and FDR told him that in 1904 he and a friend were in Caracas. One night, with nothing to do, they went to the theater to see something called *Pagliacci*, though they knew nothing about opera. They saw a marvelous unknown tenor perform. "He was wonderful," remembered FDR, "and by applauding, I feel that in some little way, I discovered Enrico Caruso."

In February 1945, Roosevelt, Churchill, and Stalin met at Yalta, on the Black Sea in Crimea. At one point Churchill quoted at length from *The Decline and Fall of the Roman Empire*.

"Oh, you and your fancy education," Roosevelt, a Harvard graduate, joked. "You're just showing off because you studied hard and I didn't."

"Studied hard?" replied Churchill. "My dear Mr. President, at school I was last in my class."

Back in Washington, FDR received a note from FDR Jr. saying a surprise awaited his father in the navy's secret file for January 30, 1945, the president's sixty-third birthday. Roosevelt ordered Fleet Admiral Ernest King, chief of naval operations, to check. It contained a note saying his son had sunk a Japanese submarine.

In one of his elections, he carried a Manhattan district by winning every vote but one. "Pretty flattering, Mr. President," an aide said. "Yes," replied FDR, "but I wish I could've met that lone Republican. I know I could've made that vote unanimous."

He once called the *New York Times* to complain about an unfavorable editorial. "Don't worry, Mr. President," said the editor. "Our surveys show only ten percent of our readers ever check the editorials."

A few weeks before his sudden death, Roosevelt got to screen Laurence Olivier's film of *Henry V*. Viscount Halifax, the British ambassador, watched the movie with FDR. Both loved the film, but the ambassador was cautionary. "Mr. President," said Halifax, "you and I are university men. I don't think ours will be a typical reaction."

Roosevelt replied, "The possession of a university degree doesn't give one an advantage appreciating something good. I know what the general public likes," said the four-times-elected president. "The public will like it."

When *Sunrise at Campobello* opened on Broadway, with Ralph Bellamy as FDR, Eleanor and daughter Anna were in attendance. Anna enjoyed the show but suggested one change. At one point, FDR and Eleanor said "I love you" to each other. "They never did that in front of anyone," Anna told the producers. The line was cut.

On the first anniversary of FDR's death, there were ceremonies at Hyde Park. Dignitaries from all over the world attended. One diplomat noticed a crowd surrounding one attendee and asked Robert E. Sherwood who it was. "That's Frank Sinatra," replied Sherwood.

"This seems strange to me," the diplomat said.

"You have Eleanor Roosevelt, cabinet members, Supreme Court justices, all here to honor President Roosevelt, and they push to see a singer named Sinatra."

Sherwood replied, "I think Mr. Roosevelt would've liked that."

In December 1945, General de Gaulle visited New York and was greeted by the governor. "We in France loved FDR," said de Gaulle to his host. "He is irreplaceable. During the last election we were hoping for the sake of the world that he'd win. By the way, what was the name of the man who ran against him?"

"That honor was mine," replied New York governor Thomas E. Dewey.

Years later, an actor told me that on several occasions, FDR couldn't take time away from running the war to give his weekly Fireside Chats on the radio, so the actor, who did a perfect imitation, substituted for him. It was Art Carney, who'd win immortality as Ed Norton on *The Honeymooners*.

DAVID SARNOFF

(1891–1971)

On the chilly night of April 15, 1912, the RMS *Titanic*, hit by an iceberg, sent out distress signals. The SS *California*, just twelve miles away, had its radio turned off. Only the SS *Carpathia*, fifty-six miles away, picked up the signal, but couldn't arrive until the next morning. The world already knew of the disaster, since the most distant recipient of the faint distress call was in the Marconi office at the Wanamaker Building in lower Manhattan. A young Russian immigrant was working the radio late that night. His name was David Sarnoff.

Sarnoff supplemented his family's income by singing in a synagogue choir during the Jewish High Holidays. He was a soprano until, inevitably, his voice changed and he lost his job. Looking for work, he saw a sign in a window. The sign read: "Wanted: Office boy for the Marconi Wireless Company."

One of the most important men of the twentieth century, Sarnoff eventually founded the Radio Corporation of America (RCA), which in turn started the National Broadcasting Company (NBC).

In November 1942, an English visitor remarked to Sarnoff, "In England, there are such cordial relations between the government and industrialists, whereas here in America, the government is continually at loggerheads with them."

"That's because in England," replied Sarnoff, "they knight industrialists; here we indict them."

Sarnoff served in the army during World War II as a communications expert, eventually rising to the rank of brigadier general. In Rome after the liberation in 1944, Sarnoff visited Marconi's widow. She told him she'd survived the past four years and now needed only one thing: a radio.

Shortly after the liberation of Paris, later in 1944, the army issued orders establishing wireless facilities for the press. But an elderly civilian wanted wireless privileges too. "I have wireless operator's license number ten," said the man proudly. "I know what I'm talking about."

The army officer who'd set up the press office replied, "Well, I happen to have operator's license number one."

"In that case," replied the man, "it's nice to meet you, General Sarnoff."

In October 1947, Sarnoff offered Albert Einstein fifty thousand dollars a year for a once-a-week broadcast. Einstein turned him down, saying, "I'd rather talk to three people who understand me than be paid for speaking to millions who don't."

Hjalmar Schacht was a German banker, politician, and industrialist who was arrested and tried at the Nuremberg war crimes trials. Authorities raided his apartment and found a framed photo inscribed by Sarnoff, who'd been his friend during the prewar Weimar Republic. At the trial, to save mutual embarrassment, neither Schacht nor Sarnoff acknowledged each other. Schacht, who'd been bravely involved in anti-Nazi activities while serving in the German government, was acquitted.

In 1952, one of Marconi's daughters, Joya, visited Sarnoff at his offices at NBC, next to Radio City Music Hall. Showing her around, he said, "If it hadn't been for your father, I'd probably still be looking for a job today."

In May of that year, Sarnoff dined with his son and eventual successor, Robert, and his granddaughter Rosita, then eight years old. He asked if she knew the meaning of the word "excellent" and she said she did; it meant the very best. "How would you rate your own brainpower?" he asked. "I'd say very good," she replied. "And your father's?" he asked. "His brain? Also very good," said the little girl. "And *my* brainpower?" asked the founder and chairman of RCA, whose vision changed the world.

"I'd say good," she replied.

In September 1953, Sarnoff reminisced about the competition he faced over the years. "I'm actually grateful for my competitors and even my enemies," he said. "In the long-range movement toward progress, a kick in the pants sends you further along than does a friendly hand. The buggy manufacturer feared the automobile, and the railroad people feared the airplane. Why not operate them all, so long as there's a market for each? This is also true of radio versus television. As long as people go to the beach or are in their cars, there'll always be room for radio."

A radio and TV executive was eager to be hired and told Sarnoff that he, the applicant, was a genius. "You're no genius," replied

Sarnoff. "You're only eccentric. All geniuses are eccentric, but all eccentrics aren't geniuses."

As far back as 1954, Sarnoff carried a tiny box in his breast pocket with an earplug. He described it as his "boredom killer." It was an early transistor radio. "When I sit at a dinner and listen to a boring person next to me," he explained, "I simply pull out the ear attachment and put it on, leaving the person thinking I'm hard of hearing. Then I listen to good NBC orchestra music." He mentioned this to a young woman before a dinner and found that, by coincidence, she was seated next to him. "Here," he said, giving her his anti-boredom device. "You'll probably need it more than I do."

When Winston Churchill received the Freedom House award, the original presenter, industrialist Bernard Baruch, was ill, so General Sarnoff read his remarks. "Tonight, Mr. Prime Minister," he told Churchill, "I've reverted to my original occupation: messenger boy."

Sarnoff owned a rare copy of a book written by Lee de Forest, the radio pioneer, inscribed "To David Sarnoff, the father of radio." Sarnoff commented, "There are so many 'fathers of radio' that there is now doubt as to the legitimacy of the offspring."

In April 1956, Sarnoff was introduced to a Soviet official in New York, who was aware that Sarnoff was born in Belarus. "I know you came to America with just a penny in your pocket," said the Russian. "No, I came *without* a penny," said Sarnoff. "If you have a penny, that's a start already. But it's tougher without a penny."

When Sputnik was launched in 1957, Sarnoff said, "Up to now, Russia put all its satellites in hell. Now they've finally put one in the heavens."

In November 1961, Sarnoff told of his schooling as a boy in Belarus. As an eight-year-old student, he had to memorize Hebrew passages, two thousand words at a time. His stern teacher stood by with pinching fingers and a tiny cat-o-nine-tails. "Let's just say mine was not a progressive school," he said.

One night at the Colony restaurant, Edward G. Robinson was challenged to confirm the Yiddish word for "umbrella." He looked around the restaurant for help. He couldn't find it at the first table, where Frank Sinatra sat with some grim-looking men with sunglasses. At the second table, Kirk Douglas said his Yiddish was limited, so he couldn't help. Assistance did come from the third table, where Sarnoff confirmed the word to be "shirem."

JOSEF STALIN

(1879–1953)

No, the brutal dictator never sat at a front table at El Morocco, supped matzo ball soup at Lindy's, or hobnobbed with a Gabor at the Stork Club. My father definitely didn't know him, but he knew people who dealt with Stalin, and those were his sources.

Harry Hopkins, FDR's perpetually sickly looking advisor, visited Stalin in Moscow in October 1941, five months into the Nazi invasion. Hopkins asked Stalin why he thought the Germans had invaded. "Did they think you were weak?" he asked.

"On the contrary," replied Stalin through an interpreter. "He knew we were strong. Hitler knew that as long as such a powerful war machine was at his back, he couldn't turn around and try to destroy England."

A former secretary of war, Major General Pat Hurley, was one of the few Americans Stalin trusted. They first met a few months after America entered the war. "You're not doing so well," said Stalin.

"You weren't doing so well in 1941 when the Germans invaded," said the general.

"That's because your country didn't help us that year," replied Stalin.

"Because you made that pact with Hitler," the general shot back.

Then Stalin replied, and when the interpreter hesitated, the general said, "Tell me what he said."

"Comrade Stalin says you're one tough guy."

Before Eisenhower was named supreme commander of the Allied forces, Wendell Willkie was sent to Moscow by FDR. He asked Stalin, "How do you tell whether a general is going to be capable?"

"You can't decide that from answers on an examination paper," replied Stalin. "Only from his experience in battle. For instance, take your Joe Louis. If you were to pick a good opponent for him, you wouldn't select the man just because his biceps, chest, height, weight, and reach were the same as the champion's. You'd pick a man who'd shown talent in the ring." Stalin was wrong: Eisenhower had never commanded troops in the field but was the right choice.

In May 1943, the tide was turning on the Eastern Front. Stalin explained, "It wasn't my leadership at all. We made every mistake that could be made until there weren't any more to be made."

At the Tehran summit, Stalin noticed the large contingent of aides and advisors FDR and Churchill had brought. "Why so many?" he asked. "They can't sway us."

The two Western leaders had never met the mysterious Stalin, and at one point Churchill asked to meet with him alone, except for their interpreters. At that meeting, Churchill asked how a person advanced in Soviet society. "Two ways," replied Stalin. "Industrially or politically."

"I don't think an industrial career would have intrigued me," said Churchill. Stalin replied, "If you'd been born in Russia, you'd have been one of the top men by now."

They spoke for nearly four hours, after which Stalin said, "Do you think I believe you two are ganging up on me?"

"Why would you say that?" asked Churchill.

"Because if I were you," replied Stalin, "that's what I'd be doing."

The summit ended with Stalin's toast to Churchill and Roosevelt: "To our two great allies, and to the extermination of fifty thousand Nazi officers." Churchill said he couldn't drink to the extermination of fifty thousand people, even Germans. FDR said, "To two great allies, and perhaps a compromise can be made between you two: to the extermination of only forty-nine thousand Nazi officers."

Eisenhower sent Stalin a box of cigars, and when he lit one, Stalin asked the British air marshal who'd delivered them, "How soon before this one explodes?"

"They're quite safe," replied the air marshal. "At least as long as I'm in the room."

At the Potsdam summit in 1946, two of the Big Three had changed. FDR had died in 1945, succeeded by Truman, and Churchill, incredibly, had been voted out of office, replaced by Clement Atlee. The three leaders concluded their meeting by offering each other cigarettes. Stalin examined the two Western leaders' cigarette cases. Atlee's was inscribed, "To Clem, from the Executive Committee of the Labour Party." Truman's case was inscribed, "To Senator Truman, from his colleagues in the Senate."

Then Atlee and Churchill examined Stalin's cigarette case. It too carried an inscription: "To Prince Dimitri, from his Tania."

Secretary of State Edward Stettinius Jr. attended a dinner at which FDR told Stalin that in the cables Roosevelt exchanged with Churchill, they referred to Stalin as "Uncle Joe." Stalin asked what that meant, then appeared offended. "Don't be deceived," Soviet foreign secretary Molotov interrupted. "We've known this for two years. All of Russia knows that."

In 1949, French prime minister Georges Bidault proposed a toast: "To Mr. Pavlov, the brilliant translator," he said. "His work has been so useful to us in these conferences." Stalin turned to Pavlov with a glower and said, "You rendered service to France?! Siberia for you!" Then he smiled and drank.

An American oilman once paid a hundred thousand dollars to the Soviet government for an option to drill. Then Russia reneged on the deal and Stalin refused to return the money. "You know, I will take this to your courts," said the American. "Go ahead," said Stalin, confident that a lawsuit would have no effect. He was, of course, correct: the American lost in the courts.

"Are you satisfied you can't get your money back through the courts?" Stalin asked. The American nodded. Stalin then returned the money.

ADLAI E. STEVENSON

(1900–1965)

In 1955, my father and I visited Governor Adlai Stevenson at his home in Libertyville, outside Chicago, and he showed me buttons from his grandfather's two campaigns for vice president: one that he won, on Grover Cleveland's ticket, and, later, one that he lost, running with William Jennings Bryan.

That fall, I ran for president of my fifth grade class at New York's Public School 9, but came in second. Soon afterward, Stevenson, who'd somehow heard about my defeat, wrote my father, "Tell Jeffrey it's not so bad. I'm sure he's recovered and that there are some advantages in being the runner-up. I hope he finds them, because I have."

Then, in a subsequent class election, I won the vice presidency. Again came a letter: "Tell Jeffrey—or should I say 'Mr. Vice President'—that I am coming to report at the first opportunity and to lay my sword at his feet. I am his to command. I tried and failed. He tried and won . . . Bravo! Onward! *Courage, mes braves*!"

Is it any wonder that in the fall of 1956, I was out there on the street corner, all of twelve years old, handing out Stevenson buttons when he ran against Eisenhower a second time? I also managed to collect virtually every Stevenson button, which I treasure.

Defeated presidential candidates usually land in the trivia section of American history, but Adlai Stevenson appealed to postwar liberals and had a fervent following. There was even a strong movement in 1960 to draft him yet again for a third try, only to be bypassed by John F. Kennedy's well-oiled campaign. Yet the former governor of Illinois still lives in the hearts of those who believe he might've won had his opponent not been *the* biggest American hero of World War II.

In May 1952, he was still undecided about running, and commented in verse: "The more I see of this terrible mess, the more I want to be president less."

By September, Stevenson was asked where he'd like a summer White House to be. "What's wrong with Libertyville?" he asked. "I

Adlai Stevenson (center) with my parents, 1962.

can find peace and quiet there." When it was pointed out that the vast fields of alfalfa on his farm might prevent reporters with hay fever from covering him there, he said, "That's why I find peace and quiet there."

Broadway actress Benay Venuta campaigned for Stevenson, singing at rallies. After he lost she asked him for an autographed photo. He complied, signing it, "Don't worry. It wasn't your fault."

Stevenson visited Swaziland and met the king, Sobhuza II. The ruler greeted the American clad in a leopard skin. Nearby were some of the king's sixty-four wives. Stevenson and the king had one thing in common: the following fall, both would have a son at Harvard.

Elvis Presley announced he was supporting Stevenson in 1956, saying, "I sometimes don't dig this cat but I'm sure he's got the Most." Stevenson's reaction? "Who's Elvis Presley?"

At one stop on the campaign, he noticed children in his audience and asked, "How many children would like to be a candidate for president of the United States?" Lots of little hands shot up. Then he asked, "How many candidates for president of the United States would like to be children again?" Then he raised *his* hand.

When New York governor Averell Harriman, who'd tried for the nomination himself, introduced Stevenson at a luncheon, the candidate was off in another room. On cue he walked in and said, "Governor, I want to thank you for the introduction, which I didn't hear. But if it's anything like the others—thanks for the exaggeration."

In August 1957, Stevenson, back practicing law in Chicago, was told statistics showed that America was prospering. "That's not enough," he said. "The tombs of great nations must've been inscribed with the slogan, 'You never had it so good.'"

In November 1958, Stevenson toured the Soviet Union and protested that the Soviets had jammed American radio broadcasts. After he left, the government gave a medal to the head jammer.

Harry Truman wasn't a fan of Stevenson's. He supported Averell Harriman. After Stevenson's second defeat, Truman announced that he'd support Missouri senator Stuart Symington in 1960, saying: "What Governor Stevenson must learn is that not all voters are Yale graduates." Stevenson, a graduate of Princeton, left Harvard Law School and earned his law degree at Northwestern. (Truman, who'd read every book in the Independence, Missouri, library by the age of sixteen only took a handful of college classes, never graduating.)

In March 1959, Stevenson and Vice President Nixon visited Bangkok separately. Both occupied rooms in the same hotel reserved for distinguished visitors. Every morning, Stevenson ordered a small breakfast and all the English-language newspapers, then he'd ask the waiter his opinions about world affairs and his family. Nixon would call, "Come in, boy," to the waiter, order a big breakfast, and say nothing more. Stevenson left a small tip, Nixon a big one.

In March 1962, Stevenson visited Dr. Albert Schweitzer in Africa and learned just how much the Nobel Prize winner revered all living things. Stevenson noticed a mosquito on Dr. Schweitzer's shoulder and managed to flick it off. Dr. Schweitzer told him, "You had no right to kill it. That was *my* mosquito!"

At a New York party, Stevenson noticed visiting dancers from the Bolshoi Ballet doing the Twist, then in vogue. Kathryn (Mrs. Arthur) Murray, half of the famous husband-and-wife dance-instructing duo, asked Stevenson to give it a try.

"Sorry, but I don't know how to do the Twist," replied Stevenson.

"It's easy," replied Mrs. Murray. "You do it as if you're drying your back with a towel."

"Sorry," Stevenson said again, "but at my age, I'm no longer able to dry my back."

He once observed, "When you're campaigning, you learn more about yourself in six months than in years of psychoanalysis."

My father introduced Stevenson to Grace Kelly.

"You know her," said my father. "She starred in *Dial M for Murder*, *High Noon*, and *High Society*."

"No, sorry, don't know her," Stevenson replied.

"How about *To Catch a Thief*? *Mogambo*? *The Country Girl*?"

Still no response. Finally, my father said, "She's the daughter of the Philadelphia Democratic official John Kelly."

"Oh, of *course*." He beamed. "Why didn't you say so?"

Then my father introduced Stevenson to Marlene Dietrich, and a few weeks later, offered to introduce the unmarried candidate to a dozen more eligible women.

"Can't," said Stevenson. "I'm off to meet Indian prime minister Nehru."

"That's why you lost," said a friend.

In early November 1963, Stevenson, now the U.S. ambassador to the United Nations, attended a memorial service for Eleanor Roosevelt, who had died one year earlier. A heavy downpour spread out over Hyde Park during the ceremonies. Stevenson looked up at the bleak gray skies and said, "I refuse to blame the bad weather on the Republicans here in Dutchess Country. That's how far I've come as a statesman."

CHIEF JUSTICE EARL WARREN

(1891–1974)

A three-term governor of California, Warren was the state attorney general when he was complicit in the shameful imprisonment of 120,000 loyal Japanese American citizens during World War II. Nevertheless, history has been kind to him for his leadership of a progressive Supreme Court. Brown v. Board of Education, in 1954, ended segregation in public schools and is his greatest legacy. People forget that he was New York governor Thomas E. Dewey's running mate in 1948, an election that incumbent President Harry S. Truman and Alben Barkley barely won.

Nominated by President Eisenhower (who later regretted it, incredibly), Warren served with distinction on the Court from 1953 to 1969.

Mrs. Warren was asked how it felt when her husband ran for vice president. "I didn't even want him to run for district attorney of Alameda County," she recalled.

In April 1959, Warren spoke at a tribute to Judge Learned Hand, probably the greatest federal judge never appointed to the Supreme Court. After Warren finished, someone said, "They gave the Hand a great big judge."

At a meeting at the White House in late February 1963, JFK said, "All three of us wanted to be president, but only one made it." Then he bowed slightly. Turning to LBJ, he said, "Two of us wanted to be vice president, but only one of you made it." Finally he turned to Chief Justice Warren, saying, "But only one of us has lifetime job security."

In May 1964, Warren was invited to a concert. The invitation read, "Black tie or white tie." Taking no chances, he donned white tie and tails. Only one other man was similarly attired: the conductor.

Warren lunched at Toots Shor's in June 1965 and pondered whether to have his roast beef hot or cold.

"Fine thing," said Shor. "The chief justice of the United States can't even make a decision over roast beef!"

In July 1966, New York State Supreme Court judge Charles Marx

Chief Justice Earl Warren (far right), wife Nina (near right), my father, and Toots Shor (left).

was flying home from Dublin with his wife. A few minutes into the flight, he learned that Warren was on board, and sent him his card.

Warren invited him over, and Judge Marx told the justice that Warren had voted to overrule Marx's decision that the book *Fanny Hill* was obscene.

Just then the captain said there was a mechanical problem that would force the plane to return to Dublin. "Wouldn't it be ironic if this plane went down, with me and you, who helped overrule my decision, on board?" Marx asked.

"Don't be so optimistic," Warren replied.

"I have sixteen grandchildren," Warren told a friend. "It's gotten so that I'm afraid to answer the phone in the morning."

PART
VI

"You

Dirty Rats"

AUTHOR'S NOTE

In my father's time, organized criminals were just as vicious and cruel as they are today—perhaps more so. But they, too, were part of the fabric of New York nightlife of that era. You might see a gangster seated with his girlfriend at a table next to a movie star, or hobnobbing with some politician, probably shooing away the house photographer.

My mother played a round of golf with Frank Nitti, not knowing, of course, that he had been Al Capone's right-hand man while Capone was in prison. It was Sunday, December 7, 1941, and my mother and grandmother were in Hot Springs, Arkansas, where the baths helped my grandmother's arthritis. Hot Springs was also a gathering place for many gangsters, who joined everyone else around the radio as they received the terrible news from Pearl Harbor.

My father knew these characters—made famous, or infamous, by the writings of his friend Damon Runyon—only as news sources, never as friends. But any depiction of New York nightlife of his era without them would be incomplete.

LOUIS "LEPKE" BUCHALTER

(1897–1944)

In April 1940, Louis "Lepke" Buchalter was sentenced to thirty years to life for extortion related to his role in Murder, Inc., the infamous murder-for-hire gang. He announced he didn't expect to leave prison alive. His health was failing and he said, "I want no notes on my slab." Asked to elaborate, he said that unlike the other members of Murder, Inc., "I want it said on my tombstone: 'I Never Did Sing.'"

While in prison, he was convicted of first-degree murder and sentenced to death. He died in the electric chair at Sing Sing in 1944.

AL CAPONE

(1899–1947)

When Jimmy Cagney starred in *The Public Enemy*, the film was screened for Capone and Vincenzo Antonio Gibaldi, aka "Machine Gun" Jack McGurn. McGurn sneered at what he thought was a phony depiction of gangsters.

Just then Capone got a call, ordered the projectionist to stop the movie, talked for a minute, and slammed down the phone. Then he signaled to the projectionist to resume. Pointing to one of the characters on screen, he said, "Okay, somebody knock that guy off."

Decades before the heyday of "The Dapper Don," John Gotti, Capone set the sartorial standard for gangsters. He never wore the same suit and tie on successive days, except during his prolonged trial for income tax evasion.

At the start of the trial, the judge barred all photographers. Nevertheless, one newspaper proudly published exclusive photos of the trial each day: Capone's photographer Harry Coleman had taken seventy-five photos of the gangster in different poses and outfits, then snapped a picture of the empty courtroom. He superimposed the posed pictures of Capone over the shot of the courtroom to create the fake "trial" photos.

After serving most of his eight-year sentence for tax evasion in Alcatraz, America's most secure prison, Capone was sent to Terminal Island, California, to serve another year for contempt of court. Just before his release in November 1939, a federal officer interviewed him. He asked Capone what part he played in the St. Valentine's Day Massacre in 1929, a crime that remains unsolved.

"It was just a coincidence I knew most of those guys," he said. Then he patted the officer's shoulder, saying, "Forget it. They were all enemies of society, weren't they?" One victim was a mechanic.

A federal officer suggested that Capone's law student son change his name. "What's wrong with 'Capone'?" replied the gangster.

Whenever anyone visited Capone in prison, the mobster, who learned the the inevitability of taxes the hard way, always said the same words to the departing visitor: "Good-bye, and don't forget to take care of your Uncle Sam."

MICKEY COHEN

(1913–1976)

ickey Cohen was the West Coast version of Chicago's Capone. Both were born in Brooklyn, Cohen fourteen years later. He too moved to Chicago, and worked for Capone's younger brother Marty before winding up in Los Angeles. "I never killed anybody who didn't deserve it," Cohen boasted. Like Capone, he went to prison on income tax evasion—twice, in fact, and he, too, was sent to Alcatraz.

Cohen fancied himself a celebrity, the best-dressed man in town. When producer-director Chester Erskine went to his usual barbershop, he noticed two burly men in tight suits giving him the once-over. Then Erskine's regular barber said he was okay, and the puzzled producer sat down, only then noticing Mickey Cohen in the next chair.

One of Cohen's legitimate businesses was a men's haberdashery store. After the ninth attempt on his life, he said, "This is hurting business; customers think my shirts come with extra holes."

When his mansion was firebombed, the hardest-hit room was the guest room. Inspecting the rubble, Cohen said, "Now I'll never be able to rent this out."

Edward "Neddie" Herbert was Cohen's bodyguard. When he took a fusillade of lead intended for his boss, Cohen found the only person in town with Herbert's blood type, a visiting radio writer from New York. The man quickly became Cohen's "guest," holed up in a hotel with food and entertainment paid for by Cohen, awaiting the call for a transfusion. It never came.

Asked how he kept his young son from misbehaving, Cohen said whenever the boy acted up, he pretended to call and complain to the boy's idol, Roy Rogers.

CHARLES "LUCKY" LUCIANO

(1897–1962)

For years after he was deported to Naples, the Italian city he'd left as a child, we received a Christmas card from Charles "Lucky" Luciano, signed only "Charles L." He signed it that way to avoid inspection by federal agents. For several years, it arrived in the same mail, ironically, as the annual card from one of those agents: J. Edgar Hoover.

"Yeah, I like Hoover," he told my father. "Hoover's no friend of the hoodlums, but I like him because he never makes announcements about what he's gonna do. He never says a guy is tied up in a racket and he's gonna grab him for it. Nah. None of that *yappity-yappity* stuff. A guy does something? Hoover grabs him. Efficiency. Hoover's got efficiency. I like that."

When my father and oldest brother George arrived in Naples in 1953, their hotel phone rang. "Lyons? Luciano. Come see me. Just get into any cab and say 'Casa Luciano.'" To make certain the first cab wasn't a plant, my father took the fifth cab and said the magic words.

My brother asked Luciano if he knew whether the Red Sox and St. Louis Cardinals—his favorite American and National League teams, respectively—had won.

"Baseball?" said Luciano. "Naaah, Not my game. I play the horses." Then he recalled hearing in prison that the New York Archdiocese had given the prison a donation to help pay for renovations. Luciano told the prison chaplain that he should bet the money on three horses running the next day.

The priest naturally declined, but the next day all three, none favorites, won.

By the time my father and brother returned to their hotel, a note was waiting for George, saying both his teams had won. Luciano still had connections back in New York.

"I have no plans," Luciano said. "What kind of plans can a guy like me make? If it rains tomorrow, I get an umbrella. Them kind of plans." The Italian government placed restrictions on his ev-

My father (left) and Charles "Lucky" Luciano,
captured on a surveillance camera in Naples, 1953.

ery waking moment. As a result, he lamented, "The money days
are over. I invite other guys who've been deported here for a meal,
maybe." He couldn't go into legitimate business, because, "the
people I meet get tailed, so they drop me. I paid my rap, but now
they choke me."

When my father used the word "Mafia," Luciano said, "I ain't
gonna be interviewed about no Mafia by no one." My father looked
out at Mount Vesuvius and said Naples was a beautiful city.

"No place is beautiful," Luciano replied, "if you're not free to
move around in it or leave it."

"MACHINE GUN" JACK MCGURN

(1902–1936)

achine Gun Jack McGurn was the subject of a conversation at the Stork Club one night in 1942. One of the patrons there admitted he'd met the gangster. Of all people, it was the scholarly two-time Pulitzer Prize winner Thornton Wilder. During Prohibition, Texas Guinan, the famous nightclub performer, introduced him to the gangster. "This is Thornton Wilder," she said. "He's not only an author, but he's now a professor, teaching English at the University of Chicago."

"I had a professor, too," replied the gangster. "Al Capone."

DUTCH SCHULTZ

(1902–1935)

When Arthur Flegenheimer, a.k.a. "Dutch Schultz," was threatened by rivals, he holed up for three weeks in a press agent's home. Eventually the agent's wife complained because to show his gratitude, Schultz had bought toys for their children: three slot machines.

On October 23, 1935, the night Schultz was gunned down, one of his henchmen was shot in a barbershop. Seated nearby and in a deep sleep was nightclub owner Monte Proser. When the bullet-riddled victim staggered and fell across Proser, Proser awoke and groggily said, "Sorry, buddy, this chair's taken."

PART
VII

"Make 'Em

Laugh"

FRED ALLEN

(1894–1956)

Born John Florence Sullivan in Cambridge, Massachusetts, Fred Allen was a huge star in vaudeville and radio. Allen made a few movies, like *Thanks a Million*, *We're Not Married*, and *O. Henry's Full House*, but radio won him millions of fans. He died of a heart attack in my father's arms on St. Patrick's Day, 1956, while they were walking together across from Carnegie Hall.

A few days before the show *Stars in Your Eyes* was to close for lack of business, Allen met the star, Jimmy Durante, and told him he'd be coming that night.

"How will I know you're out there?" asked Durante.

"Easy," replied Allen. "I'll be the one in the audience."

Of rival Milton Berle he said, "If ego were acid, Berle would've consumed himself long ago."

By 1951, television was becoming commonplace in American homes due to Berle's success. Allen said, "Television is the only medium where you rehearse two weeks—just to be awful. If you can't be awful on short notice, give it up." Later, he dismissed live comedy shows on TV: "Television humor is third-dimensional fun. You have to clear your humor through studio audiences, to convince viewers that what you're doing is really funny."

Two days after he died, my father wrote, "The luck of the Irish didn't hold for Fred Allen on St. Patrick's Day. 'How old was your husband?' the policeman asked. 'Not "was," "is,"' his wife replied, in desperation. 'He's sixty-one.'"

NBC allowed Allen to utter one "off-color" word: "Heck." He responded by saying, "At this network, they obviously don't believe in Heaven, Hell, or CBS."

Allen believed that network executives "are men who do nothing but get together and decide that nothing can be done. The fastest way to clear out a meeting of network executives is to interpose a fact. They run rather than confront a fact." Ironically, the first non–family member to arrive at the hospital was an NBC executive.

WOODY ALLEN

(1935–)

No filmmaker of any era has captured the humor, mores, and tenor of his time as well as Allan Stewart Konigsberg, aka Woody Allen. Since he wrote the screenplay for *What's New Pussycat?* in 1965, he has written, directed, produced, and often starred in several dozen films, at an average of one a year. Every new Allen film is an event.

During the run of his play *Don't Drink the Water*, the star, Lou Jacobi, gestured so hard during one performance that one of his cuff links flew into the audience. "We can't let that happen again," Allen told the actor. "I suggest you get your wrists pierced."

We attended his lavish New Year's Eve party, where he greeted us with a request to face a TV camera, "and please say something funny."

In June 1963, *Cleopatra* was the talk of the world—one of the most expensive films ever made, with little hope of recouping its cost. Woody said he'd done some calculating and figured there was one way it could make money. "Everyone in the world has to see it," he said. "Four times. Then Red China has to be admitted to the UN so everyone there can see it. That should do it."

Discussing his draft status, he said, "I'm classified '4H'—in the event of war, I'm a hostage."

When he wrote *Don't Drink the Water*, he cast six-foot-one-inch Tony Roberts in the lead role. Allen told him, "I wrote it for me, but you seemed more the type."

Allen was one of the James Bonds in the original version of *Casino Royale*. He was asked to ad-lib when he untied Daliah Lavi. Allen said to the glamorous actress, "After I release you, we'll run amok. And if you're too tired, then we'll just walk amok."

Allen was shown a cane that quickly turned into a sword for protection against muggers. But he refused it. "At home," he explained, "I have a sword which quickly turns into a cane, in case of trouble. Then I get sympathy."

The insult comic Jack E. Leonard (who was Don Rickles before

Woody Allen and Romy Schneider, *What's New Pussycat?*, Paris, 1964.
Photograph by Larry Shaw.

Rickles) saw Woody Allen perform at a New York nightclub one evening and afterward told him, "You look like a late-shift pharmacist at an all-night drugstore."

Flying home from Europe in early 1965, Allen complained about having to pay excess weight charges. He paid the fee, then said, "Next time I'll fly El Al. The Israeli airline doesn't worry if you're overweight. They only worry if you're *under*weight."

In May 1967, my father left his precious notebook in one of the nightclubs along his nightly beat. His signature was engraved on its leather cover, so the next day it arrived at our home. Inside was a note: "Be kind to Woody Allen. He's such a nice fellow."

When told that President Nixon objected to the profanity in the movie *Love Story* but liked the rest of the film, Allen replied: "I *loved* the profanity but objected to the rest of the film."

In 1969, Allen delivered a joke that mocked Vice President Spiro Agnew, later to resign in disgrace for taking a modest bribe. Allen said, "The second toughest job in the world is being Mrs. Spiro Agnew." The controversial vice president responded with a joke of his own that fell flat: "Woody Allen is always at half-mast." "Agnew obviously writes his own material," my father wrote.

When he was sued by his first wife because of jokes at her expense, he said, "The complaint reads just like my nightclub act but with the timing ruined by a lot of 'wherases' and 'aforementioneds.'"

In August 1972, Allen explained why, in his movies *Take the Money and Run* and *Bananas*, his characters' parents were depicted wearing masks: "They deserved to be shown that way. We were cast out on the streets at seven in the morning and told not to return until midnight. You'd spend the day breaking windows, setting fires."

In October 1972, Allen was giving his usual Monday night performance with his jazz group at Michael's Pub in Manhattan. But it wasn't an ordinary night. He was nervous because Benny Goodman, the King of Swing, the Babe Ruth of clarinet players, was in the audience. Allen performed flawlessly and afterward, Goodman asked him for tips on playing some of the numbers he performed.

Allen visited a nightclub where the owner asked if he could introduce Allen to the customers. "Of course," replied Allen. "Just make sure you say 'Woody Allen, the jazz clarinet player.'"

SID CAESAR

(1922–2014)

When Sid Caesar died in February 2014, a link to my childhood was broken. I remember those hilarious comedy bits on *Your Show of Shows* spoofing other programs and movies—the weekly insanity that came out of our early black-and-white TV. The set was a vertical tube, about five feet high, with the image bounced off a mirror. I guess that was appropriate for broadcasting off-the-wall humor!

For years, Caesar's wife Florence complained that they never had time to go out. He was constantly writing, rehearsing, or performing. Finally, he took her to London for an engagement, and she thought at last they'd enjoy an evening out. But his rehearsal pressure prevented that. "It's the same here as it was for us back home on Long Island," she said, "only the plumbing's not as good."

Caesar was the houseguest of a movie producer who employed a butler. Not used to seeing butlers, Caesar took him aside and said, "No one should do this job. It's menial. Here's fifty dollars. Quit working for him."

In mid-April 1955, Caesar was rehearsing his cast when a call came from Princeton University. "Professor Einstein's office calling," said the woman's voice on the line. "He's a big fan of yours, Mr. Caesar, and in particular loves your 'Professor von Votsisnehm' character. He'd love you to come out to Princeton next week for lunch."

Well, an invitation from the Most Brilliant Mind of the Century, as *Time* magazine would name him, doesn't come every day, so Caesar sprang into action. He canceled the rehearsals, saying to the writers and cast that somehow they'd wing it, and headed to the nearest library. He was determined to master the theory of relativity in two days. He pored over every book he could find, phoned scientists for advice, and put in hours studying, perhaps approaching a vague idea of the theory.

The following Monday, April 18, 1955, Einstein died suddenly.

In the 1962 musical *Little Me*, Caesar played seven characters and had twenty-three costume changes. "If it weren't for zippers, the show would run five hours," he said.

Once, when he was nearly assaulted by two men, he scared them off by spewing fake epithets in a phony Polish accent.

Caesar explained why he preferred a live audience for comedy. "Trying to make people laugh without a live audience," he said, "is like playing handball without a wall."

GEORGE JESSEL

(1898–1981)

If George Jessel had quit show business after 1927, he'd still have a footnote in history as the actor who turned down *The Jazz Singer*, the first talking feature, which made Al Jolson an immortal.

But Jessel made his own name as "The Toastmaster General of America" and as a popular Broadway actor, singer, and honorary-Oscar-winning producer. He'd starred in the stage version of *The Jazz Singer* and made an early short talkie, but rejected Warner Bros.' offer of the starring role in the screen version—based loosely on his own life—because he claimed the studio owed him money. He did invest some of his own funds in the project.

When he was a twelve-year-old member of Gus Edwards's vaudeville company, they performed in Boston. Soon after the final curtain, a representative of the local Children's Welfare Society came backstage and headed for Jessel. But the boy was prepared. He pretended to be nineteen, donning a derby and lighting a cigar. "I don't feel so well tonight," he said. "I had a date with a dame last night and maybe I stayed out too long." Unimpressed, the official said, "Sonny, how much is nine times eight?" Jessel got it wrong. He was back in school in New York the next day.

It was Jessel who renamed Frances Gumm, a young, unknown singer from Grand Rapids, Minnesota, saying she should have a garland of flowers placed on her. The young woman changed her first name to "Judy," kept "Garland," and became Hollywood's greatest singer.

Suspicious that his wife, actress Norma Talmadge, was cheating on him, Jessel arrived at their home in Florida with a gun. When he saw someone running out the back he fired, but grazed her butler, who'd been standing behind him.

At his arraignment, the judge asked, "How on earth did you hit someone standing *behind* you?"

Jessel replied, "How should I know? I'm a vaudeville comic, not Buffalo Bill!"

"I was married to Norma Talmadge for five years," he said, "but I never unpacked." The day they separated, Jessel checked into the Beverly Hills Hotel and called his friend George Burns.

"I couldn't believe it," said Burns, reacting to the news. "*Nobody* can get into the Beverly Hills Hotel without a reservation."

In October 1939, Jessel refused to wire condolences to Al Jolson when Jolson separated from his wife, actress Ruby Keeler. "Because when I left Hollywood a few weeks ago when I separated from *my* wife, Jolson said, 'You don't know how to pick a wife who'll last, Georgie. Take a lesson from me.'"

By March 1940, Jessel, then forty-one, was smitten with actress Lois Andrews, twenty-five years his junior. "So what?" asked Jessel. "When she's a young girl of seventy, I'll be just ninety-five." When someone else wondered about the wisdom of marrying a sixteen-year-old, Jessel cracked, "I have *neckties* older than she is."

When they announced their engagement, he was asked if he really believed their marriage would last. "In a world like this," he replied, referring to the gathering war clouds, "what lasts?" Then he added, "We decided to wait an extra month before marrying. Who knows? By then she may prefer a new tricycle."

Jessel produced, starred in, and cowrote the book for a musical called *High Kickers*, based on an idea by Phil Silvers, who would gain fame as Sergeant Bilko in TV's *You'll Never Get Rich*. Well into the run, attendance was high, and Jessel wrote a note to a newspaper critic who'd panned the show: "I'm writing this from my new Rolls-Royce I purchased with some of the receipts." That show set an unofficial Broadway record: six of its chorus girls eloped.

On December 8, 1941, Jessel's father-in-law, who was younger by some years, was stationed in Manila. Ten hours after the Pearl Harbor attack, the Japanese invaded the Philippines. Young Mrs. Jessel of course feared for her father's safety. "You ought to do something," she said to her husband.

"At my age," he said, "the only thing I can do is cancel tomorrow's tickets to *Madame Butterfly*."

By August 1942, Jessel's marriage to Lois Andrews was, predictably, headed for divorce. In her complaint, she alleged he was too old for her and "besides, he didn't believe in Santa Claus."

Soon afterward, at the next table at the Stork Club, a woman sat with an army officer. She turned to Jessel and said, "He's leaving for overseas, leaving me all alone, pining for him." Then she said, "I must have you meet him. Oh, darling, what *is* your name?" That's when Jessel recognized her as the starlet Peggy Joyce, who reportedly dated powerful men from Averell Harriman to Irving Thalberg and Charlie Chaplin, and eventually married six times.

When Jessel finally retired from the stage in July 1943, he moved to Hollywood permanently to produce movies from an office on the Fox lot. Then he wired his New York office to forward just three souvenirs from his life on Broadway: a portrait of his friend Mayor Jimmy Walker, another of his third wife, Lois Andrews, and a baseball autographed by his beloved Brooklyn Dodgers.

Jessel said he left Broadway for Hollywood "after five Nazi spies landed off Long Island, made their way to my opening night, and wrote the reviews."

In September 1944, Andrews, his ex, was headlining in Chicago. Jessel was upset at something she'd said about him in the press, and decided to confront her. Backstage, he caused a commotion, then stormed onstage. He suddenly stopped, turned to the audience, smiled, said, "A funny thing happened to me on my way to the theater tonight," and proceeded to do twenty minutes of comedy.

When Jessel was a guest at the White House, Roosevelt caught him pocketing a matchbook. "I still have family in the Bronx," Jessel explained. "Where else could they ever see a matchbook inscribed 'FDR'?"

George Jessel was known for his trademark monocle and toupee. He explained, "I use a monocle so I can read radio scripts better. I'd rather be called eccentric than blind. As for the hairpiece, I use it onstage when I'm doing my 'Hello, Mama' routine. I try to look younger. Otherwise people would think my mother would have to be at least a hundred years old."

Jessel escorted Eleanor Roosevelt to a Washington dinner and someone remarked, "That's the first time I've ever seen George with a woman his own age."

After a lunch at the Truman White House, he was asked about the chicken salad. "Never has so much chicken salad owed so much to so few chickens." Eleanor Roosevelt, who also attended, later told Jessel, "Confidentially, there were no chickens in that salad at all."

In August 1945, Lieutenant General James Doolittle, who'd won the Medal of Honor for his daring raid on Tokyo three years earlier, was at a Hollywood dinner party. Jessel was master of ceremonies and asked General Doolittle to speak. "What'll I say?" asked Doolittle. "Just tell 'em a few jokes," said Jessel. Doolittle replied, "Oh, okay. Then *you* fly a bomber over Tokyo."

Jessel was at El Morocco, engaged in a heated political debate with an international playboy escorting a young woman. "I knew I'd won the argument," said Jessel later, "because on her way out, his date slipped me her phone number."

A newspaper report said he was romancing a veteran actress. "Impossible," he said. "Why, she's old enough to be my wife."

He advised friends house-hunting in Hollywood, "Find a guy who's just built a big house for his beautiful young bride. But make certain it's the wife who's left *him*, so he'll be desperate to sell at any price."

"Is that the way you bought your house?" my father asked. "No," replied Jessel, "that's how I *sold* mine when Lois left me."

At a movie premiere, Jessel announced, "Ladies and gentlemen, I want to introduce you to the greatest naval hero of World War II, Admiral Chester Nimitz. Admiral, can you just say a few words?" The admiral rose and said, "Sorry, my name's Admiral Ernest King."

Jessel often boasted of his friendships with everyone from Churchill to Truman, FDR, Edison, Einstein, and every other important person over the previous half century. His office was one floor above that of Dorothy Parker, the witty writer. A visitor to her office heard a tremendous crash from the floor above. "Oh, that's just Jessel dropping a name," she explained.

On a visit to Las Vegas, Jessel tried to visit Frank Sinatra, but he was busy, so Jessel went to the casino and lost sixteen hundred dollars. He tried again in vain to see his friend, but Sinatra had brought a blackjack dealer to his suite to play undisturbed all night. So Jessel returned to the floor, recouped his loss, and flew home.

On Steve Allen's show, Jessel recalled performing in the same theater on a bill headlined by Lillie Langtry. "Just before we went on, news came that the *Titanic* had sunk."

He told the producers of *Lolita* that the movie wouldn't be a hit. "Who'd believe such a story about a middle-aged man obsessed with a girl?"

In France he entertained a small group of people and was told later that one was Picasso, who hadn't understood much of what Jessel had said. "That's okay," said Jessel. "I never understand what *he's* doing either."

"The secret of making a good speech," he said, "is all in the feet. Never to put them in your mouth."

Lunching with former president Truman, Jessel, who'd had a few, told Truman, "Mr. McKinley, please don't go to Buffalo. Something tells me you'll find trouble there."

Jessel met the man who'd paid a million dollars for Nashua, the famous race horse. "That's a lot of money," Jessel observed, "but then again I married a young girl who cost me a lot more, couldn't run, and was even younger than Nashua."

A woman threw a beer bottle at Jessel after he told her the only judge he'd allow to marry them was Joseph Force Crater, New York's most mysterious missing person, who'd disappeared in 1930.

DON RICKLES

(1926–)

In 1970, I accompanied my father on his rounds. At the Copa, Rickles was the headliner. He spotted my father and began insulting him. I couldn't have been prouder! Years later, I got a measure of revenge interviewing Rickles live on WNBC. I asked if, now that *Toy Story* (in which he voiced Mr. Potato Head) was being released on DVD, we could expect his other fine films to be released as well: *Beach Blanket Bingo*, *Muscle Beach Party*, and *Bikini Beach*.

"Jeffrey," he replied via satellite, "remind me to fly to New York and slap you!"

Born in New York—where else?—Rickles got his first break replacing a comic who didn't show up at the Slate Brothers Club in Los Angeles. He did so well in the first show, insulting gangsters and movie stars in the audience, that Henry Slate leaped onstage, impulsively removed his diamond ring, and presented it to an astonished Rickles while the audience cheered.

In the dressing room, Slate asked Rickles to return the ring. The bewildered Rickles said, "But I thought you gave this to me."

"I did," replied Slate, "and will again, during the second show."

He acted between heavyweights Clark Gable and Burt Lancaster in an excellent submarine drama, *Run Silent, Run Deep*, after the impressionist Frank Gorshin, who refused to fly from New York, was seriously injured en route in a car accident.

Rickles spent six months in Yugoslavia filming *Kelly's Heroes* with Clint Eastwood and Telly Savalas. He needed a GI's haircut and stopped into the first barbershop he saw. The barber, speaking Russian, kept saying, "Da, da."

Rickles said, "I didn't know if he was saying 'Yes, yes' or wanted me to meet his father."

"There's so little to do between scenes here," Rickles complained. "My training as a Catskills social director hasn't helped pass the time."

At a preview screening, an English woman said, "I thought your film was quite good."

"Only 'quite good'?" asked Rickles. "Not great?"

The woman replied, "If I use the word 'great' here, then how would I possibly describe Winston Churchill?"

One night he was performing at the Copa and noticed several children in the front row. It didn't deter him from using the four-letter words he often employed. In case their parents objected, he said, "What did you expect when you brought them here, Howdy Doody? Oral Roberts?"

Asked what he got by continually insulting people, he replied "Rich."

When he broke the attendance record at the Copa, Rickles explained by paraphrasing Will Rogers: "I never met a man I didn't want to insult."

JOAN RIVERS

(1933–2014)

Born Joan Molinsky, a Phi Beta Kappa graduate of Barnard College, she performed early on in a group called "Jim, Jake, and Joan." She'd been a gag writer for the old *Candid Camera* show and began appearing on *Ed Sullivan*, doing self-deprecating humor, which evolved into her trademark tart-tongued barbs at fashion faux pas on the E! Channel. She was the most successful female stand-up comedian ever.

I first saw her in 1966, at the intimate Downstairs at the Upstairs. She'd just come from an engagement in Omaha. "Omaha is a little like Newark," she joked, "but without Newark's glamour."

When she moved upstairs to perform in the more prominent room, she told her audience, "You don't get ulcers from what you eat. You get ulcers from what's eating *you*."

She observed, "Lincoln walked twelve miles to find a book. Today, on his birthday, the libraries are closed." She'd never be a society type. "I always thought a fox hunt was trying to find a fur coat wholesale."

Rivers apologized to an audience for the frizzy condition of her hair. She explained that she shared a hairdresser with Jacqueline Onassis. "It's great seeing her, except that whenever she comes into the salon, my stylist drops whatever he's doing, tells me to make the best of it, and immediately goes over to her."

Before one engagement, the owner asked her what she'd like before her performances. "Just plaster a hundred glossy photos of Elizabeth Taylor around the hotel," she said. "I want people to think I'm a last-minute replacement."

Her screen debut came in the Burt Lancaster movie *The Swimmer*. "I was asked to do a brief nude scene. We had a terrific battle about my appearance in the nude. I argued until I was blue in the face—but they still refused to let me do it."

HENNY YOUNGMAN

(1906–1998)

Quick now! What's the connection between Harry "Henny" Youngman, the King of the One-Liners, and the Beatles? All five were born in Liverpool!

His family moved to Brooklyn, where he befriended a young Milton Berle, to whom Youngman supplied jokes.

He began cracking one-liners while playing violin with the Swanee Syncopaters. This led to a career on radio, in nightclubs, in a handful of movies—and playing at bar mitzvahs and weddings. He performed for seventy years.

I once accompanied him to Radio City, for reasons I'll never recall. During the performance of the Rockettes, he called out, "Don't talk—kick!"

Youngman donated a unique item to display at the National Antiques Show: three of his old joke files.

He once walked down Broadway holding a steering wheel, explaining, "I can't afford the extras."

Youngman told the story of an eighty-year-old woman who was filing for a divorce from her husband of sixty-two years. The judge asked, "Sixty-two years? And *now* you want a divorce?" "Yes," said the woman. "Enough is enough."

During the height—literally—of the miniskirt revolution, he said, "They come in three sizes: short, shorter, and 'if it please the Court.'" He then described Twiggy, the slimmest of London's top models, as "Jayne Mansfield after paying Britain's taxes."

Youngman said he inherited his love of show business from his father, who'd been hired by a local singer to applaud at every performance. One time, however, the singer failed to pay his clappers. His father and the others took revenge at the next performance: they applauded continuously, forcing the singer to do twenty encores and lose his voice.

In December 1964, Youngman explained his fear of flying: "I'm afraid of the movie."

During the Vietnam War, New York governor Nelson Rockefeller, seeking the presidency, announced, "If drafted, I'll run." Youngman said, "Funny, my son said the same thing the other day."

When Youngman was starting out, he'd walk into Lindy's smoking a big cigar, "so people thought I was prospering. They invited me to sit with them at their tables and join them for dinner. Those cigars kept me from starving."

His theme song, which he'd play on his violin, interrupting the song with rapid-fire jokes, was "Smoke Gets in Your Eyes." He explained why: "I tried 'Flight of the Bumblebee,' but even *I* couldn't talk that quickly."

PART
VIII

"Put Up

MUHAMMAD ALI

(1942–)

When Cassius Clay beat Sonny Liston in Miami in 1964, winning by a technical knockout when Liston refused to return to the ring for the seventh round, the referee was Barney Felix, the athletic director of the Doral Country Club. Later he watched the film to assess his work.

"If I had it to do all over again," he said, "I'd have worn a different color shirt and pants."

Former heavyweight champion Gene Tunney had some trouble adjusting to Ali's new name. "Why didn't he name himself Spartacus?" he wondered. "Then he could recite that famous speech." Tunney then recited the famous speech.

Ali hosted a party at Toots Shor's shortly before his fight with Joe Frazier and was introduced to Frazier's manager, Yancey Durham, who said Frazier would "take you in six rounds."

Ali laughed, saying, "Don't even let your *fighter* dream about that."

Ali admitted he'd called himself "The Greatest" to get attention. But, he said, he came to realize that "while I'm still 'The Greatest,' I'm now more humble about it."

The night Ali fought Zora Folley in 1967, in the last fight at the old Madison Square Garden, shipping magnate Stavros Niarchos watched with some friends in Switzerland. In the second round, he dozed off, waking up just fifty seconds before Folley was knocked out. "It's an old business trick I have," the billionaire explained. "Be tuned into the biggest game around, if possible from a safe distance of at least three thousand miles, then play possum until just before the climax."

Ali's jaw was broken in his first fight against Ken Norton, in March 1973 in San Diego. By June, Ali was in New York and arrived at a restaurant to find all the tables occupied. "If you'll wait a short while, we'll have a table for you, Mr. Ali," said the owner. "Right now, we're serving members of the American Medical Association."

Ali replied, "I don't need a doctor. My jaw is healed. All I want to do is give it some exercise."

Muhammad Ali with his daughter. Photograph by Sam Shaw.

ROCKY GRAZIANO

(1919–1990)

orn Thomas Rocco Barbella in Brooklyn, the son of a fighter with a brief ring career, he fought his way to the middleweight title in 1947 in the second of his three savage fights against Tony Zale. He had a 67–10–6 record, with an amazing fifty-two KOs between 1942 and 1952. Then Graziano used his crown to become a media personality in the growing years of television. Paul Newman portrayed him in *Somebody Up There Likes Me*, based on his autobiography.

Jake LaMotta announced he was eager to fight his boyhood friend Graziano and said they'd fought once before: when they were twelve. It went on for a long time until grown-ups spotted them and put a stop to it. That would be their only bout.

In September 1949, Graziano was training for his fight with Charles Fusari at the Polo Grounds in New York. He heard that Fusari, an Italian-born middleweight, had the ability to sleep soundly anywhere: in a dressing room before a fight, in his home while a fire razed the building next door, anywhere. Graziano said, "I'll see to it that Fusari sleeps—on the canvas." Rocky won, but by a TKO in the tenth round.

After the fight, Graziano's young daughter took a look at her father's battered face and began weeping. Trying to comfort her, he said, "See what happens when you cross the street without looking?"

Early in his television career, Graziano explained why he was never nervous, even before a live nationwide telecast. "People always say, 'Good luck,'" he remarked. "Why? I never worry or need luck if I know nobody's going to throw punches at me."

A month later, he met John Garfield and regaled the actor with stories about his fights and his youth, which included brushes with the law. "I was born on Clinton Street on the Lower East Side of Manhattan," said Graziano.

Graziano learned that Garfield never went to college. He called his manager, Jack Healy, and said, "Hey, Jack. Get me a movie contract! I always thought you had to go to college to be a movie star."

Graziano allowed singer Alan Dale to get into the ring and spar a round. Manager Healy said to Hale, "If, by some miracle, you knock him down, go to a neutral corner."

"If that happens," said Graziano, "you'd better go to a neutral *country!*"

Graziano and Joe DiMaggio were introduced as "the two greatest right-handed hitters of all time."

"I can catch, too," added Graziano.

After he retired, a friend asked Graziano what drove him to hang up his gloves. "I looked in the mirror after my last fight," the champ replied, "and I decided there must be an easier way to meet congenial people my own age."

A few weeks later, he bemoaned the dearth of movie roles coming his way. "Somebody up there is knocking my brains out," he said. "Maybe I should write a sequel to the story of my life and call it *I Lied the First Time.*"

Graziano appeared on a show called *Family Living* to talk with a college professor about juvenile delinquency. "Don't you think you'll be overmatched?" Graziano was asked.

"Naaah," said the champ. "He can only talk *about* it. I *was* one."

Graziano had a nightclub act and took young Johnny Carson's advice by beginning, "Folks, a funny thing happened to me on the way to the canvas."

While appearing in a TV movie, he was asked: "Are you a Method actor? You know, from the Actors Studio?"

"Ha!" said the champ. "I went there once and watched 'em, the way they talked and moved. They were all trying to act like me! So that's how I found out I was a natural-born actor."

Once he saw the potential purses from closed-circuit telecasts, which didn't exist during his ring era, Graziano considered a comeback but was asked, "Can you make your old weight?"

"For that kind of dough," he replied, "I'll become a flyweight."

In October 1962, Graziano spoke at Gallaudet College for the deaf. He spoke the sign language he'd learned when he didn't speak for eighteen months as a child. As he ended his speech, a woman fell, and Graziano said, "Take a nine count!"

One night at Shor's, a fan mistook him for Jake LaMotta. "How could you think I was LaMotta?" Graziano protested. "Even if my face was run over by a train, I'd still look better than LaMotta."

Another woman asked him for an autograph and she too mistook him for LaMotta. Graziano took back the autograph, saying, "I'm saving this for someone who appreciates me."

A few weeks later, he watched a troupe of flamenco dancers stomping their heels on the floor at a furious pace. "I've seen that before," he said. "We used to do that to guys in the old neighborhood."

Graziano was introduced to Dustin Hoffman in 1975.

"You act like I fight," said Graziano.

JOE LOUIS

(1914–1981)

Almost no athlete from the 1930s and '40s would be able to compete with today's stars. Today's athletes are bigger, faster, stronger, and train with better equipment year-round.

But Joe Louis surely could. In any era. He was far and away the greatest heavyweight champion of his time and maybe, with apologies to you-know-who, the greatest of all time.

Born Joe Louis Barrow in rural Alabama, the grandson of former slaves, he would hold the then-coveted sports title of Heavyweight Champion of the World from 1937 to 1949, 140 consecutive months, a record that, given today's much bigger purses, will last forever. "The Brown Bomber," as he was known, nearly killed then-champion Max Schmeling, who'd defeated an out-of-shape Louis in an earlier fight. Coming on the eve of World War II, Louis's victory galvanized America.

An hour or so before his fight with Max Baer in September 1935, MGM publicist Howard Dietz, who also wrote the lyrics for "Dancing in the Dark" and "That's Entertainment," got a phone call from studio boss Irving Thalberg, who said he was considering filming *Romeo and Juliet*.

"I like the idea," said Dietz, "but I'm on my way to see Louis pummel Baer."

"Okay, go to the fight," replied Thalberg, who then told him he was considering casting his wife, Norma Shearer as Juliet. By the time Dietz expressed his objections, Louis had KO'd Baer in the fourth round at Yankee Stadium.

In 1937, Louis was in Hollywood completing his role in an autobiographical movie called *Spirit of Youth*. It all went well until a scene where the script called for him to say, "Yes, Ma." But that's not how Louis addressed his mother. He asked for a script change to "Yes, Mummy."

Late in 1939, "Slapsy Maxie" Rosenbloom, the former fighter who won 222 of his 298 fights and who held the light heavyweight championship before turning to acting, was asked if he could take Louis.

"Don't be silly," said Rosenbloom. "Louis could beat me over the telephone."

On September 29, 1941, Louis defeated Lou Nova with a TKO in the sixth round of a scheduled fifteen-round fight at the Polo Grounds. Two weeks later, Nova complained about the referee: "He never should've allowed Louis to enter the ring with those two hand grenades he concealed in his right glove."

In September 1956, Buddy Baer, a former heavyweight contender and brother of Max Baer, was asked about his title fight against Louis in 1941. Baer had shocked the world by knocking the champ out of the ring in the first round of their bout, only to refuse to come out for the seventh. He later was KO'd by Louis in the first round of a 1942 rematch.

"How tall was Louis?" Baer was asked. "He came up to about here," he replied, pointing to his chin. "And quite often."

When Louis went to see his friend Billy Eckstine perform at a nightclub, the doorman said, "I fought on the undercard the night you beat Schmeling."

"Sure, I remember you," said Louis. "You got knocked out in the first round, so I had to climb into the ring twenty minutes earlier."

Louis played golf with a pro named Porky Oliver, who spotted Louis four strokes. The champ won the match against Oliver, who had nearly won the 1953 Masters. Louis collected his money, then said, "Porky, want to get even? I have an idea. We'll go four rounds, and I'll spot you the first three."

In *Thoroughly Modern Millie*, Carol Channing was taught how to box by former heavyweight contender Lou Nova. Nova, who took a severe beating from Louis in their title fight, was asked if he thought he could take Louis in a rematch.

"Sure," said the fighter, then beaten into retirement by four lesser opponents. "Sure I could take him, but only if I were twenty-five again and he wasn't."

Louis found himself alone in an elevator at the Park Sheraton Hotel with Rocky Marciano, whose eighth-round TKO of Louis on October 26, 1951, ended Louis's seventy-bout professional career.

Marciano, who later said he hated defeating his idol, looked at Louis and said, "Sir, you look familiar. Haven't we met before?"

When Louis dined at Jack Dempsey's restaurant, someone asked the former champs who'd win if they'd faced off in their primes.

"The only one who has the answer," said Dempsey, pointing skyward, "is up there."

Heavyweight champion Joe Louis.

In June 1970 Jack Sharkey, the only man to fight Dempsey and Louis, compared their punches. "Joe floored me nine times," said the former champ. "Dempsey hit me just once. That was in 1926, but every morning when I get up, I stretch my jaw from that punch."

Much of Louis's later life was spent paying back taxes. In the 1940s, former New York mayor Jimmy Walker had suggested federal tax relief for the champ. Twice during the war Louis had waived purses, donating them to the Army and Navy Relief Funds. "In olden days," said Walker, "it was a sign of courage for a man to fight on a winner-take-all basis. But Joe showed even greater courage by fighting on a winner-take-*nothing* basis." The federal government did offer Louis some relief, but not until the 1960s.

Toots Shor took Billy Conn's sons to a Yankee game and pointed to second base. "That's where Louis flattened your father," he told the boys.

James J. Braddock, who lost his heavyweight title to Louis at Chicago's Comiskey Park in 1937, attended the Louis–Bob Pastor fight in 1939 at Briggs Stadium in Detroit, which Louis won. Braddock visited Pastor after the fight, and the loser said, "If only that blood hadn't dripped into my eye."

"Right," said Braddock. "He hits pretty hard, too, doesn't he?"

Visiting the Mayo Clinic in Rochester, Minnesota, Louis met Dr. Charles Mayo, one of the cofounders. "I'm proud to meet you," said the surgeon. "After all, you've knocked out more people than I have."

"No, I'm the one who's honored," replied Louis. "Making people well is more important than knocking them out."

In April 1974, Louis learned that both Muhammad Ali and George Foreman would receive a guarantee of $5 million apiece for their next title fight. "I got a guarantee, too, for my first professional fight," he recalled. "It was 1934. I knocked out Jack Kracken in the first round at Beacon's Arena in Chicago. I was guaranteed two ringside seats for my parents."

ANTONIO ORDÓÑEZ

(1931–1998)

He was a fighter, too—a bullfighter.

He was the most amazing man I ever knew. Ernest Hemingway, his godfather, proclaimed him the greatest matador of all. And Hemingway, who'd written *Death in the Afternoon* in 1932, had seen them all. Charismatic? Orson Welles told me in 1958 that, "Ordóñez could walk into a restaurant in Shanghai and people there would know a star had arrived."

I met Ordóñez in June 1961, a few weeks before Ernest Hemingway died. I was fifteen. Mary Hemingway had written Ordóñez an introductory letter, asking him to allow me to travel with him that summer in his cuadrilla (entourage) up, down, and across the Iberian peninsula.

It was the start of a life-changing experience. The Hemingways thought it would be for two weeks; in the end I would spend seven summers touring with the great matador. He adored Jacqueline Kennedy and the songs of Nat "King" Cole. His great rival was his brother-in-law Luis Miguel Dominguín, who had Picasso design his "suit of lights"—the matador's golden jacket—and who was Ava Gardner's lover. Hemingway wrote *The Dangerous Summer* about the rivalry of the two bullfighters in 1959. Antonio was like another older brother to me.

He knew only one phrase in English, and not a very useful one at that: "Okay, Mack." But he could find the only Spanish-speaking waiter in Idaho, where he visited Hemingway in Ketchum. He was extremely curious about America, exploring the far reaches of Brooklyn, the Grand Canyon, and all points in between.

I introduced Ordóñez to baseball listening to Phil Rizzuto's broadcasts on Armed Forces Radio while driving into the night on Spain's country roads. In New York, my father introduced him to Frank Gifford, and I took him to a Giants–49ers game.

In May 1962, he signed a deal with his friend Anthony Quinn to star in a short film Quinn was producing about matador Ignacio Sánchez Mejías, immortalized in Spanish literature by Federico García Lorca's poem "Lament for Ignacio Sánchez Mejías."

A signed photo from Antonio Ordóñez to Jeffrey Lyons, his "brother-from-another-mother."

Ordóñez insisted he could receive a letter addressed simply to "Antonio, España," making him more famous than any actor in Spain. Just then he and Quinn entered a restaurant and the crowd applauded Quinn. "Yes, I noticed," said Ordóñez, "but that's because all of Spain knows I only like to be applauded in the arena."

In November 1962, he visited Quinn backstage after taking in Quinn's performance in *Tchin-Tchin*, even though Ordóñez spoke next to no English. He told his actor friend that he was offered a small part in a Spanish movie. "There are no small parts," Quinn said. "That's as if I were entering the bullring in Madrid and saying, 'It looks like a small bull.'"

In February 1970, Ordóñez met Dr. Robert Jastrow, head of the Goddard Institute for Space Studies, part of NASA's Goddard Space Flight Center. Jastrow let him hold a piece of lunar rock. Ordóñez, pretending to be unimpressed, said, "Can you prove that rock isn't from Hawaii?"

In New York on the way home from the winter bullfight season in South America, he and his wife Carmen went to the Rainbow Room nightclub with Mary Hemingway. She asked him to dance, but Ordóñez used the Spanish peasant's excuse to decline: "I'm wearing new shoes and they're tight."

Carmen interceded, however, and revealed that a bull had stepped on his foot in Lima, Peru.

A. E. Hotchner, Hemingway's biographer and one of his closest friends, once pitched fastballs to Ordóñez, who only needed three pitches before figuring out how to hit home-run-length fly balls.

Laurence Harvey watched him perform in the bullring of Málaga and said he was studying Ordóñez in preparation for a role in a movie called *The Running Man*. "No, I won't be facing a bull in the movie. It'll be a mock bullfight I perform with children."

Antonio replied, "Be careful. Bulls are more predictable than children."

PART
IX

"Play

YOGI BERRA

(1925–)

Lawrence Peter Berra personifies all that is good in people. A beloved catcher, manager, and coach who won ten World Series rings, he is also a D-Day combat veteran. He's the father of a major leaguer and another son who played in the NFL, and is probably the most quoted American of his time.

Yogi applied for Special Services in the navy, saying he was a ballplayer. They didn't believe the short, stout Berra and assigned him as a boxer. He won nine fights, then got a chance to play in a ball game. After hitting a homer, he was switched to baseball.

He was in the third wave that landed on Omaha Beach on D-Day. "A lotta noise that morning," he told us, "like Opening Day."

In May 1955, *Damn Yankees* opened on Broadway, and the team was invited to a run-through. Yogi sat next to director George Abbott. When the "Yankees" sang in the shower, Yogi whispered to Abbott, "You have to change that number! We never do that."

In December 1955, my father returned to New York after two weeks in Russia. His first night back at Toots Shor's, he ran into Yogi. "Hey, Lenny," Yogi said, "I hear ya been to Russia. Nice town?"

In early February 1961, Yogi visited Phil Silvers backstage after a performance of *Do Re Mi*. Silvers was a huge sports fan and referred to his five daughters as "my infield." So here was a chance to ask Yogi something he'd always wanted to know.

"Yogi," he said, "when the batter steps into the box, you always seem to talk to him. What're you talking about?"

"I don't know," replied Yogi. "I'm sometimes hard to understand."

The 1961 season was one of baseball's greatest. It was the first season of expansion, but most of the attention was on the incredible home run race between the M&M Boys—Mickey Mantle and Roger Maris. Hollywood took notice; in *That Touch of Mink*, a scene was set in the Yankee dugout with Berra and the sluggers alongside Doris Day and Cary Grant. When Berra later heard the ballplayers' work described as "acting," he asked, "How can it be acting when we use our real names?"

During the 1962 New York newspaper strike, Yogi asked a baseball beat writer, "How come I haven't been seeing your stuff lately?" Told there was a strike, Yogi replied, "Oh, I didn't know. I haven't been reading the papers lately."

Jimmy Piersall, the great center fielder for the Red Sox, Mets, and Indians, and the subject of the Anthony Perkins movie *Fear Strikes Out*, recalled his first day in the major leagues. He and Yogi dined together and Piersall ordered filet mignon.

"Jimmy, you're a major leaguer now. Why don't you order a steak?" said Yogi.

In May 1964, Yogi was managing the Yankees and was asked about his other interest away from baseball. "It's called Yoo-hoo," said Yogi. "It's a soft drink."

"Is that hyphenated?" he was asked.

"No, it's carbonated," Yogi replied. (Actually, it isn't!)

In 1965, Yogi became a player-coach for the crosstown Mets and appeared in four games, holding up his Hall of Fame eligibility for a year. Manager Casey Stengel said it was hard finding the right player as a roommate for Yogi on road trips. "He can't be a light sleeper," explained Stengel, "because Yogi likes to talk a lot."

LEO DUROCHER

(1905–1991)

A great baseball trivia question: "I played for the New York Yankees. I'm a Hall of Famer. I wore a single-digit number now retired. I married a blonde movie star. And I'm *not* Joe DiMaggio. Who am I?"

The answer: Leo Durocher, a light-hitting shortstop on the 1929 Yankees, number 7 in your program, married to actress Laraine Day. He roomed with Babe Ruth that season. He was the colorful manager of the Brooklyn Dodgers, then the rival New York Giants, the Chicago Cubs, the Houston Astros, and finally the coach of the L.A. Dodgers.

In February 1945, Leo the Lip, as he was known for frequently arguing with umpires, gave a speech at a banquet. On the lectern he noticed there were two microphones. Durocher pushed both aside, saying, "With my Ebbets Field training, I don't need these."

He made a USO tour and got into a loud argument. He was reminded by an officer, "Save your anger, Leo. You're here to help these soldiers fight Germans—not umpires."

In June 1949, an American UN diplomat took his British counterpart to the Polo Grounds to see the Giants play the Pittsburgh Pirates. In the fourth inning, a close play went the way of the Pirates. Durocher came racing out of the dugout to argue.

"What's happening?" asked the Englishman.

"Oh, that's just Mr. Durocher showing off his charm," replied the American.

In 1954, after a superb Chinese dinner cooked by Danny Kaye, the short-tempered Durocher's fortune cookie read, "Your chivalry and compassion are admirable qualities."

In December 1955, Bill Rigney, who'd succeeded Durocher as manager of the New York Giants, congratulated him on his new job as an NBC-TV baseball analyst. "You no longer have to worry about pitchers, infield defense, hitting—everything during a game. You now have the best job in the world."

"No," replied Durocher. "The best job in the world is managing the New York Giants."

When Durocher was managing the Brooklyn Dodgers, a pitching prospect had a tryout at Ebbets Field. After a few throws, the skipper walked slowly to the mound. "Better look for another line of work, kid," he said, taking the ball from future Metropolitan Opera star baritone and Yankee Stadium national anthem singer Robert Merrill.

Later he heard Merrill singing in the shower and yelled, "And that goes for your singing, too!"

Before he became a TV star in *The Rifleman*, Chuck Connors had a brief major league career as a Dodger and Cub first baseman. Late in one game, Brooklyn was way behind and Connors, aware that Durocher didn't want to burn his bullpen in a hopeless cause, asked if he could pitch to a batter or two.

"Why not?" Durocher replied. "You hit like a pitcher. Maybe you can throw like one, too." Then Durocher changed his mind.

Casey Stengel once complained about having to speak before Durocher at an off-season banquet. "No matter how good my speech," he explained, "no one will remember it after Leo speaks. It's the same difference as hitting a home run in the first inning or the bottom of the ninth."

Hall of Famer Bob Feller was once asked who was the first batter he faced as a pro pitcher. "It was an exhibition game in 1936 during spring training," Feller recalled, smiling. "I was a kid of just seventeen, and we were playing the Cardinals. It was Leo Durocher and I struck him out."

HANK GREENBERG

(1911–1986)

A self-serving memory here. When I was playing center field for the Fieldston Eagles high school baseball team in the 1962 season, Hank Greenberg came to see us play against his son's Poly Prep team. He saw me make a circus catch near the fence, then throw out a runner at the plate. When the inning was over, Greenberg told me I had major league defensive ability.

Then he saw me hit. Or not. Still, it was a thrill I've never forgotten, which keeps me playing competitive softball in Central Park.

Greenberg's the greatest Jewish position player in baseball history, a five-time Detroit Tiger All-Star, two-time Most Valuable Player, and Hall of Famer whose career was interrupted by World War II. He was the first player drafted into the armed forces in 1940 and was discharged a year later. But the day after Pearl Harbor, Greenberg, who might have padded his career statistics by playing against wartime military rejects, reenlisted in the Army Air Corps. One can only imagine how he would have done if he'd decided to keep playing baseball instead of going to war!

By June 1939, Max Schmeling, the ex–heavyweight champion, had returned to his native Germany, much to Greenberg's regret. "I wish he'd come back here," said Greenberg. "The last time he was in town, I played stickball with him and won five hundred dollars."

In April 1942, Sergeant Greenberg was stationed at an army base in Florida. A visitor noticed that his cot was too short. "Half of me sleeps one day," he explained, "and the other half of me sleeps the next. This goes on for six days. On the seventh day, I go to a hotel in Tampa. Then *all* of me sleeps."

When Greenberg was traded from the Tigers to the Pirates, the perennial doormats of the National League, he sought out an unlikely source for a scouting report: Oscar Levant, often a sidekick in Hollywood musicals. Levant, a Pittsburgh native, gave Greenberg a detailed description of the spacious outfield in Forbes Field.

MICKEY MANTLE

(1931–1995)

J met Mickey Mantle twice, in one week. The first time I was reviewing movies at WPIX, which for decades had been the Yankee flagship TV station. I introduced myself, and he looked at me with that polite but distant gaze of a superstar who frequently has to pretend he's interested in meeting a fan.

Then I mentioned my father. His expression changed and he broke into a big smile, saying, "I owe your dad a lot. He was the only journalist who didn't report that I was drinking at Shor's the night before a big game."

"Mickey," I replied, "I'm a Red Sox fan, but I still want to implant this moment in my memory to tell my children." We had a moment, as they say.

A week later, we met again, at his restaurant on Central Park South, and he had no memory of our recent "moment."

Mantle was faced with the impossible task of succeeding (no one could replace) Joe DiMaggio, just as Carl Yastrzemski, a decade later, followed Ted Williams in left field for the Red Sox. Both players were up to the task, bringing their own unique skills and styles of play to forge their Hall of Fame careers. In September 1956, Mantle compared forearms with Rocky Marciano. "To me," said the just-retired boxer, "Mickey's forearms look bigger, so he must be stronger. I knocked out forty-three in my career, but Mickey's knocked out forty-seven just this season, and there's nearly a month to go!" Mickey would knock out five more home runs by the time the Yankees won the World Series that October.

Mantle shared a table at Shor's with Jackie Gleason and Eddie Arcaro, winner of five Kentucky Derbies. Toots told Arcaro that jockeys aren't really athletes. "The horse does all the running," he said. Arcaro replied, "Baseball players aren't really athletes. All they do is hit a little ball with a stick and hope it goes somewhere."

Mantle ignored that and reminded Gleason he'd beaten the comedian in a round of golf. Gleason then jokingly suggested they step outside and find out who was the real athlete.

437

"You make my weight," said Mantle, "and I'll do it." To which Toots replied, "I get that a lot from little Mr. Arcaro here."

A few days later, Anthony Newley, the quintessentially English actor and songwriter, then on Broadway in *The Roar of the Greasepaint, the Smell of the Crowd,* lunched at Shor's for the first time. He didn't know much about baseball or the Yankees, but he recognized Mantle at a nearby table."

"Oh, look," said the Englishman, "there's Mickey Mantle. He's the chap who excels at rounders."

When he got his two thousandth hit, in a game against the California Angels in late September 1964, the Angels' first baseman Joe Adcock said, "I'd like to shake your hand, but I'm afraid it wouldn't look right."

BABE RUTH (1895–1948)
AND LOU GEHRIG (1903–1941)

I recently came across my father's yearbook from the High School of Commerce, which was located where Lincoln Center is now. The baseball team of 1920 boasted a player whose nickname was "Babe." He was far better than any player anyone had ever seen. His name was Henry Louis Gehrig. My father was two years behind Gehrig, and although he stood only five foot eight, he went out for the football team, on which Gehrig also played.

The coach lined up my father against Gehrig in a drill. One tackle later, my father was on the swim team, but not before Gehrig taught him how to drop-kick—far easier with that old watermelon-shaped ball. My father passed on that skill to me.

Ruth and Gehrig were teammates on the Yankees for eleven seasons, but weren't the best of friends. Many photos of Ruth reaching home after a blast show Gehrig, who batted behind him (numbers 3 and 4 in your programs), with his back turned. It's no wonder; their personalities and lifestyles were polar opposites.

After the season, Ruth and Gehrig would barnstorm, playing exhibition games around the country. In Iowa in 1928, a nine-year-old farm boy finished his chores early to be able to see the game. He got Ruth and Gehrig to autograph his baseball, then added his own signature before covering it with shellac. He signed it "Robert William Feller." Bob Feller grew up to become one of the greatest pitchers of all time.

When it came time to cast *Pride of the Yankees* in 1942, the year after Gehrig died, Ruth overcame his reluctance to play himself. The producers also wanted Gehrig's roommate, Bill Dickey, the Hall of Fame Yankee catcher, who was still active. But Dickey ignored messages. Finally, when contacted, he explained, "I'm no actor. How can I call Gary Cooper 'Lou'?" He and Ruth ended up playing themselves convincingly.

Paul Gallico, who wrote the book on which the movie was based, was asked if Cooper was so good an actor that he was able to play Gehrig, who batted left handed, even though Cooper didn't hit that way.

439

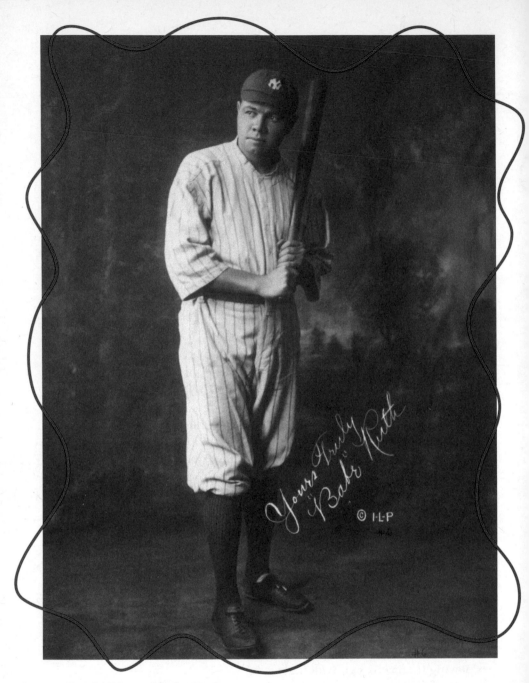

Baseball legend Babe Ruth.

"When it comes to hitting," replied Gallico, "Cooper isn't even *right* handed." A popular theory has it that Cooper swung right handed but that the film was shot with the "4" and "Yankees" on his uniform written backward, and he ran to third base. Then the negative was reversed. Some deny this.

Ruth was once asked to throw out the first pitch at a semipro game. He knew the teams were playing a double-header, so the former pitching immortal practiced an unusual drill, which he put into practice that day. He placed two catchers ten feet from each other, picked up two baseballs, and pitched perfect strikes simultaneously.

PART
X

"If Music Be the

Food of Love..."

HAROLD ARLEN

(1905–1986)

He wrote the music for some of the most memorable songs in Hollywood history. Besides "Over the Rainbow," which won the Oscar for Best Song in 1939, he composed standards like "The Man That Got Away," "That Old Black Magic," "Stormy Weather," and "Blues in the Night."

He was born Harold Arluck, the son of a cantor, in Buffalo, New York. He joined several bands and eventually wrote "Get Happy," his first hit. Ironically, its mention of Judgment Day evoked evangelical themes. After a stint at the famed Cotton Club and an engagement as a performer at the Palace Theater, he eventually moved to Hollywood and began writing songs for the movies.

In June 1943, Arlen returned to New York for the first time in six years, and soon went to Syracuse to visit his father, a rabbi. By that time, he was the toast of Hollywood. He asked his father if there was anything he'd like from New York. "Yes," replied Rabbi Arlen. "I need more marriage certificates. I've run out up here."

The following year, Arlen was back in Hollywood at Ira Gershwin's. Also present was Harold Rome, who wrote the songs for the revue *Pins and Needles* and who would later write *Wish You Were Here* and *I Can Get It for You Wholesale*. They began performing their own songs, but each, at one point or another, forgot the lyrics. Their wives then chimed in with the words.

On a December afternoon in 1952, Arlen was walking up Broadway. A few steps behind, Arthur Schwartz spotted him. Schwartz began to whistle "Stormy Weather." No response. Then Schwartz whistled "Over the Rainbow." Same result. Finally Schwartz whistled his own standard, "Dancing in the Dark." Arlen turned and greeted Schwartz.

Two years later, he and Truman Capote were working on their Broadway-bound musical, *House of Flowers*. Capote was in New York, using Marlene Dietrich's apartment, and Arlen worked by phone from Hollywood. Dietrich had phoned Arlen from a piano store in New York and had him listen to the tones of one she was considering buying. He didn't like it, so she went to the Steinway store, phoned him again, and had him listen to a few notes on one of theirs. He approved, and she bought it.

Arlen and his wife accompanied Arthur Miller and his wife to El Morocco. At one point, Arlen danced with Mrs. Miller.

"Everyone's staring at us," said Arlen.

"That's because they recognize you," replied Marilyn Monroe.

LOUIS ARMSTRONG

(1901–1971)

He was an American original, a great trumpeter, jazz ambassador, and international star. Wherever he traveled, Armstrong always took his trumpet with him in case he was asked to play. "If I use someone else's trumpet," he explained, "it's understood that I'd be playing for free. But if I'm playing *mine*, I'll get some loot."

He was absorbed in the world of jazz to the exclusion of almost everything else. In fact, during a European tour in 1955 Armstrong was told the Big Four were meeting in Switzerland. "I'd like to go dig 'em," he said. "I haven't heard a four-piece combo in a long time."

That same year, Armstrong wrote an article for *Ebony* magazine about dieting. He'd reduced his weight from 268 to 170 pounds. "Lose Weight the Satchmo Way," the article was headlined. Armstrong sent a copy to the White House, suggesting in an accompanying letter that if President Eisenhower stuck to the diet, he would feel like a ten-year-old. Armstrong received a reply on White House stationery: "Thank you, but the president is not supposed to feel like a ten-year-old."

Armstrong performed "St. Louis Blues" with a symphony orchestra conducted by Leonard Bernstein. He was asked if this would be his first performance with a symphony. "Hell, no," Armstrong said. "Twenty-two years ago, when I worked in a Chicago nightclub, the stage door faced the opera house. And when I'd go out for air, I'd hear the orchestra playing *Cavalleria Rusticana*, so I'd pick up my trumpet and join in."

In the fall of 1958, Armstrong prepared for his eleventh world tour, covering more places than any other trip he'd made. The only thing he dreaded was the endless series of inoculations he'd need. He asked his agent, "How come you keep booking me in countries where I have to get sick?"

In March 1959, his tour reached Australia. During the long flight home, Armstrong filled out the airline questionnaire. Under "Suggestions for improving the service," Armstrong wrote, "Move Australia closer to the U.S."

Louis Armstrong and his band, Paris Blues, directed by Martin Ritt and produced by Sam Shaw, Paris, 1960. Photograph by Sam Shaw.

Asked for advice for a young trumpet student, he said, "Keep blowin'."

Another young trumpet student saw Armstrong play at New York's Metropole and told Satchmo his own playing was improving.

"Do you know the scale yet?" asked Armstrong.

"I sure do," the boy replied. "Here at the Metropole, it's $125 a week for sidemen and double for leaders."

In 1960, Bing Crosby sat in the control room of an Armstrong recording session and marveled, "Satchmo is the only musician I know who can't be replaced."

When Armstrong heard that LeRoy Neiman had painted and sold two portraits of him, he decided to buy two portraits of another jazz immortal, saxophonist Gerry Mulligan. First, though, he was offered a life-size portrait of him. "No thanks, Pops," he told the gallery owner. "I don't want *that* much Mulligan."

Paul Anka did an Armstrong impression on an album, then asked Satchmo if that bothered him.

"Pops," Armstrong replied, "a lotta cats have copied the *Mona Lisa*, but they still line up to dig the original."

THE BEATLES

JOHN LENNON (1940–1980)
RINGO STARR (1940–)
PAUL McCARTNEY (1942–)
GEORGE HARRISON (1943–2001)

They arrived in New York just ten weeks after the Kennedy assassination, the perfect diversion for a nation still in mourning. Soon, they became a national obsession. They led the "British Invasion" in music and changed a generation.

Just before they arrived in New York, Shelley Winters, the two-time Oscar winner, received a letter from a British newspaperman, asking her to look after the four young musicians coming to New York for the first time. "Take them to a political meeting and to a session at the Actors Studio so they won't be bored," he wrote.

They weren't bored in New York.

Asked about his new movie *Cromwell* in June 1970, Richard Harris said, "It's a spectacular drama about a British commoner who wielded more power than any other commoner ever has—except the Beatles."

In November 1970, Erich Segal, author of *Love Story*, was teaching writing at Yale, where undergraduates began bringing their dates to his lectures. Not because of *Love Story*, but because as the screenwriter of *Yellow Submarine*, he knew the Beatles.

In 1964, Jackie DeShannon, whose biggest hit song would be "What the World Needs Now Is Love," was an opening act for the Beatles on their first American tour. "My job," she explained, "was to entertain the audience while the boys were backstage combing their hair."

When young Sid Bernstein, the future rock music promoter, was a student at the New School, he heard a lecture by journalist Max Lerner, who urged students to read British newspapers for a different perspective on world affairs. Bernstein read an account of an up-and-coming group. "I phoned their manager, Brian Epstein, and booked them into Carnegie Hall," he said. That's how Bernstein became the Beatles' American promoter.

Paul said to Ringo, "See? I told you it was Sid, not Leonard."

In August 1965, John Lennon questioned Victor Spinetti, their costar in *A Hard Day's Night* and *Help!*, saying, "Victor, I know that when the director says 'Action!' most actors change their voices and faces, but you're always the same. Does that mean you're as terrible as we are?"

Phil Silvers arrived in New York and walked along West Fifty-Fourth Street past the hotel where the Beatles were staying. Silvers, still a big TV star, waved to the mobs surrounding the hotel, then told several policemen, "Sorry to have caused all this to-do."

Before one performance, Ringo was hoarse. "Don't worry," said George Harrison. "When it comes time for Ringo to sing, all he has to do is raise one hand and everyone roars, so they'll never notice."

Leopold Stokowski conducted his American Symphony Orchestra in a series of Teenage Concerts at Carnegie Hall for six thousand students, and asked the students why they loved the Beatles.

One student put it best: "When you listen to the Beatles, it gives you something to do; when you listen to serious music, you just have to sit still."

In 1970, Yoko Ono published a revised edition of her 1964 book *Grapefruit*, urging readers to burn it when they were done. At the end, John Lennon wrote, "This is the greatest book I've ever burned."

In July 1971, director Fernando Baldi directed Ringo Starr in his dramatic film debut in *Blindman*, a spaghetti western. Baldi later said, "Ringo entered the movie as a Beatle, but left as an actor."

MARIA CALLAS

(1923–1977)

She was an international opera star who redefined the word "diva." She was also famous for being the longtime mistress of Aristotle Onassis until he dumped her for another, much more famous woman.

Callas was at a party and met an official from the British Information Services. He asked her why she'd never done a command performance for the queen. "She doesn't like opera," said Callas.

"But the queen did go to the opera to see you," he replied.

"Yes, she did," said Callas. "And I watched her. She looked like she didn't like it."

Born in New York, raised in Greece, and living in Italy, Callas was asked in which language she thought. "Let's just say," replied the highest-paid opera singer of all time, "that I count in English."

After she'd been fired from the Metropolitan Opera in New York and La Scala in Milan for her diva behavior, a Met executive said, "Maria's been fired more often than any rocket out of Cape Canaveral."

In 1960, Alfred Hitchcock had a brilliant idea for a movie scene with Callas. The setting would be the Met, where Callas is concluding an aria. Just then, she notices a man in the first box about to murder a woman. Callas screams—and immediately hears a round of applause for having hit the highest note in the aria.

When it was disclosed that she was making more money than President Eisenhower, the diva shrugged and said, "Let him learn how to sing."

Before a performance of *La Traviata* at the Met, she threw a tantrum backstage. She discovered that Gina Lollobrigida was in the audience; she considered the Italian movie star a jinx. Later it was revealed that Callas had canceled several performances in Rome attended by Lollobrigida. Callas feared audiences would look at the actress instead of the stage.

In 1959 her marriage was in trouble. She said, "I'd rather raise a family than sing another note."

She and Rudolf Bing, the austere general manager of the Met, had a reconciliation after he'd fired her for repeated missed performances. She returned to sing *La Traviata* and later heard a rumor that Licia Albanese, another star soprano, had also been in the house—just in case.

"Yes, it's true," said Bing. "Maria, I love you, but I just don't trust you."

NAT "KING" COLE

(1919–1965)

The incredibly mellow tones of this gifted jazz pianist and singer still resonate today in his recordings of "The Christmas Song," "Route 66," "Those Lazy, Hazy, Crazy Days of Summer," and his biggest hit, "Mona Lisa."

He was one of the first African Americans to have his own TV show, and in 1957 he performed on a cerebral palsy telethon where my family also appeared and met him. He died too young, of lung cancer.

Cole defined his relaxed style: "I try to make my voice sound like I'm wearing slippers."

Before a Carnegie Hall concert in 1953, he said, "I made two reservations for my flight back to California, one an hour later. In case I have to do encores."

After his engagement at the London Palladium in 1954, Cole was booked to tour the provinces. "Do you know what 'the provinces' are?" his agent asked. "Sure," replied Cole. "Anything north of 125th Street back home in New York."

In Paris celebrating his tenth anniversary with Capitol Records, Cole said, "Being a recording artist is like being the prime minister of France: you continually need a vote of confidence from your followers."

Preparing for his role in *Cat Ballou*, Cole said, "Learning dialogue is easy. They're just lyrics which don't rhyme."

Returning from a tour of Australia, he was asked the fastest way to get there. He responded, "A hit record. Two hits gets you there even faster."

When he met Van Johnson and Lana Turner on a studio back lot, he said, "This is the first time I've seen either of you without a bag of popcorn in my lap."

He defined rock'n'roll: "It's for teenagers on an allowance, not grown-ups on an expense account."

At a dinner honoring the president of Capitol Records, George Jessel said, "I came here to shake hands with the real guest of honor." Then he shook hands with Cole.

Cole played the great composer W. C. Handy in the movie *St. Louis Blues*. The plot, he said, was "nothing complicated. Boy meets girl. Boy loses girl. Boy writes the blues."

Cole explained the difference between a ballad and the blues: "A ballad is when you find the girl. The blues are when you lose her."

GEORGE GERSHWIN

(1898–1937)

n December 1955, a cable arrived at the plush Beverly Hills home of Ira and Lee Gershwin: it was from the producer of the touring company of *Porgy and Bess*, the classic 1934 George and Ira Gershwin opera, opening in frigid Moscow.

Ira was agoraphobic and hated leaving home. The cable read: "Come and see how we've improved your lyrics." He was on the next flight.

One can only imagine what other great music George Gershwin would have written had he lived a normal lifespan, instead of dying of a brain tumor at thirty-eight. But *Rhapsody in Blue*, *Porgy and Bess*, "Fascinating Rhythm," "They Can't Take That Away from Me," "I Got Rhythm," and so many other timeless works are a wonderful legacy. His music has been heard in 546 movie and TV soundtracks! (To date.)

When he was twenty, Gershwin was in an all-night poker game with Irving Caesar, who wrote the lyrics for "Tea for Two" and many other songs. Caesar would interrupt his losing streak to join Gershwin at the piano and write some lyrics for a melody Gershwin was working on, then return for another hand.

Gershwin finished composing his melody and Caesar, still behind, returned to the piano to complete the lyrics. The song was "Swanee," immortalized by Al Jolson.

Rouben Mamoulian, who directed the first Broadway production of *Porgy and Bess*, told Gershwin that a fugue was a composition in which the original theme is repeated. "A fugue," Gershwin corrected him, "is a musical theme which keeps coming in and in a while the customers keep going out and out."

While rehearsing for a musical, Gershwin received distressing news from playwright S. N. Behrman: the woman both had been wooing had married someone else.

"Well," said Gershwin, "I'm glad I'm in the middle of rehearsals; otherwise I'd be terribly upset."

While living in Paris, Gershwin approached composer Maurice

Ravel to see if he might give him lessons in serious composition. "No," said the composer of *Bolero*. "Better for you to be a first-class Gershwin than a second-class Ravel."

In April 1936, Gershwin began seeing a psychiatrist, but first asked the doctor, "Will this treatment affect my genius?"

Oscar Levant once heard Gershwin talking endlessly on the arts, composing, etc., and asked, "George, if you had to do it all over—would you fall in love with yourself again?"

Before he died, Gershwin drew an outline for a sketch of Irving Berlin, but never completed or signed it. It was given to Berlin, who considered it one of his prized possessions. Ira was in New York late in 1940, finishing work on the lyrics for *Lady in the Dark*, and visited Berlin. He spotted George's unsigned sketch and underneath wrote, "My brother George drew this for Irving Berlin—Ira Gershwin."

VLADIMIR HOROWITZ

(1903–1989)

The Russian-born classical pianist made his debut in the West in 1928, at Carnegie Hall. He was one of the greatest pianists of the twentieth century.

Only one pianist was Horowitz's equal. In a men's clothing store, the salesman greeted him, "Nice to see you again. And how is Mrs. Rubinstein?"

"Oh, she's fine," replied Horowitz. "I see her every so often."

Horowitz had three conditions for any concert: no plants on-stage, no velvet or silk drapes or backdrops, and no ads referring to him as "King of the Pianists."

"If you have to be advertised that way," he explained, "then you're no king."

Horowitz and his wife visited Arthur Miller in Connecticut. Miller told the maestro that he thought his piano was out of tune. Horowitz played an entire sonata, then said, "You're right, it *is* out of tune, but only a little."

When CBS filmed Horowitz's Carnegie Hall recital in 1968, the wardrobe department supplied ballet shoes for the cameramen and the programs had plastic covers to cut down on the noise of pages turning.

After it was broadcast a few months later, CBS vice president Michael Dann, who watched it in his office with the maestro, took him and other executives out to a celebratory dinner. He noticed Horowitz wasn't eating.

"I never eat after one of my concerts," Horowitz explained.

"But this was just the telecast of a concert you performed months ago," Dann replied.

"Doesn't matter," said Horowitz. "I played along on every note to-night, just as if I were performing."

In July 1967, Horowitz and his wife made their first visit to Ar-thur, the sensational discotheque, and listened to the Wild Ones, the house band. "If I had to make my living playing rock 'n' roll, I'd starve," he said. "I have no idea how to play that."

FRANK LOESSER

(1909–1969)

He was one of the wittiest, most talented songwriters America ever produced. "Praise the Lord and Pass the Ammunition," "Baby, It's Cold Outside," "Standin' on the Corner," and many others are standards. *Guys and Dolls*, *The Most Happy Fella*, and *How to Succeed in Business Without Really Trying* are frequently revived.

When he first came to Hollywood, Loesser drove to Paramount, met the studio's musical director, Boris Morros, and said, "Hi. Want to hire a genius?"

In September 1950, Loesser revealed his method of writing the first song after the intermission (for *Guys and Dolls*, it was "Take Back Your Mink"): "The audience is drifting in after intermission, so the song must be catchy to make 'em rush in, sit down—and behave themselves."

Producer Sam Goldwyn wanted Loesser to write more than the agreed-upon number of songs for the 1952 Danny Kaye movie *Hans Christian Andersen*, but Loesser was reluctant to discuss any revised deal.

"How can I get you to talk?" asked Goldwyn.

"Easy," replied Loesser. "Just throw a lot of money at my mouth."

Loesser told a man at the next table at Sardi's that people were referring to his new show, *The Most Happy Fella*, as an opera. "Nobody calls a show an opera unless they have to," said the man. "Nobody, that is, except me." It was Rudolf Bing, general manager of the Metropolitan Opera.

Loesser stayed at a hotel at the same time as Edwin Lester, head of the Los Angeles Light Civic Opera Company. The similarities in their last names led to frequent confusion with phone calls. Finally Lester met Loesser and said, "Never mind all that. Where's my laundry?"

By late 1956, *The Most Happy Fella* was a big hit, but Loesser was a perfectionist who often came to the theater to make sure the cast wasn't falling into bad habits.

Frank Loesser, 1960. Photograph by Sam Shaw.

"Even 'Mary Had a Little Lamb' gets stale after three hundred performances," he said.

By January 1957, Loesser had had three hits on Broadway: *Where's Charley?*, *Guys and Dolls*, and *The Most Happy Fella*. He did his best to keep the opening night tickets out of the hands of Broadway's usual first-nighters. "They're bored people," he explained. "I want a first-night audience who'll cheer at every turn. Give me an audience of chorus girls' aunts."

Loesser's favorite dinner course was caviar, blinis, and sour cream. "If scientists study meteors to see if civilized life exists there, they should make this test: just see if they have sour cream," he said. "No life can be deemed civilized without it."

Loesser advised a novice about how to write lyrics: "They should be like those of a man making love—full of exaggerated compliments and wild promises."

When Loesser heard the news that Betty Smith, author of *A Tree Grows in Brooklyn*, married a man named Joe Jones, he quipped, "Now they'll never be able to check into a motel."

BILLY ROSE

(1899–1966)

The multimillionaire lyricist, theater owner, impresario, speed shorthand champion, art collector, and investor left an amazing legacy. Mentored by the financier Bernard Baruch, Rose made millions on Wall Street and at one time was the second biggest holder of AT&T stock.

Rose penned lyrics to standards like "Me and My Shadow" and "It's Only a Paper Moon." He owned the famous Diamond Horseshoe nightclub in the Paramount Building near Times Square, bought the Ziegfeld and another theater he renamed after himself, and produced several Broadway shows, including *Jumbo*, with Jimmy Durante, and *Seven Lively Arts*. Among his four wives were Fanny Brice and an Olympic gold medalist, swimmer Eleanor Holm.

William Samuel Rosenberg was a high school sprint star and studied shorthand with John Robert Gregg, inventor of the most modern form. He could write up to 250 words a minute with either hand and won the world championship.

In 1937, Rose produced Cleveland's Great Lakes Exposition and hired Olympic swimming champion and movie Tarzan Johnny Weissmuller. Weissmuller demanded a guarantee that Lake Erie would be at least seventy degrees. Rose's reply: "Ask God."

Asked if he'd ever invest in a period play, he said, "Not on your life. I don't like plays where they write letters with feathers."

Rose was very competitive. When asked if he'd ever consider taking up painting, he said, "No. I'll never start anything at which I know I could never match the top guys."

When a theater owner didn't want to book Rose's all-black show *Carmen Jones*, Rose threatened to build a theater right next door. Realizing Rose meant business, he relented.

Opening night of *Oklahoma!* was one of Broadway's landmark evenings. But it was almost ruined for Rose and his wife by a couple seated in front of them, who constantly shuffled their programs during the first act, even holding them up to the light to identify actors. So at intermission, Rose snatched their programs, forcing them to spend the second act simply watching the show.

Rose was once offered a talking bird for a show. "I'd have loved to put it onstage," he recalled, "but it could only say one thing: 'That'll be four thousand dollars a week.'"

In March 1946, Rose attended the Nuremberg war crimes trials. He was billeted in an oversize bedroom in a large house outside the city. In the morning, he was driven to the courtroom, and the driver said, "Mr. Rose, now that you've slept well, I can tell you that the house where you stayed was Heinrich Himmler's, and you slept in his bed."

Rose commissioned Salvador Dalí to paint *The Seven Lively Arts* for the lobby of his Ziegfeld Theater. Later, it was moved to Rose's suburban mansion, only to be destroyed by a fire in 1956. Also lost were irreplaceable works by Utrillo, Vlaminck, Chagall, and Renoir.

"I'll paint you seven others to replace the burned ones," said Dalí, "and at the cost in 1944. You had faith in me. You were my friend then, you are my friend now."

Lost in the fire along with the priceless paintings were Rose's shorthand medals. "I bought the paintings, but I won those medals," he said, "so they meant more to me." He traced the manufacturer and had every one replicated, along with medals for contests he didn't win, saying, "I thought I deserved the benefit of the doubt."

Assuming the largest canvases must be the most valuable, the firefighters saved an enormous one by a living artist, Thomas Hart Benton, while irreplaceable Impressionist masterpieces burned. Benton wrote the firefighters, commending them on their taste.

Rose once considered buying the New York Yankees. "My shows relied on nostalgia," he said. "I'd have put Joe DiMaggio back in the lineup."

After summering on the Riviera he stopped off at his fifty-five-room Manhattan town house, studied his rich portfolio, then was chauffeured in his Rolls-Royce to his newest home, on an island off Connecticut, to celebrate his birthday. After blowing out the candles, Rose was asked what he'd wished for. "More of the same," he replied.

Rose learned to swim when he was fifty-eight, years after making a fortune producing aquatic shows. "It was probably better back then that I couldn't swim," he said. "That way I could ask my swimmers to perform the impossible."

A writer about to sell his script to a movie studio came to Rose for advice. He asked the difference between a percentage of the net and the gross profits. "It's simple," replied Rose. "In the movie business, 'gross' means sure money. But 'net' means a lawsuit."

Billy Rose and my father.

In May 1963, Rose won the rights to the play *The Deputy*, about the Vatican's role in the Holocaust. When asked why he wanted it produced Rose explained: "I have six million reasons why." He won the bidding by recalling his mentor Bernard Baruch's advice, "When you're sure you want something, strike quickly and let everybody get a little rich."

A houseguest once beat Rose repeatedly on his pool table. A few weeks later, Rose invited the guest back and beat *him* decisively. In the interim, he'd hired pool champion Willie Mosconi for lessons.

In 1964, he married Doris Warner Vidor, daughter of one of the Warner brothers. Beforehand, she asked the judge to present his credentials. "I wouldn't put it past Billy to hire someone from Central Casting to portray a judge and in a week or so reveal that we're not married," she explained.

Rose suggested they leave their respective fortunes to each other: "Think of the odds. I'm older and richer."

ARTURO TOSCANINI

(1867–1957)

If you think Fletcher, the music teacher in the recent movie *Whiplash*, had a short fuse, he pales alongside Toscanini, the most famous conductor of all. The native of Parma, Italy, played the cello in an orchestra touring South America in 1886. One night, when the conductor of the local orchestra was ill prepared, the young musician, who'd memorized the entire evening's program, took up the baton for the first time and performed flawlessly. He was nineteen.

In 1915, Toscanini was booked on a May 1 voyage from New York back to Italy via Liverpool, but he left a week earlier than planned on an Italian liner. He thus avoided the fatal voyage of the SS *Lusitania*, whose sinking helped to precipitate America's entry into World War I.

When Giacomo Puccini died in 1924, he hadn't finished *Turandot*. Another composer, Franco Alfano, completed it two years later. When a young Toscanini led the orchestra at Milan's La Scala in the opera's debut performance, he suddenly stopped, twenty minutes before the end, turned to the audience, and said, "Here died the maestro."

In 1938, Toscanini, by then conducting the NBC Symphony Orchestra, was in the elevator at 30 Rockefeller Center headed to a rehearsal. The young page running the elevator was whistling absent-mindedly. After a few floors, Toscanini said, "You're flat."

During a rehearsal, Toscanini became so enraged at the orchestra that he threw down his watch and stomped on it, smashing it to pieces. An assistant quietly gathered the remnants. The watch had been a gift from NBC. Two days later, the assistant delivered the repaired watch to Toscanini, along with two cheap watches marked "For rehearsals only."

In December 1938, Toscanini wanted to stay overnight at a hotel near rehearsals in New York City. To accommodate him, the management moved a guest from the room Toscanini wanted—bandleader Tommy Dorsey, who was understandably displeased. To retaliate, Dorsey scheduled early-morning rehearsals for his band in the adjacent Paramount Theater, deliberately blowing his trombone straight up at Toscanini's bedroom window.

Arthur Rubinstein was asked if he'd ever performed with Toscanini. "No, never," the piano virtuoso replied. "That could never happen. Toscanini is an autocrat, and so am I."

An army captain asked Toscanini to lead the orchestra at a military function. "Do you remember me?" asked the captain.

"Oh, yes," replied Toscanini. "You were my second flute player in 1927. When the first flutist was sick you asked to step in. And I remember that night you made two mistakes."

That captain, Meredith Willson, went on to compose *The Music Man*.

Oscar Levant, a concert pianist by trade, was a guest soloist with Toscanini. "You don't play *with* Toscanini," he explained, "you play *under* Toscanini."

American troops liberating Rome discovered a penniless Pietro Mascagni, composer of the famous 1890 opera *Cavalleria Rusticana*. New York opera lovers quickly established a fund for him and asked Toscanini to donate. "A fund to help Mascagni?" he said. "No! Mascagni was and still is a Fascist."

In 1945, Toscanini was conducting another orchestra and noticed the absence of its prominent first violist, Milton Katims, who was a respected conductor in his own right. "Why isn't he here?" Toscanini asked. He was told Katims was conducting another show. "Conducting?" asked Toscanini. "Why does such a fine artist on the viola want to lead an orchestra? After all, *anyone* can wave a stick."

The cake for his eighty-second birthday was decorated with chocolate notes from his favorite musical works. Ever the perfectionist, he studied the notes and said, "They're wrong."

In 1951, Toscanini went to see the first Technicolor Mickey Mouse movie. In one scene, Mickey was shown conducting an orchestra in the *William Tell* Overture, constantly disturbed by the antics of his rival, Donald Duck. Toscanini sighed and said, "I too have my Donald Ducks."

After repeated bows one night, Toscanini told opera star Jan Peerce, "This is always the ugliest moment of the evening for me."

When he was presented with a silver breakfast tray as an award, he responded, "I never eat breakfast."

His orchestra gave him a unique birthday gift when he turned eighty-six: a clock that needed to be wound only once every fifty years. He wound the clock, then said, "Strange, isn't it? All of you will be dead the next time I wind this."

By his next birthday, he'd mellowed. At a rehearsal, the orchestra's playing didn't satisfy him. But instead of the expected outburst, the maestro said, "I am not enthusiastic about your intonation."

Toscanini once sent a check to fund a singing scholarship for a group called the Joy of Singing. One year later, without receiving a solicitation, he sent another check, with a note reading, "Did you think I'd forget?"

AFTERWORD

BY DOUGLAS B. LYONS

After reading this book, you might get the impression that our father was a workaholic. He was always working—lunch places, dinner clubs, nightclubs, after-theater clubs, parties, Broadway openings, off-Broadway theaters, and many trips abroad. How much did he travel? Two anecdotes can tell that story: He once had to get a new passport because there was no room left for more stamps. And when he flew into Idlewild (later John F. Kennedy International Airport), he frequently saw the same customs agent, who greeted him *by name*. No matter where he went, he kept a dime in his pocket, so he could call home from a pay phone at the airport to let us know he had landed.

But I never got the feeling that he was too busy us. Although he had dined at the great restaurants of the world, his absolute favorite place to eat dinner was at home with his family.

On Saturdays and Sundays he always went across the street with us to Central Park with baseball or football equipment. I never heard him say, "I'm too tired. I worked until one a.m. last night" or "I just got off a ten-hour flight." His attitude was "Let's go!" He was the best batting practice pitcher ever—he never struck *anybody* out!

A school show? He was there. Parent-teacher night? He came. A piano recital? Sledding in Central Park? He was there.

And he included my brothers and me in his work. He must have taken me to a hundred Broadway openings. He also took us to many screenings of new films and to fancy opening nights. (I bought a tuxedo for the premiere of *Lord Jim* in 1965.)

If it was something new, he wanted to be there. We went to a "happening" at the former Loew's Eighty-Third Street Theater. When the discotheque Arthur opened on East Fifty-Fourth Street, he was there almost every night, although he was not a fan of loud music and his idea of dancing involved people touching each other. But interesting and newsworthy people were there, so he was there. He took me to a screening of Orson Welles's *The Trial*. There, he introduced me to two of his friends: Abe Beame, the New York City comptroller and future major, and Larry Fine of the Three Stooges. What a headline, I thought: "The Three Stooges Meet Franz Kafka!"

Whatever unusual experiences he exposed my brothers and me to—whether it was taking us to the World's Fairs in Brussels in 1958, Seattle in 1962, and Montreal in 1967; watching gamblers at a Las Vegas casino (he watched but didn't gamble); ball games at the Polo Grounds, Ebbets Field, and Yankee Stadium; or introducing me to ballplayers at Toots Shor's after an Old Timers' Game—he'd say, "It's part of your education."

When he and my two oldest brothers, George and Warren, were going to see Lili St. Cyr, a famous stripper, I was told that I was too young to go. I disagreed: "I am SO old enough to see him!" (Some years later he took me to see her in Lake Tahoe.)

Reading these stories that Jeff has unearthed and organized, I am reminded of the people our father introduced me to, such as Justice William O. Douglas of the Supreme Court of the United States, for whom I was named; Chief Justice Earl Warren (I didn't wash my hand for a week after meeting him); and Joe DiMaggio, who came to my bar mitzvah. One day at the Palace Hotel in San Francisco, where Harding died, Pop and I had lunch with three giants (not Giants): Joe DiMaggio; Carlos P. Romulo, former president of the Philippines and aide to General Douglas MacArthur; and Jake Ehrlich, one of America's most prominent defense attorneys. (Pop never put his pocket notebook away during that lunch.)

Another time, when Pop visited me at Berkeley, we had lunch with Joe DiMaggio and two of his friends: Lefty O'Doul and Ernie Nevers. O'Doul batted .398 in 1929 and later helped popularize baseball in Japan. Nevers, who played briefly in the major leagues, is a member of the Pro Football Hall of Fame.

In New York one day, I had lunch with Pop and three of his friends: Ben Shahn, Marc Chagall, and John Steinbeck. Steinbeck told the story of the toast he gave all over the USSR, where his books were very popular but earned him no royalties. Everyplace he went, he was toasted. As the guest of honor, he had to offer a return toast. What could he say in a country that was cheating him out of millions of dollars? He used a variation on the first line of "The Birth of the Blues": "Natchez to Mobile, Memphis to St. Joe!" If said quickly it sounded profound, but was actually gibberish.

Pop introduced me to Roger Baldwin, the founder of the American Civil Liberties Union; Helen Keller; Nathan Leopold, the most infamous killer in America in 1924; Robe

rt Frost; Nobel Peace Prize winner Dr. Ralph Bunche (a frequent guest at our Passover seders); downstairs neighbors Phil Silvers and Abe Burrows; Frank Loesser; Richard Rodgers; and Isaac Stern. While walking through the World's Fair in Seattle, he encountered two friends: Van Cliburn and Igor Stravinsky.

On one of his rare trips to Los Angeles, we went to a very small, out-of-the-way restaurant. There we met Jack Lemmon, who was playing the piano, and William L. Shirer, author of *The Rise and Fall of the Third Reich*.

My father introduced me to many true pioneers of television: David Sarnoff, Steve Allen, Johnny Carson, Ernie Kovacs, Lloyd Bridges (*Sea Hunt* is still my favorite show of all time), Edward R. Murrow, and Walter Cronkite.

All part of my education.

And, of course, when my parents flew from London to San Francisco, a relatively new "over the pole" flight, for my graduation from Berkeley in 1969, they got to watch me walk out on one of their friends: an honorary degree was presented to Arthur Goldberg, then LBJ's ambassador to the UN, whose job was to defend the U.S.'s involvement in the Vietnam War. I wore a gas mask as I walked out.

Two years later, on March 8, 1971, Pop introduced me to Goldberg at the annual dinner of the New York Democratic Party, where the festivities consisted of erecting a giant screen and showing the first Ali-Frazier fight—two undefeated heavyweight champions meeting in the ring. I told Goldberg how much I admired his decisions on the U.S. Supreme Court, before he became the UN ambassador, and I remember his exact response: "Hey, some fight, eh?"

I worked for the NAACP Legal Defense and Educational Fund on abolishing the death penalty, which we thought we did when Furman v. Georgia was decided on June 29, 1972. In fact, we had an impromptu party at the Fund's headquarters in New York. My father came and introduced himself as my father. He was very proud.

I think about him almost every day—the things we did, the places we went, the people we met. I remember many of the stories that Jeffrey has put together for this book. I read his column every day. When I was away at school, his secretary sent them to me, so I knew where he was going and who he was seeing. What a life! What a time it was!

ACKNOWLEDGEMENTS

As was the case with *Stories My Father Told Me: Notes From The Lyons Den*, this book would've been impossible without the help, support, and encouragement of my wife Judy. I don't come close to deserving her.

My brother Douglas, who lived through many of these incidents with me, was the first editor, calling on his skills learned at Doubleday, to make vital corrections and suggestions. We shared an amazing childhood, along with our late older brothers George Martin and Warren Hay Lyons. I owe my love of baseball to George and of show business to Warren.

As was the case with the earlier book, my thanks to Edie and Meta Shaw for lending me more of their father Sam Shaw's incredible photos of some of the people in this book, and to Shannon Connors, Greg Villepique, and Misha Beletsky at Abbeville Press for their invaluable help. Also to Bob Abrams, the president and publisher of Abbeville Press and my Fieldston football teammate in 1961; my leader then, my leader now. And thank you to my literary agent, Karen Gantz, for believing in this book. She and my publisher Bob Abrams have been the driving forces behind one of the most rewarding experiences of my life.

Finally, to my colleague and friend Rex Reed for his introduction. We've shared many a dark screening room over the years—too many to count.

INDEX

Index

Index

Mountbatten, Lord Louis, 118
Mountbattens, 16
Moynihan, Pat, 293
Mulligan, Gerry, 447
Muni, Paul, 341
Murray, Arthur, 213–214
Murray, Mrs. Arthur (Kathryn), 384
Murray, John, 369
Murrow, Edward R., **277–278**, 468
Mussolini, Benito, 121

Nathan, George Jean, 34
Nathan's Famous, 26
N B C, 400
Nehru, Jawaharlal, 385
Neiman, LeRoy, 447
Nelson, Barry, 181
Nelson, Byron, 76
Nepal, King of, 353
Nesbitt, Cathleen, 129
Nevers, Ernie, 467
Newhouse, Mitzi, 118
Newhouse, Sam, 118
Newley, Anthony, 352, 438
Newman, Paul, 153–154, 180, 239, 242, 288, 291, 292, 420
Newman, Phyllis, 351
Niarchos, Stavros, 418
Nichols, Mike, 205–206
Nimitz, Chester, 409
Nitti, Frank, 390
Niven, David, 24, **167–170**, 168
Nixon, Patricia, 268
Nixon, Richard M., 68, 120, 266–267, 268, 292, 319, 384, 403
Nizer, Louis, 310
Norgay, Tenzing, 18
Norris, Clarence, 344
North, John Ringling, 34, 229
Northeast Airlines, 21
Norton, Ken, 418
Nova, Lou, 424
Novak, Kim, 119, 278, 292
Novarro, Ramon, 235
Nureyev, Rudolf, 67

Oak Room, Plaza Hotel, **31–32**
Obama, Michelle, 359

Oberon, Merle, 153
O'Brian, Hugh, 218–219
O'Brien, Pat, 44, 368
O'Casey, Sean, 73
Odets, Clifford, 135, 148, 222, **279–281**, 280
O'Donnell, Emmett "Rosie," 43
O'Doul, Lefty, 467
O'Hara, John, 262, 264
O'Hara, Maureen, 182
Oliver, Porky, 424
Olivier, Laurence, 42, 127, 132, 133, 153, 181, 195, 244, 350, 374
Onassis, Aristotle, 46, 108, **355–356**, 358, 450
Onassis, Jacqueline Kennedy, 352, **357–358**, 413
O'Neill, Eugene, 21, 25, 140, **282–283**
Ono, Yoko, 449
Ordóñez, Antonio, **427–429**
Ordóñez, Carmen, 428–429
Osato, Sono, 214
Oswald, Lee Harvey, 270
Oswald, Marina, 269–270
O'Toole, Peter, 126, 128, **171–174**, 172, 196, 206
Ouspenskaya, Maria, 125

Pacino, Al, 242
Page, Geraldine, 244
Palance, Jack, 281
Paley, William S., 33
Paley Park, 33
Palmer, Arnold, 350
Parker, Dorothy, 264, **284–285**, 409
Pasternak, Joseph, 31
Pastor, Bob, 426
Patterson, Floyd, 18, 334
Patton, George S., 309, 321, 322
Paul (news dealer), 350
Pavlov (translator), 381
Paychek, Johnny, 57
Peck, (John) Gregory, **175–177**, 176, 292
Peck, Eddie, 336
Peckinpah, Sam, 137
Peerce, Jan, 464
Pegler, Westbrook, 36
Peppard, George, 214
Peppermint Lounge, 71
Perelman, S. J., **286**

Perkins, Anthony, 106, 433
Peron, Eva, 119
Perona, John, 16, 20, 35, 168
Peters, Jean, 145
Petrillo, James C., 140
Philip, Prince, 52, 325, 330
Phillips, Siân, 173
Picasso, Pablo, 233, 290, 296, 339, 409, 427
Pickford, Mary, 57, 256
Piersall, Jimmy, 433
Pike, Dr., 288
Pinter, Harold, 300
Pissarro, Camille, 203
Plaza Hotel, Oak Room, **11–12**
Plummer, Christopher, 72, 161
Podell, Jules, 28, 29, 30
Poitier, Sidney, **178–180**, 179
Pompidou, Georges, 312
Porter, Cole, 127
Post, Mrs., 370–371
Powell, Eleanor, 360
Powell, Thomas, 313
Powell, William, 169, 191, 260
Power, Tyrone, 79, **181–182**, 254
Power, Tyrone, Sr., 181
Prager, Stanley, 304
Preminger, Otto, 165, 166
Prentiss, Paula, 132
Presley, Elvis, 383
Preston, Frances Folsom Cleveland, 323
Preston, Robert, 141
Prince of Wales (later Edward VIII), 121
Proser, Monte, 397
Puccini, Giacomo, 463
Puleo, Johnny, 146
Purvis, Melvin, 289

Quinn, Anthony, **183–185**, 184, 228, 427, 428

Rabb, Maxwell, 12
Radford, Arthur W., 310
Rainer, Luise, 269, 279, 280
Rainier, Prince, of Monaco, 209, 356
Rains, Claude, 345
Rank, J. Arthur, 28, 195, 321
Raphael (artist), 299

477

Index

Index

PHOTOGRAPHY CREDITS

All photographs are from the Lyons family archive, with the exception of the following:

Alfred Eisenstaedt/The LIFE Picture Collection/Getty Images: cover and page 38

Shaw Family Archive/Sam Shaw: pages 14–15, 80, 83, 93, 110, 114, 146, 154, 168, 184, 212, 217, 220–21, 233, 240, 243, 247, 255, 258–59, 275, 298, 331, 353, 398–99, 416–17, 419, 442–43, 447, 458
Shaw Family Archive/Larry Shaw: pages 172, 402

Library of Congress Prints and Photographs Division, LC-USZ62-62334: page 425
Library of Congress, Prints & Photographs Division, photograph by Harris & Ewing, LC-DIG-hec-22989: pages 430–31
Library of Congress Prints and Photographs Division, LC-DIG-ppmsca-39089: page 440